Alternative Educational

EDUCATIONAL FUTURES
RETHINKING THEORY AND PRACTICE
Volume 21

Scope
This series maps the emergent field of educational futures. It will commission books on the futures of education in relation to the question of globalisation and knowledge economy. It seeks authors who can demonstrate their understanding of discourses of the knowledge and learning economies. It aspires to build a consistent approach to educational futures in terms of traditional methods, including scenario planning and foresight, as well as imaginative narratives, and it will examine examples of futures research in education, pedagogical experiments, new utopian thinking, and educational policy futures with a strong accent on actual policies and examples.

Alternative Educational Futures

Pedagogies for Emergent Worlds

Marcus Bussey
University of the Sunshine Coast, Australia

Sohail Inayatullah
Tamkang University, Taiwan

Ivana Milojević
University of the Sunshine Coast, Australia

SENSE PUBLISHERS
ROTTERDAM / TAIPEI

A C.I.P. record for this book is available from the Library of Congress.

ISBN 978-90-8790-511-8 (paperback)
ISBN 978-90-8790-512-5 (hardback)
ISBN 978-90-8790-513-2 (e-book)

Published by: Sense Publishers,
P.O. Box 21858, 3001 AW
Rotterdam, The Netherlands
http://www.sensepublishers.com

Printed on acid-free paper

TABLE OF CONTENTS

MARCUS BUSSEY AND SOHAIL INAYATULLAH

1. PATHWAYS

Alternative educational futures

INTRODUCTION

If you have this book in your hand you are probably dissatisfied with education today. You may be a teacher looking for directions beyond the classroom and authoritarian, top down, passive learning; or an academic interested in the epistemological foundations of coherent and transformative resistance to the mainstream industrial worldview; or perhaps an administrator looking for ways to 'disorganise' out of the bureaucratic nightmare of educational administration and ineffective policy; or a concerned parent who intuitively knows there is a better way for your child than education that kills curiosity and creativity while it disseminates competitive individualism, consumerism and shallow democracy; or a business leader frustrated with the lack of passion, innovation and creativity in school or university graduates. No matter who you are, you have seen the link between a profound rethinking of education and personal and social renewal.

For us—Bussey, Inayatullah and Milojević—this book is another small step towards rethinking the present in the light of possible futures because whatever steps we take as a species towards the future—be it a proto-global civilisation, a fractal cosmopolitanism, a Gaian technolopoly, or a return to the past—education both as an institution and as a social process is key to how we get there, remembering that the future is created and changes with every step we take.

Education is central to how any future is to be realised. How we teach children today determines the values, attitudes, personal and social awareness and skills of tomorrow's citizens. Furthermore, schools and their curricula are templates of today's priorities. If a school building was the subject of an archaeological dig 2000 years from now, much about our values and social order could be adduced. For a start, a cultural need for order, uniformity and linear social process would be evident; hierarchy too would become clear with headmaster's (or University President's) rooms being in one place, nested at the centre of a hive of social beings. The flag pole would be the subject of learned papers on tribal/national affiliations and, if text survived in the form of curriculum documents, the pole—like the *omphalos* at the centre of the ancient universe—would be found to inform the concrete structure of the school with unity and purpose. Just as we observe of ancient Egypt, where nothing changed over millennia (Wright, 2006, p. 145), so those distant archaeologists would point out that industrial age schooling changed little from its inception in the nineteenth century until the twenty-first century. Perhaps it will change little over the next 100 years. But if you are holding this

M. Bussey, S. Inayatullah and I. Milojević (eds.), Alternative Educational Futures: Pedagogies for Emergent Worlds, 1–9.

book then probably you are part of that shifting consciousness—the cultural creatives (Ray, 2000)—ready to make change but looking for tools, inspiration and a rationale for it. Whoever you are, this book invites you on a journey into the alternative futures of education. Our intent, however, is not just to map the futures of education but to enable the creation of alternative pedagogies that challenge the current educational trajectory.

In Chapter One political scientist and futurist, Sohail Inayatullah notes that "Futures studies seeks to help individuals and organisations better understand the processes of change so that wiser, preferred futures can be created". Change is ubiquitous today, yet in the area of education it tends to be cosmetic. As mentioned above, the purpose behind this book is to explore alternative educational futures that engage, in the spirit of Inayatullah's definition, the deeper transformative potential of self and culture as a new preferred educational template emerges from the ruins of late modernity. That such a template is real, not just a figment of our utopian imaginings, is attested by chapters that approach in many unique ways the issues facing education and educators today. The diversity of such approaches also allows us to appreciate the openness of this endeavour. As we move from unstructured hope to empowerment we do not need more road maps or blue prints but rather visions that create new categories that change the direction of reality. That these 'visions' are plural is essential as we draw in unique ways on the collective, heterotopic potential of the present as it is embodied in each of us.

Futures thinking is about developing such maps within contexts such as education (Slaughter & Bussey, 2005). It uses time as an epistemological category rather than accepting it as a reified objective natural phenomena (Shapiro, 1992). In this, futurists demonstrate a sensitivity towards the social construction of experience in which both time and space are 'read' as no longer natural but historically produced, culturally maintained and qualitatively different both across cultures but also within more localised structures such as communities and institutions. How futurists use time is determined by a range of concerns relating to the nature of the cultural product being explored and the identified, and sometime unidentified, needs of their client/target group. Creating temporal distance from the present has been one strategy used by futurists to problematise the present. Just as an anthropologist seeks to study culture by being 'in it but not of it', so the futurist seeks to look at society from a temporal distance.

Such a position is described as allochronic and refers to what Johannes Fabian, in his landmark study *Time and the Other*, termed the "denial of coevalness" between the observer and his/her object (Fabian, 1983, p. 31). A range of concepts and techniques are applied in futures thinking to generate a sense of critical distance from the present in order to facilitate creative and innovative responses that might, under the pressure of the present, distort our ability to anticipate and respond. Inayatullah summarises these in his chapter 'Mapping Educational Futures'. It is customary to ask questions about the short, medium and long term future, to apply temporal postures that open up, problematise or contradict current perceptions of the world and experience as we know it. The logic behind such temporal strategies is that, as cultural historian Pitirim Sorokin put it, "Time is the basic category of any becoming" (Sorokin, 1957/1970, p. 317).

EDUCATIONAL FUTURES

Futures studies as an approach to social process and meaning production in education can be seen to fall into three broad categories, with their own priorities, understandings of time and context along with different senses of agency. Each category concerns a specific orientation, focus and epistemological grounding and can be thought of as levels or layers of the same field.

The Future of Education

The first concerns the teaching of the 'official' future. This tends to assume that there is one future out there in the external world. This is often the official fact-based future. Milojević has argued in her *Educational Futures: Dominant and Contesting Visions* (2004) that when the chant of the futures of education is evoked, the mantra used is not transformative but tied to the status quo. Information is required not to challenge ministerial policy but to use futures information for strategic purposes. The executive at every level of government wishes for inform-ation that can ensure that graduates gain employment, that their nation's competitive advantage is enhanced, and that political leaders are kept out of the daily newspapers. The future of education assumes that the sole externally objective future can be, to some extent, accurately predicted. Risk is reduced by using a range of predictive methodologies. Previously situated in the national development discourse, this future is now inextricably tied into the globalisation and new technologies discourse in which students need to globalise, virtualise and learn the new life sciences. The future is obvious. The purpose of education is to ensure that one's nation (or school or university) is the most successful.

When futures studies is brought into curriculum in this context it appears in its most timid genotype—quantitative trend analysis, images of the techno-utopian future, with texts on how students and ministries must adapt to THE future.

Alternative Futures of Education

The second is teaching and learning about alternative futures. Central in this pedagogical approach is that the future cannot be predicted with any accuracy because the extent of uncertainty is too high. This is because of multiple factors: that there is rapid technological and economic change; that humans are complicit in the futures they are creating; and that the future is epistemological: an open space being created by our inner and outer realities. Thus there cannot be THE future but a range of alternative futures. Central to this approach is the notion of alternative futures—that there is more than one possible future. James Dator (2002) has made this point continuously and forcefully since the late 1960s. Richard Slaughter's work on foresight is a fine example of such work (Slaughter, 1995, 2004) as is

3

Ziauddin Sardar's *Rescuing All Our Futures: The Futures of Futures Studies* (1999).

For ministries and political leaders, at one level, this approach is problematic in that instead of fixing the future, it opens up alternatives. Instead of certainty, we are given paradox. Instead of the correct future, we are given agency. Instead of an objective external world, our inner worlds are complicit in the world we construct—we make the world.

Futures studies courses in this approach tend to be layered, focused not just on the predictive dimensions of futures thinking but also on the interpretive (the different meanings individuals give to the future), the critical (what is missing in particular nominations of the future, how the future is colonised by various class and institutional interests) and anticipatory action learning (wherein those who are being impacted by the future—students, for example—use their own categories of the future to invent desired futures).

Futures studies as well takes a macro view. This is where episteme and history meet in order to explore the philosophy and practice of education within the civilisational context of post modernity, globalisation and the post-Western horizon. The temporal frame is long term and open ended. It subsumes the short and medium terms within its overarching exploration of the civilisational discourse of education and the human journey.

However, it is alternatives that are first and foremost; it is not acceding to a particular view point of the future, be it industrial or sustainable, nuclear or solar, materialistic or religious or spiritual, individual or structure, but rather ensuring that educational futures explores, are as much as possible, the full terrain of possibilities, and in doing so, even challenges the metaphor of "terrain". This involves the teaching and learning of futures theories, methods and approaches in school or university curricula. How should futures studies be best taught—what is the doxa of knowledge? What is the best balance between process and content? are some guiding questions.

Studying the alternative futures of education is central to our social engagement with the future of learning. It allows practitioners and stake holders to engage with education in order to first identify possible, probable and preferable futures for learning (Bell, 1994). It then provides tools and concepts to engage with the forces currently shaping the educational terrain in order to clarify the values underpinning education and steer our schools and institutions of higher learning in more socially equitable, flexible and creative directions. Agency in this context resides with all those with an interest in the outcomes of education and is therefore not restricted to the professional elite. Agency as well, pertains not only to the inner world of the individual but also to the inner world of the collective (Sarkar, 1982).

Furthermore, the teaching of futures of education does not limit itself to rational teaching models. This is creating—whatever the nature of the future—an embodied experience of the future (Bussey, 2008). Such work involves non-linear teaching strategies that embody the experience of the future for students. Such 'in the future' contexts are experimental and affective and can involve drama, music, the visual arts and media, along with meditation and experiments in stillness and non-verbal communication.[i]

Alternative futures of education is a powerful vehicle for developing critical literacies, an appreciation of historical, social and cultural forces and in supplying the skills for anticipatory social engagement. However, and this is a crucial point, official educational establishments engage with this deeper perspective on the future by taming it via scenario planning. By developing four different scenarios, and determining the implications for education in each scenario, they believe they have opened up pedagogical space; they believe they have innovated. Alternative futures if far deeper than mere scenario planning—it involves movement between epistemologies, it involves foundationally challenging assumptions, particularly challenging the coherence of the knowing self that is constructing the future. It also involves embodying the futures so that the dominant self can be opened to alternative ways of knowing. This tension between the official and the alternative is unlikely to disappear. The challenge is not however for more surveillance or vigilance, but for enhanced presence (Senge, 2004).

Education For the Future

The third approach is teaching for the future. This is pedagogy that is currently focused on sustainable development. The future is seen as something that must be saved for future generations. It is a prophetic approach to the future and to futures teaching, warning us of disasters ahead unless we change our ways. It challenges the alternative futures approach by warning us that no alternatives are indeed possible if nature is destroyed on the planet, if we do not immediately pursue the path to deep sustainability. This approach thus tends to have a more social and environmental dimension (as compared to teaching and learning about THE future). David Hicks's work on sustainable futures exemplifies such an approach (Hicks, 1994, 2002, 2004).

Agency is understood as collective and temporal (and beyond temporal) in that it is not only those in the Western modernist present who participate in the processes of futures thinking but also those who have gone before, remain silent today and are still unborn that are invited to representation. It is thus not simply the dominant species called into this futures nexus, but all life and what Loren Eiseley once colourfully called "Earth ... the mightiest of the creatures" (1969/1994, p. 148). Such education for the future work involves an ethical commitment to what Marcus Bussey calls, in Chapter Two, a neohumanist stance which speaks for the silent majority: past, present and future. This approach is politically empowering, or at least has the potential to be so, as it covers a wide range of social literacies. Of particular concern are issues of identity, social and gender equity, cultural and economic globalisation and environmental degradation and activism.

"For the future" is also futures generations oriented, sensitive to how non-Western cultures construct the future. For the future differs by culture. For the future, for Maori, for example, maybe be centred around cultural values. Within Islam, for nstance, 'for the future' means ensuring that Islamic categories of knowledge are represented in the future and futures discourses (Inayatullah, 2003; Sardar, 1985).

While the "for the future" has strong positivist roots, it quickly moves into the realm of questions of existence and meaning (existential and metaphysical), defining and exploring social structures within the context of students' lives and, more broadly, the experiences of humanity on the planet.

The chapters in this book have implications for all three aspects of educational futures but in its overall trajectory we have sought to bring together work that is focused on the *alternative* futures of education, though, certainly, the futures for education perspective is not silent, particularly in the latter chapters where the challenges of the planet are engaged.

Alternative Educational Futures: Pedagogies for Emergent Worlds falls into three sections. In Part One are placed three chapters that map and challenge current thinking and assumptions about education. Sohail Inayatullah sets the scene by outlining the foundational futures concepts employed in this text. He then describes what he calls the six pillars of futures studies. He links this overview with implications for educators and examples from his own practice as a futurist. In the second chapter Marcus Bussey uses music as a metaphor to explore three constructions of educational contexts for the coming century. In this he offers an assessment of the global educational context via three visual texts that capture the essence of each context. Richard Slaughter offers an overview of a future education programme run by a State Department of Education in Australia in the 1990s. Central to this overview is his interest in what lead to it being discontinued. There are lessons to be learnt in his analysis yet he chooses to focus on what futures education has to offer as a catalyst for personal and collective self understanding and as a process of engaging with the deeper issues that constitute our problematic future.

In Part Two the focus is on policy and issues relating to implementing alternative futures education. In this spirit, David Hicks offers a clear overview of the nature of a futures programme and its constituent parts. His focus is practical and hands on but driven by the need to move from dreams to action. Jim Dator and Sohail Inayatullah both offer chapters focused on the university as an education provider. Dator takes a critical eye to how the university sector is functioning. In his chapter he questions the layered nature of the term 'quality' and explores how paradoxically universities today are both achieving it and loosing it simultaneously. Inayatullah follows this with an analysis of the forces at work on the university sector and offers both macro and meso level scenarios for its future and the future of the academic profession in general.

The next three chapters look at specific developments and issues facing the educational community. Erica McWilliam and Shane Dawson take on Wikipedia, exploring how the shape of knowledge is being reconfigured and what the implications are for educational institutions. Marcus Bussey looks at the question of access and equity and how our thinking about it has been shaped by a long elitist tradition in education. Kathleen Kesson focuses on democracy and what it will take for us to deepen it via more participatory forms of educational practice.

In Part Three, alternative futures thinking and practice are showcased. Both Patricia Kelly and Basil Savitsky build their chapters around transformative pedagogic encounters that affirm the praxis orientation of futures work. Kelly reflects on her work with young engineering students and how transformative work is possible within a first year course. Satvitsky outlines nine tools he uses on a futures course he runs and reflects on how the weave of these with practical contexts deepens students' understanding and confidence. The chapters by Julie Matthews and Robert Hattam, and Martin Haigh introduce an inter-civilisational strand into alternative pedagogical thinking. Matthews and Hattam, through the lens of Zen Buddhism, explore the role of humour as an antidote to prevailing pedagogical templates that privilege linear rationality over student's own awareness that life is paradoxical. Haigh draws his inspiration from Neovedanta and examines the implication of this Indian response to British colonialism for sustainable education. Jennifer Gidley looks at the contribution of Steiner (Waldorf) education to thinking about alternative futures. She brings Steiner education to the table in order to provoke dialogue between, and creative engagement with, learning possibilities that promote diversity and foster creativity and spirit. Billy Matheson looks at the potential for narrative approaches to deepen futures oriented education that empowers individuals and communities and promotes sustainability, creativity and diversity. In their chapter, Jennifer Gidley and Gary Hampson explore Ken Wilber's integral theory as a model for thinking about transformation of contexts bounded by fragmentation and competition. They offer his process of "transcending *and* including" as a bridging tool to facilitate the emergence of an integral consciousness both pedagogically and socially.

All authors in this collection are committed to transformation of assumptions about education and its social function. All too often alternatives to mainstream hegemonic educational narrative are dismissed as out of touch. Yet there is a growing voice that asserts that, given the current environmental and social stress being experienced at a global level, calls for change are deeply in touch. That creative and spiritual responses to this context are recurrent themes in this text also indicates some essential features of a coherent resistance to the dominant educational narrative. Alternative futures thinking gives such dissent a voice.

Peter Senge, C. Otto Scharmer, Joseph Jaworski and Betty Sue Flowers note in their book *Presence* that:

> The fate of the human species is still very much in our hands. Certain things have been set in motion that will be difficult to reverse. But we have two openings that are immensely helpful. First, there is a higher ecological awareness of our interdependence with other life and our mutual responsibility. And second, there is an earth-based spirituality building at a very rapid pace. (2004, p. 66)

These chapters bear witness to various manifestations of this emerging resistance. It is particularly relevant to note that the ecological awareness of interconnection is expressed culturally and technologically, i.e., virtually, as human consciousness expands beyond vested interest and embraces more holistic and integral (spiritual) visions of knowledge potential and meaningful learning. Such a dynamic process is described frequently in these chapters as a neohumanistic drive toward integral being/knowing. Edward Said, in his essay on humanism charts this relationship—a very *neohumanistic* relationship—of expanding horizons and local, context bound responses to this global imperative. It is worth closing this introduction with his observation that:

> Education involves widening circles of awareness, each of which is distinct analytically while being connected to the others by virtue of worldly reality. A reader is in a place, in a school or university, in a work place, or in a specific country at a particular time, situation, and so forth. But these are not passive frameworks. In the process of widening the humanistic horizon, its achievements of insight and understanding, the framework must be actively understood, constructed, interpreted. And this is what resistance is... (Said, 2004, p. 75)

NOTES

[i] Two examples of the use of create pedagogy to are to be found in the work of Debra Robertson and Gretal Bakker of Performance Frontiers www.performancefrontiers.com and Marcus Bussey at www.futuresevocative.com.

REFERENCES

Bell, W. (1994). The world as a moral community. *Society*, July/August, 17–22.
Bussey, M. (2008). Embodied education: Reflections on sustainable education. *The International Journal of Environmental, Cultural, Economic and Social Sustainability (forthcoming)*.
Dator, J. (2002). *Advancing futures: Futures studies in higher education*. New York: Praeger.
Eiseley, L. (1969/1994). *The unexpected universe*. New York: Harcourt Brace & Co.
Fabian, J. (1983). *Time and the other: How anthropology makes its object*. New York: Columbia University Press.
Hicks, D. (1994). *Educating for the future: A practical classroom guide*. Weyside Park, Godalming, Surrey: WWF, UK.
Hicks, D. (2002). *Lessons for the future: The missing dimension in education*. London and New York: Routledge/Falmer.
Hicks, D. (2004). Teaching for Tomorrow: How can futures studies contribute to peace education? *Journal of Peace Education*, 1(2), 165–178.
Inayatullah, S., & Boxwell, G. (Eds.). (2003). *Islam, postmodernism and other futures: A Ziauddin Sardar reader*. London: Pluto Press.
Milojević, I. (2005). *Educational futures: Dominant and contesting visions*. London and New York: RoutledgeFalmer.
Ray, P. H., & Anderson, S. R. (2000). *The cultural creatives: How 50 million people are changing the world*. New York: Three Rivers Press.
Said, E. W. (2004). *Humanism and democratic criticism*. New York: Palgrave.
Sardar, Z. (1985). *Islamic futures: The shape of ideas to come*. London: Mansell.
Sardar, Z. (Ed.). (1999). *Rescuing all our futures: The future of futures studies*. Westport, CT: Praeger.
Sarkar, P. R. (1982). *The liberation of intellect: Neohumanism*. Calcutta: Ananda Marga Publications.

Senge, P., Scharmer, C. O., Jaworski, J., & Flowers, B. S. (2004). *Presence: Exploring profound change in people, organizations, and society*. New York: A Currency Book.

Shapiro, M. J. (1992). *Reading the postmodern polity: Political theory as textual practice*. Minneapolis, MN: University of Minnesota Press.

Slaughter, R. A. (1995). *The foresight principle: Cultural recovery in the 21st century*. London: Adamantine Press.

Slaughter, R. A. (2004). *Futures beyond dystopia: Creating social foresight*. London and New York: Routledge/Falmer.

Slaughter, R. S., & Bussey, M. (2005). *Futures thinking for social foresight*. Tamsui, Taiwan: Tamkang University Press.

Sorokin, P. (1957/1970). *Social and cultural dynamics: A study of change in major systems of art, truth, ethics, law and social relationships* (Revised and abridged in One Volume by the Author ed.). Boston: Porter Sargent.

Wright, R. (2006). *An illustrated short history of progress*. Toronto: Anansi.

cities did generations ago (Inayatullah, 2004). And yet many, if not most, Western mayors now believe that they were mistaken. Instead of spending billions on unplanned growth, or development without vision, they should have focused on creating liveable communities. They should have kept green public spaces separating developed regions. They now understand that their image the future—of unbridled growth without concern for nature or liveability—led to the gigantic megacities where many had jobs, yet suffered in almost every other way. Asian cities have unconsciously followed this pattern. They have forgotten their own traditions, where village life and community were central, where living with nature was important. Now they must find ways to create new futures, or continue to go along with the future being discarded elsewhere. This used future is leading to a global crisis of fresh water depletion, climate change, not to mention human dignity.

School systems—from design of playgrounds, to school rooms, to the relationship between the principal, teacher and student—remain locked into an image from the agricultural and industrial era. Surveillance, a clear hierarchy, seeing students as widgets and, most importantly, examination systems based on the 'mass' view of education dominate. The cost of this used future is the unique nature of the individual learner. Graduates, as well, when they enter the workforce, continue this future. It becomes the uncontested norm, even while failing to produce the desired results.

The second concept is the disowned future (see Stone & Stone, 1989; Inayatullah, 2007). Our excellence is our fatal flaw, said the Greek writer Homer. What we excel at becomes our downfall. And we do not see this because we are busy focusing on our strategic plans. It is the self disowned, the future pushed away, that comes back to haunt us. The busy executive, focused on achievements, only in later life remembers his children. It is later in life that he begins to think about work–life balance, about his inner life. The organisation focused on a strategic goal denies the exact resources it may need to truly succeed. In the story of the tortoise and the hare, we often focus on the hare—wanting to be the quickest and the smartest—but it is the tortoise, our reflective self, that may have the answer to the future. Plans go astray not because of a lack of effective strategy but because the act of creating a particular direction ignores other personal and organisational selves. The challenge is to integrate our disowned selves: for the school principal to remember what it was like to be a child, to use her child–self to create curriculum; for the army general to discover the part of him that can negotiate, that can learn from others. This means moving futures closer: from a goal oriented neo Darwinian approach to a softer and more paradoxical Taoist approach.

The third concept is alternative futures. We often believe that there is only one future. We cannot see the alternatives, and thus we make the same mistakes over and over. But by looking for alternatives, we may see something new. We are not tied into in the straitjacket of one future. As well, if our particular future does not occur, we do not die from emotional shock, rather, we learn how to adapt to changing conditions. Many in the former Eastern Europe remain in a state of future shock. They believed there was only one future—the socialist one. When that disappeared, they did not know what to do, where to look. Alternatives had not been mapped, the mind had become inflexible.

Alternative futures thinking reminds us that while we cannot always predict a particular future accurately, by focusing on a range of alternatives we can better prepare for uncertainty, indeed, to some extent *embrace* uncertainty. Career planning for schools often is based on training students for one job, instead of multiple jobs, or portfolio careers, or other variations of work. Related to the concept of alternative futures is the notion of alternative pasts. For pedagogy, this would mean questioning history, asking what–if certain events did not happen— such as China's abandoning its naval strategy in the fifteenth century—how might history have unfolded differently. By opening up historical space, futures space is created. Alternative futures thinking in the class room would constantly challenge approaches that focused on education for the future. Such approaches tend to construct the future as almost predetermined, focussing on the future being global and technologically driven. Education for alternative futures intends to enable learners to see different futures—collapse futures, for example, or spiritual transformation. Or it might attempt to construct scenarios currently considered impossible: a world without war, for example.

The fourth concept is alignment. We need to align our day–to–day problem-based approach with strategy. And we need to align strategy with the broader big picture, and the bigger picture with our vision and the vision with our day–to–day. Often we envision a particular future, and yet how we measure this future and our organisational indicators, have no relationship to that vision. Thus the vision fails, because everyone knows the vision is there for show so as to appear modern. While enabling and ennobling us, the vision must link to the day–to–day realities; our day–to–day measures must reflect the vision. For educational institutions, this concept suggests that a vision for the future is crucial, and that the vision needs to be linked to strategy and indicators. As well, the vision should not become written in stone but remain flexible, adapting to changing conditions.

There is also inner alignment. Often an organisation or individual has a particular strategy of the future—to achieve a certain goal—but its inner map does not reflect that strategy. The inner map may even be in direct contradiction to this external reality. Thus there is a disconnect between what the leader may say or do, or wish others to do, and the inner map of the organisation. The challenge is first to discern the inner map—how the organisation sees itself. Is it youthful or mature? A tiger or an elephant? As well, how does the organisation imagine the future? Does your organisation believe the future is random; or that you are rushing down a rapid stream with rocks all around; or the future is like a game of snakes and ladders; or like a family? The inner map needs to reflect the outer map, and vice versa. In strategy sessions with schools, I have found that it is the inner story that often does not allow innovation. "It can't be done here", is a common response that ensures that innovation fails. Tired of pushing against bureaucracies or resistant parents, innovate teachers give up. The system then reinforces the fatigue. Another story of school for administrators is that of seeing their other school as Camelot surrounding by barbarians (the school boards, the media, parents, government ministers, and even students). This story is one of an impending deluge. The story also creates a cycle of distrust where the outside criticises the inside, and the inside attempts to protect its own. Innovation is stifled.

The fifth concept is your model of social change. Do you believe that the future is positive and you can do something about it? Or is the future bleak and there is nothing you can do about it? Or is the future created by the one-hundredth monkey? Or is the future already given, created by prophecy? Or perhaps you believe that the future is cyclical, everyone has a turn and the most effective strategy is to be patient. Or do you believe the future is not given, but created by our daily actions, and thus we must take the "bull by the horns"? Or ... In an educational setting, the challenge is that the model of social change differs dramatically amongst the stakeholders. The principal is likely to have a different model (more toward grabbing the bull by the horns) than parents, who see school in far more conservative and incremental terms. Teachers are likely to be caught in the middle.

The sixth concept is the use of the future. Futures thinking can simply be about foresight training, helping individuals and organisations with new competencies and new skills. At a deeper level, futures thinking can help create more effective strategy. By understanding the alternative, used and disowned futures, organisations can become far more innovative. At a deeper level, futures thinking can create capacity. It is not so much predicting correctly or getting the right strategy, that is, using the right tools, but about enhancing our confidence to create futures that we desire. Futures methods thus decolonise the world we think we may want—they challenge our basic concepts. They deconstruct. Enhancing capacity empowers individuals; this liberates and is scary for many as the safety of having others make decisions for one is taken away.

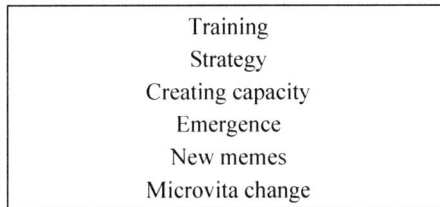

Training
Strategy
Creating capacity
Emergence
New memes
Microvita change

Figure 2. Uses of the future

For schools, futures projects generally tend to be focused on tools and methods. Principals and teachers are already overwhelmed by the demands of the state, school boards, parents and the changing world (web technologies, research in genetics, changes in health paradigms, issues around safety and risk); opening up the future creates even more chaos. To work beyond such demands and pressures invites educators to go to the deeper levels of emergence. Futures thinking helps create the conditions for a paradigm shift. The organisation imagines a new future, creates a new strategy, enables stakeholders, uses tools and then a new future emerges. Even deeper levels are about meme (Dawkins, 1989; Blackmore, 1998,

p. 2; www.scholars.nus.edu.sg/cpace/infotech/cook/memedef.html)[ii] and microvita change (Sarkar, 1991). Meme change is about changing the ideas that govern institutions (life long learning, for example) and microvita is about the non-local field of awareness that makes sense of reality (inner change instead of just strategy). Futures thinking ultimately can go far as mapping and changing memes and fields of reality.

There is a seventh concept, but that is the no-concept: that all listing of concepts becomes yet another cookbook that limits creativity, instead of allowing innovation. Being present to changing sensitive conditions, allowing futures to emerge, is central here.

THE SIX PILLARS OF FUTURES STUDIES

These six pillars of futures studies (Figure 3) provide a theory of futures thinking that is linked to methods and tools, and developed through praxis. They can be used as theory or in a futures workshop setting. The pillars are: mapping, anticipation, timing, deepening, creating alternatives and transforming.

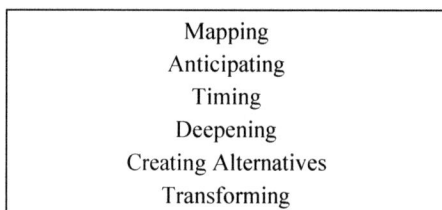

| Mapping |
| Anticipating |
| Timing |
| Deepening |
| Creating Alternatives |
| Transforming |

Figure 3. Six pillars of futures studies: MATDCT

Mapping

In the first pillar, past, present and future are mapped. By mapping time, we become clearer on where we have come from and where we are going. Three tools are crucial.

The method, shared history, is the first tool and consists of having participants—in a futures workshop—write down the main trends and events that have led up to the present. A historical time line is then constructed to the present. Shared history asks: What are the continuities in our history, what is discontinuous? Has change been stable or have there been jumps in time? This opening tool creates a framework from which to move to the future.

The second tool is the futures triangle. This maps today's views of the future through three dimensions: the image of the future, the push of the present and the weight of history. This is represented pictorially as Figure 4.

The image of the future pulls us forward. While there are many images of the future, five or so are archetypal. These are:

- Evolution and progress—more technology, man as the centre of the world, and a belief in rationality. In education, this is the modernist industrial vision of education. Schools should teach basic skills (reading, writing, mathematics) and prepare students for becoming consumers, workers and citizens of the nation–state (and the best as producers and leaders).
- Collapse—a belief that humanity has reached its limits, indeed we have overshot them. This is evident in world inequity, fundamentalism, tribalism, nuclear holocaust, climate disasters, which all point to a worsening of the future. In educational settings, there is a general sense that education is failing, that schools and universities are unable to meet the changing needs of the world. They are unable to adapt to new technologies; they are unable to manage the loss of state subsidies (for universities) because of globalisation; and they are unable to create new minds focused on world citizenship.

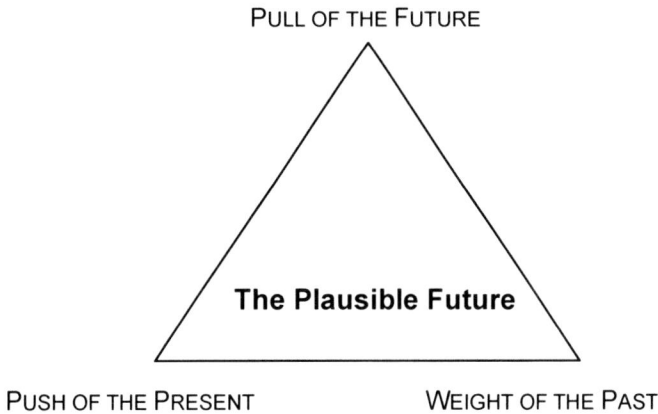

Figure 4. The futures triangle

- Gaia—the world is a garden, cultures are its flowers, we need social technologies to repair the damage we have caused to ourselves, to nature and to others; becoming more and more inclusive is what is important. Partnership between women and men, humans and nature, and humans and technology is needed. This is challenging the very notion of 'man'. This is the sustainability image in education—schools and universities moving from silos of learning to an ecology of mind, to an ecology of selves and pedagogy. The purpose of education in this image changes dramatically, becoming far more idealistic and future focused. The image is of the garden school or university where all learn from each other, and create value by finding their unique skills.
- Globalism—we need to focus on ways to come closer as economies and as cultures. Borders need to break down; technology and the free flow of capital can bring riches to all. Traditional 'isms' and dogmas are the barriers stopping

us from achieving a new world. This image has been the one educational systems have started to focus on—preparing students for a global–tech world, adapting to new technologies and to becoming global corporate and non-governmental organisation players.

– Back to the future—we are past our prime; we need to return to simpler times, when hierarchy was clearer, when technology was less disruptive, when the Empire was clear. Change is too overwhelming; we have lost our way, and must return. In this future, education is about the return to foundational texts—Greek, Indian, Sinic or Islamic, for example. Each culture requires a return to the basics, whatever these basics are. Generally, however, the basics focus on morality, clear roles around gender, strong leadership (often male) and communitarian values—identity is collective and generally singular, be it religious, national or ethnic based.

An additional image that faces education today is the breakdown of the public—whether from globalisation, new technologies, gender politics, multiculturalism, terrorism, the notion of a public with a shared ethos; that is, mass culture, has broken down. This is leading to a multiplicity of learning spaces, from home schooling, to alternative schools, to new universities, to corporate education, to … The public has become contested and new possibilities for public verses private are still emerging. This is the postmodern educational system—perhaps the *à la carte* model of schooling and university.

Along with images are the pushes of the future. These are quantitative drivers and trends that are changing the future. An aging population is one such trend. We are living longer and having fewer children. Which future will this trend push us towards? Along with living longer, increased military spending and export—especially by the five permanent members of the UN Security Council—is making the world a more dangerous place, as are the activities of terrorists.

There are also weights. These are the barriers to the change we wish to see. Each image has differing weights. Those who imagine a globalised world are weighed down by nationalists and the brutal fact that while capital may be freer, labour is still tied to place. The Gaian image is weighed down by the dominance of hierarchy—male, empire or expertise. "The boss (the teacher, the principal, the government minister) is always right" is the guiding myth.

By analysing the interaction of these three forces, the futures triangle helps us develop a plausible future.

The third tool is the futures landscape. This tool helps us audit where our organisation is. The landscape has four levels which can be presented visually as shown in Figure 5 below. First is the jungle, a dog–eat–dog competitive world, wherein the goal is to survive. Second is the chess set, where strategy helps us enhance our effectiveness—we succeed by being clear about our goals and creating more responsive organisations. Third are the mountain tops—these are the big pictures, the broader social contest we find our organisations in. Finally is the star, the vision. Is your school or university engaged only in day–to–day survival, or is it using strategy to move forward? Has it developed scenarios of alternative futures, different assumptions of how the world might be? Does it have a vision of the desired future? If so, does it link the vision to strategy?

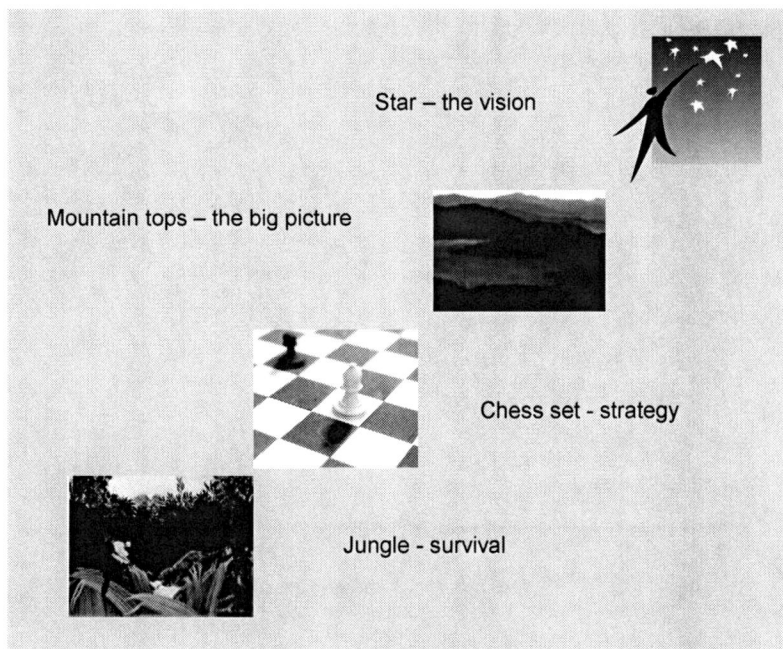

Figure 5. The futures landscape

This leads us to the second pillar of futures studies.

Anticipation

The second pillar of futures thinking is Anticipation. There are two main methods here. Emerging issues analysis (Molitor, 2003) seeks to identify bell-weather regions, where new social innovation starts (Figure 6). It also seeks to identify issues before they become unwieldy and expensive, while searching for new possibilities and opportunities. Emerging issues include disrupters such as: will robots have legal rights soon? Will meditation be part of every school curriculum? Will peer to peer mediation become a core skill for every school in the world? Will meat be banned from schools (as soft drinks have been in some American counties) (CBS Worldwide Inc., 2002, par. 1)? Will schools and universities redesign curriculum and their buildings to reflect the challenges of climate change? Will brain science advances lead to far more targeted learning in schools? Will we develop pharmacies in our bodies? Will the smart toilet help us with early diagnostics?

While solving emerging issues leads to little political pay off—that is, voters will not reward the leader for solving tomorrow's problems—it can help minimise harm and indeed help organisations respond far more swiftly to emerging challenges. While too expensive for a particular school to engage in, ministries of education can use this method to develop new opportunities and avoid future problems, as can consortiums of universities.

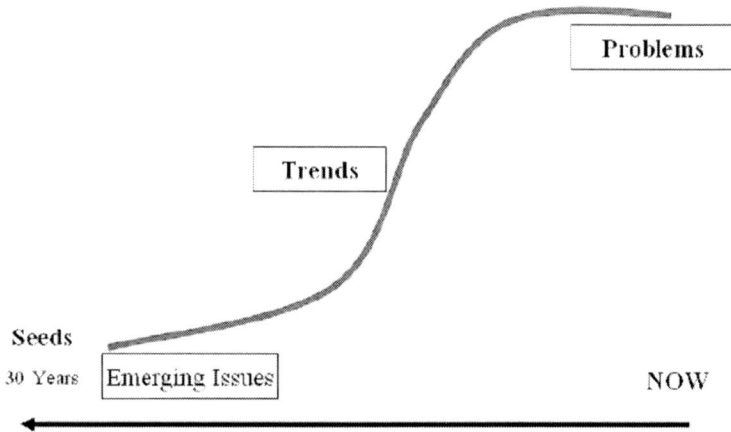

Figure 6. Emerging issues analysis

Along with emerging issues analysis is the futures wheel. The futures wheel seeks to develop the consequences of today's issue on the longer term future. We can ask how a particular new technology might influence us 20 years from now. The futures wheel does not stop at first order impacts, but rolls along to second order impacts, and beyond. It intends to explore and deduce unintended consequences. For example, using the future wheel we can map logical implications of having daily meditation sessions for school children in the public system. This would likely lead to enhanced IQ and EQ over time, as well as better grades. Sick days would be reduced and, in time, the wellness paradigm would become dominant. In another trajectory, some parents might object, leading to political and social tensions. This could however be resolved by children who have experienced the benefits. Or it could lead to parents taking their children away, seeing meditation as too radical an intervention.

The futures wheel helps anticipate future issues, create the possibility of new products and move from seeing the world at a simple unconnected level to a complex connected level (as illustrated in Figure 7). How the parts interact with the whole becomes clearer ...

Timing the Future

The third pillar is timing the future. This is the search for the grand patterns of history and the identification of each one of our models of change. Do we believe that it is the creative minority that generates the new system? Or do we believe that you can't fight the school system hall, that is, deep change is impossible. Humans are essentially past-based, every parent believing they are the world's expert when it comes to education. We can only resign ourselves to the fate of history. Or do we believe that change comes from inner reflection and spiritual practice? Or that changing the outside world is next to impossible—*plus ça change, plus c'est la même chose*? Or that by changing our consciousness we can change the world? Or is institutional change the key—if we can change laws and social structures then we can affect real change? It is not just enough to, for example, go to a higher level of consciousness to stop war or smoking; rather, peace forces are needed for stopping war. To reduce tobacco consumption, financial disincentives are required as well as social support networks to help individuals make the transition. Or is it really technology that counts most of all—we create technology and then it creates... ? We create the Internet and now we define how we work—flexible but 24/7; how we play—gaming; and even how we meet partners. Technology creates new economies and tension results when society lags behind, when power relations do not change.

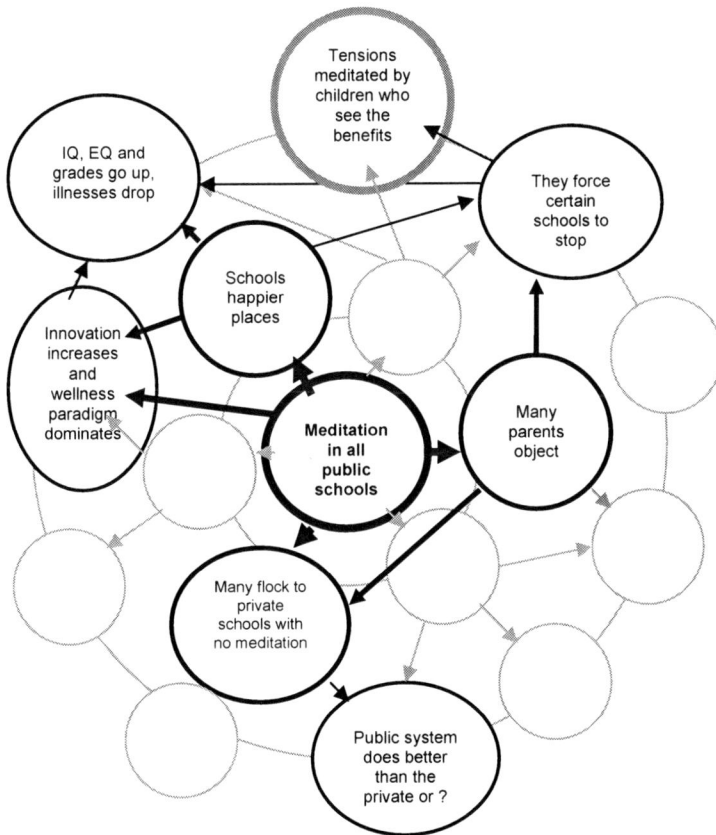

Figure 7. The futures wheel

23

How do you time the future? We can also ask, what is your metaphor of the future? Do you believe the future is just luck or good *karma*? Or is the future a planned rational activity created by choice and risk analysis? Or is the future totally open, anything is possible; the world is a magical place? Or is there is 'syncrodestiny', as Deepak Chopra writes (2005)? Or is the future like a game of snakes and ladders—there is hard work but the world is a scary place and at any second, all the gains can disappear? Or is the future like a machine, regular, predictable, clockwork—there are patterns which once seen can help identify what will happen?

Macrohistorians or grand thinkers have been wrestling with these questions for thousands of years (Galtung & Inayatullah, 1997; Voros, 2006; Special issue, *Journal of Futures Studies*, 2004). From their thinking, a few foundational ideas result:

- The future is linear, stage–like, with progress ahead. By hard work, we will realise the good future.
- The future is cyclical, there are ups and downs. Those at the top will one day find themselves at the bottom. Because they are on the top, they are unable to adapt and adjust as the world changes. Their success was based on mastery of yesterday's conditions. Few are able to reinvent their basic values.
- The future is a spiral—parts are linear and progress-based, and parts are cyclical. With leadership that is courageous and has foresight a positive spiral can be created. The dogmas of the past are challenged but the past is not disowned, rather it is integrated in a march toward a better future.
- New futures are more often than not driven by a creative minority. They challenge the notion of a used future. Instead of imitating what everyone else is doing, they innovate. This can be social, political, cultural, spiritual or technological innovation. These change agents imagine a different future, and inspire others to work toward it. When there is no creative minority, instead of sustainable systems what results are bigger and bigger empires and world–states. Power and bureaucracy continue unchallenged, charisma becomes routinised and the hunger for something different, that can better meet human needs, drifts away. Size or growth takes over, inner and outer development disappear.
- There are hinge periods in human history, when the actions of a few can make a dramatic difference. It is in these periods, especially, that old ways of behaviour are no longer helpful: what succeeded before no longer works now. We are likely in this phase at present.

The social Darwinian notion of competition now endangers us all—but Darwin also wrote about love (Loye, 2000, 2004). For Darwin, this human sensitivity is far more important than the survival of the fittest. Evolution is perhaps moving from randomness to conscious, visioned direction. Such a change is because we are now no longer able to keep on pushing crises back, focusing only on the litany, the superficial, instead of resolving the deeper issues. Our current worldview is not up to the challenge. Man over nature may have brought technological progress but it now threatens to extinguish us all. The creation of the nation–state was a wonderful solution to the problem of empire *versus* localism, of the knight *versus* the priest, however, nationalism threatens us all, and thus new governance systems are needed. Masculinist reductionist science has truly been a miracle but now a move toward holism is required. For schools, this means moving to an ecology of learning, what in other chapters has been called the neohumanist model of education.

What worked in previous eras—the agricultural and the industrial—is unlikely to help us in a global postindustrial era. Indeed, in this view of history, the image leads reality—the image is of a transcendental jump, but the reality is lost in industrial modernist masculinist reductionism.[iii]

Conscious evolution is the key in this approach (Sahtouris, 2002). The world is a complex adaptive system—once we map the future, it changes. Thus, while we need a vision, we do not need a blueprint. Education is therefore about developing the capacity to adapt to novelty and to create novelties. This is a crucial change in purpose, as education generally has been focused on social control or creating consumers (and some producers) for the market.

Deepening the Future

Pillar four is deepening the future and uses Causal layered analysis (Inayatullah, 2004) to unpack the future. Causal layered analysis (CLA) assumes four levels of analysis.

The first level is the 'litany'—quantitative trends, problems, often exaggerated, often used for political purposes—(e.g., safety in schools) usually presented by the news media. Events, issues and trends are not connected and appear discontinuous. The result is often either a feeling of helplessness (What can I do? It is too overwhelming. My child is in danger.) or apathy (Nothing can be done, as demographic patterns cannot be easily changed.) or projected action (Why don't they do something about it? It is government's responsibility. What are they the educators doing?). This is the conventional level of most futures research that can readily create a politics of fear.[iv] The litany level is the most visible and obvious, requiring few analytic capabilities.[v] Assumptions are rarely questioned.

The second level is concerned with social causes, including economic, cultural, political and historical factors (weak laws, breakdown of community, economic rationalism). This type of analysis is usually articulated by policy institutes and published as editorial pieces in newspapers or in not–quite academic journals. This level excels at technical explanations as well as academic analysis. The role of the state and other actors and interests is often explored at this level. The data is often questioned, however the language of questioning does not contest the paradigm in which the issue is framed but rather, remains obedient to it. In the safety issue, causes may cluster around the following: overpopulation particularly via new migrants entering the school system; poor building design, and lack of funding for schools; congestion caused by cars; violence shown on television and in movies and video games.

The third deeper level is concerned with structure and the discourse/worldview that supports and legitimates it. The task is to find deeper social, linguistic, cultural structures that are actor–invariant (not dependent on who the actors are). Discerning deeper assumptions behind the issue is crucial, as are efforts to revision the problem. At this stage, one can explore how different discourses (the traditional, modernist, feminism, technological, for example) do more than cause or mediate the issue, but constitute it. A traditional response may be to look for who are the strangers—stranger danger. A modernist solution to safety may be to install guards, while a feminist may teach children mediation skills (in case the violence is coming from within the school). A technological response may be to install surveillance cameras throughout the school and surrounding areas. Or it may be to give each child a mobile phone, so they can call in case of danger.

The fourth layer of analysis is at the level of metaphor or myth. These are the deep stories, the collective archetypes—the unconscious and often emotive dimensions of the problem or the paradox (e.g., students as tabula rasa, *vs.* students as plants to nurture, *vs.* students and teachers as different species in an ecology of learning, *vs.* elders know best). This level provides a gut/emotional level experience to the worldview under inquiry. The language used is less specific, more concerned with evoking visual images, with touching the heart instead of reading the head. This is the root level of questioning. Questioning itself, however, finds its limits since the frame of questioning must enter other frameworks of understanding—the mythical, for example. In the safety issue, one dominant metaphor is that of stranger danger. For the feminist it is about 'dialogue'. Use of new technologies is framed by "better safe than sorry", while for critics of surveillance it is "1984".

In one workshop for an educational ministry in Australia (Inayatullah, 2005), CLA was applied to concerns including safety in schools, behaviour management in schools, industrial relations, and public school enrolments. Solutions to school safety ranged from more surveillance to creating strong local communities. Behaviour management issues had varied solutions depending on participant's perspectives. A traditionalist on stronger values, a modernist on behaviour modification and other interventionist programs, and a postmodernist perspective called for new technologies and an understanding of power relations between schools and their communities, teachers, students and families.

Depending on one's worldview or myth, the solutions offered differed. If the myth was that teachers were lazy, then more flexible industrial relations policy to increase efficiencies were suggested. If the myth was that teachers are worked too hard, then unions were the solution so as to ensure a 'fair go'.

Marcus Bussey in his chapter in the *Causal Layered Analysis Reader* provides the following analysis of the litany issue he terms "fear and intensification" (see Table 1):

> Futurists seeking to engage with the educational possibilities facing schools today can begin by first examining the dominant image of schools as depicted within media and political debate. Such an examination would produce an analysis like CLA: Fear and Intensification. As can be seen, while antagonistic to the more hopeful aspirations of parents, children and educators, yet its hold on populist educational debate today is formidable. (Bussey, 2004, p. 332)

Table 1. CLA of 'fear and intensity'

CLA: Fear and Intensification	The Dominant Model
Litany	Schooling is out of control; blame children, parents, teachers, politicians
Systemic	Increase levels of surveillance, more testing, computers
Worldview	Effective managerial controls will enable schools to function at optimum, all problems can be solved
Myth/metaphor	Schools are knowledge factories

CLA also can be employed to better understand different futures and different images of the future. Bussey offers this analysis of the new spirituality (and see Table 2):

Layered vision of knowledge promoted in spiritually values-oriented learning communities. A deep view of mind as 'body–mind–spirit' is promoted and facilitated. The emphasis shifts from content to process. Valid knowledge is seen in terms of its spiritual/individual, social and cultural worth with meditation as part of the research process. Character becomes central to school curriculum.

Small groups and team learning that follows action learning principles become the mainstay of education—shifting emphasis from individual as solitary to individual as connected member of a learning community.

Knowledge as personal and social quest that ultimately leads to greater welfare of all and augmentation of one's sense of spiritual self. Thus, learning becomes more visceral and at the same time more subtle—a process of self making. Defining metaphor is taken from the Wisdom tradition and is the wise–one as Homo tantricus. (Bussey, 2004, p. 336)

Table 2. CLA of 'new spirituality'

CLA: Wisdom Culture	
Litany	Life is full of lessons, information helps but so does moral courage, ignorance is the enemy, purposeful effort leads to wisdom, information and knowledge are not the same thing
Systemic	Decentralised and community–based learning, relational with mentoring, teaching and learning are social responsibilities, we need different teachers for body–mind–spirit continuum
Worldview	Life a journey to the Centre, knowing is layered
Myth/metaphor	*Homo tantricus*

Education can also be a litany solution to many of today's problems, as demonstrated in the following unpacking of health mistakes.

If we examine health care (Table 3) we know that there is a high rate of medical mistakes leading to serious injury or death. At level one, litany, the solution is more education and training (focused on anatomy, for example) for health practitioners, particular doctors. At level two, system, we search for causes for these mistakes. Is it lack of communication between health professionals? The state of the hospital? Lack of understanding of new technologies? Mis-administration of medicine? Systemic solutions seek to intervene by making the system more efficient, smarter, ensuring that all parts of the system are seamlessly connected. The goal is not the education of a particular stakeholder but to make the entire system smarter.

Table 3. CLA of 'medical mistakes'

Causal Layered Analysis Level	Medical Mistakes
Litany	High rate of medical mistakes
	Solution: More GP Training
Systemic causes	Audit on causes of mistakes: communication, new technologies, administration
	Solution: more efficient smarter systems
Worldview	Reductionist modern medical paradigm creates hierarchy
	Solution: enhance power of patients
	Solution: move to different health systems
Myth/metaphor	"Doctor knows best"
	Solution: "Take charge of your health"

But if we move to a deeper, worldview level, we see the problem may in fact be the paradigm of Western medicine itself: its reductionism, its focus on technique and the disowning of its softer and holistic potentials. The doctor remains far above, the nurse below and the patient even lower. It is the hierarchy of knowledge that is the root problem at this level. Merely more training or more efficient systems ignore the question of power. The solution is to empower patients, or a move to different health systems—complimentary health systems, for example. Certainly, alternative health is the disowned self of modern medicine (though now many researchers are integrating these opposites—using modern and ancient medicine to develop better outcomes). At this worldview level, the goal is to create learning and healing organisations—wherein the entire system is reflective of its purposes and errors. The system thus becomes more complex and co-adaptive.

At the myth level, the deeper problem is the notion of "doctor knows best". Patients give up their power when they see medical experts—patients enter the hospital system and immediately regress to their child selves. Doctors resort to expert selves—

and with dehumanised bureaucracies ensuring a focus on efficiency, mistakes keep on happening. Education at this level is about empowerment.

CLA seeks to integrate these four levels of understanding. Each level is true, and solutions need to be found at each level. Thus policy solutions can be deeper. Litany interventions lead to short term solutions, easy to grasp, packed with data. Systemic answers require interventions by efficiency experts. Governmental policies linked to partnership with the private sector often result. Worldview change is much harder and longer term. It requires seeking solutions from outside the framework in which the solution has been defined. And myth solutions require the deepest interventions, as this requires telling a new story, rewiring the brain and building new memories and the personal and collective body. The entire exercise is intended to work with all parts of the system to develop preferred futures—to move the individuals and systems toward ideal states.

After the future is deepened, we can then broaden it, using the fifth pillar.

Creating Alternatives

The fifth pillar is creating alternative futures. There are two important methods in this pillar. The first is nuts and bolts.[vi] This consists of undertaking a structural functional analysis of the organisation and then finding different ways of doing what it does. If it is an educational organisation, one may challenge current models: administrators (what are some other ways to manage information and competencies, can AI replace humans, for example?); teachers (who should teach, should jobs be tenured); students (from the locale, global, web, part time, only humans, all ages); location (from campus, or remote, or …); and curriculum (why not action learning; should students design the curriculum themselves?). The key is to create an organisational functions chart and then search for new structures to engage in those functions.

The second way to create alternative futures is via scenarios. Scenarios are the tool *par excellence* of futures studies. They open up the present, contour the range of uncertainty, offer alternatives, and even better, predict.

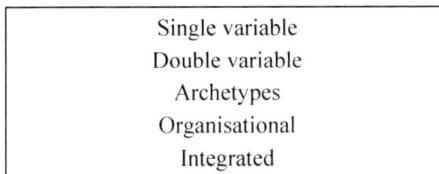

Single variable
Double variable
Archetypes
Organisational
Integrated

Figure 8. Multiple scenarios method

There are multiple scenario methods (Figure 8). The first is the multi-single variable. This is derived from the futures triangle. Based on the images or the drivers, a range of scenarios or stories/pictures of the future are created. Scenario one could be: "Return to traditional values" where students engage in rote learning, obedience to teachers and principals is paramount, and testing is the main criteria for success. A postmodern scenario would be the university or school as an *à la carte* menu—students pick and choose what they wish to study. A "global virtual or invisible school/university" scenario would be totally technologically driven. Students would rarely physically assemble, preferring webcams, wikis and other virtual meeting spaces.

The second method—the double variable method—identifies the two major uncertainties and develops scenarios based on these. This method, among others, has been developed by Johan Galtung (1998; www.transcend.org). For example, for the futures of education, two critical uncertainties are the site of change (global *vs.* tribal) and the level of change (status quo or transformation). Based on these uncertainties, four futures are possible (Figure 9). The first future is "Corporatopia".

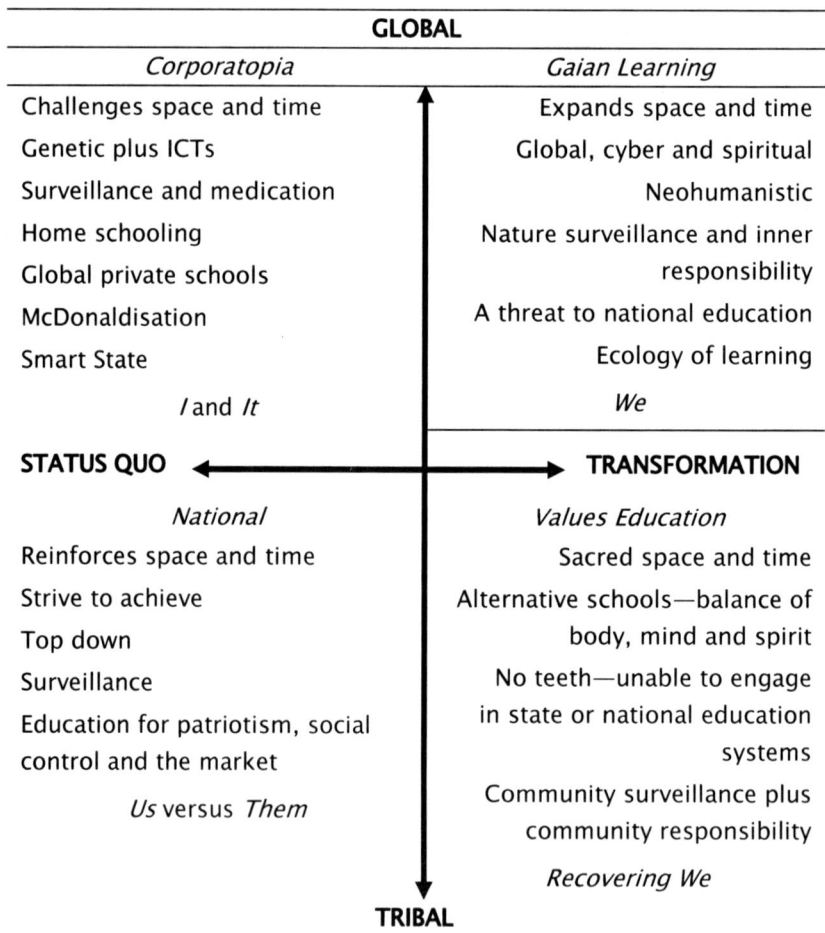

	GLOBAL	
Corporatopia		*Gaian Learning*
Challenges space and time		Expands space and time
Genetic plus ICTs		Global, cyber and spiritual
Surveillance and medication		Neohumanistic
Home schooling		Nature surveillance and inner
Global private schools		responsibility
McDonaldisation		A threat to national education
Smart State		Ecology of learning
I and *It*		*We*
STATUS QUO ←		→ **TRANSFORMATION**
National		*Values Education*
Reinforces space and time		Sacred space and time
Strive to achieve		Alternative schools—balance of
Top down		body, mind and spirit
Surveillance		No teeth—unable to engage
Education for patriotism, social		in state or national education
control and the market		systems
Us versus *Them*		Community surveillance plus
		community responsibility
		Recovering We
	TRIBAL	

Figure 9. Four futures

In this, education is global and focused on creating economic wealth. National boundaries are transcended through the new information and communication technologies. The inner story is: "I and It". The second is "National". This is education for national competition. The goal is to win against other nations by enhancing the skills and intelligence of the populace. The inner story is "us *versus* them". The third is "Values education". The present seeks to transform the future by rediscovering the past. Traditional values of honour and trust are primary—it is these values that are most important for creating a good society. The inner story is: "Recovering we". The final scenario is "Gaian learning". This is education that is planetary in scope, challenging traditional disciplines and seeking global solutions. The inner story is "we".

Developed by James Dator, the third method articulates scenario archetypes (1979; http://www.futures.hawaii.edu). These are:

– Continued Growth—where current conditions are enhanced: more products, more roads, more technology, and a larger population. Technology is considered the solution to every problem. Education in this scenario is about preparing students for a globalised technological world. However, the context of this competition is national, thus, the goal is education for national competitiveness in the world economy.

– Collapse—this future results as Continued Growth fails. Collapse is inevitable as the contradictions within and between the following are too great: between the economy and nature; between men and women; between the speculative and the real economy; between religious, secular and postmodern approaches; and between technology and culture. In this scenario, educational systems are unable to keep up with the pace of change. Universities, for example, are outflanked by multinational corporations. Educational subsidies (or investment) are reduced as nations attempt to become more competitive. The best professors leave the public sector as they search for higher salaries and more autonomy. Public education becomes irrelevant, no longer linked to emerging futures.

– Steady State—this future seeks to arrest growth and find a balance in the economy and with nature. It is a balanced, softer and fairer society. Community is decisive in this future. Steady State is both back to nature and back to the past. Human values are first here. Technology is often seen as the problem. In education, this future would be about focusing on community and environmental values. The purpose of learning is to create a better society. The exaggerations of globalism—consumerism, market failures (climate change, for example)—are reduced. Education is seen as an investment and not as a cost. Individual and collective discipline are seen as critical values for moving forward.

– Transformation—this future seeks to change the basic assumptions of the other three. Transformation comes out either through dramatic technological change (artificial intelligence eliminates the courts, bureaucracy, much of schooling, and many forms of governance; genetics changing the nature of nature, for example) or through spiritual change (humans change their consciousness, not just values, but the experience of deep transcendence). In the technological variant of this future, education would be foundationally transformed. Schools would disappear, students would learn from everywhere and anytime, the limits of space and time would be dramatically reduced. In the spiritual variant, meditation, yoga, emotional intelligence and mediation would be the focus. The purpose of education would be self-realization and planetary transformation. This would not be a return to the traditional ashram, however, rather, the ashram would be transformed as well—becoming far more global and embedded with new technologies.

Taking these four scenarios, one can incast or articulate how one's organisation (school or university) would look in each of these scenarios. I will focus here on a particular part of the world economy, East Asia. Will East Asia (Table 4) continue to grow, becoming more and more the centre of the world economy, or will there be a collapse because of lack of transparency, because of overgrowth leading to SARS-like diseases, or because an open economy challenges authoritarian leadership systems? Or will East Asia find a neo-Confucian balance, focusing neither too much on material values nor on tradition? Or can East Asia transform: will dramatic changes in science and technology (robotics and gaming) change culture; will a Taoist/Zen resurgence deeply transform the patriarchy of Confucian culture?

Table 4. Incasting East Asian education

Scenarios	Continued Growth	Collapse	Steady State	Transformation
Description	East Asia continues to grow, becoming the centre of the world economy	Overgrowth, lack of transparency, SARS-like diseases, and authoritarian system lead to a collapse	Neo-Confucian balance created, balancing material values and tradition	Dramatic changes in science and technology transform East Asia. Resurgence of Taoist Zen culture transforms Confucian culture
Education	Testing and global competition. East Asian universities on the rise	Education is part of the problem—does not challenge the paradigm	Education is about virtue and balance	Education is student and technology driven, and even run. Meditation practices are central and spiritual intelligence is foundational.

In Continued Growth, education would be about testing, graduating so one could get a job in the right corporation or ministry. Education is a commodity—one works hard, sacrifices for the future, so that one can become wealthy. East Asian universities compete globally. In Collapse, education ceases to be of utility, what has been taught has only made the world worse—knowledge has become reductionist, unable to deal with the global challenges. Instead, education would be far more survival-based, passing on skills to survive long term economic downturns. In Steady State, education would be about the balance between material and spiritual; nation and globe; instrumental and ethical values. In the Transformation scenario, education would be created by students, they would produce knowledge. New technologies would transform schooling and universities in East Asia. In the spiritual variant, meditative practices would form the basis of a good education.

Developed by Peter Schwartz (1995, 1996) of the Global Business Network, the fourth model of scenario writing is organisational focused. The scenario structure is composed of four variables: best case (where the organisation desires to move towards); worst case (where everything goes bad); outlier (a surprise future based on a disruptive emerging issue); and business as usual (no change). In a project for the Australian Government Pharmaceutical Industry Alliance, this method was used (Table 5).[vii] The preferred scenario was "Science Olympics" wherein the educational system is focused on a science curriculum that is attractive and engaging. It is valued the way sports currently are. There is investment and winners are rewarded. The worst case was a long term recession where investment for biotech dries up, and companies are saddled with decreased sales even while they have to meet societal obligations for delivering affordable pharmaceuticals. The brightest would leave the country for brighter horizons elsewhere (Singapore, South Korea or the UK).

Table 5. Four scenarios of education

Scenarios	Best Case	Worst Case	Outlier	Business as Usual
Description	Science Olympics The education system is focused on science. The best and brightest pursue degrees in science. Scientists are like sports stars.	Long term recession. Investment dries up and best and brightest leave for overseas. Those who stay, pursue safe government jobs, or are unemployed.	Genetics and digitalisation change the nature of drugs, i.e., gene therapy eliminates numerous diseases. Education for science and technologies—research leads to products.	No clear strategy, losing out to other nations and pharmaceutical industry criticised by the public. Education loses its way, direction comes from a variety of conflicting stakeholders.

Science education lags dramatically behind other areas (information and communication technology and business education). In the outlier scenario, genetics and digitalisation change the nature of drugs (a pharmaceutical factory in your body, monitoring your daily needs, or gene therapy eliminating many diseases and thus the need for drugs). Education uses the products from the science and technology revolution in dramatic ways—intelligence drugs and even gene enhancement. Research is translated into products. Business as usual would be no clear strategy, other nations steaming ahead, pharmaceutical being criticised by the public and science not considered an attractive field for young persons.

The fifth scenario methodology has four dimensions: the preferred, the world we want; the disowned, the world that we reject or are unable to deal with; the integrated, where owned and disowned are united in a complex fashion; and last is the outlier, the future outside of these categories. For example, in a workshop for Brisbane City Council[viii] on refreshing the vision for Brisbane 2026 (Table 6), in the preferred, employees desired a more multicultural organisation, gender partnership, a green city focused on sustainability, a strong balance between work and home, a learning and healing organisation, and even a focus on spiritual practices and values. The combination of these characteristics would make Brisbane unique. The disowned, they believed, was the economic (how will we make money) and the strategic competitive—can we compete if we are more balanced in a dog–eat–dog world— and the material: issues of engineering, roads and garbage. In the integrated scenario, they saw that sustainability may give them a competitive edge; green technology principles could be applied to waste disposal and to road construction (focused not just on roads but on enhancing travel choices *vis a vis* bikeways, light rail, cars,

Table 6. Four scenarios for Brisbane

Scenarios	Preferred	Disowned	Integrated	Outlier
Description	Multicultural Gender partnership Work-home balance Sustainability Spiritual values Learning and healing	Economic—how to make money Strategic competitive Material—engineering, roads, garbage Skills-based education	Sustainability gives the competitive edge Green technologies can be applied to waste disposal and road construction Transformative learning that includes reflection and skills.	New diseases challenge the city Education for alternative futures—for ensuring tomorrow problems are identified today

buses, taxis and walking). The integrated scenario would decrease pollution, enhance longevity. Spiritual practices would likely increase productivity as individuals had more clarity about their goals. A learning and healing organisation that was skills-based would increase productivity and retraining would ensure that the city was efficient, adapting to changing conditions. The outlier was new diseases challenging the nature of the city. Education in this future needed to be about frameworks that ensured that tomorrow's problems were identified.

Transforming the Future

The final pillar is transformation.

In transformation, the future is narrowed toward the preferred. Which future do individuals desire? The preferred future can result from scenarios. It can also be created by a process of questioning. Questioning consists of asking individuals about a preferred day in their life in the future. What happens once they wake up? What does their home look like? What type of technologies do they use? Who do they live with? What is the design of their home? What types of building materials were used? Do they go to work? What does work look like? Do they travel to work? How? What do they eat? How does one learn? Where does one learn? Through which technologies? These questions force individuals to think in more detail about the world they would like to live in.

The preferred future can also be discerned through a process of creative visualisation. In this process, individuals are asked to close their eyes and enter a restful state. From there, in their minds' eye, they take steps to a hedge or wall (the number of steps is based on how many years into the future they wish to go). Over the hedge is the preferred future. They walk into that future. The facilitator asks them for details such as: Who is there? What does the future look like? What can they see, smell, hear, touch, taste? Intuit? This exercise articulates the future from the right brain—it is more visual.

The three visioning methods—the analytic scenario, the questioning and the creative visualisation—are then triangulated to develop a more complete view of the future.

In a workshop for a state government ministry of education, the vision that emerged (Inayatullah, 2005) (after three days of workshops using the six pillars approach and based on the three visioning methods) had the following attributes:
– No differentiation between teacher and student—flexible roles and deep learning environments;
– Technology embedded in classrooms (not as an externality but merged with the environment);
– Global education—direct contact with other children, multiple languages, multiple cultures—true appreciation of different ways of knowing;
– Student-based , happy children, learning-based;
– Multi-age, not grade controlled;
– No school uniforms, flexible; and
– Community, truly local, and global, truly planetary.

When groups go through such a process, they are inevitably inspired. However, *a loss of hope can quickly set in if pathways to achieve the vision are not set in place.* That is, the system has numerous weights and from CLA, we know that there are inner stories that mitigate against transformation ("it won't work here", for example). To overcome these weights, backcasting is used (Figure 10) (Boulding & Boulding, 1995).

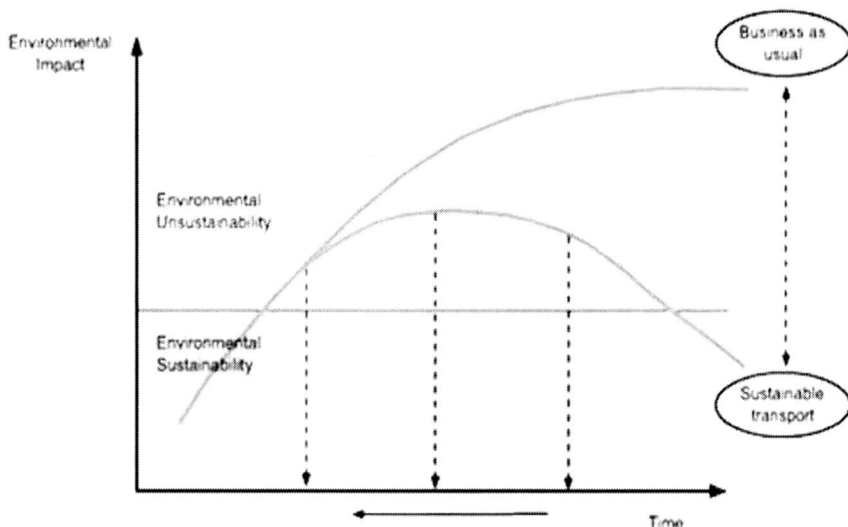

Figure 10. Backcasting

This method works by moving individuals into the preferred future. I then ask, in the instance of the preferred, what happened in the last 20 years to bring us to today? What are their memories of the last 20 years? What needed to happen? What were the trends and events that created today? Backcasting requires imagination ... but as well logic—a sense of cause and effect—what has to have happened to create the desired future. Backcasting fills in the space between today (the future) and the past. Doing so makes the future far more achievable. The necessary steps to achieve the preferred future can then be enacted. This can be done via a plan or, far more effectively, via action learning steps, where a process of experimentation begins to create the desired future. This can be a budgeted for transition strategy or a full scale re-engineering. Backcasting can also be done with any particular scenario, for example, the worst case. Events and trends that happened to create the worst case are articulated. From there, pathways are developed to avoid that particular future.

What happens though when there is conflict between visions of the future? Johan Galtung's transcend method (www.transcend.org) is an excellent way forward. It focuses not on compromise, or far worse, withdrawal, but on finding win–win solutions. To do so, all the issues that are contested in the two visions need to be spelled out. And then, through a process of brain storming, alternatives creating, new ways to integrate the visions can occur. In one case, one group desired a green sustainable city; another group a far more exciting modern international glamorous city. Through the transcend method (Figure 11), the Greens understood that their city would become boring. They thus realised that the glamorous vision was a way to recover that aspect of their disowned personalities, but also that the modern dimension of the city could help them innovate. The modernists understood that without sustainability as a guiding principal there would be no way forward for anyone—both aspects of the vision needed each other.

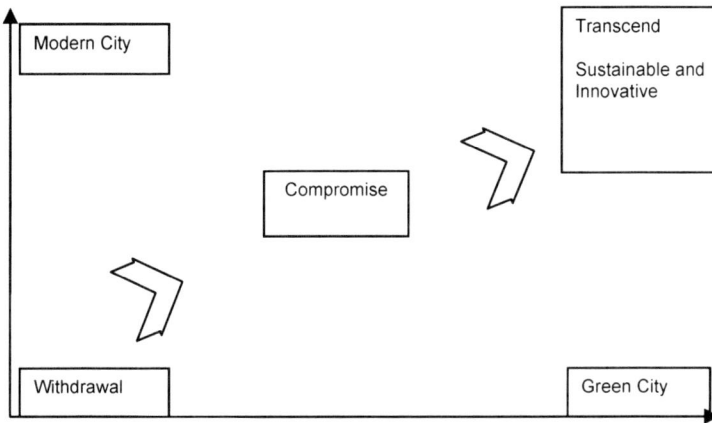

Figure 11. The transcend method

In an educational context, there may be conflicts between a "Corporatopian" vision and a "Gaian learning". It may be that each needs each other—the corporatopia providing the capital and the Gaian providing the necessary pedagogy to ensure the thrival of the planet. A corporatopia would provide efficiency, as the Gaian learning provides slower and deeper reflective time.

The study of the future thus has six foundational concepts and six pillars. As the world becomes increasingly heterogeneous, as events from far away places dramatically impact how, where, when, why and with whom we live and work, futures studies can help us recover our agency. By mapping the past, present and future, anticipating future issues and their consequences, being sensitive to the grand patterns of change, deepening our analysis to include worldviews and myths and metaphors, creating alternative futures, and choosing a preferred future and backcasting ways to realise it, we can create the world we wish to live in.

Futures thinking does not wish to condemn us to hope alone.[ix]

NOTES

[i] The Indian steel company Mittal is even eying purchasing the football club, Red Star Belgrade.

[ii] The *Oxford English Dictionary* defines meme as: "An element of a culture that may be considered to be passed on by non-genetic means, esp. imitation".

[iii] The work of Riane Eisler is exemplary—www.partnershipway.org.

[iv] The Club of Rome's *Limits to Growth* and other studies are modern examples of this.

[v] Of course, those who develop the litany require great—not only analytic—capability, but also the capacity to touch the system, the worldview and myth/metaphor level. A litany is not a litany unless it has something to rest on. For example, the litany of economism rests on the world financial system which rests on the worldview of capitalism which rests on the myth of greed, the invisible hand, and self-interest.

[vi] This was developed at the Hawaii Judiciary, particularly as input into the Hawaii Judiciary Foresight Conference, Honolulu, 6 January, 1991.

[vii] August to October, 2001—Melbourne, Brisbane and Sydney. The full project report is available from the Australian Government's Department of Industry, Science and Resources.

[viii] Organized by Jennifer Bartlett of Brisbane City Council, 3 March, 2006, Brisbane, Australia.

[ix] To paraphrase John Cleese from his movie *Clockwork*: "despair I can handle, it is hope that is the killer".

REFERENCES

Blackmore, S. (1998). Imitation and the definition of a meme. *Journal of Memetics—Evolutionary Models of Information Transmission, 2,* 11–.

Boulding, E., & Boulding, K. (1995). *The future: Images and processes.* London: Sage.

Bussey, M. (2004). Educational scenario building: CLA as a tool for unpacking educational futures. In S. Inayatullah (Ed.), *The Causal Layered Analysis (CLA) reader: Theory and case studies of an integrative and transformative methodology* (pp. 331–337). Tamsui, Taiwan: Tamkang University Press.

CBS Worldwide Inc. (2002, August 28). *Soda pop to be banned in L.A. schools—Health worries prompt new rule, to take effect in 2004.* Retrieved, January 5, 2008, from http://www.cbsnews.com/stories/ 2003/06/25/ health/main560372.shtml

Centre for Women's Business Research. (2001). *Number of minority women-owned businesses expected to reach 1.2 million in 2002.* Washington, DC: Centre for Women's Business Research. Retrieved, July 4, 2007, from http://www.cfwbr.org/press/details.php?id=54

Chopra, D. (2005). *Syncrodestiny.* London: Rider and Co.

Dator, J. (1979). The futures of cultures and cultures of the future. In T. Marsella et al. (Eds.), *Perspectives on cross cultural psychology* (pp. 369–388). New York: Academic Press.

Dator, J., & Seo, Y. (2004). Koreas as the wave of a future: The emerging dream society of icons and aesthetic experience. *Journal of Futures Studies, 9*(1), 2004.

Dawkins, R. (1989). *The selfish gene.* Oxford: Oxford University Press.

Galtung, J. (1998). *Essays in peace research* (Vols. 1–6). Copenhagen: Christian Ejlers.

Galtung, J., & Inayatullah, S. (Eds.). (1997). *Macrohistory and macrohistorians.* Westport, CT: Praeger.

Inayatullah, S. (2004). Cities create their future. *Journal of Futures Studies, 8*(3), 77–81.

Inayatullah, S. (2005, May). Report of the Queensland Education Futures Scanning Workshop, Brisbane, Australia.

Inayatullah, S. (2007). Alternative futures of occupational therapy and therapists. *Journal of Futures Studies, 11*(4).

Inayatullah, S. (Ed.). (2004). *The Causal Layered Analysis (CLA) reader: Theory and case studies of an integrative and transformative methodology.* Tamsui, Taiwan: Tamkang University Press.

Karoly, L., & Panis, C. (2004, March). *The 21st century at work: Forces shaping the future workforce and workplace in the United States.* Prepared for the US Dept of Labor. Santa Monica, CA: Rand.

Loye, D. (Ed.). (2004). *The great adventure.* New York: State University of New York Press.

Loye, D. (2000). *Darwin's lost theory of love.* San Jose: Iuniverse.com.

May, G., & Jones, D. (2001). *Futures toolkit.* United Kingdom Local Governmental Association (www.lga.gov.uk). Retrieved 2007, from http://www.lga.gov.uk/lga/toolkit/futures%20methods.pdf

McGray, D. (2002). Japan's gross national cool. *Foreign Policy,* June/July, 44–54. Retrieved December 5, 2007, from http://www.douglasmcgray.com/grossnationalcool.pdf

Molitor, M. (2003). *The power to change the world: The art of forecasting.* Potomoc, MD: Public Policy Forecasting.

Sahtouris, E. (2002). *Earth dance: Living systems in evolution.* San Jose: Iuniverse.com.

Sarkar, P. R. (1991). *Microvitum in a nutshell* (3rd ed.). Calcutta: Ananda Marga Publications.

Schwartz, P. (1995). Scenarios: The future of the future. *Wired, Special issue.*

Schwartz, P. (1996). *The art of the long view.* New York: Doubleday.

Stone, H., & Stone, S. (1989). *Embracing our selves: The voice dialogue manual.* Novato, CA: New World Library.

Ura, K., & Galay, K. (2004). *Gross national happiness and development.* Thimbu, Bhutan: Centre for Bhutan Studies, 2004.

Voros, J. (2004). Nesting social-analytical perspectives: An approach to macro-social analysis. *Journal of Futures Studies, 11*(1), 1–22.

Sohail Inayatullah is a Professor of political science/futures associated with Tamkang University, Taiwan (Graduate Institute for Futures Studies), University of the Sunshine Coast (Faculty of Arts and Social Sciences), and Prout College (www.proutcollege.org).

He has authored/co-edited eighteen books and CDROMs, including Six Pillars *(a CGI DVD);* Youth Futures, Macrohistory and Macrohistorians, Questioning the Future, The Causal Layered Analysis Reader, *and* The University in Transformation. *Inayatullah has authored over 300 refereed journal articles, book chapters and magazine editorials. He is also theme editor (Globalization and World Systems) of the* UNESCO Encyclopedia of Life Support Systems.

MARCUS BUSSEY[i]

3. GLOBAL EDUCATION

A musical exposition

As a musician I often find myself thinking about society, culture, history and
education via analogies with music. I know there are certain limitations in doing
so: the most obvious for a poststructuralist being that music imposes an artificial
order on any moment that is read 'musically', while, for instance, a structuralist
might express doubts over music's romantic proclivities that somehow blur the
distinctions between rational and somatic categories. So, having had some months
to think about the question of "Global education from a Neohumanist perspective",
and knowing that I am going to be meeting some friends who had gathered with me
in Israel last year just before the 'disaster' of the Israel–Lebanon action and just
after Daniel Barenboim had given the last two Reith Lectures in Jerusalem on music
as a form of socio-political engagement, I thought to pick some of the thematic–
melodic strands of that meeting and work them here into something resembling a
fugue.

EDUCATION AND CAPITALISM

Firstly, I will pick up on Barenboim's (2006) observation that:

> It is very difficult for the human being to truly have the courage and the
> ability to start from scratch, to start from zero, to take experience from the
> past and yet think it anew. And yet this is essential, in music as well as in life.
> (Lecture 5)[ii]

His argument is that every time a musician comes to a piece to play it, the music is
fresh, new and ephemeral, yet it is also the product of years of disciplined work
and interpretation. It is both new and old. The same applies to life. 'Today is the
beginning of the rest of your life', may be a cliché, but it carries a real truth. The
individual and the collective, when freed from the 'iron cage' of historical, social,
and personal *karma*, can begin afresh. The moment, every moment, is paradoxically
both stale and fresh. Similarly, the question of globalisation is both new and old, as
is my own perspective: neohumanism.

Barenboim identifies courage as something necessary when facing any new
context, musical or otherwise. Certainly, courage is required if we are to think beyond
the conditions that determine global educational priorities as they are currently
understood. Almost universally such priorities are taken to be discrete components
of an unarticulated yet necessary historical narrative. Australian academic Gordon

*M. Bussey, S. Inayatullah and I. Milojević (eds.), Alternative Educational Futures: Pedagogies for
Emergent Worlds, 41–56.*

Tait (2004) says of this narrative that it is shared and self evident; he sums it up with some irony as follows:

> The more civilised we became, the more we pushed back the school leaving age, until we eventually developed schools that clearly reflected the values and ambitions of the wider community. After all, are schools not simply microcosms of society at large? In addition to this, the form that modern schooling takes is regarded as an unproblematic part of the same story. Of course we should organise our learning in the way we do, with the emphasis on formalised learning spaces, graded curricula, timetables of activities, various forms of assessment, and a clear hierarchy of authority. These features of the contemporary education merely reflect the fact that this is self-evidently the best system available. After all, how else could education possibly be organised? (Tait, 2004, p. 13)

Tait's point is that much that we take to be natural about schooling, is unnatural. Things could be otherwise. The current momentum behind the globalisation of the neoliberal metanarrative is contained in the subtext to the story Tait presents here. The mythic story, discretely hidden by the intelligibility of this narrative of human progress towards an enlightened education system, and citizenry, is that the individual is the basic unit of society and that when enculturated via disciplinary education, they will govern/police themselves. The beauty of the system is that it is self regulating, and heavily invested in by private capital. The "pedagogic family" (Tait, 2004, p. 20) willingly carries the emotional, and increasingly, the financial burden of producing well-educated and disciplined citizens.

At the risk of conflating positions I see parallels, counterpoints, between Tait's essentially Foucauldian analysis and that of Peter McLaren (the wild boy of Marxist revolutionary critical pedagogy). McLaren sees the global progress of neoliberal education as a form of pedagogy for capital (McLaren, 2006). He points out that such education facilitates capital's grounding of social mediation in forms of value (ibid, p. 241). In this he argues that our subjectivities are constituted through the pedagogic lens of capitalist education and expressed in a social universe driven by the logic of advanced capitalism in which all things are simultaneously both commodity and labour.

FROM CRITIQUE TO POSSIBILITY

I have little doubt that both Tait and McLaren are right (remembering the paradox Niels Bohr points to that the opposite of a great truth is another truth) when assessing the key elements of modernity's global educational project. Yet there is another story we can tell in which the deconstructive and revolutionary energy of such analyses turns, as Henry Giroux (Giroux, 1988, p. 204) would have us turn, from critique to possibility.

This, as a story of possibility, Barenboim tells through a musical analogy:

> Now, when you play music, whether you play chamber music or you play in an orchestra, you have to do two very important things and do them

simultaneously. You have to be able to express yourself, otherwise you are not contributing to the musical experience, but at the same time it is imperative that you listen to the other. You have to understand what the other is doing. (Lecture 4)

A neohumanistic perspective takes this interactive quality from music and applies it to social contexts in which the layered and multiple are grounded in a pedagogical ethic of the other. In this living context education implies the other; it implies community, culture, history, myth and continuity; it simultaneously looks back and forward; it is the heartbeat of the moment stretched out before and behind the student in various unique and general syncopations of mind and soul as it encounters its own and others' traditions in unique yet paradoxically general settings. Education, rather than simply focusing on the transmission of information and the learning of narrow social disciplinary rules can, when run through a neohumanist lens, leads us to consider the frontiers of our humanity where coherence dissolves into mystery. Judith Butler (2004), when reflecting on vulnerability and how it grounds the human condition, points to this liminal quality observing:

> If the humanities has a future as cultural criticism, and cultural criticism has a task at the present moment, it is no doubt to return us to the human where we do not expect to find it, in its frailty and at the limits of its capacity to make sense (ibid: 151).

She goes on to suggest that if we are to enact such a form of critical awareness that we would need to: "... interrogate the emergence and vanishing of the human at the limits of what we can know, what we can hear, what we can see, what we can sense" (ibid).

This in essence is the neohumanist invitation. In this context rationality is expanded to embrace the spiritual (sure, I am pushing Butler beyond her comfort zone) and critique emerges as an engaged critical spirituality that both expresses and facilitates dimensions of the global encounter that a truly global education might provide.

From the perspective of this symposium I have no doubt that the phrase "global education" indicates the positive potential behind processes of globalisation which seem from our perspective to be unstoppable and irreversible. Despite shared misgivings we feel ourselves to be caught in an ineluctable process of global significance. The question before us is: Can we reclaim our personal and collective agency?

CRITICAL SPIRITUALITY

The critically spiritual approach of neohumanism short circuits the dichotomy upon which this question is based. Global, from a neohumanist perspective, is both an expression of the unique subjectivity of each of us while simultaneously being the objective expression of universal fields of consciousness that map the subtle and physical universe. Prabhat Rainjan Sarkar, who developed the concept of neohumanism, points out that such an understanding of consciousness and our global possibilities grounds our actions in a subjective approach to the real while we adjust objectively to the material and social concerns of the moment (Sarkar, 1987, pp. 24–27).

Thus by presenting consciousness and being as a continuum we have both ontological and epistemological tools for rereading the social and reengaging our pedagogy from a transformative perspective. The following image, Figure 1, developed by Sohail Inayatullah (Inayatullah, Bussey & Milojević, 2006) captures the layered nature of the neohumanist worldview.

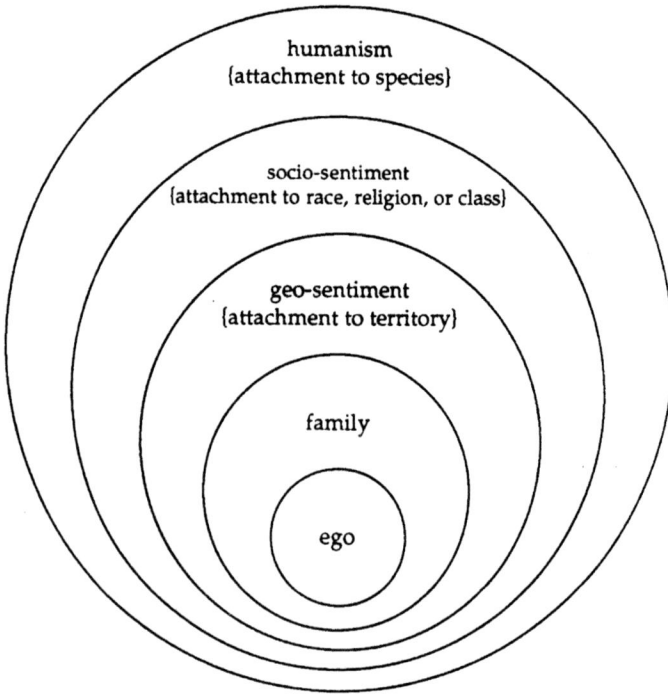

Figure 1. Map of neohumanism's co-incentric circles (love and respect for all beings, animate and inanimate, in the universe)

With reality configured to validate the intersection of subjective–objective space, we find the *between* of which Michel Serres speaks (1995)—a space of hybrid interactivity or what Foucault called heterotopic possibility (Foucault, 1986). Sure, you say, education is all about interaction and the grey zone in which value and information collide with the unique context of the individual. But … there are two other models of education that hold centre stage. The neohumanist vision for global education is better understood when placed along side these powerful alternative visions.

FLAT EDUCATION: NETWORKED MONO-KNOWLEDGE

This contrasts greatly with the model of capitalist being which lies at the heart of much globalising education. In this the needs of the centre are exported to the periphery in order to access the dynamic energy of desire. Thomas Friedman sums this insight up well:

> One cannot stress enough the fact that in the flat world the frontiers of knowledge get pushed out farther, faster and faster. Therefore, companies need the brainpower that can not only reach the new frontiers but push them still farther. That is where the breakthrough drugs and software and hardware products are being found. And America either needs to be training the brainpower itself or importing it from somewhere else—or ideally both—if it wants to dominate the twenty-first century the way it dominated the twentieth … (Friedman, 2005, p. 274)

Here Friedman is playing on the tension inherent in such words as 'frontier'. In his "flat world" the frontier is anywhere someone has a computer and is savvy enough to turn it on. His vision of a globalising education is one in which science and mathematics are taught uniformly and centrally in schools all over a country (ibid, p. 273). This he assures us is not happening in the United States. Regardless of the accuracy of his claims, the vision is one of education that is uniform and "flat". There is only one playing field for Friedman, and it is global in dimension and uninterested in the local or parochial. Thus he warns:

> This flattening process is happening at warp speed and directly or indirectly touching a lot more people on the planet at once. The faster and broader the transition to a new era, the more likely is the potential for disruption, as opposed to an orderly transfer of power from the old winners to the new winners. (ibid, p. 46)

Friedman's flat world still has a centre—the United States—but he sees that centre under attack from both within and without. His flat education is also clearly scientific and utilitarian in nature—it has a centre too; though he does acknowledge the essential extra ingredient for success here: imagination (ibid, p. 443). Yet imagination is a double edged sword—it can imagine a 9/11 or a world of harmonious cooperation. Thus he argues, "We have to be the masters of our imaginations, not the prisoners" (ibid, p. 448).

So Friedman imagines a flat world in which there is a relative centre, anywhere there is a computer, and an absolute centre, currently the United States but who knows? The relative centre is built around the willingness to creatively and positively engage with the opportunities bursting into our awareness; it is anchored in the capacity to access a flat education in which the skills and values of the absolute centre are channelled throughout the flat world.

Some lessons from Friedman's flat classroom are that access to education determines access to the centre; the absolute centre may be reconfigured as fractal centres in which process—a knowledge economy—takes the place of a centralised geo-political space; take the initiative, don't wait for the centre to come to you: "Do whatever it takes, but get out of the door" (ibid, p. 449). A map of his flat networked education might look like Figure 2, below, which is one of Marc Lombardi's[iii] images.

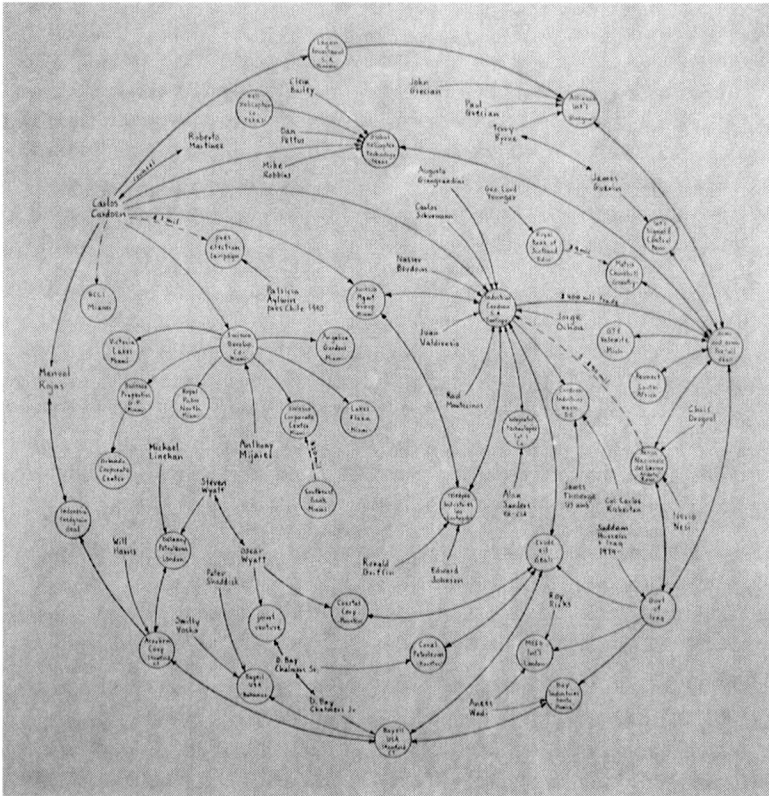

Figure 2. Map of the flat classroom and mono education as 'networked' space

THE MULTICULTURAL EDUCATION: PARALLEL TOLERANCE AND THE INTERACTIVITY OF CENTRE AND PERIPHERY

Contrasting with Friedman's flat education there is the well known model of multicultural education. One in which the central space is purportedly open to all and around which orbit, cultural contexts which are validated by their participation in the political and pedagogical life of the collective. Such an approach to collective engagement is mapped in Figure 3[iv] as a forum.

Conte Forum
Chestnut Hill, MA

Gate C

JJ KK LL MM NN OO

I J K L M N O P

H Q

G R

F S

E T

D C B A X W V U

CC BB AA XX WW VV

1 2 3 4 5 6 7 8 9 10 11 12 13 14 Luxury Boxes

Gate B

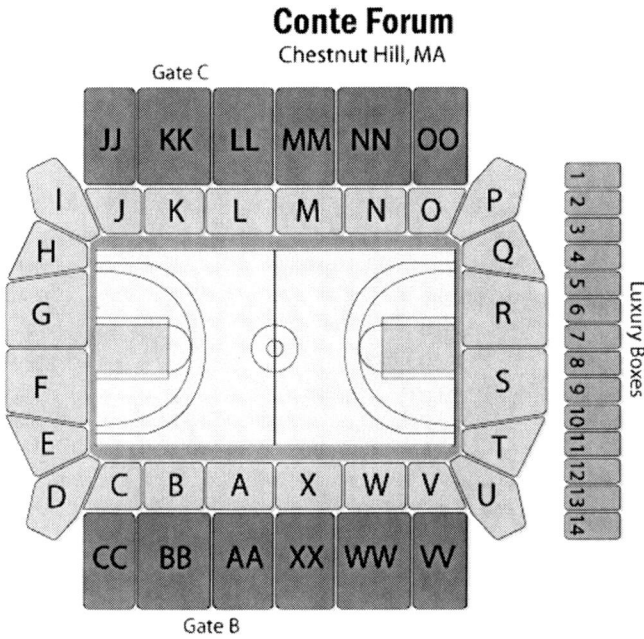

Figure 3. The multicultural forum

This is a broadly humanistic map of the global 'family' with educational units that promote tolerance (each family does its own 'thing'), understanding and engagement being built around the same core model described by Friedman—the maths, science and literacy trinity which acts as a kind of forum (historical and architectural overtones are intended), in which all citizens come to speak the same language, leaving individual differences aside. This division is presented as rational and reflects the values of what John Ralston Saul calls "positive nationalism" (2005). For Saul, this is:

> ... a belief in the positive tension of uncertainty and the central importance of choice. It is not wedded to narrow absolutes. It is particularly dubious about broad answers to utilitarian questions. Thus, the conviction that one market view must prevail in all considerations—whether it be Marxist or neo-liberal—is of little interest. (ibid, p. 271)

For Saul, this solution works because it is the way people have organised themselves throughout history. Thus he concludes that, "The desire of people to organise their lives around the reality of where they live is central to the return of nationalism" (ibid, p. 272). Such reasoning leads Saul to conclude that the globalist myth is evaporating (ibid, p. 274) and that the local is taking back its own and that this humanist response to the irresponsibility of market ideologues is the way of the future. Such pragmatism, some might call it wishful thinking, will see many peoples coming together in limitless configurations of "people, separate and interwoven" (ibid, p. 279) and the breaking down of "an artificial tension between a theory of global economics and a reality in which people live" (ibid, p. 277).

Here difference is presented as a life style choice and the most appropriate response, the most democratic response, is tolerance and the celebration of difference. What is fundamental to difference in this context is that it only makes sense when contextualised by our sameness—our common humanity, just as Derrida notes democracy only makes sense when contrasted with the undemocratic potential it holds within its own process (Derrida, 2005, pp. 30–31). Yet this balance tends to be overlooked in the melee of educational administration and curricula approaches to knowledge that are linear, piecemeal and driven (at warp speed) by often competing images of the future and the past.

The weakness of this model is that in a bureaucratised educational context, and a bureaucratised/McDonaldised culture of hyper-individualism, differences tend to be compartmentalised with tolerance becoming a euphemism for ignorance and laziness, and 'multi' covering for segregation and exclusion. Communities as a result are fragmented with the emergence of centre–periphery configurations that map the same disparities experienced at the global level.

THREE MODELS

What emerges from these rather brief overviews are three distinct models.

The first is the neohumanistic concept of the 'global' as a holistic and interactive space in which agency and structure are mutually reinforcing and the creative space of cultural renewal emerges from the point of interaction. Such a point could be described as liminal or aporetic. Firstly, it is on the border between two conceptually distinct 'realms', hence its liminality; and secondly, the paradox of the agency–structure dialectic producing creative energy experienced as heterotopic possibility accounts for its aporetic profile. The end result is a global that is local/personal and heavily dependent on the uniqueness of learning encounters which indigenise global pedagogic imperatives (Figure 1).

Second is the monoeducation of the flat classroom in which learning is networked, both figuratively and literally, around the imperatives of the market as it transforms from hard to soft learning. In soft learning, science/maths is linked to creativity and ultimately centralises not in geo-political arrangements but in aggregates of knowledge–productivity that may be corporate or nation based (Figure 2).

Finally, the multicultural compartmentalised family model which in many ways offers a replay of global inequality at the local level. It can be read as a cultural version of Friedman's flat schooling in that it does not challenge the central educational process, rather seeking to append cultural tolerance and understanding through the curriculum. As such it disempowers itself by not challenging and reconfiguring the epistemological assumptions that drive Western globalising education (Figure 3).

MUSICAL METAPHORS

So, back to music. Each possible reading of global education suggests a different future. There are overlaps and partial truths in all three positions but the starting points, the intention, the *telos* of each is different. What is clear is that at this moment in time we are faced with some very real choices and that a transition is inevitable. Barenboim reminds us that transitions are central to both being and musical thinking:

> Transition, let us not forget, is the basis of human existence. In music it is not enough simply to play a statement of a phrase, it is absolutely essential to see how we arrived there, and to prepare it. One plays a statement one way at the beginning of a piece, but when the same statement returns later, in what we call in musical terminology the recapitulation, it is in a completely different psychological state of mind. And therefore the bridge, the transition, determines not only itself but what comes after it. It is important to recognise that the present does not exist without the past, and that the present would be different with another past. At the same time, what we do in the present is inevitably the prelude to what the future will be. And the future is determined not by something that we passively wait for, but it is the inevitable outcome that we prepare for from the present moment. (Lecture 5)

What we have here is three different musical transitions in which theme and form weave according to the inner logic of the 'dance'. The neohumanist is a truly contrapuntal work in which each voice is valued and lives both as a single line and a member of a musical relationship which is simultaneously whole and part. Here the harmony is less established, less demanding or prescriptive than the powerful diatonic chords which establish a tonal centre and punishes divergence. Think of the motets and masses of Josquin des Prez (1455–1521) with the long melismatic lines and free use of harmony—structure and form are present but offset or counterbalanced by the freedom allowed the voices. Transition here is a negotiated dialogical affair and there can be many of them.

The flat classroom vision of Friedman and other globalism enthusiasts is a monodic piece in which we encounter a single voice or texture, or if thinking instrumentally, *à la* techno music that offers a single silken musical fabric of networked rhythmic sound that synthesises difference into a unified sonic wave. Here I am thinking of the pulsating dance music of a band like "Kraftwerk" and some of the more trance-oriented techno variants of the 1980s and early 90s. This music is compulsive and can be either ambient or driven. Transitions tend to be subtle and rarely move away from a defining music texture from beginning to end.

The multicultural classroom is a fine example of centralising Western harmony at work. Here texture, invention and direction are paramount. Transition is prescribed and usually in the form Barenboim describes. Think the first movement of a symphony by Mozart and you have the idea. Melodic lines are clear, harmony centralises and satisfies the ear. The democracy of the orchestra is all harnessed to the inner logic of the piece and the outcome, given everyone listens and respects, is a magnificent expression of social purpose. Yet, the rules are clear and the appearance of democracy belies the fact that the order determines all expression. The thing about a melody by Mozart is that it seems so perfect we all feel it could not have been otherwise. The centre of power is in the harmony and though no one can be said to hold the power—it appears to be shared by conductor, composer and musicians—it is in the very essence of the process itself and transition can only occur if and when rules are followed. This is how we experience forms of aesthetic fascism.

Future Harmonies

Each process follows rules of harmony, meter and form yet the end results are strikingly different. Nevertheless, it is important to acknowledge the fact that music, like society and education, is an organised process. What I want to underscore is that all forms of music, society and education presuppose a value base, a structure, and a process, yet the neohumanist vision is most open, functioning like an Indian *raga* in deep resonance with context.

Thus the neohumanist global vision is the most inherently tolerant of difference as the building block for any future is the individual, not as an isolated being but as a being–in–context. The critical terrain of this context is both spiritual and material, simultaneously. The educational possibilities here are, therefore, more complex and more tantalising. For Friedman the starting place for transitions is a global–in–context which inverts the neohumanist approach. Thus for the neohumanist, liberation comes from the individual's personal quest being identified with collective welfare; for Friedman, the welfare of a global collective can, in some way, guarantee the welfare of individuals. For Saul, the positive nationalism of his humanism creates a safe central forum in which difference meets; the space itself guarantees the freedom of the group and the individual.

Each possible future makes sense in the light of Barenboim's comment. But which do we want? Which also is most possible? The most plausible? Well Barenboim has an opinion on this too:

> Music in this case is not an expression of what life is, but an expression of what life could be, or what it could become. Music itself should not be used for political or any other purpose. But although you cannot make music through politics, perhaps you can give political thinking an example through music. As the great conductor Sergei Celibidache said, music does not become something, but something may become music. (Lecture 4)

The future harmonies inherent in the various visions of global education can indeed be understood via musical metaphors. While all represent structure and hierarchy, they do so in quite different ways. Barenboim takes up this point and how difficult it is to strike the balance here between structure, hierarchy and the individual: "in music there is a hierarchy, a hierarchy if you want with equality. And that is what of course is much easier than in life. How difficult it is to achieve equality and yet to find a hierarchy" (Lecture 4).

With this in mind, neohumanism can be described with reference to the pre-modern work of des Prez or the non-Western *raga*. The flat classroom by contrast inverts this worldview offering the total synthesis of synthesised sound, while the multicultural classroom creates the spaciousness of a sonic forum in which equals meet in a predetermined space in which the rules are set (by the West) and are invariant.

Neohumanist Possibilities

Like Derrida, I feel the future, *la futurité*, is something that acts as a horizon beyond which we cannot see (Derrida, 1978/2002, p. 95; 1990, p. 969). It is a limit position. Yet we can and do every day assume things about the future. These assumptions are shaped by fears and hopes, by a sense of those forces acting upon us as societies and individuals, and by the burden of our *karma*—personal and collective history. When we engage strategic hope we are able to challenge the passivity we often inherit with our assumptions. Neohumanism with its mix of spiritual vision and pragmatic common sense can be taken and applied as a form of such strategic hope. It is a utopic, as Louis Marin would say (1984), through which we can better understand ourselves in the present, and become active agents for the future.

What I have found with students and teachers is that when we start thinking globally hope diminishes. The global is just too BIG! Well, neohumanism makes the global personal and returns a sense of agency to us all. It is not that we are faced with the kind of choice captured so elegantly by John F Kennedy when he said: "Ask not what your country can do for you—ask what you can do for your country". Rather, it is that through a spiritual grounding we come to recognise that self-interest and the common good are indistinguishable.

With this in mind the question of how we perform global pedagogy itself becomes somewhat less confronting: neohumanist pedagogy is global pedagogy. It is not a matter of going online and gaining a degree over the Internet, or a matter of teaching about countries far from home, or engaging students in respectful interactions, or environmental studies. These can all be part of both a technocratic flat world, a multicultural world or a neohumanist one. What *is* different is how authority is enacted, how knowledge is constructed and how we communicate this.

Vinay Lal notes that:

No future can be promising unless it entails a thoroughgoing critique, and dismantling, of modern knowledge systems that have given us the interpretive devices with which we have sought to make sense of our lives and the world around us. For much too long, the spokespersons for the West have not merely pretended they had the solutions to the world's problems, but they have been allowed to exercise a monopoly over what kinds of questions are asked and the manner in which they are to be asked. (Lal, 2002, p. 181)

To be honest I do not really know what a neohumanist classroom is. But I know what it is not: it is not limited, it is not violent and punitive, it is not teacher driven and authoritarian, it is not about learning as dull transmission and idle memorisation, it is not selfishly individualistic or segregated, it is not exclusive, fundamentalist or closed, it is not time driven, output obsessed and assessment oriented. In short is not a classroom we would recognise today.

I acknowledge here that the list I just gave is at the heart of any number of real and apparent dissenting pedagogies. It is in short both useful (as a guide) and useless (as rhetoric). What can be said of neohumanism is that it embodies the holistic aspiration by linking the educative process to the lived practice of teachers, curricula planners, and associated staff. At the heart of neohumanist practice is a direct and sustained spiritual endeavour to establish a relationship with the Divine. Only when we begin to see everything as an expression of divinity do we begin to act and think globally. This spiritual orientation generates a deepened critical faculty which strips away power and the psychological and epistemological glosses that distort social action. A continuum emerges here that is simultaneously linear and singularly immanent: we practice neohumanism, we accept it as the principle behind all we do and we also recognise it as a goal as it is always, from the human and relative stance, unattainable.

Certainly we need to be, as Lal urges, asking new questions that are expressive of a wider range of concerns relating to and inspired by the kind of inter-civilisational issues explored by Ananta Kumar Giri (2006) and Fred Dallmayr (2002). Giri for instance identifies a new social ethic which draws upon the Vedic wisdom of his own country, India. His linking of servanthood to social action is founded on his analysis of the India *varnas* (Giri, 2006, p. 335ff) and has relevance for the neohumanist recognition that social service linked to local needs must be part of any pedagogy.

It is not that science, mathematics or literacy is taught that is problematic—these are correctly identified as essential to any prosperous global future. It is the cultural context of learning that needs real sustained attention. As Theodor Adorno lamented: How could one of the most 'enlightened' cultures on the planet have committed the holocaust (Adorno, 2003)? This is a real question that education must face. Neohumanist pedagogy specifically engages with the issue of ethics and reason. It challenges the supremacy of instrumental rationality and offers a benevolent rationality which is armed, critically prepared, with a critical spirituality (Bussey, 2000, 2006) grounded in real life contexts.

As it emphasises a spiritual reflective turn, linked to a clear ethical base and an engaged, on the ground, hands on process, neohumanist pedagogy pushes teachers and students, and all school support staff, to transcend their preconceptions and begin to teach/learn in effectively global ways. Getting individuals to work both for and within collective structures begins the grounding of ethics in service. It is through such actions that we push our consciousnesses beyond self interest and the trap of alienated individuality. Truly global education is about this journey. And it is also about much more than extending the humanist parameters to include all people. As Jeremy Rifkin, in his foreword to Kim Stallwood's book on animal rights (2002) notes, something much deeper is going on:

> The human journey is, at its core, about the extension of empathy to broader and more inclusive domains. At first, the empathy extended only to kin and tribe. Eventually it was extended to people of like-minded values. In the 19th century, the first animal humane societies were established. The current studies open up a new phase, allowing us to expand and deepen our empathy to include the broader community of creatures with whom we share the Earth. (ibid, pp. xi–xv)

Sohail Inayatullah, in a recent essay, observed that the likelihood of neohumanism becoming the new 'hegemony' any time soon is not great (2006). Yet he saw that its seeding capacity was rich and historically part of an emergent sensibility. There is a timeliness to neohumanism, an awareness that, as Rifkin notes, things are rapidly moving to a new stance and whether that stance is explicitly called a neohumanist stance or not seems to me irrelevant. What is clear is that there are numerous voices, as Ivana Milojević observes (2006), working in concert stating basically the same thing: current educational vision is limited and needs to be augmented with a good shot of ecumenical spirituality.

ENABLING TRADITIONS AND APPLIED HOPE

In this way, seeing an ecumenical language and thought emerging, I am reminded again of music and of the balance and tensions of voices in search of a global harmony. Certainly new hybrid forms are emerging from the interaction of civilisations in a global scene that offers rich possibilities for encounter, synthesis and new learnings. The hybridity of the term 'neohumanism' itself illustrates this process. It has a Greek prefix linked to a Latin root and was devised by an Indian mystic–philosopher. It draws on both critical and poststructural insights into reality while retaining its normative commitment to the social, economic and spiritual growth of all that is on the planet and in the universe.

For global education to rethink its priorities and thus escape from the flat hegemonic classroom described by Friedman and to overcome the tensions inherent in the humanist model at the heart of multicultural education, we need a post material sensibility. In this I am reminded of Cornel West's elegant description of prophetic pragmatism (1999, p. 149ff). An approach to life that is practical and grounded while cherishing and maintaining the deep connection to spirit that sustains us when the world seems set on its own destruction. Yet, like West, I am aware of the vulnerability of my position when subject to the harsh gaze of a predominantly material and consumption oriented world that cherishes the individual as a token of an empty freedom. I think West's subjective, highly 'rational' defence is worth noting:

> I do not think it possible to put forward rational defences of one's faith that verify its veracity or even persuade one's critics. Yet it is possible to convey to others the sense of deep emptiness and pervasive meaninglessness one

feels if one is not critically aligned with an enabling tradition. One risks not logical inconsistency, but actual insanity; the issue is not reason or irrationality, but life or death. (ibid, p. 171)

Life and death are worth considering. From a neohumanist perspective there is no heaven or hell other than that which we create, collectively, in the here and now. What emerges from this insight is a cosmology of hope that empowers us to move from the "As above: so below" worldview of transcendental dualism (a.k.a. capitalism) to an "As within: so without" sense of agency that is not merely a New Age placebo to get us through a bad day but both a challenge to engage with our own mythic structures and an invitation to dive deep into the enabling traditions that give form and meaning to daily experience.

So the fugue draws to a close and I return to Barenboim. His vision of hope anchored in music profoundly touched me. Sure, I can see that his thinking is in many ways shaped by the Western musical tradition, but, as Cornel West would observe, there is much that is enabling in that tradition. It is not all about domination, violence and predatory capitalism. If we listen closely we can hear the open strand of an Indian *raga* and the whistled tones of a Maori conch. Barenboim's message is that we must practice hope, it is to be applied in the present not stripped of use-value by being projected into the future. This is why he and his friend, the late Edward Said, formed the Palestinian/Israeli youth orchestra, the West Eastern Divan, as a vehicle that symbolises the potential unity that exists between the most alienated of peoples. Thus he notes:

In the West Eastern Divan the universal metaphysical language of music becomes the link, it is the language of the continuous dialogue that these young people have with each other. Music is the common framework, their abstract language of harmony. As I have said before in these lectures, nothing in music is independent. It requires a perfect balance between head, heart and stomach. And I would argue that when emotion and intellect are in tune, it is easier also for human beings and for nations to look outward as well as inward. And therefore through music we can see an alternative social model, a kind of practical Utopia, from which we might learn about expressing ourselves freely and hearing one another. (Lecture 4)

CONCLUSION

For me, neohumanism has the potential to negotiate the challenge posed in Barenboim's vision of a "practical utopia". Is such an idea an oxymoron? Perhaps. Certainly Ashis Nandy wisely warns against utopian dreams as they inevitably turn into other's, and frequently our own, nightmares (Nandy, 1987)—we must remember that capitalism is the expression of the utopian aspirations of many 'reformers' in the eighteenth and nineteenth century (Hetherington, 1997; Perkins, 2001). Yet, if we soften the term, shifting the emphasis from the future to the present tense, from salvation to process, the utopic of neohumanism, open-ended, ethical, grounded in practical action and spiritual striving, has much to offer any discussion relating to global education. Such a discussion is not about answers but about framing questions that give form to our aspirations and about trying from today to enact these questions in the classroom and everywhere else learning occurs.

NOTES

[i] Talk given at the 'Symposium on Globalization and Global Education' hosted by Seattle Pacific University, 17–19 May, 2007.

[ii] Barenboim's Reith lectures, number 5. The last two were given in Jerusalem. I indicate which lecture I am taking his comments from simply with their number.

[iii] Marc Lombardi (1951–2000) "reveals the intricate web of connections that lurk beneath current headlines draws on the major political and financial scandals of the day to create large-scale linear diagrams that at first glance look like celestial maps; a closer reading reveals the intricate web of connections that lurk beneath current headlines" (http://www.albany.edu/museum/wwwmuseum/work/lombardi/).

[iv] I like this image as not only are the stalls all clearly bounded but it also includes 'Luxury Boxes'—something often left out of the more enthusiastic multicultural narratives. This image is of the Conte Forum a multipurpose sports stadium in the U.S. The image can be found at https://files.gotickets.com/cached/_images/443.443.conte_forum.fit.8e7a5a0 d6f2e7f5c8d25b0ff921e1caa.gif

REFERENCES

Adorno, T. W. (2003). Education after auschwitz. In T. R. (Ed.), *Can one live after auschwitz?* (pp. 19–33). Stanford, CA: Stanford University Press.

Barenboim, D. (Writer). (2006). In the beginning was sound. *The Reith Lectures.* UK: BBC 4. Retrieved from http://www.bbc.co.uk/radio4/reith2006/

Bussey, M. (2000). Critical spirituality: Neo humanism as method. *Journal of Futures Studies, 5*(2), 21–35.

Bussey, M. (2006). Neohumanism: Critical spirituality, tantra and education. In S. Inayatullah, M. Bussey, & I. Milojević (Eds.), *Neohumanist educational futures: Liberating the pedagogical intellect* (pp. 80–95). Tamsui, Taiwan: Tamkang University Press.

Butler, J. (2004). *Precarious life: The powers of mourning and violence.* London and New York: Verso.

Dallmayr, F. (2002). *Dialogue among civilizations: Some exemplary voices.* New York: Palgrave Macmillan.

Derrida, J. (1978/2002). *Writing and difference* (A. Bass, Trans.). London: Routledge.

Derrida, J. (1990). Force of law: The 'Mystical Foundation of Authority'. *Cardozo Law Review, 11,* 919–1045.

Derrida, J. (2005). *Rogues: Two essays on reason.* Stanford, CA: Stanford University Press.

Foucault, M. (1986). Of other spaces. *Diacritics, 16*(1), 22–27.

Friedman, T. L. (2005). *The world is flat: A brief history of the twenty-first century.* New York: Farrar, Straus and Giroux.

Giri, A. K. (2006). *New horizons of social theory: Conversations, transformations and beyond.* Jaipur: Rawat Publications.

Giroux, H. A. (1988). *Teachers as intellectuals: Towards a critical pedagogy of learning.* New York: Bergin & Garvey.

Hetherington, K. (1997). *The badlands of modernity: Heterotopia and social ordering.* London and New York: Routledge.

Inayatullah, S. (2006). The futures of neohumanist education. In S. Inayatullah, M. Bussey, & I. Milojević (Eds.), *Neohumanist educational futures: Liberating the pedagogical intellect* (pp. 335–353). Tamsui, Taiwan: Tamkang University Press.

Inayatullah, S., Bussey, M., & Milojević, I. (Eds.). (2006). *Neohumanist futures education: Liberating the pedagogical intellect*. Tamsui: Taiwan: Tamkang University Press.

Lal, V. (2002). *Empire of knowledge: Culture and plurality in the global economy*. London: Pluto Press.

Marin, L. (1984). *Utopics: Spatial play*. London: Macmillan.

McLaren, P. (Ed.). (2006). *Rage and hope: Interviews with Peter McLaren on war, imperialism and critical pedagogy*. New York: Peter Lang.

Milojević, I. (2006). Visions of education: Neohumanism and critical spirituality. In S. Inayatullah, M. Bussey, & I. Milojević (Eds.), *Neohumanist educational futures: Liberating the pedagogical intellect* (pp. 55–79). Tamsui, Taiwan: Tamkang University Press.

Nandy, A. (1987). *Traditions, tyranny and utopias: Essays in the politics of awareness*. New Delhi: Oxford University Press.

Perkins, M. (2001). *The reform of time: Magic and modernity*. London: Pluto Press.

Sarkar, P. R. (1987). *Neohumanism in a nutshell: Part 1*. Calcutta: Ananda Marga Publications.

Saul, J. R. (2005). *The collapse of globalism and the reinvention of the world*. London: Viking/Penguin Books.

Serres, M., & Latour, B. (1995). *Conversations on science, culture, and time* (R. Lapidus, Trans.). Ann Arbor, MI: The University of Michigan Press.

Stallwood, K. W. (Ed.). (2002). *A primer on animal rights: Leading experts write about animal cruelty and exploitation*. New York: Lantern Books.

Tait, G. (2004). What is the relationship between social governance and schooling? In B. Burnett, D. Meadmore, & G. Tait (Eds.), *New questions for contemporary teachers: Taking a socio-cultural approach to education* (pp. 13–24). Sydney: Pearson/Prentice Hall.

West, C. (1999). *The Cornel West Reader*. New York: Basic Civitas Books.

Marcus Bussey lectures in World History at the University of the Sunshine Coast. He is also a member of that university's Regional Sustainability Research Group and an associate of Prout College (www.proutcollege.org). He has written widely in the area of futures, education, policy, culture and transformative pedagogy and has over 50 published papers (journal articles, book reviews, book chapters, magazine articles and an encyclopedia entry for UNESCO's Encyclopaedia of Life Support Systems) *and has co-authored* Futures Thinking For Social Foresight *with Richard Slaughter (Tamsui, Tamkang University Press, 2005) and co-edited* Neohumanist Educational Futures: Liberating the Pedagogical Intellect *with Sohail Inayatullah & Ivana Milojević (Tamsui, Tamkang University Press, 2006).*

RICHARD A. SLAUGHTER

4. FUTURES EDUCATION

Catalyst for our times

PREAMBLE

The study of Futures is intellectually stimulating and seeks to empower
students. It draws on the innate capacity of the human mind to engage in
foresight, or futures thinking enhanced by concepts, tools and techniques.
When this enhanced capacity to engage with 'the future' is implemented in
specific areas ... Futures can contribute substantially to social and economic
well-being. Students who take this course will be encouraged to transform their
view of the world. As they develop informed foresight about the 21st century
they may experience many shifts of value, focus and attitude and they should
discover that most fears, negative attitudes and 'doomsday' images of the future
rest on misperceptions. In learning how present actions will shape future consequences, students gain access to new sources of understanding and action ...

Futures also address the critical issues of late adolescence and provides a
valuable preparation for working life. Therefore, instead of looking ahead to
the world beyond school with anxiety and fear, students will be able to look
ahead with much greater clarity and confidence. Such attitudes and skills
clearly provide a sound basis for decision making ...

Citizens of tomorrow need to be prepared for a world which will be
significantly different from the world of the 1990s: a world characterised by
rapid technological change, major environmental challenges, globalism and
expanding information networks. This syllabus provides the opportunity
for students to develop the skills that will enable them to develop leadership
in shaping their own future and Australia's. (Pre-Pilot Senior Syllabus in Futures,
Board of Senior Secondary School Studies, Brisbane, April 1998, pp. 1–2)

INTRODUCTION

It is startling to realise that the first attempts to teach in a specifically futures-
oriented mode took place in the 1960s, half a century ago. Back then, far-sighted
individuals could clearly see some of the challenging global issues and problems
that have since become daily news. What is striking, however, is that despite many
attempts to bring futures education (FE) fully into the mainstream of educational
thinking and practice, it still remains surprisingly rare. This chapter therefore
begins with a brief overview of the global outlook. Next it considers some of the

*M. Bussey, S. Inayatullah and I. Milojević (eds.), Alternative Educational Futures: Pedagogies for
Emergent Worlds, 57–72.*
© *2008 Sense Publishers. All rights reserved.*

ways bureaucracies de-focus this outlook and marginalise innovations intended to address it. Finally it reviews what FE offers schools, teachers and students in the early twenty-first century—a catalyst for deeper understanding of the world and ways out of humanity's self-constructed trap.

THE STORY THAT CONNECTS

Over the last 30 years a reliable and, one might say, 'scientifically informed', series of publications has appeared that describes the human predicament with increasing clarity and precision. For example, beginning with the *Limits to Growth* (Meadows, 1972) and currently ending with *Beyond the Limits: a Thirty Year Update* (Meadows, 2005) the Meadows team provided an evolving perspective that tracks our growing understanding of global change and also what this means for human life and culture. More recently the International Geosphere Program (IGP) sponsored another series of publications that brought together the work of many scientists from around the world. One of these is called *Global Change and the Earth System* (Steffan, 2004) and it also provides vital new depth understanding about the context in which human life is framed. Here is a sample:

> Many human activities that reached take-off points sometime in the 20th Century have accelerated sharply towards the end of the Century. The last fifty years have without doubt seen the most rapid transformation of the human relationship with the natural world in the history of the species. (p. 258)

As a consequence:

> The Earth is currently operating in a no-analogue state. In terms of key environmental parameters, the Earth System has recently moved well outside the range of the natural variability exhibited over at least the last half million years. The nature of the changes now taking place simultaneously in the Earth System, their magnitudes and rates of change are unprecedented. (p. 262)

Overall, works of this kind describe how, over the last 100 years, our species has grown fundamentally out of balance with its world. It follows that we need to understand this in some depth and discern wise, informed, society wide strategies of response. I call this 'the story that connects' because the perspective brings together hitherto separate pieces of information, creating the clarity that necessarily precedes action. But, of course, what has been called the 'blizzard of change' confronting us is not limited to humanity's many impacts upon the external world, significant as these are. The range of change processes can appear bewildering because they operate across many different domains. That is why change analysts and foresight practitioners have adopted various methods for managing this complexity.[1]

Two other works provide a flavour of the rich web of understanding that has arisen in relation to a variety of change processes, including social, economic and political ones. The first is by Mikhail Gorbachev, former President of the Soviet Union. His book, *Manifesto for the Earth*, sets out a brief, but coherent, analysis of the global situation along with some clear recommendations for change (Gorbachev, 2006).

Gorbachev is no idealist. As one who lived through the multiple privations of life in war-torn and post-war Russia, his view of the world is grounded in the realities of life as seen from a small farm in the Stavropol region of the North Caucasus. As Russian President he is known for initiating certain democratic reforms that opened up the Soviet Union, bringing it forward out of the totalitarian era. He is therefore well qualified to state that "the opportunities on offer at the end of the cold war were for the most part not taken up" (p. 31). And he is clear about why: lack of vision, lack of political will and the spread of economic liberalism around the world. This was demonstrated at the 2002 Johannesburg World Summit on Sustainable Development where a variety of progressive measures (such as investment in renewable energy by the OPEC countries and measures to curb excessive consumption in the rich West) failed to be taken up and implemented. For these and related reasons he considers that global politics is in a genuine crisis.

Gorbachev writes about how the Chernobyl disaster affected him personally. It was "a decisive test for glasnost" (openness), it "shattered" his belief in the "absolute reliability of technology" and it radically changed the time-scales that he'd been implicitly using. "What right have we to burden our descendants with such a problem?" (p. 22). In the book he writes succinctly about the "three crises": economic, social and ecological. After lamenting the widespread failure of the UN and governments to respond, Gorbachev calls for a rejection of the consumer society (which he regards as "a disaster"), a re-assessment of economic liberalism ("the growing ecological crisis shows that a liberal economy functioning mainly according to the criteria of profitability and a return on capital is not capable of coping with the ecological challenge" (p. 41)) and a wholesale commitment toward re-thinking and re-prioritising human activities on the Earth. "What we need is not a revolution but an evolution of the idea we harbour about ourselves and about how the world might be organised and what its new shape in the age of globalisation might be" (p. 53). We may note in passing that it is just such questions that have considered within the futures domain for some time.[ii]

Gorbachev's solution is to put his energy into initiatives like the Earth Charter, Green Cross International and the Earth Dialogues process. He's accepted that governments *per se* and the UN simply will not act in the ways that will achieve sustained change. Therefore the only route left is direct engagement with people around the world and, especially, through the NGO movement. He does, however, overlook the role of education.

The second example is a work that explores the dilemma of the US and, by extension, other technically developed societies. *The Long Emergency* is a challenging book that employs an uncompromising cultural analysis of the US to take issue with nearly all of the underlying myths and cultural assumptions that have become widely accepted, not only there, but around the world. (Kunstler, 2005, Sardar & Davies, 2004) Kunstler, a US citizen, thinks that the US has been "sleepwalking into the future" for many decades by adopting and promoting a short-termist, exploitive and self-defeating set of policies and practices that will cost it dearly. These include:
− the 'fad' of globalism and a 'magical' market economy;
− present-day profiteering at the expense of future well being;

- a "colossal mis-investment" in suburbia;
- the creation of an unsustainable economy from a formerly sustainable one;
- dishonest government where vital trends are dismissed as "unthink-able"; and, overall,
- a Las Vegas-type culture of dependency and purposeless dissipation.

Underlying all this are issues of modernity and the projected decline of fossil fuels. Kunstler suggests that the former is much more dependent upon the latter than anyone is prepared to admit. He points out that the peaks of US and world oil discoveries were in the 1930s and 1960s respectively. The significance of subsequent oil 'shocks' and temporary shortages was overlooked due to an inherent American complacency, its belief that it could secure supplies from overseas and then by the emergence of new fields in Alaska and the North Sea. But the figures from the Middle East are uncertain and the growth of China has helped to accelerate demand right at the point when supply is fully stretched. In this view, we have already reached the period of 'peak oil', and the ride "down from the peak", as it were, will be far more difficult than current decision makers realise. There's also a deeper and more vexing issue that is seldom considered anywhere. Kunstler views the oil era as having permitted the world's population to rise to its current level, a level that cannot possibly be sustained. He writes:

> The current world population of 6.5 billion people has no hope whatsoever of sustaining itself at current levels, and the fundamental conditions of life on earth are about to force the issue. The only questions are: what form will the inevitable attrition take, and how, and which places, and when? (p. 61)

About half of the book deals with the post-oil world that he believes will occur before mid-century. He suggests that:

> eventually all nations will have to contend with the problems of the Long Emergency: the end of industrial growth, falling standards of living, economic desperation, declining food production, and domestic political strife. A point will come when even the great powers of the world no longer have the means to project their power any distance. Even nuclear weapons may become inoperable, considering how much their careful maintenance depends on other technological systems linked to our fossil fuel economy. (p. 98)

Unlike some other commentators he believes that, with the possible and temporary exception of nuclear power, there are simply no viable alternatives to oil. For a variety of reasons, the so-called 'renewable' sources of energy such as solar, wind, wave, hydro and hydrogen, will not replace oil and gas. Nuclear power may produce some base load electricity but this will fail to serve the wider spectrum of energy needs. The underlying theme of the book, therefore, is that of a culture that lost its grip on reality, created a fantasy world predicated on cheap, easily transported energy, and now faced with chronic entropic decline.

Clearly this is a powerful and challenging thesis. There is, however, one very significant omission: he says virtually nothing about the many sources of vitality, creativity and depth innovation within US culture, including those found within a variety of educational settings. I will return to this point below.

What we have in these brief samples from an extensive futures literature is the beginnings of a diagnosis of the 'state of the planet' in the early twenty-first century. A central claim of this chapter is that, equipped with this resource, it is well within the capacity of human societies to respond. A well-grounded and informed futures perspective goes a long way beyond allowing us to propose a variety of actions to preserve the environment, vital as this is. It also provides the tools to understand deeper issues like the fallacies of economic growth and discerns some of the more subtle drivers of unsustainable outlooks within the heart of the Western worldview itself (Berman, 1981; Slaughter, 2004). Is all this too difficult for young people? Well, expressed in that manner, perhaps. Yet, the starting points for a futures discourse are quite straightforward. Again, we'll return to this later. First I want to consider how educational bureaucracies have responded to this unprecedented outlook and to some of the innovations intended to address it.

HOW BUREAUCRACIES DE-FOCUS THE FUTURE AND UNDERMINE INNOVATION

The first, fairly obvious, point to make is that bureaucracies are not designed to be forward thinking. They exist to carry out a range of administrative tasks in the here and now as dictated by past practice and current political realities. The Directors and CEOs of such organisations must first and foremost serve their current political masters or they are quickly out of a job. In working with such entities it is striking to see how the focus of attention is not only short term but also largely internal. Broadly speaking they are not densely connected to the wider world but operate unthinkingly within a pre-defined sense of what has been called 'bounded rationality'. They are profoundly rational, and there are reasons for everything, but reality is deeply filtered and simplified. There are two immediate implications for the topic under discussion. First, approaches to 'the future' when they do occur, tend to be stereotypical. Second, as I will show below, innovations with any potential for deep-seated change are quickly marginalised.

Over several decades it becomes clear that government departments, bureaucracies, decision-makers in school systems are far more comfortable with initiatives addressing the futures of education. The basic reason for this is that such exercises are largely extrapolative, tend not to question bureaucratic assumptions and do little to question or challenge existing educational practice. On the other hand, approaches that consider futures in education introduce dynamic new features into present-day administration, theory and practice. Thus, overall, it tends to end up in the 'too hard' basket despite its many positive implications (Hicks, 2002; Gidley et al., 2004).

A second point about bureaucracies is that they do not welcome innovations 'from the outside', as it were. Many futures initiatives I've known of, or been involved in, worked very well at the school level and were enthusiastically embraced. But as soon as one moves beyond particular schools to the system level everything changes. Here futures in education initiatives seem to vanish like smoke on a windy day and are seen no more. Perhaps the central reason for this is that school systems are governed, in turn, by two powerful sets of background forces that have no real interest at all in education or, indeed, our collective futures. Those forces are politics and economics. In fact education, politics and economics are themselves mediated through an ideological framework that has become hegemonic over recent decades (Milojević, 2005). This managerialist, market oriented, growth-addicted view of the world has actively worked to de-focus and hold back many useful social innovations, not only this one (Fisher, 2006). The result is that teachers in schools (and let us not forget, teachers and learners in very many other locations) have been undermined by these background forces that all–too–often lie out of sight and unregarded. Bringing futures work in education back into focus and freshly comprehending its individual and cultural value is indeed a challenging task. Yet it is a vital step toward a worthwhile future for humankind.

A specific example occurred in Queensland, Australia, during the mid-1990s when I made many trips from Melbourne to Brisbane to chair a committed convened by the then Board of Senior Secondary School Studies (BSSSS). The committee had been formed following a government report that had recommended a more explicitly futures-oriented approach (Queensland Government, 1994). The result, after about two years' work, was a detailed outline of a two-year subject for Years 11 and 12 called: *Futures Personal, Social, Global* (BSSSS, 1995). The subject was put out for trial in a number of Queensland schools and a formal evaluation was undertaken (Underwood, 1996). It's worth noting some of the reasons provided to the official evaluator *by the schools* for choosing to trial the draft subject:
- at each school there is a teacher or teachers enthusiastic about the challenge of this innovative syllabus;
- the subject is seen as a means of making available the skills of the humanities' disciplines as students move from traditional disciplines to new technology-based subjects;
- Futures is seen as being relevant to the needs of students in a changing world. They will learn to cope with change by understanding it; and
- The subject offers opportunity for students to acquire and develop in the areas of basic competencies and the core curriculum elements. (p. 3)

Equally interesting are the reasons given *by students* themselves for wishing to take the subject:
- the content of the course is appealing;
- the belief that students should develop an active relationship with the future;
- (it is) the best subject available on the subject choice line;
- the belief that it would help them to get an overall position in the Student Evaluation Profile needed to obtain tertiary entrance; and
- the expectation that it would be helpful or needed in a future job. (p. 4)

While it can be argued that creating a new Futures subject is not the only—nor even the best—option, clearly this one was going to be a success. The summary of the evaluation highlighted the following points:

- an "encouraging number of students" had taken part;
- the teachers involved were "highly qualified in a number of disciplines";
- there was "favourable parent reaction" to the work carried out;
- the trial subject offered "attractive and innovative learning experiences";
- teachers were having "some difficulties with the assessment of students in group work";
- there were some concerns about "insufficient detail in the curriculum document";
- also, "locating and adapting resources for classroom use are concerns";
- yet there was also "an impressive enthusiasm for the new subject amongst Administrators, Heads of Department and Teachers"; and, finally,
- "this new and innovative subject is being enthusiastically received in the trial schools and, though there have been some difficulties and concerns, is progressing satisfactorily". (p. 10)

The results of this evaluation are given in some detail because they show very clearly that, with some predictable and routine teething issues, the new subject was enthusiastically received by schools, teachers, students and parents. You'd think, therefore, that the innovation would be well enough established to enter into common practice. Yet that is not what happened (see box, below).

How to Kill a Curriculum Innovation: 1988–1999

1987-88	Futures curriculum project initiated within the Catholic Education Office, Brisbane.
September 1993	B. P. O'Rourke, principal of Corinda High School, publishes Futures and the Curriculum discussion document.
March 1994	Review of the Queensland School Curriculum (the *Wiltshire Report*) published. Recommends that 'every syllabus in every subject should have a futures perspective'.
1994—1995	Subject Advisory Committee (SAC) meets under auspices of the Board of Senior Secondary School Studies (BSSSS) to develop Futures curriculum framework.
12 May 1995	BSSSS votes unanimously to adopt the new Futures subject.
June 1995	Trial of Senior Syllabus in Futures confirmed.
6 October 1995	Teacher's Conference on Senior Futures held at Education House, Brisbane. Trial schools selected soon thereafter.
June 1996	Favourable first evaluation report on trial of Senior Futures subject.
December 1997	Final report on trial of Senior Futures. Recommends subject continue to full pilot stage.
April 1998	Pre-Pilot Syllabus released by BSSSS. Intended for use in 'approved schools' commencing with Year 11 in 1999.
1999	BSSSS under threat from 're-organisation'. Pilot abandoned.

Following the successful trial, and for reasons never openly explained, the BSSSS shelved the new subject indefinitely. And it has remained shelved ever since. This is not unusual for such would-be innovations—it is more often the norm. The result has serious individual and social implications. A generation of young people has been denied access to the field and thus also the chance to acquire many of the skills of proactive citizenship. A little of what has been thus far lost is evoked by this statement from a Year 11 student in one of the trial schools. She wrote:

> This has been a very empowering experience for myself, as this (subject) created an opportunity for the advantages of the internet to be experienced first-hand. The due date provided just that little bit of extra inspiration. However, this driving force was ultimately eclipsed by the motivation from the desire to achieve something that I have never tried before. It really opened my eyes. Having the occasion to teach others about the Futures Field forced me to re-think what it means to me, and my relationship with its role now and in the future. In a sense it restored a feeling of 'awe' that I initially experienced when I first encountered the field, and has cleared away a lot of the baggage and associations that accumulated throughout the year. The fact that it has occurred through a blossoming and thriving new medium has been a bonus and I feel that I have learned a great deal about my own capabilities … (Rundle, 1996)

Responses of this kind are not uncommon when FE work is carried out sensitively and well, and when teachers are adequately supported in these tasks. The fact that the innovation was set aside is evidence of an acute systemic difficulty that thrives in state bureaucracies, i.e., their long-standing habit of eliminating the very innovations that would have enhanced the human and social ability to address what is clearly an unprecedented and challenging global outlook. This remains a scandal and an embarrassment to the teaching profession, to the authorities responsible and to any meaningful vision of healthy and forward-looking civil society. But the good news is that this state of affairs can be changed very quickly where the point of so doing is understood.

'JOINING THE DOTS' THROUGH ENVIRONMENTAL SCANNING AND STRATEGIC FORESIGHT

If there is a summary statement that describes the predicament of school systems today it is that they are still caught up in 'past perceptions of problems'. This was demonstrated very clearly in Australia during 2007 when there was a politically driven and nationwide shift away from various progressive innovations—including futures—in school curricula and a strong call for 'back to basics'. The states came under severe pressure to bring back traditional disciplines such English, history and geography. Some indication of the depths to which the education debate had fallen was suggested by the former prime minister's willingness to personally become associated with the kind of crass and negative opinionising normally found only in the tabloid press and to launch a book that was not only spiritually and ethically arid but also betrayed a deep ignorance of the wider context of human life.[iii]

As time goes by it becomes increasingly clear that the lack of an explicit futures perspective in any curriculum—be it 'traditional' or 'progressive'—leads to the same general consequences, i.e., a new generation of students lacking any real grasp of the human predicament and of the ways it can be addressed. This is not simply a lost opportunity, it actively undermines any notion of a viable wider social project as it passes from generation to generation. Clearly this dilemma will not be solved overnight.

I mentioned above how short term politics and conventional economics, in a sense 'conspire' to restrict educational thinking, practice and administration very much to the here–and–now (Slaughter, 2004, Chapter 13). We do not have to look far to find a telling a comparison from another domain that contrasts in almost every detail with currently accepted practice in educational settings. While I in no way condone the values and culture involved, the following example demonstrates two vital points. First, for any organisation interested in understanding broad processes of change, systematic scanning of the environment (a precursor to disciplined forward thinking) is both possible and highly desirable. Second, the skills involved have been around for some time, are not particularly esoteric and could easily be widely adopted if the will was there to do so. Consider, therefore, the following passage that describes a typical early morning meeting at a large international merchant bank:

> ... Seated round the table are people who have got to the top of their product speciality at the world's biggest financial players. These people know what they are doing, and they know everything there is to know about their product area. They get together daily; they are not discussing the weather or the sports scores, they are discussing business threats and opportunities, 'anticipated market movements' to use one of their favourite phrases. These are real-life, dynamic meetings not dull bureaucratic risk-control affairs. These are firms in a state of 'constant communication' ... not just in the meetings but outside too, using the informal networks that the organisational structure develops ...This is an industry taking a great deal of trouble to join up the dots at every conceivable level. (Augar, 2005, p. 113)

Although I've not visited more than a tiny fraction of the world's educational bureaucracies, I'd venture to suggest that not one of them has meetings of this kind anywhere, at any time, whose purpose is to scan broadly and "connect the dots". We've already seen why. Like the governments they serve, they are simply not alert to dynamic shifts in the macro-environment. Nor, on the whole, do they have the skills that this alertness requires. Bureaucracies serve as agents of government policy for social administration in the here and now. In this role of 'minding the shop' they have no interest in, nor any capability for, forward thinking. It is simply not within their remit or job description. One could argue that they are concerned with continuity, not with change. So when ideas, people, books, curriculum innovations with some of these features appear, a well-oiled 'immune system' not dissimilar to the white cells in the human bloodstream, is activated and the 'invaders' are repelled. Yet for those with eyes to see, historically unprecedented changes can be clearly discerned 'in the pipeline' or, to change the metaphor, 'tsunamis of change' can be seen moving steadily toward us from the near future (Dator, 1992). What therefore are some appropriate responses?

FORWARD-LOOKING EDUCATIONAL RESPONSES

A number of educational thinkers and writers have addressed this issue and come to similar conclusions. For example, Peters covers much of the relevant territory in his paper on "Educational Policy Futures" (Peters, 2005). What is clear from this and similar sources is that the grounds for including explicit futures perspectives within educational administration and school curricula are now compelling. Ironically, this case was made quite explicitly in what became known as the *Wiltshire Report* commissioned by the Queensland Government in the 1990s (Queensland Government, 1994). An overview document states very clearly that "the Panel recommends that every syllabus in every subject should have a futures perspective, tackling new timely topics and crucial current social issues" (p. 5). One reason this did not occur is that there was no real support for it in the bureaucracy, which continued along its well-worn 'business–as–usual' path, with the results discussed above.

In contrast to this sad and familiar picture it seems rather obvious to suggest that educational bureaucracies need to be re-designed (not re-structured along similar lines) for a very different world. It is a world that is, or should be, informed by what I termed 'the story that connects'. *It is simply no longer good enough for large-scale economic interests to draw on advanced thinking and innovative practice for commercial gain while educational interests continue to lag decades behind. The environmental scanning capabilities, the same global connectivity and the sense of urgency to 'connect the dots' should now be designed into school systems.* This means new structures, new operational units, new job descriptions and a new, or renewed, sense of 'what education is about' in the early twenty-first century (Beare & Slaughter, 1993).

Another way to approach this question at the system level is to consider how strategic foresight differs from old-style planning. One definition of strategic foresight is:

> The ability to create and maintain high quality, coherent and functional forward views and to use the insights arising in organisationally useful ways. For example, to detect adverse conditions, guide policy, shape strategy, and to explore new markets, products and services. (Slaughter, 1999, p. 287)

Most, if not all, educational bureaucracies have some sort of planning and/or strategy function, albeit one that is inward looking and stereotypical. On the other hand our understanding of foresight has developed rapidly in recent years and we can now regard it as a human capacity with considerable power when it is properly developed and applied. Thus, the process of adding 'foresight' to planning and/or strategy is profoundly enlivening and can readily be seen to 'refresh' the latter. It does so by bringing into play ideas, methods and capabilities that had earlier been overlooked. Moreover, there are sufficient case studies available to demonstrate these gains in capability very clearly (Slaughter, 2007). Such changes are needed at the highest levels—from ministers to department heads to professors in universities—before innovations at the school level can thrive.

Thus far I've argued that FE is mandated by threats to human civilisation that are now rebounding upon humanity from an over-stressed global system. But we should also be clear that the intrinsic value to young people provides equally powerful grounds for innovations of this kind.

WHAT DOES FUTURES IN EDUCATION OFFER YOUNG PEOPLE?

Again, this is not new. The many constructive consequences of teaching and learning explicitly within a futures mode are well understood and documented (Hicks, 2002). It has long been understood that for young people 'the future' is a topic of deep and abiding concern. For example, one researcher looking at the experiences of teenage girls recently reported that: "every single girl had these massive feelings of doubt. A lot of them ask: 'what am I doing here? Do I have a future and what is it?'" (Sullivan, 2007). All are, quite reasonably, interested in the unfolding of their own lives and not a few can see that there are a number of issues that give rise to concern, if not outright fear.

Unfortunately, however, it has been the case that young peoples' images of futures are largely and one-sidedly derived from the mass media: films, computer games, TV and Internet subcultures, with few resources available to process or mediate their implicit and explicit content, and with all-too-familiar results. A 2007 survey found that:

> The future most young Australians want is neither the future they expect nor the future they are promised under current national priorities … Most … see the expected or probable future of humankind largely in terms of a continuation or worsening of today's global and national problems and difficulties. The probable future is also the problematic future. (Eckersley et al., 2007, p. 13)

While such images are certainly not without value when considered carefully, they also tend to exert a distinctly negative influence. Hence many young people grow up fearing the future, learning to avoid it, and unaware of either its positive potentials or the many ways that they could act to address issues of concern. On the other hand, FE provides the perspectives and understandings that provide a basis for many long term solutions to the human predicament: active foresight, sustainable cultures, stewardship of the Earth. If we recall the "feeling of awe" and the "clearing away of (mental) baggage" mentioned above by the student from a trial school, one can readily detect the kind of fruitful engagement between alert youngsters and the challenges ahead that stand at the heart of 'effective schooling'.

What's currently missing from educational thinking and practice is a specifically futures discourse. It is absent from the highest levels of executive decision making,

from universities and professional associations and also from classrooms. Yet it is growing mastery here that actually provides the symbolic starting points to move 'the future' from being a domain of fear and avoidance to one of agency and personal power. The point is that even a very basic familiarity with, and competence in, a futures discourse has catalytic effects. In a nutshell, and most centrally, *it 'unlocks' the Futures domain and catalyses human and social potential.* What does this mean? Ideas that seemed vague are clarified (e.g., how human foresight can become a principle of great social utility and power); global problems that seemed 'too hard' now admit a range of solutions (e.g., peak oil and alternatives for an over-dependent world); the links between individual and collective action are revealed (e.g., how political systems can be influenced through various forms of 'right action') and so on. It is appropriate, therefore, to return to the 'good news' mentioned above, i.e., *the starting points for a futures discourse are simple, straightforward and well within the capacity of every young person.* Given the chance, all young people can understand concepts such as the following:
- the use of foresight in everyday life;
- the use of different time frames for different purposes;
- exploring the 200 year present (stretching 100 back and forward);
- the use of simple tools such as time lines and futures wheels; and
- how to change fears into motivation.

This is merely a small sample of the resources available (Slaughter & Bussey, 2006).

At first sight, and without the symbolic support of a futures discourse, the futures domain may appear either threatening or 'empty'. Yet the latter is an illusion woven from habit, linguistic traps (such as past, present, future tenses) and cultural assumptions that have not been clearly reflected upon, problematised and re-framed. Solutions are not distant but, in fact, surprisingly close at hand. Anyone who looks at daily life carefully enough soon discovers that without a very personal mastery of applied foresight no one would rise from their bed each day. No one would go to school or work because they'd have lost all motivation and purpose. It's the fact of having an open future that makes it possible, indeed, requires us, to think, evaluate and plan ahead in virtually everything we do. Understanding this makes it a good deal easier to explore the implications of futures enquiry and informed action at the organisational and social levels.

The key point is this: exploring the futures domain at a range of levels provides some of the most valuable ways to get to grips with human life and culture in time. *Despite a current preoccupation with 'back to basics' in school curricula around the world and the false sense of security that it provides to some, forward thinking should be seen as a core skill, requirement and focus at every level of every school system.* This was the conclusion reached by the *Wiltshire Report* in Queensland in 1994 and subsequent events have only served to confirm its veracity. Executive decision-makers need an immersion in Futures so that they can become attuned to the meaning of signals of change in the wider world. Teacher educators need it because successive generations of teachers are preparing young people for a progressively altered world. Young people themselves need it because they face a number of powerful systemic challenges, any of which could bring the species to its knees, and they need to be prepared (Slaughter, 2006).

BEYOND DENIAL, AVOIDANCE AND REPRESSION

It was suggested above there have been many curriculum innovations directed at bringing futures thinking and perspectives into educational thinking and practice but hitherto they have generally been marginalised. The Queensland trial subject in Futures is a case in point. The common strategies of denial, avoidance and repression of unwanted knowledge screen out uncomfortable truths at every level and in every sector of society. Now, however, 'signals' from the global system regarding conflict, climate change, water supply, chronic over-dependence on cheap oil—these and many others—are confronting everyone with facts that can no longer be ignored. We are living through the most profound, many-stranded, global transition in history. It is one in which the human species needs to pay close attention to the many 'signals' emerging from the global system. According to the Meadows team three basic responses are available:
– deny, disguise or confuse the signals;
– alleviate the pressures from limits by technical or economic fixes; or
– acknowledge that the human socio-economic system as currently structured is unmanageable and seek to change the structure of the system. (Meadows, 2005, pp. 235–236)
Any look at the mass media will find the first solution highlighted clearly and often. A particularly obnoxious example is *The Australian* newspaper's monthly glossy high-end publication called *Wish Magazine*. At an estimated cost of perhaps AUD$2 million per year, it engages the best visuals and advertising talent to, in effect, push the message that 'you, too, deserve the very same lifestyles as the rich and famous'. It is a futile and counter-productive message that perversely works against any shared social interest in a more sane and equitable world. Why? Because, if we were smart, we'd not be expending wealth generated during the temporary summer of oil's peak on further stimulating yet higher levels of consumption. Instead we'd be investing those very same temporary riches in adapting to a changed world. Similarly, a quick scan of the news will reveal many technical and economic fixes designed to facilitate more growth and development in an already-stressed system. The third response—changing the structure of the system—is currently beyond the capability of present day decision-making, even though it is where we need to go. The fact is that it may only be invoked when one or more sufficiently serious 'inflections' in the world system (such as a stock market crash, a human pandemic or a large-scale environmental catastrophe) reveal the poverty of present practices. Clearly 'social learning' of this magnitude will be a very expensive exercise indeed. But we would be foolish to merely sit back and wait …

To deal successfully with global challenges of the scale we are facing requires much broader understanding of the human context than currently exists in governments and bureaucracies anywhere. Societies need time to respond. *If it is only through the careful use of informed foresight that we can create time and space to deal with such complicated and challenging issues, then the sooner school systems begin using and teaching it at every level, as appropriate, the better.* Clearly, we're not speaking here merely about a curriculum change but changes in the deep structures of our understanding of the world (Wilber, 1995).

CONCLUSION

School systems have been run, by and large, as if the future remained open and unproblematic. That was once a reasonable assumption but it no longer is. The future of humanity is currently under greater threat than most are willing to admit. Yet as the costs of not understanding the 'great transition' progressively mount, so the rationale for thinking ahead becomes increasingly obvious. School systems need to face these facts. They need a more dynamic and responsive structure, including their own environmental scanning systems that are different from, but as effective as, those routinely operated in commercial environments. They need to value and use the futures frameworks, methods and tools that have been available for some time. Beginning teachers need to be introduced to futures concepts and tools suitable for classroom use. They also need to develop their own specifically futures-oriented understanding more fully than ever before.

It is only when changes of this kind are well under way that school systems can legitimately claim that they are preparing young people appropriately for their future lives. Only then will young people begin to be properly equipped for the manifestly challenging tasks ahead. The 'bottom line' is that there is nothing inevitable about the journey of the human race from its origins in the distant past onward into the future. Equally, however, there is nothing inevitable about the current 'overshoot and collapse' trajectory, the 'fall into Dystopia', either. While schools are by no means the only, or even the most powerful, actors involved, it seems to me that they have a pivotal role to play in helping humanity decide just how to respond to the growing global dilemma that surrounds us.

NOTES

[i] The term STEEP was developed to track 'signals of change' in relation to: Social, Technological, Economic, Environmental and Political factors. There are, in fact, several such acronyms but all have the same underlying purpose.

[ii] Wendell Bell's opus, *The Foundations of Futures Studies*, volumes 1 and 2 (Bell, 1997, 2003), and especially volume 2: on values, objectivity and the good society, provide a valuable and informed overview of some of the 'big questions' of our time as viewed from a specifically futures viewpoint.

[iii] The work in question is Donnelly's *Dumbing Down* (2007), a barely literate polemic purporting to identify a left-wing conspiracy to take over the school curriculum. Soon after publication its thesis was convincingly rebutted by historian Stuart Macintyre (Macintyre, 2007).

REFERENCES

Beare, H., & Slaughter, R. (1993). *Education for the 21st century*. London: Routledge.
Bell, W. (2003, 2004). *Foundations of futures studies* (Vols. 1 & 2). New Brunswick, NJ: Transaction Press.

Berman, M. (1981). *The reenchantment of the world.* Ithaca and London: Cornell University Press.

Board of Senior Secondary School Studies Queensland. (1995). *Trial syllabus in futures.* Brisbane: BSSSSQ.

Dator, J. (1992). *Surfing the tsunamis of change, paper for symposium 'Construction Beyond 2000'.* Finland: Espoo.

Donnelly, K. (2007). *Dumbing down: Outcomes-based and politically correct-the impact of the culture wars on our schools.* Melbourne: Hardie Grant.

Eckersley, R., Cahill, H., Wierenga, A., & Wyn, J. (2007). *Generations in dialogue about the future: The hopes and fears of young Australians.* Canberra: Australia21.

Fisher, F. (2006). *Response ability.* Melbourne: Vista.

Gidley, J. (2004). *Futures in education: Principles, practice and potential, Australian foresight institute monograph 5.* Melbourne: Foresight Institute. Retrieved from http://www.swin.edu.au/agse/courses/foresight/monographs.htm

Hamilton, C., & Denniss, R. (2005). *Affluenza.* Sydney: Allen & Unwin.

Hicks, D. (2002). *Lessons for the future.* London: Routledge.

Kunstler, J. H. (2005). *The long emergency.* London: Atlantic Books.

Macintyre, S. (2007, March 7). Polemic fails its own test. *Australian Literary Review,* 12–13.

Milojević, I. (2005). *Educational futures: Dominant and contesting visions.* London: Routledge.

Peters, M. (2005). Educational policy futures. In R. Slaughter et al. (Eds.), *Knowledge base of futures studies, Vol. 5: Synergies, case studies and implementation.* CD-ROM. Brisbane: Foresight International.

Queensland Government. (1994). *Shaping the future, overview of the review of the Queensland school curriculum.* Brisbane: Queensland Government (AKA the *Wiltshire Report*).

Rundle, K. A. (1996). *Curriculum futures experiment in Queensland.* Unpublished ms.

Sardar, Z., & Davies, M. W. (2004). *American dream—global nightmare.* London: Icon.

Slaughter, R. (1999). *Futures for the third millennium—enabling the forward view.* Sydney: Prospect.

Slaughter, R. (2004). *Futures beyond dystopia: Creating social foresight.* London: Routledge. Available on CD-ROM at http://www.foresightinternational.com.au

Slaughter, R. (2006). *Living in a world on the edge.* Paper for ideas festival, Brisbane, 2006. Retrieved from http://www.foresightinternational.com.au

Slaughter, R., & Bussey, M. (2006). *Futures thinking for social foresight.* Tamsui, Taiwan: Tamkang University Press. Available on CD-ROM at http://www.foresightinternational.com.au

Slaughter, R. (Ed.). (2007). *AFI monograph series* (Vols. 1–10). Melbourne: Swinburne University. Available in pdf form from http://www.swin.edu.au/agse/courses/foresight/monographs.htm

Steffan, W., Sanderson, A., Tyson, P. D., Jäger, J., Matson, P. A., Moore III, B., et al. (2004). *Global change and the earth system: A planet under pressure.* Berlin: Springer Verlag.

Sullivan, J. (2007, April 21). Schoolgirl crushers. *The Age,* A2 section, 12–13.

Underwood, F. (1996). Evaluation of the trial syllabus in senior futures, Interim Report 1. Brisbane: BSSSSQ.

Wilber, K. (1995). *Sex, ecology, spirituality: The spirit of evolution.* Boston: Shambhala.

Richard Slaughter is a writer, practitioner and innovator in futures studies and applied foresight. He completed a PhD in Futures at the University of Lancaster (UK) in 1982. Since then, he has explored the futures domain through educational work, institutional innovation, social foresight, integral futures and the identification of an evolving knowledge base. During 1999–2004 he was Foundation Professor of Foresight at the Australian Foresight Institute, Melbourne. During 2001–2005 he was President of the World Futures Studies Federation.

RICHARD A. SLAUGHTER

He is currently Director of Foresight International, an independent company dedicated to building the futures field and facilitating the emergence of social foresight. He is the author or editor of some 20 books and many papers on a variety of futures topics. For more details, including extracts and info on related works, please go to: http://www.foresightinternational.com.au.

PART TWO

POLICY ISSUES IN EDUCATION

5. A FUTURES PERSPECTIVE

Lessons from the school room

In this chapter I firstly set out some of the problems faced by practising teachers in relation to the academic field of futures studies and then clarify the educational rationale for developing a 'futures perspective' in the school curriculum. Whilst schools have a crucial role to play in helping young people think about the future what is actually possible and appropriate is dependent on children's ages. I outline some of what is currently known about children and young people's perceptions of the future and then give an example of how teachers and students who intend to be teachers can be introduced to these concerns. Finally I indicate some of the areas of futures education that require further research.

PROLOGUE

Teachers as professionals

All good futurists would probably like other professionals to be enthused about their field. This is because it seems self-evident to us that the insights from futures studies could be of benefit to most other academic fields. Wendell Bell (1997, p. xxi) thus argues that specialists in other disciplines would benefit from futurising their thinking and I would agree with this. Why, therefore, do I find social commentators generally and teachers in particular so uninformed about futures studies? I suspect Jim Dator (1998, p. 298) had the answer when he addressed readers of the *American Behavioural Scientist*:

> ... the chances are very good that ... you have never taken a course in futures studies; never met a person who teaches it at the university level; teach or study on a campus where futures studies is not offered; and probably associate *futures studies* (if the term means anything to you at all) either with astrology and charlatans or with Alvin Toffler, John Naisbitt, or Faith Popcorn ... Your most fundamental images of the future are almost certainly shaped primarily by films and videos you have seen.

This would certainly be true for most school teachers but it would also be reinforced by other forces relating to the professional context in which they work. Most teachers consider themselves to be first and foremost educators, that is, they feel they have an obligation to educate rather than proselytise. They thus feel it would be wrong to add things to the curriculum simply because other professionals feel they should and, anyway, the content of the curriculum may not be up for negotiation if the education system is a highly centralised one. Secondly, many teachers in industrialised countries have been suffering from 'curriculum fatigue' in particular as a result of neoliberal policies which have lead to increasingly utilitarian and market driven forms of education. Thirdly, teachers may unwittingly resist innovative change because schools are but one of the many sites of cultural reproduction which reflect prevailing hegemonic forces. They, as well as their pupils, are often unable to think 'outside the box' whether socially or culturally, as Apple (1993) and Giroux (1992) have argued at length, or ecologically, as writers such as Orr (1994) and Bowers (1997) have argued. Western forms of education, whether as practised at home or exported, thus tend to reflect white, male, neoliberal views of the world (Apple, 2001)—and of the future (Milojević, 2002).

Children and Youth

If we believe that adults can benefit from the insights of futures studies in their personal lives, their work and their communities, then what they might or might not have learnt about futures in their youth and childhood needs to be of vital interest too. I use the term futures education, as against futures studies, to distinguish what may or may not go on in schools and formal education up to the age of 18. Whilst culture, ethnicity, gender and class will affect young people's views of the future (as it also does for adults), what in particular affects them is the process of childhood socialisation and development.

How children conceptualise the future varies with age. In early childhood we are dealing with quite different notions of the future to those held by older children (Page, 2000). As they enter the middle years of schooling (7–14), children's views begin to take on some aspects of adult understanding (Hicks & Holden, 1995) and these mature with age. Youth futures (15–25) have also been noted as a specific category differing in crucial ways from adult views (Gidley & Inayatullah, 2002). A range of important changes are thus taking place in youth and childhood which makes futures education a distinctly different enterprise to that of futures studies. How adults conceptualise the future is largely a result of what did, or did not, happen to them during this crucial formative period.

The Problem with Futures Studies

The problem with futures studies for teachers is that most of them will never have heard of it for the reasons given by Dator above. If they do come across the field, it appears to be an academic and research-based activity carried on in universities. This puts most teachers off because universities seem remote from their daily life in classrooms. The nature of futures studies is thus likely to be misunderstood and, even if understood, not seen as immediately useful to teachers in schools. There is nowhere I can point to at the moment in the UK as an example of good practice in futures education. Whilst the English Qualifications and Curriculum Authority has a Futures Programme (www.qca.org.uk/11232.html), on closer inspection this turns out to be primarily about the future of the curriculum and contains little that specifically helps teachers think more critically and creatively about a range of alternative futures, whether for society or education.

Many other issue-orientated academic fields *have* given rise to lively and innovative educational fields. Examples include global education, development education, environmental education, peace education, intercultural education. Whilst each maintains its own distinct identity, many see these fields as potential allies with overlapping interests. When educators refer by name to these issue-based educations what is generally missing, however, is any reference to futures studies or futures education. In other words, we have as yet to gain widespread credibility with natural educational allies. One of the few exceptions is Pike and Selby's (1999) model of global education which argues that the spatial and temporal dimensions of the curriculum are of equal importance.

FUTURES EDUCATION

Educational Rationale

Whilst 'futures education' or 'futures in education' are useful shorthand terms to designate the application of futures ideas to formal schooling and teacher training, it is important to recall that this is not generally part of the everyday vocabulary of teachers. They are more likely to talk about 'preparing children for the future' and, if urged to be more specific about the future in their teaching, would probably demand a clear educational rationale for this. This is an appropriate request for an educator to make and one that can easily be answered in the professional language of teachers as shown below in Table 1.

Aims of Futures Education

In exploring the elements of such a rationale with teachers it then becomes possible to talk about the need for a 'futures dimension' within the curriculum and the need for pupils to develop a 'futures perspective', i.e., the ability to think more critically and creatively about the future. The specific aims of futures education can be formulated as helping teachers and pupils to:
- develop a more future-orientated perspective both on their own lives and events in the wider world;
- identify and envision alternative futures which are just and sustainable;
- exercise critical thinking skills and the creative imagination more effectively;
- participate in more thoughtful and informed decision making in the present; and
- engage in active and responsible citizenship, both in the local, national and global community, and on behalf of present and future generations

Aims such as these are of interest to a wide range of educators concerned with subjects such as English, maths, science, technology, geography, history, modern languages, business studies and religious education. They are also of particular relevance to equal opportunities, multicultural education, and cross-curricular themes such as education for sustainability, citizenship, and personal and social education.

Table 1. Rationale for a futures dimension in the curriculum

Pupil motivation

Pupil expectation about the future can affect behaviour in the present, e.g., that something is, or is not, worth working for. Clear images of desired personal goals can help stimulate motivation and achievement.

Anticipating change

Anticipatory skills and flexibility of mind are important in times of rapid change. Such skills enable pupils to deal more effectively with uncertainty and to initiate, rather than merely respond to, change.

Critical thinking

In weighing up information, considering trends and imagining alternatives, pupils will need to exercise reflective and critical thinking. This is often triggered by realising the contradictions between how the world is now and how one would like it to be.

Clarifying values

All images of the future are underpinned by differing value assumptions about human nature and society. In a democratic society pupils need to be able to begin to identify such value judgements before they can themselves make appropriate choices between alternatives.

Decision making

Becoming more aware of trends and events which are likely to influence one's future and investigating the possible consequences of one's actions on others in the future, leads to more thoughtful decision making in the present.

Creative imagination

One faculty that can contribute to, and which is particularly enhanced by, designing alternative futures is that of the creative imagination. Both this *and* critical thinking are needed to envision a range of preferable futures from the personal to the global.

A better world

It is important in a democratic society that pupils develop their sense of vision, particularly in relation to more just and sustainable futures. Such forward looking thinking is an essential ingredient in both the preserving and improving of society.

Responsible citizenship

Critical participation in democratic life leads to the development of political skills and thus more active and responsible citizenship. Future generations are then more likely to benefit, rather than lose, from decisions made today.

At the same time, discussion with teachers and teacher educators in various countries reveals that the future is largely a missing dimension within education. Gough's (1990) investigation into the portrayal of futures in educational discourse is invaluable here. After examining a range of educational documents he identified three common types of reference to the future—tacit, token and taken–for–granted. *Tacit futures* are all those which are assumed and never brought out into the open. They remain hidden and unexplicated but nevertheless present. Thus the future may not even be mentioned in an educational document but assumptions about it are still tacitly present. *Token futures* often involve clichés and stereotypes presented in a rhetorical fashion. Gough (1990, p. 303) notes, "When one finds 'the future' (or a futures-oriented inference) in the title of an educational document it usually means much less than might be expected". *Taken–for–granted futures* occur whenever a particular future, or range of futures, is described as if there were no alternatives. Discussion of the future framed solely in terms of science and technology or work and leisure would be in this category.

Insights from Futures Studies

It is interesting to reflect on which insights and concepts from futures studies have been taken up by teachers and used in their work and also how they have been developed for use with children. Whilst the teaching materials available to schools are still relatively limited, it is nevertheless still possible to give some idea of the concepts that have been taken up. The following examples are fairly representative of responses over the last 25 years in Western education.

Amongst the concepts used in a seminal booklet from the US National Council for Social Studies (Fitch & Svengalis, 1979) are: possible, probable and preferable futures; utopian and dystopian writing; assumptions about time; scenarios; trend analysis; forecasting; cross-impact matrices; and futures wheels. Riley's (1989) resource book for teachers includes: possible, probable and preferable futures; trend extrapolation; futures wheels; Delphi technique; cross-impact matrices; scenarios; values and the future; imaging; and timelines. Pike and Selby's (1999) resource book on global education refers to: possible, probable and preferable futures; futures wheels; intergenerational justice; and sustainability. A resource book on citizenship education (Hicks, 2001) contains: images of the future; futures wheels; probable and preferable futures; rights of future generations; scenarios; and sustainable futures. Contributors to Gidley and Inayatullah's (2002) book on youth futures further confirm that a wide range of futures tools are being used with young people as does Slaughter and Bussey's *Futures Thinking for Social Foresight* (2006).

YOUNG PEOPLE AND THE FUTURE

Understanding how children and young people develop their ideas about the future is crucial since it is from this formative period that adult perceptions emerge. The importance of futures education in schools lies in its capacity to challenge often unconscious processes. The literature on children and young people's views of the future has been growing slowly since the mid-90s and a flavour of this will be given under the headings primary, secondary and youth. (NB. Since 'secondary' encompasses 11–18 and 'youth' 15–25, there is an overlap between these two categories.) As you will notice the research still has a very Western bias so one should be cautious about generalising from this.

Primary Level

It is a common assumption amongst many teachers that younger pupils have little conception of issues in the wider world. However, Fountain (1990) points out that nursery and infant children (age 4–7) regularly: call each other names (prejudice); arbitrarily exclude others from their play (discrimination); argue over materials (resource distribution); protest that rules are not fair (human rights); quarrel and fight (peace and conflict); waste consumable materials (environmental awareness); find out that more can be accomplished by working together (interdependence). Issues that might initially be considered national or global are thus present in many classrooms and need to be recognised and worked with.

One of the few educators to explore how young children conceptualise the future is Australian early years specialist Jane Page (2000), who notes that futures educators generally ignore this age group. Her work with 4 and 5 year olds, however, shows that futures concepts are beginning to be developed at this age. The children she studied have a fundamentally different attitude towards the future, time and change than older children. Time is viewed purely in terms of the child's own activities, i.e., in four sleeps rather than four days time. They cannot understand that time exists independent of themselves, but there is a growing sense of progression beginning with notions of 'before' and 'after' and moving on to 'yesterday' and 'tomorrow'.

The 'future' means being older or things changing. There is a growing awareness of societal issues, for example the environment, war, music, places and events in the news. Thinking about the future at this age involves imaginative fantasy, past and future often get mixed up (they are both the 'not now'), and there is a great sense of control and freedom over the future in such play. Whilst this may seem idiosyncratic and unrealistic from an adult point of view, this is a vital developmental stage. Young children are developing positive feelings about their place in the future and their role in its creation and are more positive than older children about the future.

Whilst different levels of ability are found in conceptualising the future at 7–8, this is when initial manifestations of an 'adult' understanding of time begin to appear. Research by Hicks and Holden (1995) in England shows the emergence of an ability to think ahead and the realisation that the future may be something to work towards as well as something to be concerned about. Reality and fantasy may still sit side by side and children sometimes fear that their own area may be subject to violence and wars seen in other places on TV. There is a growing awareness of social and environmental issues and children are generally optimistic that the future will be better both for themselves and others. However, some think problems such as pollution and poverty may get worse. Boys often fear global disasters, for example the world exploding or aliens landing.

Secondary Level

Understandably, young people's concerns for the future tend to reflect current national and global events although these may change over time. In the 90s Hicks and Holden (1995) found that in relation to their personal futures English adolescents were concerned about getting a good job, having a good life, issues of health, good relationships and doing well at school. In relation to the futures of their local community they identified crime and violence, jobs and employment, the range of amenities, and environmental threats as their main concerns. In terms of the global future, they were worried about issues of war and peace, environmental damage, poverty and hunger, and relationships between countries. Pessimism increased with age and most felt that they had not learnt enough about these issues at school.

Oscarsson's (1996) work with Swedish teenagers showed similar findings. A majority of pupils had a positive view of their own future, although many reported what he called 'uncertain optimism' in relation to work. Unemployment was seen as the main threat to their personal futures and, to a lesser extent, environmental problems. They had a less optimistic vision of Sweden's future, however, often expressing concern about economic conditions. Nearly two-thirds had a pessimistic view of the global future, particularly in relation to environmental issues and to a lesser extent warfare. Their views of the global future were more pessimistic than those of personal or Swedish futures. Brunstad's (2002) research in Norway and Rubin's (2000) in Finland echo some of these 'European' themes. Rubin also examines in some depth the relationship between young people's concerns and the wider socio-cultural context.

Hutchinson's (1996) work with Australian teenagers focused in particular on the nature of their probable and preferable futures. Their probable futures fell into six broad categories: i) an uncompassionate world (depersonalised and uncaring); ii) a physically violent world (with a high likelihood of war); iii) a divided world (between 'haves' and 'have-nots'); iv) a mechanised world (of often violent technological change); v) an environmentally unsustainable world (with continued degradation of the biosphere); and vi) a politically corrupt and deceitful world (where voting is a waste of time). Their preferable futures fell into four broad categories: i) technocratic dreaming (uncritical acceptance, especially amongst boys, of techno-fix solutions for all problems); ii) demilitarisation and greening (of science and technology to meet genuine human needs); iii) intergenerational equity (accepting responsibility for future generations); and iv) making peace (with people and planet via a reconceptualisation of both ethics and lifestyles). These are very powerful images for young people who said they had learnt little about futures in school.

Youth Futures

A most welcome addition to this comparative research is Gidley and Inayatullah's (2002) *Youth Futures* in which Eckersley (2002) has a chapter on Australian youth. He reports that the future most young Australians want is neither the future they expect, nor the future they are promised. Most do not expect Australian society to be better than today in 2010. They see a society driven by greed whilst what they would like is one motivated by generosity. Their dreams are for a society that places less emphasis on the individual, material wealth and competition, and more on community and family, the environment and co-operation. The belief that life would improve is a minority position and pessimism increases with age; those in their 20s are more negative than those in their teens. In an earlier account of this research, Eckersley (1999) concludes "Young people's preferred futures are undoubtedly idealised and utopian. Their significance lies in what they reveal about fundamental human needs ... and what they expect and what is being offered to them by world and national leaders".

It is clear from the above that much of the existing research on young people and the future relates to Western societies so that, as yet, limited cross-cultural comparisons can be made. Research on youth futures is also, by definition, less likely to look at age differences than work done in schools. Two contrasting studies deal with Japan and Singapore. Wright (2002) examines the role of contemporary Japanese youth in challenging traditional values and argues that their 'cool resistance' may enable them to rewrite a future that has already been colonised by their parents' culture. In a different vein, Oehlers (2002) explores how political and cultural pressures in Singapore have largely stifled any youth disaffection so that any debate about alternative futures is almost impossible.

TEACHER EDUCATION

A Global Dimension

For futures education to have a greater impact on schools it is clear that initial and on-going teacher education are crucial arenas to influence. The obstacles in teacher education, however, are likely to be similar to those in schools. I thus think it is tactically easier, in schools and teacher education, to get people thinking first about the need for a 'global dimension' in the curriculum (where are we now?) and then to go on to consider the need for a 'futures perspective' (what may happen as a consequence?). Thus, rather than starting with the future and explaining its importance in relation to the global issues in the present, one begins by looking at the state of the world in the present which automatically leads on to questions about the future (Hicks & Holden, 2007). What's happening now will always be more tangible than what has yet to come. An example of this in terms of educational policy and practice comes from my own institution, Bath Spa University in the UK.

Traditionally, undergraduates training to be teachers in England used to take a degree which focused rather narrowly on the National Curriculum and the professional training of teachers. Increasingly, a number of universities have replaced this with a 3+1 route, i.e., a three-year degree (Education Studies as single honours or Education with a subject specialism as joint honours) followed by a one-year post-graduate Certificate in Education—which is where their professional training now occurs. Those who do this at Bath Spa are guaranteed a global perspective in their modular programme because it forms a key strand in the Education Studies degree. The School of Education specifically chose this strategy in order to bring breadth and depth back to the study of education.

Modules are arranged in three strands ~ A: Learning and curriculum; B: Teaching, settings and structures; C: Global and international. Education students have to choose modules from each of these groups, so all of them will have some understanding of the need for and nature of a global perspective. In their first year all students take a compulsory module entitled Education for Change which explores three main themes: i) the nature and purposes of education; ii) the current state of the world; and iii) the need for a global and futures dimension in the curriculum. The 'international' modules explore the nature of education in different cultural settings. The 'global' modules focus on contemporary global issues and concerns. These include futures, citizenship, human rights, and sustainability.

A Futures Perspective

Each year around 25 second year students take module ED2013 Education for the Future. The time allowed for this module is a one-hour lecture and a two-hour seminar each week for 12 weeks. A flavour of the module is conveyed by the following details (Table 2).

EPILOGUE

Issues Arising

There are two quite different issues that I would like to raise here. The first is to do with the significance of what we are learning from the research and the second is procedural in the sense of how best to influence teachers and educational policy makers.

Whilst we now know more about *what* young people think about the future, we are only just beginning to engage with what that might *mean*. Eckersley (2002, p. 32) highlights the difficulties when he writes:

> There is little doubt that many qualities that future fears might intuitively be expected to influence—hope, purpose and meaning in life, coherence, efficacy, or agency—are important to well-being. However, we may never be able to do more than suggest this because of the difficulty of disentangling

concerns about the fate of the earth from the many other factors that influence these qualities, and hence well-being.

He further notes important qualifications to the belief that global pessimism might be eroding young people's well being. Firstly, the direction of any causal relationship between future pessimism and diminished well being can run two ways. Young people may feel pessimistic about the future because of their experience of the world now; at the same time, if depression levels are increasing in society then future visions are likely to become more pessimistic. Secondly, the wider research on well being shows that most people report satisfaction with their lives and that

Table 2. ED2013 Education for the Future

Description

'Futures in education' is the shorthand term used internationally by educators who believe that one of the main tasks of education is to prepare young people for a future that will necessarily be very different from today. In the UK teachers are more likely to talk about 'education for the future' when they express this concern. This module will introduce you to the crucial need for a futures perspective in schools and the ways in which this can be used to enhance pupils' learning. It will look at how young people feel about the future, locally and globally, and ways in which images of the future affect what we feel is worth doing in the present. It will explore the nature of both probable and preferable futures in the early 21st century and encourage you to think more critically and creatively about your personal and professional futures.

Learning outcomes

By the end of this module you should be able to:

Understand the need for a futures perspective in the curriculum

Think critically and creatively about futures related issues

Reflect critically on both the meaning and practice of futures education

Develop classroom activities that encourage futures-orientated thinking

Outline programme

Facing the future

Popular images of the future

Understanding futures studies

Whose futures?

The nature of futures education

A futures perspective (primary)

Young people's views (secondary)

Envisioning preferable futures

The need for sustainable futures

Course review and evaluation

this is most influenced by family, work, friends and leisure. Thirdly, pessimism is only one of several cultural traits in modern Western society that are inimical to well being, including consumerism, deconstructive postmodernism and individualism.

Futures education has as yet to make a significant impact in schools despite a range of important initiatives instigated by committed educators in different countries (e.g., Gidley et al., 2004; Morgan, 2006). In this respect, unfortunately, I have to take issue with Slaughter (2002) who argues that there has been a shift from 'rhetoric to reality' in schools and that futures is emerging into the educational mainstream. The list, however, is still the 'usual suspects'—a handful of innovative educators in the US, Australia and the UK—but not yet a sea change in the wider educational system. One of my measures of this, as I mentioned earlier, is that futures education still seldom makes it into the list of 'issue-based educations' that socially committed educators around the world are conversant with.

Global education is an interesting case in point. It is an international educational field that has at least a 30 year history, its own professional organisations and publications, conferences, alliances, documents, agendas, official policies and curriculum frameworks (Oxfam, 2006; Pike, 2000; DfES, 2005). Most of this effort is aimed at primary and secondary schools and teacher education. If there are lessons here for futures education, it could be that it may take years of dedicated work before the need for a 'futures perspective' is as widely accepted as the need for a 'global dimension' in the curriculum. This requires a younger generation of futures educators to be also involved in that struggle. An alternative, of course, is that futures educators should infiltrate other issue-based educations and ensure that they each contain a futures element (Hicks, 2004).

A good example of this can be found in environmental education, where a recent review of empirical studies of learners and learning (Rickinson, 2001) included a section on young people's views of the future. Conversely, I was intrigued to read a recent biography of Elise Boulding (Morrison, 2001) which was written in terms of her contribution to peace education and feminist research but made no reference to her vital work on futures. One of the most useful entry points for those educators interested in a 'futures perspective' could still be global education. Pike and Selby, influential theorists in this field, have long argued for a model of global education that contains four main elements: an issues dimension; a spatial dimension; a temporal dimension; and a process dimension. This model is described in Pike and Selby (1999) together with a range of practical classroom activities.

Research Needed

The field of futures education is still under-researched and there are many crucial issues and themes awaiting investigation. Even an initial list of basic research that needs to be done (Hicks, 2006) is quite a long one (see Table 3).

Table 3. Research needed in futures education

Images of the future

How do children conceptualise time and the future and how does this vary with age?

- How do children's views of the future vary by gender?
- How do children's views of the future vary by social class?
- How do children's views of the future vary by ethnic group?
- What is the nature of children's probable and preferred futures?
- What emerges from cross-cultural comparisons of the above?

NB. Views of the future could be broken down into personal, local, national and global.

Media influences on images

What images of the future are conveyed by children's books, comics and computer games?

What images of the future are conveyed by TV advertising?

What images of the future have been conveyed by popular movies over the last 25 years?

How do such images relate to issues of gender, age, class and Western culture?

Image and action

How do images of the future affect attitudes and behaviour in the present?

What determines reactive or proactive stances in relation to the future?

What changes in attitude and behaviour arise from extended futures-orientated work in a school or classroom?

What do teaching materials that encourage skills of participation and responsible action look like for different age groups?

Resources and policy

What do appropriate teaching materials look like for different subject areas and how can subject specialists be encouraged to develop them?

Which futures methodologies are most useful in the classroom and how can they be related to a range of other learning outcomes?

How can head teachers, school governors and parents be persuaded of the need for a futures dimension in the curriculum?

What educational bodies and which key players would need to be influenced in order to gain official backing for such a dimension in the curriculum?

This is in no way intended to be a complete list but it highlights a range of initial research possibilities.

And Finally

There is no clear body of opinion within mainstream education that understands or supports the need for a futures perspective in schools. It is still the domain of a loose international network of socially committed educators. Future steps that need to be taken could include the following:

- Creation internationally of a seed group of educators specifically committed to futures education, possibly as an offshoot of the World Futures Studies Federation.
- Creation nationally of networks of teachers and teacher educators committed to futures education.
- Setting up alliances, nationally and internationally, with colleagues working in global education, social education, education for sustainability.
- The development of teaching materials for different age groups and subject areas that embody the principles of futures education.
- Working with professional groups (e.g., teachers, head teachers, subject specialists) to incorporate a futures perspective in policy documents.
- Offering professional development programmes to schools, local authorities, curriculum development bodies and other national bodies.
- Identifying key players in education who need to be inducted into the principles and practice of futures education.
- Circulating nationally and internationally, via conferences and newsletters, examples of successful practice at all levels of education.

If official recognition of a global perspective in the UK is anything to go, by achieving the same for a futures perspective could yet take some time. Is there enough commitment internationally to attempt this? Who are the key players and where are they now? Who would be natural allies? What and where are the pressure points which need to be worked on? And how can the wider field of futures studies support those working in schools and teacher education to begin such a programme?

In discussing William Morris's great utopian novel, *News from Nowhere*, Coleman and O'Sullivan (1990, p.10) write:

> Let us imagine that life is not as it is, but as it one day might be. Let us inspect the unknown terrain of the future, as if we are about to inhabit it ... the imagined future is a subversive force: the more who imagine a different kind of future, and imagine constructively, materially and determinedly, the more dangerous utopian dreams become. They grow from dreams to aims.

Morris, I suspect, would be delighted to know that in the early twenty-first century these concerns are still alive and at the heart of the academic field of futures studies— and futures education in schools.

REFERENCES

Apple, M. (1993). *Official knowledge: Democratic education in a conservative age*. London: Routledge.

Apple, M. (2001). *Educating the 'Right' way: Markets, standards, god, and inequality*. London: Routledge/Falmer.

Bell, W. (1997). *Foundations of futures studies* (Vol. 1). New Brunswick, NJ: Transaction Publishers.

Bowers, C. (1997). *The culture of denial: Why the environmental movement needs a strategy for reforming universities and public schools.* Albany, NY: State University of New York Press.
Brunstad, P. (2002). Longing for belonging: Youth culture in Norway. In J. Gidley & S. Inayatullah (Eds.), *Youth futures: Comparative research and transformative visions* (Chapter 12). Westport, CT: Praeger.
Coleman, S., & O'Sullivan, P. (1990). *William Morris and news from nowhere: A vision for our time.* Bideford: Green Books.
Dator, J. (1998). The future lies behind! Thirty years of teaching futures studies. *American Behavioural Scientist, 42*, 298–319.
Department for Education and Skills (DfES). (2005). *Developing the global dimension in the school curriculum.* London: Qualifications and Curriculum Authority.
Eckersley, R. (1999). Dreams and expectations: Young people's expected and preferred futures and their significance for education. *Futures, 31*, 73–90.
Eckersley, R. (2002). Future visions, social realities, and private lives: Young people and their personal well-being. In J. Gidley & S. Inayatullah (Eds.), *Youth futures: Comparative research and transformative visions* (Chapter 3). Westport, CT: Praeger.
Fitch, R., & Svengalis, C. (1979). Futures unlimited: Teaching about worlds to come. *Bulletin 59.* Washington, DC: National Council for Social Studies.
Fountain, S. (1990). *Learning together: Global education 4–7.* Cheltenham: Stanley Thornes.
Gidley, J., & Inayatullah, S. (Eds.). (2002). *Youth futures: Comparative research and transformative visions.* Westport, CT: Praeger.
Gidley, J., Bateman, D., & Smith, C. (2004). *Futures in education: Principles, practice and potential.* Melbourne: Australian Foresight Institute, Swinburne University of Technology.
Giroux, H. (1992). *Border crossings: Cultural workers and the politics of education.* London: Routledge.
Gough, N. (1990). Futures in Australian education: Tacit, token and taken for granted. *Futures, 22*, 298–310.
Hicks, D. (2001). *Citizenship for the future: A practical classroom guide.* Godalming: World Wide Fund for Nature UK.
Hicks, D. (2006). *Lessons for the future: The missing dimension in education.* Victoria, BC: Trafford Publishing.
Hicks, D. (2004). Teaching for tomorrow: What can futures studies contribute to peace education? *Journal of Peace Education, 1*(2), 165–178.
Hicks, D., & Holden, C. (1995). *Visions of the future: Why we need to teach for tomorrow.* Stoke-on-Trent: Trentham Books.
Hicks, D., & Holden, C. (Eds.). (2007). *Teaching the global dimension: Key principles and effective practice.* London: Routledge/Falmer.
Hicks, D., & Slaughter, R. (Eds.). (1998). *Futures education: The world yearbook of education 1998.* London: Kogan Page.
Hutchinson, F. (1996). *Educating beyond violent futures.* London: Routledge.
Milojević, I. (2002). *Futures of education: Feminist and post-western critiques and visions.* PhD thesis, Brisbane: University of Queensland.
Morgan, A. (2006). Teaching geography for a sustainable future. In D. Balderstone (Ed.), *Secondary geography handbook* (Chapter 23). Sheffield: Geographical Association.
Morrison, M. (2001). The life of Elise Boulding: Educating towards a culture of peace. *Vitae Scholasticae*, Spring, 7–21.
Oehlers, A. (2002). Imagining the future: Youth in Singapore. In J. Gidley & S. Inayatullah (Eds.), *Youth futures: Comparative research and transformative visions* (Chapter 9). Westport, CT: Praeger.
Orr, D. (1994). *Earth in mind: On education, environment and the human prospect.* Washington, DC: Island Press.

Oscarsson, V. (1996). Pupils' views of the future. In A. Osler, et al. (Eds.), *Teaching for citizenship in Europe* (Chapter 18). Stoke-on-Trent: Trentham Books.

Oxfam. (2006). *A curriculum for global citizenship*. Oxford: Oxfam.

Page, J. (2000). *Reframing the early childhood curriculum: Educational imperatives for the future*. London: Routledge/Falmer.

Pike, G. (2000). Global education and national identity: In pursuit of meaning. *Theory into practice*, *39*(2), 64–74.

Pike, G., & Selby, D. (1999). *In the global classroom* (Vol. 1). Toronto: Pippin.

Publishing Qualifications and Curriculum Authority. (2006). *Futures progamme*. Retrieved from www.gca.org.uk/11232.html

Rickinson, M. (2001). Learners and learning in environmental education: A critical review of the evidence. *Environmental Education Research (special issue)*, *7*(3), 207–317.

Riley, K. (1989). *Towards tomorrow*. New York: Scholastic.

Rubin, A. (2000). *Growing up in social transition: In search of a late-modern identity*. Turku: University of Turku.

Slaughter, R. (2002). From rhetoric to reality: The emergence of futures into the educational mainstream. In J. Gidley & S. Inayatullah (Eds.), *Youth futures: Comparative research and transformative visions* (Chapter 14). Westport, CT: Praeger.

Slaughter, R., & Bussey, M. (2006). *Futures thinking for social foresight*. Tamsui, Taiwan: Tamkang University Press.

Wright, D. (2002). Japanese youth: Rewriting futures in the 'no taboos' postbubble millennium. In J. Gidley & S. Inayatullah (Eds.), *Youth futures: Comparative research and transformative visions* (Chapter 7). Westport, CT: Praeger.

David Hicks is Professor in the School of Education at Bath Spa University. He is internationally recognised for his work on the need for a global and futures dimension in the curriculum and is particularly interested in ways of helping students and teachers think more critically and creatively about the future. He has published widely in the fields of futures education and global education. His most recent books are Teaching the Global Dimension: Key Principles and Effective Practice, *with Cathie Holden (RoutledgeFalmer, 2007),* Lessons for the Future: The Missing Dimension in Education *(Trafford Publishing, 2005), and* Citizenship for the Future: A Practical Classroom Guide *(World Wide Fund for Nature UK, 2001).*

JAMES DATOR[i]

6. UNIVERSITIES WITHOUT 'QUALITY' AND QUALITY WITHOUT 'UNIVERSITIES'

Today I will talk about universities and quality. My title is intended to stress that neither is absolute or eternal. Each changes with changing times, needs, and possibilities. What is deemed poor quality at one place and time might be impossibly high quality at another. Quality has the characteristic that Marshall McLuhan alleged was a saying of the Balinese: "We have no art. We do everything as well as we can" (McLuhan & Fiore, 1967).

Quality is thus a very relative thing, changing according to who 'we' are, what 'everything' actually is, and what technologies and techniques are available for us to do it at all, and hence to do it as well as we can.

Similarly with education—or rather, with learning, since I would rather focus on how and what people learn which is a much broader topic than is formal education and the professional teacher. People learn constantly. They are only consciously taught (educated) by teachers (educators) some tiny fraction of the time.

So the first thing for us to consider is: What is the purpose—the social function—of education? That usually boils down to determining whether people are educated for *their* own sake, or for the sake of some broader purpose or community. Is the purpose of formal education social development or personal growth, for example? Is education supposed to allow each of us to 'be all we can be', or are we educated so we can better serve certain functions required by the church, or by the state, or by business and commerce, or by the military?

Answers to that fundamental question help then determine what is taught, and what is not taught; who 'teachers' are and how they are educated; who pays for education, and how much; who decides what is taught, and in what sequence; what the educational 'delivery system' is like; and who determines whether what ever is to be taught has been taught "well" or not—its quality.

THE PAST OF LEARNING AND TEACHING

One thing futurists should do before they begin to think about the futures is to reflect on the pasts. So let's do that for a few brief moments.

And since I believe the present and the futures are strongly influenced by the distant as well as the more recent past, let's go back to that long stretch of time when humans lived in small, face–to–face, genetically and cosmologically homogeneous hunting and gathering societies. There was plenty of learning going on

M. Bussey, S. Inayatullah and I. Milojević (eds.), Alternative Educational Futures: Pedagogies for Emergent Worlds, 91–112.

then, but very few—or is it very many?—teachers, and almost no formal educational structures.

This is the natural and normal way for all of us to learn—continuously and unconsciously, by watching, imitating, playing, and fooling around. We generally don't even know we are learning, and no one is consciously being a teacher. We are just going about the normal routines of life, as proscribed by our culture, and as enabled and limited by our language and our technologies. There may be various rites of passage along the way where a kind of formal testing takes place, but for the most part, there is no separation of learning from life. And as for 'quality'? Well, we do everything as well as we can.

What I just said is primarily true for an oral—that is to say, a preliterate—society. Before the invention of writing, almost all learning was direct and informal. With the invention of writing several thousand years ago, formal education eventually became possible for some members of society. I say, 'eventually' because it seems to have taken about 1000 years from the invention and first use of writing as labels and signs for systems of writing and knowledge, and hence formal learning in schools, to emerge (Goody, 1977).

With writing it finally became possible to decontextualise information—to stop it, hold it, look at it, arrange and rearrange it, codify it, and teach it in a decontextualised, rote, boring, drill-based way.

And even though most people—many kings and generals, in fact—in early print-based societies did not know how to read and write, some small number of scholars did, and they were able to accumulate and pass on tried and true information that enabled the elites of print-based societies to dominate, destroy, and/or transform oral societies through the magic of the word alone.

We present-day word-worshippers tend only to focus on the positive aspects of literacy. We tend uncritically to believe that it is better to know how to read and write than to be illiterate. But in fact literacy is destructive as well. Merely forcing members of a preliterate culture to learn how to read and write destroys that culture. Learning through reading and writing is profoundly different from learning through watching, listening, and doing. And the teachers and learners differ as well—never mind the content of what one is forced to learn to read and the insipid stories one is expected eventually to write, compared to the chants, dances, and totems of oral societies (Goody, 1977; Havelock, 1986; Olson & Torrance, 2001; Ong, 1982).

Listen to a portion of "The Song of Lawino" by Okot p'Bitek of Uganda:

Listen, my clansmen,
I cry over my husband
Whose head is lost.
Ocol has lost his head
In the forest of books.

When my husband
Was still wooing me
His eyes were still alive,

His ears were still unblocked,
Ocol had not yet become a fool
My friend was a man then ...
My husband was still a Black man
The son of the Bull
The son of Agik...

The papers on my husband's desk
Coil threateningly...
They are tightly interlocked
Like the legs of the giant forest climbers
In the impenetrable forest.

My husband's house
Is a mighty forest of books,
Dark it is and very damp,
The steam rising from the ground
Hot thick and poisonous
Mingles with the corrosive dew
And the rain drops
That have collected in the leaves...

O, my clansmen,
Let us all cry together!
Come,
Let is mourn the death of my husband...
For the Prince
The heir to the Stool is lost!
And all the young men
Have perished in the wilderness!
And the fame of this homestead
That once blazed like a wild fire
In a moonless night
Is now like the last breaths
Of a dying old man!
...

Bile burns my inside!
I feel like vomiting!
For all our young men
Were finished in the forest,
Their manhood was finished
In the class-rooms,
Their testicles
Were smashed
With large books!

I rather suspect many a lament like that has been wailed by the native people of this continent as well, as their wisdom and ways of learning have been destroyed by large men bearing large books.

Then, with the emergence and proliferation of the printing press only a few hundred years ago, the written word reached a level of power and dominance that continues, more or less, to the present day. Until very recently—and that is the story shortly to be told—all formal knowledge was fixed in and communicated by reading and writing. Learning to read and write (and reckon) was the basis of all information, knowledge, and wisdom, 'higher' as well as 'lower'. Collecting written records in libraries, and pouring over them so as to produce more written records based upon them became the essence of all learning: the difficult art of turning words into other words without plagiarising.

At my university, we are still totally captivated by the magic of the written word. Not only do we insist that young adults take four or five courses about their native language—in spite of the fact that they have taken similar courses of English every year since they entered school more than a decade earlier—but we also require that those of us who teach courses in other subjects—like physics, or chemistry, or art, or, in my case, political futures studies—to offer so-called 'writing intensive' courses, on the argument that young Americans don't know how properly to read and write their native language after many, many years of the study of English as she is taught and wrote, but seldom as she is spoke or texted (Ming, 2004; Paglia, 2004; "Technology", 2004).

Even though you guys may not believe it, we Americans have been taught 'proper' English incessantly. But we have learned something else. We have learned that English as she is taught is as vital for our expressive lives as Esperanto or 'church' Latin. We have learned to think and communicate by other means, means largely ignored by the formal school system at all levels, high and low. We learn from the data-rich environment around us while our schools still focus on reading and writing in a manner no one does—or should (Sax, 2003).

Now, from a 'quality' point of view much of what we learn from what are called 'the media' may be factually wrong and morally reprehensible. Certainly, as a professor at the International Space University—devoted to educating people who will enable humanity to begin settling the solar system by the mid twenty-first century—I cringe when I look at the 'science' underlying such movies as *The Day After Tomorrow*, or *Armageddon*—much less *The Matrix*, or *Harry Potter*.

And careful public opinion polls do show that the average American and European, at least, indeed have rather horrifying views of the way the world works, in spite of (or is it because of?) years of formal science education.

Polls conducted regularly by the US National Science Foundation and recently by the European Commission show that 60 per cent of Americans and 50 per cent of Europeans believe humans and dinosaurs lived at the same time, whereas barely a majority of either could say how long it takes for the Earth to go around the Sun. Interestingly enough, over 80 per cent of both understood plate tectonics (National Science Foundation, 2004).

Try as we might, the boring science boringly presented in schools and universities does little to dispel folk beliefs, and so people persist in believing the darndest things because of what they see on TV and in the cinema. And, as I shall argue later, more and more young people are learning from interactive electronic games which routinely break even such fundamental natural laws as gravity, and which require behaviour that would be forbidden in any school and university I am aware of.

With the invention of writing and certainly with the invention of the printing press, most of the schools and universities that arose, basing their factual teaching on the word, also based their moral teaching on the Word—the Word of God. Not only the schools, but the cosmos itself was believed to be based on the Word. The Western God said, "let there be light" and there WAS light. "In the beginning was the Word and the Word was with God and the Word was God".

And not just Islam, Christianity, and Judaism: all of the so-called Great Religions became great by enshrining their beliefs in sacred texts. These texts—the words in them—often came to be more important and powerful than what the words represented (Andersen, 2005; LaFleur, 1983). For example, merely saying "*Namuyoho, Rengekyo*" is sufficient for salvation. It is not necessary to understand what you are saying, or even to believe it. Just say it.

Seldom has a technology been the subject of more worship than the word is in literate cultures. It is small wonder that my students are expected to take writing intensive courses all their lives long, until they get the words right.

But by mentioning the Word of God I also mean to call attention to the fact that there has been a strong moral, ethical, and/or religious content to most formal education based on reading and writing. The earliest schools, and scholars, typically were bent on learning and commenting on religious texts. This is still the case in many parts of the world.

However, by the nineteenth century, and the emergence of industrialism, colonialism, and the dominance of the nation–state system, a new form of education emerged—state-funded elementary and higher schools. Unlike earlier forms, these modern schools had one overarching purpose—to transform peasants into workers and soldiers, and aristocrats into managers and generals, so that the nation–state could develop, prosper, and conquer. While this is true of all early state universities, nowhere is it made clearer than with the creation of the universities of Tokyo and Kyoto in Japan, and the series of prefectural universities thereafter. During the first heady years of the Meiji Restoration, Japan was bent on becoming a modern nation as soon as possible. They sent their emissaries all over the world and quickly established impressive universities that emulated the essence of German state, and the American land grant, universities. Higher education in Japan was solely put to the service of the modernising state. And boy, were they successful as a result (Lincicome, 1995; Marshall, 1994; Ministry of Education, 1980; Passin, 1982)!

With few if any exceptions, at no time were any of these modern systems of education *per se* focused on 'the pursuit of truth' or on 'knowledge for knowledge's sake'. Neither were any of them intended primarily to help the individual learner grow and learn for her own sake. The pretence of 'a liberal education', focused on elevating and cultivating—truly *liberating* the individual learner from the blinders and shackles of her day–to–day commonsense life—was a wonderful conceit nurtured by some scholars, including myself, but largely a foggy delusion.

Neither legislators nor religious congregations nor philanthropists nor parents were willing to pour substantial portions of their wealth into institutions of higher education just so some few pointy-headed intellectuals could 'pursue truth'. What the funders wanted were obedient, competent *workers* and capable, effective *managers*. And if they were willing to fund research, even research that appeared to have no immediate earthly purpose, it was only in the hopes that an earthly purpose would in fact emerge in due time, and the sooner the better. Indeed, after World War II, 'R & D' became a routine, necessary activity of any successful nation–state, expending considerable funds for research in the certain expectation that eventually there would be a true bang for the buck.

As Bertolt Brecht put it very clearly in his poem, "1940":

Out of the libraries come the killers.
Mothers stand despondently waiting,
Hugging their children and searching the sky,
Looking for the latest inventions of professors.
Engineers sit hunched over their drawings:
One figure wrong, and the enemy's cities remain undestroyed!

Now, you need to understand that I am a 'University Brat'. My mother was a professor of humanities at Stetson University, a small liberal arts college in Florida. My stepfather was professor of geography, dean of men, and baseball coach. Before them, my great uncle had been professor of history there. The house in which I spent most of my childhood was so close to the university that it ended up in effect being on the campus itself as the university grew up around it.

Many of the evenings of my childhood were spent listening to my family and their academic colleagues talk about how dumb the students were, how inept the administration was, how venal were the board of trustees, and how the faculty in the regrettable 'college of business'—as though 'business' was a proper subject for a university!—weren't all that swift either.

When I graduated from Stetson, I had the marvellous good fortune of securing a Danforth Fellowship aimed specifically at funding, through a PhD, selected scholars who intend to become university professors. Every summer while I was a graduate student, the Danforth Fellows would gather at Camp Winamonka on the shores of Lake Michigan, and learn what it meant to be a university professor from some of the wisest, most humane, and inspiring scholars in the world.

For the first several years, old man William H. Danforth himself was with us with his little red book, titled, *I Dare You*. He would challenge each of us to be the best teachers we could possibly be. If you made the mistake of replying, "I'll try", he would hit you with the book and thunder: "No! You WILL!" and then lead us in the chant, "good better best, never let it rest, until your good is better, and your better best!!"

That is quality education! Danforth dared us to do everything as well as we can. And we did.

I got my undergraduate degree in three, instead of the normal four years, my MA in one year, and could have gotten my PhD in three more had I not taken the opportunity that the Danforth Foundation then made available—it does not any more—of spending a year studying something completely different from the field of my PhD. Nonetheless, I did obtain my PhD at the tender age of 26, and began teaching fulltime in 1958. It may bemuse some of you to learn that in all that time—from 1958 to the present—I have never gone on sabbatical leave. I have not wanted to. I travel a lot as part of my work, and never wanted to be away from my students for a whole semester, much less an entire year.

I have been a university student or professor all of my adult life, and I love it. I have loved every minute of it—except for grades. I just hate grading. I get physically sick every semester around grading time. But other than that, I love all aspects of university life, including the faculty meetings!

I would be very, very happy indeed if my students, the PhD candidates I have helped mentor over my life, could have the kind of life I have had, if they want it. Some few perhaps will, but I expect most of my students will not be able to enjoy the freedom I have enjoyed.

So please understand that as I now offer some alternative futures of higher education. I am not introducing these alternatives because I am disgruntled with colleges as I have known them. To the contrary. But I just don't see that they are easily sustainable. And they may not be all that desirable either, after all. The system of higher education I lived and loved in my lifetime is now just one frail alternative future among many others.

THINKING ABOUT FUTURES OF HIGHER EDUCATION

Futurists use a variety of theories and methods to anticipate, envision, and invent alternative and/or preferred futures (Bell, 1996; Dator, 2002). Today I want to mention briefly only three that I think might be especially useful to you.

One is trend analysis. The second is emerging issue analysis, and the third is alternative futures creation which is a specific kind of scenario writing.

Trend analysis is so well known that I don't need to spend much time on it other than to say the following:

- Most things that are tracked by trends are already so big and powerful that there is little that decision makers can do with them other than hope to utilise their power effectively. Over the years, I have identified a series of such trends that I call 'tsunamis' to emphasise their size, power, and consequence. They are things that we ought to have identified sooner and begun to develop anticipatory strategies for sooner. But we didn't, and now they are almost upon us. The most that we can hope to do at this late stage of maturity is to 'surf' them—to use their power to go where we want to go, and to have fun, though we will wipe out in the end.
- The future of a trend cannot be 'predicted'. The best we can do, and we should do it, is to forecast alternative futures of trends. Forecasting is not predicting and while no futurist can predict anything of consequence, she can and should

forecast several alternative futures based upon different theoretical and factual assumptions about the structure, environment, and interaction of the trends.

- Trends do not continue forever. In fact, they seldom continue at all. Looking for and analysing what might cause a trend to alter is also a major task of any futurist.
- Trends are never alone. They always interact with other trends, continuities, emerging issues, events, and decisions in varying and unpredictable (but fully forecastable) ways. This is where alternative futures scenarios come in. Scenarios are, in part, bundles of trends moving in varying ways—varying according to varying theories of social change and empirical facts. More will be said of alternative futures scenarios in a moment.
- Finally trends should be identified *before* they become trends. And this leads us to the second technique I wanted to mention today—emerging issue analysis.

Emerging Issue Analysis

Everything that exists now at one time did not exist. Everything that exists now will not exist forever. Everything that exists came into existence at a certain time for a certain reason, grew slowly, and then more rapidly for a while, then reached its limits to growth, and either plateaued, or died, either to stay dead forever, or to lie in slumber until it arose again as a new emerging issue at a later time, and the cycle of growth and death occurred again (Molitor, 1977).

Thus, many futurists attempt to look for what might later become trends in their earliest stage of development as emerging issues—while they are still weak, obscure and fragile, assessing how they might grow, and whether their growth should be encouraged, discouraged, or ignored.

Because emerging issues are weak, obscure, crazy, and fragile, good practical people usually ignore or ridicule them. Since these 'useful' ideas are not part of their commonsense, people conclude they are nonsense. And this fact led me to formulate Dator's Second Law of the Future which you will greet you on the first page of my website, if you were to visit it. Namely, "Any useful idea about the future should appear to be ridiculous".

Good futurists must be willing to appear to be ridiculous by showing people things they cannot otherwise see, and often don't want to see. Perhaps one reason there are so few good futurists is because we want to be loved, like everyone else, and we want to be useful. But it is impossible to be both.

I urge you to judge the 'quality' of my comments today by Dator's Second Law. The more stupid I sound, the more useful I might be. And if you agree with what I say, then either you are crazy or I am wrong.

Be aware that I intend to judge the quality of what you say by the same standard.

Emerging issue analysis requires a further technique called 'scanning' (often 'environmental scanning'). Scanning is basically a way of looking for the very beginning of emerging issues. How to scan is itself a skill that very few people have, and that almost all schools fail to teach—which is yet another story.

So the futurist then combines continuities from the past and present, with trends, emerging issues, and decisions, and, according to different theories of how the world works, frames and forecasts several alternative futures.

Now when I teach my students how to do scanning and emerging issue analysis, one of the things I have them do—before I set them loose on finding some emerging issues—is to have them develop confidence in the technique by taking something that is big, dominant, well-known, and fully established now, and finding the origin of it—when it first appeared in the world as a crazy idea, or as a flimsy, obscure reality—and then trace its growth up to the present.

When they do that, they discover, almost without exception, that indeed the world around them emerged according to various kinds of 'S' curves of growth— from nothing but some crazy idea, to a frail and flimsy emergence, through a slow initial growth and then rapid middle growth, to a hardy omnipresence, to steady prolonged, 'commonsense' existence, and/or to eventual decay and death.

Take, for example, the history of universities in England (Graham, 2002). While universities existed earlier in Paris, Bologna, and throughout the Confucian, Hindic, and Islamic worlds, the first university in England was Oxford, in roughly 1167, followed shortly thereafter by Cambridge in 1207. Or if you are from Cambridge, then it is the other way around, and Cambridge emerged first, followed by Oxford.

So universities in England would seem to have been around for a long time. But in fact, for most of British history there were only those two universities, Oxford and Cambridge (the story is different for Scotland and Ireland, but never mind for now). Indeed, any sane futurist in, say 1250, or 1350, or even 1750, if asked then to speak about the future of universities in England, would surely have said that universities are interesting but inconsequential things that have no future. They are just one of many minor ideas that somehow got a toehold long ago, never completely died out, but never really caught on either.

But then, in the mid nineteenth century there was a brief flutter of activity when the London University was organised in 1827, followed soon thereafter by King's in 1831 and Queen's in 1843, in order to broaden access to higher education somewhat. There were lots of arguments at that time about whether these were really universities, or not, and about the quality of their educational product as well.

While colleges were formed within the London federation, things were then basically quiet for almost half a century until the creation of what came to be called the 'red brick' universities in the late nineteenth century. As you know, the red brick universities were controversial and quite different from the previous institutions. They were clearly set up to satisfy the needs of a growing industrial and imperial state in ways the old universities could not, or would not. Arguments about 'quality' and authentic education were very prominent at that time as well.

But again, things quieted down for almost a century until the 1960s when the 'plate glass' universities were created and the old mechanics' institutes elevated to 'polytechnics' with equal if not even greater furore and controversy. This furore and controversy was renewed again very recently when these polytechnics suddenly were declared universities—thus doubling the number of universities—in the general educational upheaval of neoliberalism in its Thatcher-era version in the late 1980s and early 90s.

So you see a marvellous example of a typical 'S' curve in action: from nothing, emerging as barely something with basically no change except monotonic growth for 600 years (that is to say, new faculty and colleges were created within Oxford and Cambridge, but nowhere else), to significant growth and innovation in the industrial era, to an explosion of growth in the early postindustrial period, to the uncertainty, diversity, and funding and control controversies of the present.

WHAT'S NEXT IN HIGHER EDUCATION?

So have we reached the end of the line? Is there nothing new under the sun for higher education?

When I reviewed the literature for this presentation, I concluded that most of it—80 per cent if not 90 per cent of it—seems to assume that indeed there is nothing new in higher education. There seem to be only two 'real' alternatives: either continued growth of the present system of higher education—half to three quarters of the literature is focused on very marginal discussions of how—or whether—to arrange the deck chairs on the Titanic, with most of the remaining literature bemoaning the death of quality education because of the decline in the public's willingness or ability to pay for it through taxes, on the one hand, and the insistence of treating students as though they were paying customers and clients, on the other (Blass, 2003; Bok, 2003; Damrosch, 1995; Devlin & Meyerson, 2001; Duderstadt & Womack, 2003; Fish, 2004; Graham, 2002; Hirsch & Weber, 1999; Noguera, 1998, originally published in 1993; Rhodes, 2001; Rich & Merchant, 2003; Scott, 2004; Snyder, Taylor et al., 2002; Williams, 2002).

But you know very well that there are more than these two alternatives for higher education even today.

The story that I told above about the emergence and growth of higher education in England failed to mention one significant feature, the Open University. The OU can be said either to herald the emergence of universities without walls as the dominant form of higher education in the future—now exemplified most clearly by the University of Phoenix in all its worldwide virtual and shopping mall manifestations (Blumenstyck, 2003; Symonds, 2003). Or else the Open University is just a flash in the pan (as Phoenix itself eventually might become), striving to be just another brick and mortar, tenure- and research money-obsessed university yearning for respect and ranking equal to Oxbridge; desiring to be perfectly normal, and nothing weird or startling at all.

There does seem to be something very rock-steady, long-lasting, and appealing about place-based education—the dream of you on one end of a log and Plato (if not Mark Hopkins) on the other; or at least of a gaggle of robed scholars 'peripateting' around after Aristotle in search of an open classroom.

ALTERNATIVE FUTURES

Just as it is important to realise that *the* Future cannot be 'predicted', so also is it important to understand that 'alternative' futures can and should be forecast, and the consequences of the alternatives considered before 'preferred' futures are envisioned and created.

While the concept 'Alternative Futures' is similar to that of scenarios, the particular feature of alternative futures is that they are indeed substantially different from one another, in terms of theories of social stability and change, what the major trends and emerging issues are, and how they should be monitored. When people consider different scenarios, they most frequently just contemplate variations around a common theme. For example, population scenarios, and economic, energy, resource and similar scenarios typically show high, medium and low growth (or decline) based on identical theories but differing data assumptions.

Alternative futures are different. Long ago, I concluded that there are basically four generic futures facing all institutions and society:
— Continuation (in the modern case, Continued Economic Growth).
— Collapse (from one or more reasons).
— Disciplined Society (since 'continuation' is not possible and 'collapse' is not desirable, then we need to organise societies or institutions around a set of guiding values in order to survive).
— Transformational Society (the assumption that fundamental changes are taking place similar to the phase change from ice, to water, to steam; or the butterfly that emerges from the cocoon that the caterpillar spun) (Dator, 2002).

Whenever I work with groups who wish to think usefully about their futures, I insist that they contemplate at least these four generic possibilities in ways specific to their situation.

Thus, in the case of higher education, both in general and for each part of it, one should develop alternative futures based first of all on the continuation of what we currently have, modified only slightly to cope with things that do not fundamentally alter the substance, structure, and mission of higher education today. As I previously noted, most people thinking about futures of higher education are very good at doing this.

But they strongly avoid looking collapse fairly in the face. And yet various collapse scenarios should be envisioned as a consequence of a profound and prolonged global economic depression, for example; or a population- or terror-induced cultural shift away from the dominance of Western science and rationality to different knowledge bases and systems; or environmental challenges and failures of response that bring on a new kind of dark ages; or students voting with their feet and simply leaving the old brick and mortar universities empty. You can think of more reasons for collapse, I am sure. Or at least you should!

I will consider some disciplined and a possible transformational response later— at the end of my talk—which is coming. Hang in there a while longer.

There are many other formulations of alternative futures of higher education. For example, in Inayatullah and Gidley's book *The University in Transformation*, Peter Manicas (2000) writes that:

... one must take very seriously the new taxonomy of higher education offered by the National Center for Postsecondary Improvement, based at Stanford. Instead of the Carnegie schema (with 'Research I' institutions, community colleges, and so on), we have 'brand name,' 'mass provider,' and 'convenience institutions' ... 'Convenience institutions' are on the cutting edge of both the new technologies and new markets for education. They are user-friendly, operate fully as businesses ... and serve 'job-minded students for whom liberal-arts degrees hold scant appeal'.

By contrast, as Chester Finn writes, "Brand name campuses are selective, high-status places where market power comes from their very status and selectivity. They cater to mostly full-time students from traditional age groups and have a commitment to traditional academic values." In the US, the Ivy League schools such as Harvard, Princeton, and Yale are obvious examples.

The best-known state universities will strive to be in this select group but most will fall into the third category, 'mass provider' institutions. Mass provider institutions, beholden to legislators, with obligations to educate as best they can the citizens of their states, try to be all things to all people, but ultimately fail. (p. 34ff)

More recently, the National Education Association (NEA) of the US developed a set of alternative futures for higher education based on two clusters, one said to be quality-driven and the other market-driven.

According to the quality-driven cluster, higher education is a public good, an important investment in societal well being. In the market-driven cluster, higher education is no longer primarily the government's responsibility or for the public's good. It is something that allows each individual consumer to get the kind of higher education she wants for whatever private purposes she wants it.

Now, I think labelling public education 'quality-driven' is really very biased, showing clearly the preferences of the NEA, while at the same time certainly no markets are truly 'free'; they are all rigged by some policy preference or another. Nonetheless, under the '*market-driven*' label, the NEA outlines five different types of universities:

- McUniversity: which is a cheap and cheerful franchise of community colleges;
- Educational Maintenance Org: where higher education is owned or strongly guided by the needs of major corporations;
- Outsourced U: whereby all services—libraries, food, sports, dormitories, and education—are provided by outside contractors, according to student demand, with only a handful of fulltime administrators;
- Warehouse U: established to deal with rising unemployment, and the decline for the need of mental as well as manual labour, as a way to keep youth, and the not-so-young, in schools and out of the job market studying fun but harmless things as long as possible; and finally
- Wired U: featuring media-based delivery by star faculty performers, specialising in 'edutainment' with high production values.

In contrast, the '*quality-based*' cluster assumes that the US Congress passes the *Universal Access Act* (UAA) in 2006, guaranteeing each resident of the nation the right to the equivalent of two years of higher education paid for by the government. The states then create a seamless articulation between their secondary and postsecondary systems. They also establish a system of two year and then four year community-based colleges that maintain a residential orientation, but with the students less homogenous in age because they leave school intermittently to complete external service. As part of the UAA, students can extend their access to free public education by two years through participation in concentrated community service activities. Sports are largely intramural and co-ed, with an emphasis on team development and sportsmanship. The young adult energy that once went into sport spectacles and subsequent celebrations is channelled into the construction of community gardens.

Finally, in the quality-based scenario, consortia of universities eventually link into a global system of education at the graduate level. Most classes are conducted as seminars held by video-conferencing, although campuses remain, and students are expected to complete a residence requirement. Upper-level students are assigned faculty mentors and, themselves serve as mentors to lower-level students. As workers find their jobs changing, they increasingly turn to distance learning to update their skills. Each student is provided with a faculty tutor who functions much like a graduate advisor and whose responsibility is to seek out new materials to challenge the adult learners.

SOME PREFERRED FUTURES OF HIGHER EDUCATION

If the first universities in Asia, the Middle East, Europe and North and South America served the needs of the religious and political elites of the time, and if early modern universities served the needs of the protestant clergy and democratising bourgeois elite of their time, while the great modern universities of Europe, Asia, Oceania and the Americas served the needs of the industrialising and militarising nation–state, what needs might universities of the futures serve?

Again, the answer found in almost all of the literature on the futures of higher education says we will continue to serve the industrial, military, and increasingly commercial needs of the modern nation–state, in an increasingly globalised system, in place-based forms and consumer-based ways; we will reform and tweak what we already have to deliver whatever is needed new, and to continue whatever is tried and true.

However, at this point it is not clear that globalisation—based on neoliberal economic and political theories which dominated the world since the Second World War—is quite the wave of the future it was a few short years ago. Until 11 September, 2001, it was a safe bet that at least one of the major alternative futures was education and research for the continued globalisation and dominance of neoliberal institutions and values. Now, with 'terrorism' and the American-led 'war on terror' in full voice, both neoliberalism and globalisation are in retreat.

Of course, it could be that the next national elections, in this country [Australia] as well as mine, will throw the state terrorists out and bring the neoliberal globalisers back in. Time will tell.

It is also entirely possible that America, Australia and the UK will continue to be successful in ruling the world by force, might, and narrowly-defined national interest, and not only get away with it, but find more converts to—or at least semi-loyal spear-bearers in—their neoimperial Coalition of the Willing. The next US presidential election will perhaps make that aspect of the futures a bit clearer.

But for now, don't count on globalised neoliberalism being restored to its place of pride any time soon. Defending national borders and confining most activities inside them might triumph, as many people fervently desire.

But old time nation-based protective industrialism, the more recent globalised neoliberal postindustrialism, and Anglo neoimperalism are all alike in their overwhelming focus on economic growth and disdain for the environment and traditional values and ways of life.

As I said before, all major universities in all countries of the world have had but one purpose since modern times: to create an industrially and militarily strong nation–state-based, and then global, economic system. While some universities may tolerate some effete faculty members who fret about sustainability or indigenous cultures, the universities *per se* strive for only one future—continued economic growth.

But this could change. It could change because younger cohorts are more environmentally aware and concerned than are the older generations and will want the change. Or formal education may be forced to become focused on sustainability when the current economic house of cards collapses, based, as it is, entirely on consumer, corporate, and national debt, and not on anything remotely approaching the supply and demand of a 'free market'.

In his recent book, *Beyond the Modern University: Toward a Constructive Postmodern University*, Marcus Peter Ford writes that "the world is on the verge of an ecological and social catastrophe … virtually unimaginable in its scope". A total restructuring of the modern university is necessary to prevent this. Instead of focusing on "the acquisition of job-related skills characterised by intellectual and moral relativism", and a structure "based on independent academic units with each discipline having its own foundational principles and notions of reality", Ford argues that higher education should "provide students an awareness of the value of all things in nature". The modern university must "abandon its attachment to philosophical materialism and 'economism'—the faith that infinite economic growth is both possible and desirable". The "artificial boundaries separating disciplines" would be eliminated and "problem-based learning, directly embracing the teaching of human values" should be offered instead (based on a review by Barbara Beigun Kaplan in *Thought & Action*, Winter 2004, p. 123ff.)

Now if you can recall the four generic futures that I mentioned briefly earlier, you can see that Ford puts forth a 'Disciplined Society' future: he believes that there are basic fundamental values that should be taught rather than ignored (if not actively destroyed). Moreover, it should be the task of higher education to do the research and teaching that will produce a sustainable, humane, and just world, and not the ruinous, cancerous, greedy, dog-eat-dog world (though perhaps dog-eat-dog *films*) of the present.

Quality education in Ford's future seems to be almost the opposite of what it is now since he aims at instilling the values and skills necessary to preserve the world rather than to 'develop' it (see also Nandy, 2000).

There is much in this view that is appealing to me. We are facing ecological and social collapse and our universities are current contributing to both, full bore. Our current academic departments are historical accidents and not reflections of the way the world actually works. These disciplines do prevent universities from contributing to the solution of many environmental and social problems.

I believe a very good example of what a true transdisciplinary and global university should be can be seen in the International Space University (ISU) (http://www.isunet.edu/), where I also teach. ISU offers a Masters degree in Space Studies through its headquarters in Strasbourg, France, but it also holds what it provincially calls 'summer sessions' annually somewhere else. It just so happens that the ISU has recently convened an eight-week session here in Adelaide, hosted by the University of South Australia, the University of Adelaide and Flinders University. I urge you to find out something about it while you, and it, are here. Not only does ISU have as its goal helping humanity get out of its cradle—Earth— and find its proper place among the nooks and crannies of the solar system and beyond, but also it intends to see that humanity does so in peace and unity. The ISU staff and students literally come from all academic and economic backgrounds and ways of life from every part of the world. And the curriculum is firmly based on the Three I's: It is Interdisciplinary, Intercultural, and International. Nothing is taught unless it fully embodies the three I's. Engineering is not more important than ethics. Science is not more important that policy and law. All activities embrace all disciplines and cultures. Space must be in the service of all humanity— indeed, all life—and not for one country or set of elites. Though certainly not flawless, ISU is a very impressive futures-oriented institution in many ways.

Similarly, I am in full sympathy with those small number of individuals, such as Rodrigo Carazo, former president of Costa Rica and founder of the University of Peace there (Kittrie, 2003), and Glenn Paige of the University of Hawaii (Paige, 2002), who seek to turn our universities away from the builders of perfect bombs and bombers, as Brecht evoked in his poem I read earlier, and become true learners and creators of peace. Peace is not a negative thing, the mere absence of war. It is a condition and skill that needs to be taught and learned. What a wonderful world it would be, Paige has said, "if academia funded peace makers as fully as they do war makers, and if the Department of Defense had to have a bake sale every time they wanted a new aircraft carrier".

However, neither Ford, nor ISU, nor Carazo, nor Paige fully captures my preferred future.

I long have argued that it is too late to save the world from ecological collapse. Nature is dead and dying everywhere. Our challenge now is, to use the title of a book by Walter Truett Anderson, *To Govern Evolution*. We need to learn that we live in a largely, and increasingly, artificial world, a world that does not need to be 'saved' but invented.

Moreover, given developments in electronics, robotics, artificial intelligence, artificial life, genetic engineering, nanotechnology, space exploration and settlement, and the rest, humans are no longer the only (more or less) rational entities on the planet—and inner solar system. More and more work, including mental and imaginative work, is being done and increasingly will be done by the myriad of intelligent and adept entities increasingly working for and eventually working with or instead of humans over the twenty-first century and beyond.

It is often said we live in an 'information age' and that universities need to prepare their students for it. Recently, some people have begun to ask what kind of a world might lie ahead, after the information age has matured and run its course.

For example, Ernest Sternberg (1999) calls it *The Economy of Icons*:

It is still widely believed that we live in an information society in which the most valued raw material is data, production consists of its processing into information, efficiency depends on computing and scientific reasoning, knowledge and rational calculation underlie wealth, and society is dominated by an educated elite. These were revealing ideas when they were proposed almost thirty years ago, but as we begin the twenty-first century, the concept of the information economy has become a kind of collective wisdom, obscuring another economic transformation that has already overtaken us. The driving force in this newer economy is not information but image. Now the decisive material is meaning, production occurs through the insertion of commodities into stories and events, efficiency consists in the timely conveyance of meaning, celebrity underlies wealth, and economic influence emanates from the controllers of content.

Similarly, Rolf Jensen (1999) wrote:

The sun is setting on the Information Society—even before we have fully adjusted to its demands as individuals and as companies. We have lived as hunters and as farmers, we have worked in factories, and now we live in an information-based society whose icon is the computer: We stand facing the fifth type of society: the Dream Society. (p. vii)[ii]

Very importantly, Jensen sees society finally moving from a dependence on writing to the dominance of audiovisual images: "Today, knowledge is stored as letters; we learn through the alphabet—this is the medium of the Information Society. Most likely, the medium of the Dream Society will be the picture" (p. 40). Jensen concludes that Henry Ford was the icon of the Industrial Age while Bill Gates is the icon of the Information Age.

The icon of the Dream Society has probably been born, but she or he is most likely still at school and is probably not the best pupil in the class. Today, the best pupil is the one who makes a first-rate symbolic analyst. In the future, it may be the student who gives the teacher a hard time—an imaginative pupil who is always staging new games that put things into new perspectives ... He or she will be the great storyteller of the twenty-first century. (Jensen, 1999, p. 121)

With help from a colleague at the University of Hawaii, Yongseok Seo, I have come to see that South Korea may be the first country to take seriously the transition from an 'information society' to a 'dream society' of icons and aesthetic experience. Korean movies, TV dramas, pop music bands, and electronic games are sweeping Asia. But unlike similar and earlier products from Hollywood or even Bollywood and Hong Kong, those from Korea are all products developed and exported as a consequence of official governmental policy. Korea seems to be consciously leading the global transition to a Dream Society. We have convincing evidence that top Korean governmental leaders—including the recently impeached and then overwhelmingly re-elected President Moo-hyun Roh—are furthering this. Korean institutions of education at all levels are also being challenged by the government to assist in this transformation.

Once, Korea was the isolated 'Hermit Kingdom'. Then it became a source of raw products for industrial development elsewhere. Then it began to manufacture basic industrial products and soon began producing world-class automobiles. Next, Korea moved into high tech electronics and biotechnology. Now, their leaders say, the future world economy lies in the production of globally-appealing icons and dreams: movies, anime, soap operas, pop music groups, and especially electronic games. South Korea may become the first nation consciously to move from measuring its wealth by its GNP (Gross National Product) and begin to measure it by that true indicator of a dream society of icons and aesthetic experience: the GNC (its Gross National Cool) (Dator & Seo, 2004).

If other nations wish to follow suit, then their educational institutions, too, will need to change in many ways, not least of which is by shifting from learning via reading and writing, to learning via interactive electronic games.

The Massachusetts Institute of Technology (MIT) has already risen to the challenge. MIT:

recently launched the Education Arcade initiative aimed at exploiting the educational benefits of videogames. The project plans to harness the talents of scholars, international game designers, publishers, educators and policy makers to develop videogames that would be fully incorporated into existing curricula. 'We want to lead the change in the way the world learns through computer and video games,' says MIT professor Henry Jenkins. 'Our mission is to demonstrate the social, cultural and educational potential of games by initiating game development projects. We will also begin informal public conversations about the broader and sometimes unexpected uses of this emerging art form in education'. ("Education", 2003)

Keith Devlin, Executive Director, Center for the Study of Language and Information, Stanford University, also observed:

The digital revolution has led to major changes in the way [many of us] organise our societies and live our lives ... A consequence of being digital is that the word, both spoken and written, is no longer the sole primary glue of society or its culture ... [T]he word has become just one medium among several for expression and communication ... Being digital ... has given rise to an even more significant development: being interactive ... What will it mean to be an 'educated person' in the being interactive world? What will constitute the core curriculum in the new liberal arts of the twenty-first century and beyond? ... The being interactive world is so different from the world of the word that there are as yet no agreed norms and metrics as to what is 'good'. (Devlin, 2002, p. 15)

But Marc Prensky (2002) thinks he may know, and I agree:

We live in a time when long-range goals and promised rewards are a whole lot less certain and therefore less motivating that they used to be ... In the world of education, providing motivation has been one of the teacher's traditional roles ... (but) How motivating is the process of higher education in today's environment? Mostly, the 'curricular' part of college is painful, and often drudgery ... Most college teachers—and administrators—would not only agree, but think that this is a good thing. But is it? (p. 5)

College students devote a huge proportion of their time to playing computer and video games ... One college student recently confided to me he had skipped an exam because he was so close to 'beating' a video game ... The reason computer games are so engaging is because the primary objective of the game designer is to keep the user engaged ... The true twenty-first century learning revolution is that learning is finally throwing off the shackles of pain and suffering that have accompanied it for so long. I am certain that within most of our lifetimes pretty much all learning will become infinitely more learner-centered and fun: fun for students, for teachers, for parents, and even for supervisors and administrators. The huge wall separating learning and fun, work and play for the last few hundred years is beginning to tremble and will soon come tumbling down ... When it finally does fall, there will be a huge stampede to freedom. (p. 6ff)

Prensky quotes Marshall McLuhan as saying, "anyone who makes a distinction between education and entertainment doesn't know the first thing about either." (p. 8, citing Eric McLuhan)

The most important thing that educators can learn from game designers is how they keep the player engaged ... One basic rule of good gameplay, for example, is to always provide the player with clear, short term goals. Another is to make the game easy to learn, but hard to master. (p. 9)

As soon as individual course accreditation happens, the marketplace will take over. And academic institutions, I predict, will start having a really hard time. A student will no longer have to enroll in any institution to major in, say, chemistry. He or she will merely go to the standardised curriculum online, and choose his or her e-course ... from among the highest rated ones in the world, regardless of institution, just like a gamer selects his or her games regardless of publishers ... Sure, the academic world—which today accredits institutions, not courses—will resist, raising great cries about 'brands', 'learning communities' and 'standards' ... But as the barrier crumbles, professors, publishers and institutions will rush in to ... create the learning experiences rated 'five stars' by the reviewers. (p. 10f)

As a not–so–distant future student will put it, 'Show me the fun'. (p. 11)[iii]

Or, to modify what I said earlier, quality education in my preferred future will strive to raise the gross individual cool and not the gross national product. Performance and shtick will replace labour and product, and 'the Word is out!'

Or maybe not.

Let's see what we can do for quality education over our next few days together. And let's do everything as well as we can.

Thank you.

NOTES

[i] Paper presented to the Australian Universities Quality Forum 2004, Wednesday 7 July, 2004, Adelaide, Australia.

[ii] See also Pine & Gilmore (1999); Pink (2004); Postel (2003).

[iii] See also Prensky (2001); "Special issue" (2004).

REFERENCES

AAP. (2004, April 23). Technology marches ahead, grammar gets worse. *The Age*. Retrieved from http://theage.com.au/articles/2004/04/23/1082616314126.html

Andersen, P. (2005). Scriptural traditions West and East: Foundation of belief versus frameworks for the transmission of meaning. In P. Andersen & F. Reiter (Eds.), *Scriptures, schools, and forms of practice in daoism: A Berlin symposium*. Wiesbaden: Harrossowitz Verlag.

Anderson, W. T. (1987). *To govern evolution: Further adventures of the political animal*. Boston: Harcourt Brace Jovanovich.

Bell, W. (1996). *The foundations of futures studies* (two volumes). Rutgers, NJ: Transaction Press.

Blass, E. (2003). The future university: Towards a normative model from an emerging provision of higher education in Britain. *Futures Research Quarterly*, Winter, 63–77.

Blumenstyk, G. (2003). Spanning the globe: Higher-education companies take their turf battles overseas. *Chronicle of Higher Education*, *49*(42), A21. Retrieved from: http://chronicle.com

Bok, D. (2003). *Universities in the marketplace: The commercialization of higher education*. Princeton, NJ: Princeton University Press.

Damrosch, D. (1995). *We scholars: Changing the culture of the university*. Cambridge, MA: Harvard University Press.

Dator, J. (Ed.). (2002). *Advancing futures: Futures studies in higher education*. Westport, CT: Praeger.

Dator, J. (2005). Assuming 'Responsibility for your Rose'. In J. Paavola & I. Lowe (Eds.), *Environmental values in a globalising world*. London: Routledge.

Dator, J., & Seo, Y. (2004). Korea as the wave of a future: The emerging dream society of icons and aesthetic experience. *Journal of Futures Studies*, *9*(1), 31–44.

Devlin, K. (2002). Media X: The new liberal arts? *On the Horizon*, *10*(2), 15–17.

Devlin, M., & Meyerson, J. (Eds.). (2001). *Forum futures: Exploring the future of higher education.* San Francisco: Jossey-Bass.

Duderstadt, J. J., & Womack, F. W. (2003). *Beyond the crossroads: The future of the public university in America.* Baltimore: Johns Hopkins Press.

Herald Sunday (2003, December 10). Education arcade seeks to merge Learning, gaming [at MIT]. *Herald Sunday.* Retrieved from http://www.heraldsun.news.com.au/common/story_page/ 0,5478,8101066%255E11869,00.html

Eisenstein, E. (1979). *The printing press as an agent of change: Communications and cultural transformations in early modern Europe.* New York: Cambridge University Press.

Fish, S. (2004). Give us liberty or give us revenue! *Chronicle of Higher Education, 50*(10), C4.

Ford, M. P. (2002). *Beyond the modern university: Toward a constructive postmodern university.* Westport, CT: Praeger.

Goody, J. (1977). *The domestication of the savage mind.* New York: Cambridge University Press.

Goody, J. (1986). *The logic of writing and the organization of society.* New York: Cambridge University Press.

Goody, J. (2000). *The power of the written tradition.* Washington, DC: Smithsonian Institution Press.

Graham, G. (2002). *Universities: The recovery of an idea.* Thorverton, UK: Imprint Academic.

Havelock, E. A. (1986). *The muse learns to write: Reflections on orality and literacy from antiquity to the present.* New Haven, CT: Yale University Press.

Hirsch, W. Z., & Weber, L. E. (Eds.). (1999). *Challenges facing higher education at the millennium.* Phoenix, AZ: Oryx Press.

Jensen, R. (1999). *The dream society: How the coming shift from information to imagination will transform your business.* New York: McGraw-Hill.

Katsh, M. E. (1989). *The electronic media and the transformation of law.* New York: Oxford University Press.

Kittrie, N. N., Carazo, R., & Mancham, J. R. (Eds.). (2003). *The future of peace in the twenty-first century.* Durham, NC: Carolina Academic Press.

LaFleur, W. (1983). *The karma of words.* Berkeley, CA: University of California Press.

Lincicome, M. E. (1995). *Principle, praxis, and the politics of educational reform in Meiji Japan.* Honolulu, HI: University of Hawaii Press.

McLuhan, M. (1962). *The Gutenberg galaxy: The making of typographic man.* Toronto: University of Toronto Press.

McLuhan, M. (1964). *Understanding media: The extensions of man.* New York: McGraw-Hill.

McLuhan, M., & Fiore, Q., with Agel, J. (1967). *The medium is the massage: An inventory of effects.* New York: Random House.

Manicas, P. (2000). Higher education at the brink. In S. Inayatullah & J. Gidley (Eds.), *The university in transformation: Global perspectives on the futures of the university* (Chapter 3). Westport, CT: Bergin & Garvey.

Marshall, B. K. (1994). *Learning to be modern: Japanese political discourse on education.* Boulder, CO: Westview Press.

Ming, V. T. K. (2004). The death of the art of writing: Myth or reality? *Ubiquity, 5*(4).

Ministry of Education. (1980). *Japan's modern education system: A history of the first hundred years.* Tokyo: Research and Statistics Division, Minister's Secretariat, Ministry of Education, Science and Culture, Government of Japan.

Molitor, G. (1977). How to anticipate public-policy changes. *S. A. M. Advanced Management Journal,* Summer, 4–13.

Morrison, J. (2003). US higher education in transition. *On the Horizon, 11*(1), 6–10.

Nandy, A. (2000). Recovery of indigenous knowledge and dissenting futures of the university. In S. Inayatullah & J. Gidley (Eds.), *The university in transformation: Global perspectives on the futures of the university* (pp. 115–124). Westport, CT: Bergin & Garvey.

National Education Association (US). (n.d.). *Future of higher education.* Retrieved from http://www.nea.org/he/future/index.html

National Science Foundation (US). (2004). Public understanding of scientific terms and concepts: 2001. *Science and Social Indicators*, Figure 7–6. Retrieved from www.nsf.gov/sbe/srs/seind04/c8/c8.cfm

Noguera, P. A. (1998). Confronting the challenge of privatization in public education. Retrieved from http://www.inmotionmagazine.com/pnpriv1.html

Olson, D. R., & Torrance, N. (Eds.). (2001). *The making of literate societies*. Oxford: Blackwell Publishers.

Ong, W. J. (1982). *Orality and literacy: The technologizing of the word*. London: Routledge.

Paglia, C. (2004). Word and picture in a media age. *Arion*, Winter. Retrieved from http://www.bu.edu/arion/Paglia_11.3/Paglia_Magic%20of%20Images.htm

Paige, G. D. (2002). *Nonkilling global political science*. Philadelphia: XLIBRIS.

Passin, H. (1982). *Society and education in Japan*. New York: Kodansha International.

p'Bitek, O. (1968). The song of Lawino [Uganda]. In G. Moore & U. Beier (Eds.), *Modern poetry from Africa*. Penguin Books.

Pine II, B. J., & Gilmore, J. H. (1999). *The experience economy: Work is theatre and every business a stage*. Boston: Harvard Business School Press.

Pink, D. H. (2004). The MFA is the new MBA. *Harvard Business Review, 82*(2), 21–22.

Postel, V. (2003). *The substance of style: How the rise of aesthetic value is remaking commerce, culture and consciousness*. New York: HarperCollins Publishers.

Prensky, M. (2001). *Digital game-based learning*. New York: McGraw-Hill.

Prensky, M. (2003). Escape from planet Jar-Gon: Or what video games have to teach academics about teaching and writing. *On the Horizon, 11*(3). Retrieved from http://www.marcprensky.com/writing/Prensky%20-%20Review%20of%20James%20Paul%20Gee%20Book.pdf

Prensky, M. (2002). The motivation of gameplay: The real twenty-first century learning revolution. *On the Horizon, 10*(1), 5–11.

Rhodes, F. H. T. (2001). *The creation of the future: The role of the American university*. Ithaca, NY: Cornell University Press.

Rich, P., & Merchant, D. (Eds.). (2003, January). Higher education in the twenty-first century. *Annals of the American Academy of Political and Social Science, 585*.

Sax, B. (2003). Academic tradition in a digital age. *On the Horizon, 11*(3), 5–8.

Scott, G. (2004, February). *Change matters: Making a difference in higher education*. European University Association Workshop, University College, Dublin.

Snyder, D. P., Edwards, G., & Folsom, C. (2002). The strategic context of education in America 2000 to 2020, part 1. *On the Horizon, 10*(2), 6–12.

Snyder, D. P., & Edwards, G. (2003). The strategic context of education in America 2000 to 2020, part 2. *On the Horizon, 11*(2), 5–18.

Special issue on games/simulations in education. (2004, May). *On the Horizon, 12*(1).

Sternberg, E. (1999). *The economy of icons: How business manufactures meaning*. Westport, CT: Praeger.

Symonds, W. C. (2003, November 17). Cash-Cow universities [about the University of Phoenix]. *Business Week*. Retrieved from http://www.businessweek.com/magazine/content/03_46/b3858102_mz021.htm

Taylor, R., Barr, J., & Steele, T. (2002). *For a radical higher education: After postmodernism*. Buckingham, UK: Open University Press.

Williams, R. (2002). Education for the profession formerly known as engineering [adapted from *Retooling: A historian confronts technological change*. MIT Press, 2002].

James Dator is Professor, and Director of the Hawaii Research Center for Futures Studies, Department of Political Science, and Adjunct Professor in the Public Administration Program and the College of Architecture, of the University of Hawaii at Manoa; Co-Chair, Space and Society Division, International Space University, Strasbourg, France; former President, World Futures Studies Federation. He also taught at Rikkyo University (Tokyo, for six years), the University of Maryland,

Virginia Tech, and the University of Toronto. He researches, writes, and consults widely on the futures of governance, education, tourism, and space. Amongst his recent publications are:

Democracy and Futures *(with Mika Mannermaa and Paula Tiihonen). Helsinki: Parliament of Finland, 2006*

Fairness, Globalization and Public Institutions: East Asia and Beyond *(with Dick Pratt and Yongseok Seo). Honolulu: University of Hawaii Press, 2006.*

Advancing Futures: Futures Studies in Higher Education. *New York: Praeger, 2002.*

SOHAIL INAYATULLAH[i]

7. IMAGES AND TRENDS IN TENSION

The alternative futures of the university

The university is undergoing dramatic transformations. These include challenges to
the traditional image of the university as organised by a community of scholars as
well as trends increasing demands on the university. While there are likely to be
some continuities—the categories of student, professor, and administrator, for
example—the relative roles, governance structures, as well as how, when, where
and why students learn and professors teach and research, are likely to be
discontinuous.

IMAGES IN TRANSITION

This chapter maps the pulls, pushes and weights of the futures of the university
(see Figure 1); examines emerging issues that may disturb or reinforce this map;
analyses the tensions academics face in this changing future; articulates macro
global scenarios for the futures of the university; and presents meso scenarios with
respect to the capacity of universities to respond to the challenges facing them. The
chapter concludes with comments on the futures of the academic profession.

I first focus on the pulls of the future, the images of the future. These images
define what is important, what is seen as the norm, the model from which more
narrow politics emerge (who gets what, when, and how).

The classical image of the university as organised by a community of scholars
has been under challenge for centuries (Spies, 2000). The modern industrial model
with clear lines of division, a clear hierarchy, a growing bureaucracy, and research
driven not by knowledge for the sake of knowledge but for national research
interests has been in ascendancy for the last 150 years or so. However, the
industrial vertical structure did not destroy the previously dominant classical
model. Rather, it was included in the latter, leading to two parallel organisational
structures within the university. This was especially so in Europe and the US,
wherein academics generally have been left to govern themselves especially with
regards to the academic cannon. In Asia and Africa, the state has been far more
intrusive. The guiding image has not been that of an autonomous academic but of
the dissenting professor and student leader challenging dictatorship. To be sure, the
university has been a site of tension in the West as well, but in Asia, the modernist
development project has clashed head on with the quest for freedom. Order and
discipline have been in foundational contradiction to dissent and autonomy.

*M. Bussey, S. Inayatullah and I. Milojević (eds.), Alternative Educational Futures: Pedagogies for
Emergent Worlds, 113–131.*
© 2008 Sense Publishers. All rights reserved.

The industrial and classical images have been challenged also by the drivers (the pushes) of corporatisation/globalisation, virtualisation and sustainability. These have created new understandings and images of what the university can and should be. First, is the university—as a commercial (corporatist)[ii] centre—market driven, globally aggressive, in search of the 'student-dollar' wherever it may be. Rising up in the Academy is gained largely by the capacity to bring in research dollars, to demonstrate that one is a good entrepreneur. However, this image is directly in tension with the image of the community of scholars. The community is democratic and all voices must be heard; in the commercial model, on the other hand, it is not egalitarianism that is primary, but reward structures that favour financial knowledge. Courses that are taught must have not only national rationale (helping the economic development of the country) but be globally competitive, raising the competitive advantage of the nation. If the student numbers are not there, then courses are cut: each course must be able to financially justify itself. Humanities courses, and those not directly related to the global knowledge economy, are generally the first to go (Neubauer, 2000; Manicas, 2000).

There is as well tension between the imagination of the university as an industrial structure and as a site of global innovation. The former is focused on cost saving through obedience and regimentation, while the latter demands the capacity to find new products, and new niches and is focused on discovery science. The former is funded through state subsidies, that is, carving up tax payer's wealth, while the latter survives through creating wealth (and enhancing inequity).

However, the battle between defining images is not just restricted to the commercial *versus* the industrial *versus* the classical, but also rages between these three and the newly emerged virtual university. While the virtual university is run on commercial grounds—courses that bring in new students and dollars—the reach is global and the structure or organisation that supports this image, this future, is flatter. It is not corporatist *per se*, at least, not yet. The hierarchy of the professor is challenged (and eventually of the administrators as well, but that is still in the distance) and networked organisations and teaching practices result. Global reach changes the nature of the student body (no longer a physical community) and the nature of the professoriate (one can teach from any where and need not be full-time based on the campus, or even in the country of the university). As virtual technology keeps on developing, place and hierarchical power will continue to diminish. The industrial image will be strained to its limits also by classical notions of the community of scholars. However, the industrial may return via new surveillance technologies. Telecommuting may be allowed if the administration can keep an eye—via web-bots and other new technologies—on academics and students. Further, face–to–face community may be reinvented in electronic agoras. These may be global and local, inter and trans-disciplinary. The half-life of knowledge also transforms in this image of the university—the classics are less important and 'just–in–time'-knowledge far more important—as knowledge continues to exponentially increase, new knowledge becomes ever more possible, important and indeed defining of purpose (Abeles, 2000). The half-life of the career changes, too, with students and professors regularly changing employment. This means moving from one career to multiple careers or to the 'portfolio career': holding many jobs simultaneously and living in many countries during the academic year. One can be a virtual professor during the evenings and business executive during the day, or research scientist during the day, and virtual professor in the evening.

Those who prefer teaching and learning at night, too, would be liberated from synchronous learning. Time also shifts dramatically in this image of the future. In the classical image, time is shared time, when colleagues and students meet. It is generally slow. In the industrial image of the university, time is regulated and controlled, divided by semesters and seasons. In the colonial and postcolonial state dominated image of the university, time is in tension with community life and the power of administrators and Ministries of Education. Time is used as power, as a way to control others. In the commercial image, time is a commodity, bought and sold.

A more recent imagination of the university is the *world university* or perhaps more accurately *world–as–university*. For this to occur, we must first have a world, an Earth. This requires knowledge for ensuring that humanity survives the current global crises: addressing the problem of sustainability. Can humanity move from non-renewable resources to renewable resources? Can humanity move from tribal nation–states to global governance? Can humanity move from a patriarchy-driven culture to gender partnership? Can humanity move from single ways of knowing (generally the victory of the Western way of thinking) to multiple ways of knowing (borrowing from, for example, Indic, Sinic, indigenous and women's ways of knowing)? Can humanity move from survival to thrival? [iii] Answering these questions requires a new mission for the university—one focused on the global problematic and global solutions, one focused on trans-disciplinary approaches to knowledge, and one focused on knowledge cooperation. This new image requires an evolutionary jump in the nature of the university—the entire world becoming a university—and its ultimate demise, there being no particularly site for a university, since humanity has created a true democratic knowledge economy. This could be the university's final success.

This image—possible future—is in tension with the image of community of scholars (since this image tends to be parochial); with the industrial image (since the hierarchical and standardised industrial model of production is largely the cause of the current crisis, that is, flatter knowledge organisations are needed); with the commercial image, since it is not just the bottom line but the triple bottom line—prosperity plus social inclusion plus environmental sustainability—that is required. Indeed, one could argue that the fourth bottom line—that of the spirituality of humanity—is the essential ingredient in moving from survival to thrival. This image (the world–as–university) is also in tension with the virtual image in that while virtual networks are part of the solution, the challenge of the natural world—environmental pollution, global warming, and so forth—must be dealt with in the terms of the real (as opposed to virtual) world.

The realisation of this image requires dramatic new partnerships between universities (as for example with Universitas 21[iv]) and regional rules for universities (as with the Bologna process in the EU), potentially leading to new global protocols. Ministries of Education at national level are the biggest losers if this image becomes reality: they will lose their power to define curriculum, labour relations, and funding.

A final image of the future of the university is perhaps its deepest past: as a site of dissent against power (e.g., Nandy, 2000). This can be feudal power, religious power, bureaucratic power, technological power, or global power. The university has been the site where official power is contested, where alternatives are explored, where that which is not comfortable to Left and Right, tradition and novelty, is challenged. The circulation of truth and power are challenged, ensuring that "power has nowhere to hide" (Shapiro, 1992). This image has had more currency in developing nations where state power has been more extreme and intrusive. This is not to say that Western states allow universities to function in neutral power-free zones. Rather, it is hegemonic power, the power to define what is true, real and beautiful, that is more pervasive. The universalising mission of the Western state and university as expressed in the religious, Enlightenment and now in the security (war against terror) discourse has been the vehicle for the oppression of alternatives.

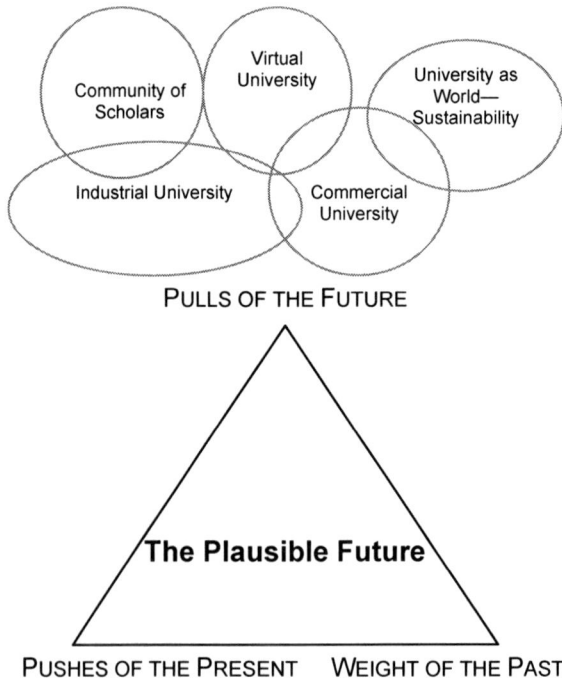

Figure 1. The futures triangle—University futures

Which of these images will become the dominant, the central image? This question has no easy answer. We know that the image of the university as community of scholars and the university as industrial national research centre is being dramatically challenged by the commercial/corporate university, the virtual university and the world–as–university (with the current problem of sustainability). Will a *mélange* result? Or will one prove dominant, for example, the commercial? Or will parts of the emergent merge—the commercial with the virtual with the world–as–university—creating a new global organisation of teaching and learning?

Pushes

While these images pull us forward, there are pushes that are equally important. These pushes include:
- Globalisation and corporatisation: in terms of the mobility of capital and labour and quickening time. Corporatisation in higher education includes both the corporate paradigm as a way of organising the university and knowledge, as investment in traditional higher education, and as a political battle over state subsidies for higher education. In the longer term, corporatisation—the commercial university—means multinationals themselves running universities. This will lead to a dramatic blurring of the classic public–private division.
  The following trend data is worth noting:
- By 2010, there will be between 100- and 185-million people qualified for tertiary education.
- The total market for higher education is US$250 billion globally, with the largest share being that of the US (US$140 billion).
- In 1991 there was one for-profit degree granting accredited institution listed on US stock exchanges and by 1999 there were 40. One of them, the University of Phoenix with 49 400 part time students had a profit of US$64.3 million (Jaschik, 2005).[v]
- In the U.S. corporate funding for the University has increased from US$850 million in 1985 to $4.25 billion less than a decade later. In the last twenty years it has increased by eight times. It is likely that East Asian nations will follow this pattern. So far it is the state that has exclusively engaged in education. However, globalisation is opening up this space in East Asia with foreign and local education. These trends certainly reinforce the image of the university as a site of global commerce (Odin & Manicas, 2004, pp. xiii-xix; Perkinson, 2003).

The implication is that corporatisation will create far more competition than traditional universities have been prepared for.[vi] As mentioned above, corporatisation is the entrance of huge multinational players into the educational market (Wiseman, 1991). Total spending in education in America was US$800 billion in 2001, estimates *The Economist* (2001, p. 71). The estimate for 2003 was that private capital invested in the US totalled $10 billion, just for the virtual higher education market and $11 billion in the private sector serving the corporate market. Jeanne Meister, president of Corporate University Xchange (CUX), expects that by 2010 there will be more corporate universities in the United States than traditional

ones. They are challenging and will continue to challenge the academy's mono-
polisation of accreditation. Globalisation thus provides the structure, and the Net
the vehicle. Pearson, for example, a large British media group that owns 50 per
cent of *The Economist*, is betting its future on it, hoping that it can provide the
online material for the annual two million people that will be seeking a degree
online (*The Economist*, 2001, p. 71). Motorola, Accenture, Cisco and McDonalds
as well as News Corporation all seek to become respectable universities. Cisco
Networking Academies have trained 135 000 students in 94 countries. Motorola
has a new division called Motorola Learning and Certification which resells
educational programs. Accencture has purchased a former college campus and
spends 6.5 per cent of its revenue on educating employees (*The Economist*, 2001,
p. 71).

Structurally, globalisation is linked to corporatisation, including the casualisation
of the work force and the creation of 'Dean, Inc.'—that is a mobile senior managerial
class, focused on its own needs, with its own stories (often heroic, dealing with this
or that problem, academic or student), its own discourse. This trend, too, favours
the university as a site of profit (see Press & Washburn, 2000).

- Digitalisation/virtualisation includes both new forms of delivery and learning,
  and a metaphor for knowledge and the brain. Both are crucial: the external
  empirical dimension (how courses are taught, where university funding goes to)
  but also the new lense, the framework that we use to understand the world. As
  McLuhan argued many years ago, we create tools, and thereafter they create us.
  This trend pushes us toward the virtual university and the university as world.
  Indeed, John Chambers, CEO of Cisco systems calls "online education the killer
  application of the internet" (cited in Svetcov, 2000).
- A third major push or driver is sustainability as a social movement   as a new,
  planetary purpose for the university. The Talloires Declaration (http://www.ulsf.org/
  programs_talloires.html) and the Lüneburg Declaration (http://www.lueneburg-
  declaration.de/downloads/declaration.htm)—both focused on the responsibility
  universities have toward solving the global environmental crisis—are directions
  in this process, as are some United Nations meetings (as with the Kyoto Protocol).
  This trend pushes us toward the university–as–world, world–as–university. The
  argument is that the university has a global, indeed, a planetary purpose that is
  beyond public and private, West and non-West, state and corporate, and especially
  beyond the narrow technical concerns of disciplines.
- Demographic shifts: aging population, the rise of new demographic groupings
  such as the cultural creatives (see Ray & Anderson at www.culturalcreatives.
  org) and digital natives (Prensky, 2001), as well as in the longer term a relative
  shift in European/North American populations favouring Asian and African
  populations by 2150. One immediate result is that workforce planning, once
  about predicting student enrolment, is now dramatically changing. The nature of
  the student (age, values, learning style, and geographic location) has become as
  important as the demographic nature of the administrative university. Standardisation becomes far more difficult as cohorts segment. Perhaps being adaptive
  will become a critical success factor? Are we moving toward a new image of the

university: the adaptive university that can shift strategy and metaphor toward the appropriate future of the university as external conditions change?

While these are current trends, there are emerging issues just on and beyond the horizon that may also influence the plausible university future.

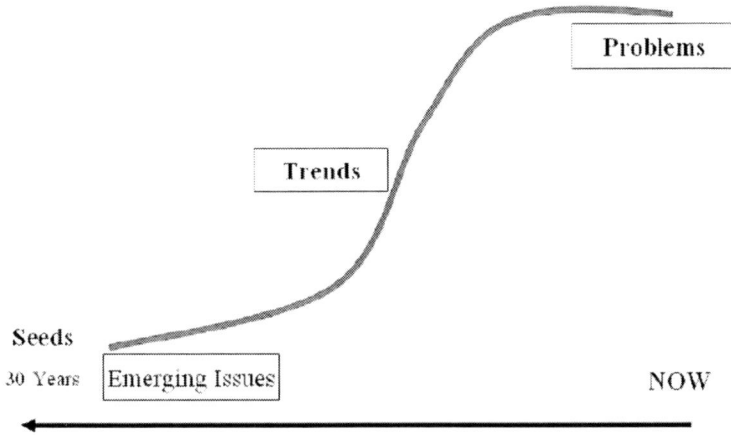

Figure 2. Emerging issues analysis

Emerging issues (see Molitor, 2003) include:
- The truly global student—this is far different from international student semester exchanges—whose learning and degrees are derived from a variety of universities. This may begin in elite universities—cooperative ventures—but could spread globally. This is the Star Alliance model of education (where air points and service are easily transferable).
- Related to this is the truly global professor, teaching at multiple campuses and negotiating salary contracts with multiple universities. Loyalty is not to a particular institution, but to knowledge and the image of the university as world–as–university. This shift in the site of the professor would require cooperation between universities and ultimately would require dramatic reorganisation. Will this create the 'star professor' or professor–as–university with students from around the world signing up to his or her virtual and physical courses (Galtung, www.transcend.org)?
- A third issue is the change in the model of how we think about learning and curriculum. Gaming could be the future framework for the future university. Already, gaming is central to the future of learning: recently Universitas 21 employed as curriculum designer someone with gaming experience (Agahi, pers. com., 2005, 18 February).
- More broadly, Clark Aldrich, James Gee, Marc Prensky, Seymour Papert (www.muzzylane.com/education/links.php; see also Van Eck, 2006) and many others have argued that the designers of video game technologies are blazing the

path that instructional technology will eventually follow. They ask us to imagine 3D learning worlds (in stand-alone and multi-student online versions) programmed to identify students' skill levels and learning styles, build accelerated learning paths, bring the students into a 'flow' state, and monitor and continuously assess their performance. As video games become ever more advanced and video game development and research programmes make their way into the nation's universities, is this the future vision? What social or market dynamics will enable the positive synthesis of video game technology and education? Certainly this push leads us toward virtuality as the future imagination of the university. We should not make the mistake of imagining this future with current value and knowledge frames. Rather we need to take the views of digital natives seriously.

Writes Prensky (2001), digital natives have different expectations, including the following:

- Interaction with editors/authors.
- Editing built into what they do, i.e., the text is interpretive and malleable. Wikipedia is a great example of this.
- Connectivity—working with others to create products.
- Levels—gaming levels, moving through lower skill sets to higher skill sets.
- From library to search engines, indeed, seeing the library as a search engine.
- Global and Local (massive multi-player on-line games), i.e., seeing many intentional communities throughout the world, some totally open and some closed.
- Finally, we should not see the future of gaming and the university from old style games. Rather, new types of games are emerging. These include social impact games, as for example, linked to meditation/biofeedback (www.wilddivine.com/) and games linked to sustainability or other values sets (www.socialimpactgames. com/).
- Genomics. Advancements in genomics may also change the university. As the model of knowledge and the self moves toward the genetic (nature as the primary force, not nurture), the politics of equity will be crucial. In a world of genetic therapy and genetic enhancement, will genetic modification become the new barrier for entry? Will courses be designed for different genetic aptitudes? As significant, will today's disciplines and faculties change as the genetic (biological) paradigm overhauls the industrial?
- Developments in the new science via meditation and learning experiments are equally profound. They suggest that the brain can be altered, new neural pathways created, and old traumas resolved. The brain thus is seen as more malleable than previously thought. IQ can be enhanced via meditation and other soft brain technologies. Will meditation be central to the pedagogy of the university as is currently the state with Gurukul University (www.gurukul.edu) and the TM University (www.tm.org; Grant 2000)?

The trajectory of these issues is speculative and thus while these issues are likely to dramatically change the nature of the university; we can not reasonably forecast in what direction and to what degree.

Mid-level Analysis—The Deep Tensions

In the nearer term, there are dramatic tensions occurring in the university. The first is the challenge of innovation and democracy. The democratisation of the university is not just difficult for administrators but is so also for senior academics. They tend to desire democracy for government but not for the university: the student is there to learn, not to exercise deep democracy, and the university thus remains feudal. For example, while the economy in East Asian nations has transformed, that is feudalism was destroyed, the feudal mind has not changed. The grand question for East Asian nations is this: how to create a culture of innovation, how to go to the next level of economic development, and—instead of copying— how to create? To create an innovative learning organisation, the culture of fear must be transformed. This means real democracy in details such as the type of seating arrangement in rooms (the round table *vs.* the lecture theatre). It means renegotiating to what extent students can challenge professors. Can junior professors challenge senior academics without fear of reprisal? The argument is that innovation comes from questioning. Questioning is a critical literacy that is central to creating a robust civil society, and, indeed, crucial to attracting international students. It is this democratisation of the mind and society that is the current challenge for Asian and African universities.

In the British system, too, the university structure is profoundly feudal. A strong distinction is made between the professor and the lecturer. Indeed, the professor is high, on top of the pyramid with others way below (and the president of the university resides on the mountain top). However, in the British system, even though the university is feudal, society itself is democratic and dissent is expected.

More democracy in the university means creating a learning organisation wherein academics, students, administrators, and other stakeholders reflect not just on the purpose of the organisation, but on how each person can improve its effectiveness. What can be changed? What is not working? But this is only half the story. The other half is integrating emotions into the project of the academy: returning the body and heart to the intellect of the academic.

Merely focusing on learning forgets that much of our life is spent on relationship: with our inner self, with colleagues, with nature and cosmos (Inayatullah, 2003–04, p. 20) and with the university itself. As universities change their nature—reducing tenured positions, increasing teaching loads—health becomes an issue. Sick institutions can emerge quite quickly, unless there is a focus on creating ways to learn and heal, and to develop sustainable and transformative relationships.

Democratisation can thus mean creating learning and healing organisations. These can then sustain civil society and begin to create society–as–university; university–as–society, expanding outwards to create the world–as–university.

However, there are antagonistic forces to this. For the Asian academic, for example, the choices as to what he or she has the capacity to do shrink daily. He or she can choose between the following alternatives—the 4 big M's. The first M is the Ministry of Education. Choosing this career means grant research focused only on the Ministry's needs, and it means being dependent on government. When states go wrong, or punish dissent—as in Malaysia or Indonesia, or Pakistan and India— losing one's job and a stay in prison are real possibilities. Texts are written with the other nation as the enemy, as in India and Pakistan. The professor must teach these texts or lose his or her position. One Pakistani academic, for example, was jailed for giving a lecture on alternative futures that contested the notion of Pakistan as an eternal state.[vii]

The second M is the Mullah, or the cleric. This is funding not from the corporation or state but from the competing worldview to the modern, the Islamic. In real terms this has meant soft and strong version of Wahibism—the creation of international Islamic universities with Saudi funds as in Malaysia. Freedom of inquiry can be a problem here as well, as boundaries of inquiry are legislated by the university's charter. Instead of spiritual pluralism what can result is uncritical traditionalism.

If we combine the first two choices we get a mix of religious hierarchy with feudal and national hierarchy, creating very little space for the academic. In the Indian context, this would be the Brahmin who goes to Oxford to study economics, joins the World Bank and returns to Delhi to work with the Ministry of Economic Development. Epistemological pluralism narrows each step of the way.

The third M is "Microsoft": focusing one's career on developing content for the new emerging universities. This is the most rapidly developing area of Net education. The costs for the academic here too are high: it is contract work, often a loss of face–to–face, of collegial relationships, and of the academy as a moral mission. Volume and speed are likely to become more important than integrity and the inner life.

The final M is McDonaldisation. This is the move to the convenient, 7/11 university, the direction many universities are being forced toward given the realities of the world economy. The basic model is to have large student volume, in and out, with academics having heavy teaching, research, community, administrative and grant writing loads. A professorship can essentially become merely a money gathering expedition, not a position for the creation of new knowledge or mentoring the young.

Leaving these M structures is a possibility, dependent on the nature of the state one lives under. However, the traditional imagination of the university—as a community of colleagues—is not a possibility. For the Asian and African academic, the route in the last 50 years was the escape to the Western university, but with these universities also in trouble, this route seems blocked.

For the Western university, the mid-level problems are, as described earlier, corporatisation leading to casualisation. With casualisation, the lecturer becomes a wage labourer.[viii] This challenges the notion of university as community of scholars, diminishes the scholarly mission of the university, and is a significant contribution to the breakdown of traditional civil society, as work–family balance is threatened. That there is a gender dimension to this tells us a great deal about the linkage of globalisation and corporatisation to patriarchy. Finally, dissent becomes problematic as lecturers can be fired if they do not toe the political line. Fortress

Europe, America or Australia demands new loyalties from academics: first to the nation and second to freedom of inquiry.

Along with casualisation, another challenge is posed by the organisational corporatisation of the university: it is run as a firm instead of as a guild (though managed by the Ministry of Education). The Vice-Chancellor becomes the CEO, the Deans become vice-presidents, professors become managers (but holding a dual position, still maintaining privilege because of access to secret knowledge) and students become customers. This leads to the end of loyalty. The university demands loyalty but cannot give stability and security, thus the feudal contract becomes emotionally void.

What then should academics in the West do? For the elite academics, the consequences are easy to map out. The professor moves from being located at a university to being a professor at multiple universities (not allowing any university to take over) and then ultimately the professor becomes the university. An alternative trajectory is the creation of an academic cooperative or group of professors creating their own university. Only national accreditation stops this innovation. And since industrial jobs are still based on accreditation, even as the walls become more porous, the university remains.

For most other academics, the costs become higher and higher. What results is loss of agency, relative salary deprivation (compared to other professions: in OECD nations even to trades such as plumber and electrician) and over time loss of respect; the university seen more and more as irrelevant to the future. In contrast, it is the media oriented technologist that is seen as where the real action is: new media technology creators (the iPod, for example), website creators (youtube.com or myspace.com, for example), the content creators, and the marketers and distributors, not the analysts (see the works of Mark Prensky, http://www.marcprensky.com/writing/default.asp).

POSSIBLE FUTURE STRUCTURES

Given the above images, trends, emerging issues and mid-level analysis, there are three possible structures. One is being a university leader, joining the world's elite, such as Harvard, Stanford or Oxford. The focus then is: "We are only going to get the best and brightest students from around the world". But the challenge to this model comes from the dotcom world. The big money is unlikely to be in teaching but in content design. The issue though is that once you *en masse* put your name on CD-ROMs and on Internet content, does that diminish your brand name and its exclusivity? If everyone can enter an elite university's web course, is the university still elite? This is the issue of franchising. Should you focus on a small customer base that can pay a lot or become like the University of Phoenix and offer "just–in–time" education?[ix]

For large universities, there are two clear choices—elite university or low cost producer with hundreds of millions of new students all over the world as potential purchasers.

For the smaller university the only choice left is the niche university—focused in a particular area of excellence or in a particular locale—not trying to be too much, knowing one's student market well.

The challenge to the traditional university is new competition from global players: multi-media corporations, elite universities that are expanding and branding, as well as low-cost producers. This makes their survival tenuous at best. With subsidies from states drying up, the writing appears to be on the wall.

These issues are already of concern in the US and European nations. While it may be harder to see this in East Asian nations (and those colonised by England) since the state plays a much stronger role in education, eventually in five or ten years educational services will be privatised there as well. All universities will likely find themselves in a global market of students and other higher education (and primary education) providers.

However, a clever and robust university may find ways to combine all these structures, for example, by developing different campuses. One campus could focus on life-long learning and short courses. A second campus could be research focused, linked to government and industry, far more practical and action oriented. A third could be elite-based, having student friendly teacher–student faculty ratios, focusing on grand questions of meaning and purpose. The Net could link them all, or there could be a fourth virtual campus, a Net university.

SCENARIOS FOR THE FUTURE

The next question is, what are the probable scenarios for the future of the university. We use scenarios to reduce uncertainty, to define alternatives. Scenarios are also important in that they also help us rethink the present—they distance us from today.

Centre–Periphery Reversed

The six largest Internet-based distance-learning universities in the world are located in developing countries—Turkey, Indonesia, China, India, Thailand and Korea. While mainly aimed at university-level education of adults, Net education is spreading to primary and secondary education. As Asia continues to rise—with India and China being the two new stars—we can well imagine a world where universities in Asia are the best.

However, to achieve this they need to i) challenge feudal societal structures, that is create capacity so the university can lead instead of mimic society; ii) move away from ethnicity and toward more global sentiments; and finally, iii) universities in Asia need to be futures-oriented. They need to move away from lamenting past injustices or historical grandeurs and instead use tradition to create new futures. But one aspect of tradition is no longer helpful: male domination (see Eisler's work at www.partnershipway.org). For Asian universities to prosper globally, gender partnership is a necessary factor.

Centre–Periphery Enhanced

In this second future, business as usual continues, only more so. Western universities continue to rise. They already have edges in gaming, digitalisation, globalisation, not to mention patenting[x] and university entrepreneurship. They will use their prestige and wealth to leap further ahead. Asian universities will continue to fall behind as there is neither talent nor tolerance, and indeed, in some places, little technology.

Global Market—Multiple Markets, Fluid

In this third scenario, centre–periphery distinctions disappear quickly, as the world is far more malleable. Indeed, the leaders may be Western universities in Asia! In terms of structure, elite universities, though having high costs, will stay ahead because of their extensive use of high technology (for research, management and communication), star professors (giving them everything they want to stay at the university, building mini-universities around them), and by virtue of building on previous branding.

At the mass level, the market is likely to segment. Some universities will go on-line, many will be battered by new multinational players and start to disappear or swim downward to the community college level (the professionally oriented two year system). This is the market most ripe for change.

At the niche level—short courses, new fields, inclusion of high school—there are many opportunities. In times of transition, many new niches are created in the evolutionary landscape. Niches are often safe, and they can be experimental. However, they may or may not survive when a new dominant paradigm for the university emerges.

Global Governance Model

In this future, the Bologna process currently underway in Europe becomes a global process. Ministries around the world cooperate, allowing agreement on credit transfers. There is far more of a fluid movement of students and professors. A global WHO type organisation results, called the World University Organisation (WUO). While bureaucratic, it ensures standardisation across the planet. Funding helps poorer areas innovate and the world–as–university image thrives. However, as with UNESCO, there are many problems. To make up for states withholding funds, private universities jump on the global bandwagon.

The End–of–the–University

Over time, the university as we know it disappears (see Tehranian, 1996, p. 446). The WUO cannot manage the complexity of knowledge and learning. New forms of learning—tele-presence and sensor telemetry (see www.accenture.com), dramatic discoveries in brain-mind science, in virtual learning—all lead to a new world. The entire world becomes a university.

These futures are certainly broad; they give us a sense of the overall possibilities. And of course for the university planner, policy analyst, they are too broad. More important are *meso level scenarios*. In partnership with Martin Fitzgerald, Pro Vice-Chancellor of the University of Newcastle (Australia),[xi] I present these meso scenarios.

To develop these futures, our first question was, what are the critical drivers? Two were identified:

– The capacity of the academics to respond to the various changes; and,
– Corporatisation–globalisation and other financial challenges universities are facing.

Based on these two variables, two axes are created: Traditional/Feudal to Corporate/Global, and Reactive to Responsive. From these two variables, four scenarios were created (Figure 3) (see Inayatullah, 2005).

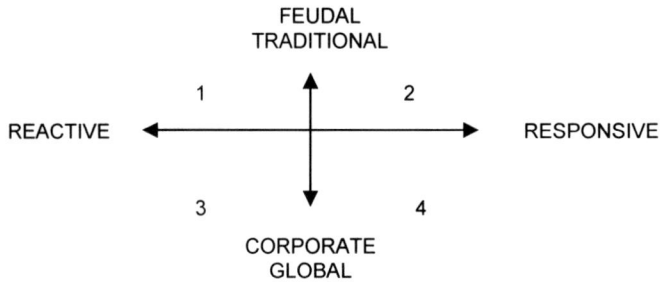

Figure 3. Capacity to respond and nature of the university

1. Corporatised—Responsive (Quadrant 4). This is the university where both administrative and academics understand the world has changed, and that new agreements must be negotiated. Governance moves from guilds to learning organisations. New sources of revenue are sought, generally from the market. The administration seeks to facilitate the creative potentials of academics. Academics do not see themselves as selling out to the corporate world. Rather, they integrate their entrepreneurial selves into their identity.[xii] New technologies are used in ways that meet the changing needs of professors, administrators, and students.

2. Feudal–Traditional—Responsive (Quadrant 2). This is the niche university. The hierarchy of the professoriate—the elitist Harry Potter nature of the university—remains and the rituals of graduation continue, but it becomes more and more restricted in terms of number, though not in terms of funding. The Vice-chancellor remains known for his scholarship and leadership capacity, not just for his capacity to earn. Academics respond to the changing world, but discriminate as to what needs to change, and what traditions must be stable.

3. Corporate—Reactive (Quadrant 3). This is the mass situation: the staff are passive aggressive, resistant to change. There is superficial adoption of new technologies (putting entire books or courses on line instead of more interactive tailored learning methods). The industrial model is torn down but not in collaboration with academics. It is done by fiat. Tenure is slowly eliminated and freedom of speech is diminished. Students are seen as customers even when they may prefer to keep the classical scholar–disciple formulation. Department chairs have little understanding of communication skills, of multiple ways of knowing. Health indicators are poor throughout the organisation.

4. Traditional–Feudal—Reactive (Quadrant 1). This is the insular university, more and more impossible to retain. In this future, the hierarchy and the feudal nature of the university are maintained. There is a lack of willingness to respond to globalisation, virtualisation and corporatisation. Governance remains top-down and financing remains a problem. The deep myth is that of Cinderella, hoping for a fairy godmother (the state or a benefactor) to save the day.

Which scenario will result? Certainly any are possible, however, creating responsive scenarios requires facilitative leadership, leadership that listens to all stakeholders and includes them in mapping alternative futures and creating desired futures.

THE FUTURES OF THE PROFESSION

Let me now return to the future of the academic. What is the role of the academic in this dramatically changing world? The first possibility is the traditional professor. This is the agent of authority, great in one field but knowing less about other fields and with low levels of communicative intelligence. Adapting to wide scale changes would be difficult for the expert academic. Corporatisation, virtualisation and even trans-disciplinary projects would be resisted.

The second potential role is the professor as web-content designer. This is actively engaging in the development of new technologies. Keeping a critical eye on issues of equity and inclusion but also being innovative in their use. While the current age-cohort is unlikely to engage in these activities, younger academics may be more amendable. They are more likely to be able to see knowledge as quick, interactive, multi-disciplinary, and always changing. They want to be web-designers and information designers. While the old role for academics was to write books, the new role is that of creating novel types of interactive content. And the content will likely be far more global and multicultural than we have so far seen (see Inayatullah, Bussey & Milojević, 2006).

The professor as web-content designer creates a third potential role: the knowledge navigator. In this role, the student (and his or her worldview) becomes paramount. For this to occur, action learning methodology is crucial. Action learning means that through an iterative process, the content of the course is developed with the student. While the professor may have certain authoritative/ expert knowledge, his or her role is more of a mentor, a knowledge navigator, to help the student develop his or her potential within categories of what is important to the student. Indeed, the categories of 'student' and 'professor' are seen as narratives, to be used but not used by. Thus, it is not the technology *per se*, though this is important, but using the technology to enable the student/professor to create desired futures.

A fourth role is that of traditional corporate man, the salary man. In this future, the lecturer understands the new corporate game, delivers research funds to the university and moves up the ladder: from student, to lecturer, to professor, to assistant Dean, to Dean and then eventually to Vice-Chancellor.

However, the traditional stable world of the academic—quiet space in the library, to reflect and to research problems that are not immediately relevant—may be gone. As the university continues to casualise, the research and community climate that long term positions (and friendships) create will begin to disappear.

In any role, the key for the academic in a disruptive and changing world is to understand the inner dimension of what it means to be an academic, to explore one's root metaphors: Is learning about co-creating with others? Is learning about filling empty minds? Is learning about helping others have access to tools? Finding a role in a changing world can emerge best when there is clarity of one's inner purpose. This is true for the university as well: what is the deeper purpose and mission that can sustain during changing and sometimes difficult times?

CONCLUSIONS

The university is not dead but transforming. For my personal perspective, I would like to retain the notion of community of scholars but with far more sensitivity to market, to student, to communities, and to planetary problems.

While respectful of others, I also want to keep the notion of dissent. This is what leads to social and physical innovation. Dissent challenges power and the normal way of doing things in every generation. In a religious system, the scholar must challenge the power of God; in a secular system, the scholar must challenge the power of the state; in a materialistic system, the power of wealth; and in a technopolis, the instrumental power of technology.

Finally, I believe that, as academics, our work is not only external, but internal, integrating our various archetypes: the *worker*, serving the student, community and market, but especially planet; the *warrior*, challenging what is wrong in the system, and creating better rules; the *intellectual*, creating new ideas and innovation, understanding, communication, creating and transforming the world; and the *entrepreneur*, creating new value, creating new wealth, applying what we learn.

This means integrating our disowned selves—the entrepreneur, for one, but also the playful aspect of life, often neglected by the serious academic. A further challenge will be to recover the spiritual dimension of the academic and of the university. This is moving toward deep reflection, seeing the intellect as only one tool of the mind. As the Indian philosopher Sarkar argued (Inayatullah, 2002), the intellect must be liberated if we are to create a new world.

Can we do all that?

If we do not respond to the challenges facing universities then what will happen? Most likely, it will be business as usual, muddling through, things getting worse and worse, more and more labour/management conflicts, and more and more loss of respect for the academic and the university.

I would prefer creative responses to the challenges to corporatisation, virtualisation and globalisation. The industrial and classical images of the university are changing. Resisting this is futile. However, merely adopting corporatisation, globalisation and virtualising uncritically would be a tragic error. A creative entanglement of outside and inner world is required.

NOTES

[i] This article is based on presentations in Luxembourg, Vienna and Penang in 2005 and 2006, organized by ASEM, ACA and University Sains Malaysia respectively. I would like to thank the organizers and participants of these conferences for their comments.

[ii] Commercial and corporate have been used interchangeable in this chapter, though one could argue that corporatist is a type of structure within the commercial umbrella. One could be commercial and eschew the vertical corporatist structure as with dot-com enterprises.

[iii] This term comes out of the work of the Foundation for the Future—particularly see their project, Humanity 3000 (www.futurefoundation.org).

[iv] http://www.u21global.edu.sg/cgi-bin/corp.dll/portal/ep/home.do. The CEO is Dr Mukesh Aghi.

[v] Net income in 2003 for Apollo Group was 78.4 million (http://www.bizjournals.com/phoenix/stories/2003/12/15/daily43.html). In 2005 it was 443.73 million. The Apollo group includes multiple universities and has over 300,000 students in 90 campuses in 29 American states. But is the University of Phoenix the future (http://www.insidehighered.com/workplace/2005 /03/28/phoenix)?

[vi] http://www.e-learningcentre.co.uk/eclipse/Resources/corpu.htm for more on corporate universities.

[vii] Najam Sethi, editor of the *Friday Times*. See http://www.saja.org/sethi.html for more on his imprisonment.

[viii] As Philip Altbach (1997, p. 332) has noted: "the American university is becoming a kind of caste system, with the tenured Brahmins at the top and lower castes occupying subservient positions".

[ix] The largest university in the US, offers no tenure, uses short courses as well as flexible delivery; a kind of just–in–time education.

[x] The *Human Development Report 1999* (UNDP, 1999, p. 68) reported that 97 per cent of all patents worldwide were held by industrial countries.

[xi] These were developed at the Applied Futures Learning Course, Mt Eliza Centre for Executive Education, 21–25 November, Melbourne, Australia. Dr Robert Burke is the director of futures thinking there.

[xii] Essential here is the work of Hal and Sidra Stone. They focus on the disowned selves—selves that we push away as we focus on particular identities. For academics, in the search for the purity of truth, the business self is pushed away. Classically for the corporate world, the ethical self is pushed away in the drive for profits. Integrating these various selves may be the most important challenge for academics. See http://www.enotalone.com/authors.php?aid=14.

REFERENCES

Abeles, T. (2000). Why pay for a college education? In S. Inayatullah & J. Gidley (Eds.), *The university in transformation: Global perspectives on the futures of the university* (pp. 79–90). Westport, CT: Bergin and Garvey.

Altbach, P. (1997). An international academic crisis? The American professoriate in comparative perspective. *Daedalus, 127*(4), 332.

Grant, J. (2000). Consciousness-based education: A future of higher education in the new millennium. In S. Inayatullah & J. Gidley (Eds.), *The university in transformation: Global perspectives on the futures of the university* (pp. 207–220). Westport, CT: Bergin and Garvey.

Inayatullah, S. (2002). *Understanding sarkar.* Leiden: Brill.

Inayatullah, S. (2003–2004). The learning and healing organization. *Executive Excellence, 19*(12), 20.

Inayatullah, S. (2005). *Questioning the future: Futures studies, action learning and organizational transformation.* Tamsui: Tamkang University Press.

Inayatullah, S., Bussey, M., & Milojević, I. (Eds.). (2006). *Neohumanistic educational futures: Liberating the pedagogical intellect.* Tamsui, Taiwan: Tamkang University Press.

Jaschik, S. (2005, March 28). Is phoenix the future? *Inside Higher Ed.* Retrieved from http://www.insidehighered.com/workplace/2005/03/28/phoenix

Manicas, P. (2000). Higher education on the brink. In S. Inayatullah & J. Gidley (Eds.), *The university in transformation: Global perspectives on the futures of the university* (pp. 31–40). Westport, CT: Bergin and Garvey.

Molitor, G. (2003). *The power to change the world: The art of forecasting.* Potomac, MD: Public Policy Forecasting.

Nandy, A. (2000). Recovery of indigenous knowledge and dissenting futures of the university. In S. Inayatullah & J. Gidley (Eds.), *The university in transformation: Global perspectives on the futures of the university* (pp. 115–124). Westport, CT: Bergin and Garvey.

Neubauer, D. (2000). Will the future include us: Reflections of a practitioner of higher education. In S. Inayatullah & J. Gidley (Eds.), *The university in transformation: Global perspectives on the futures of the university* (pp. 41–54). Westport, CT: Bergin and Garvey.

Odin, J. K., & Manicas, P. T. (Eds.). (2004). *Globalization and higher education.* Honolulu, HI: University of Hawaii.

Perkinson, R. (2003). *World bank presentation to the world education market.* Lisbon (see www.ifc.org).

Prensky, M. (2001). Digital natives, digital immigrants. *On The Horizon, 9*(5). Retrieved from http://www.marcprensky.com/writing/Prensky%20-%20Digital%20Natives,%20Digital%20 Immigrants %20-%20Part1.pdf

Press, E., & Washburn, J. (2000, March). The kept university. *The Atlantic Monthly,* 39–54. Retrieved from http://www.colorado.edu/Sociology/gimenez/papers/keptu.html

Shapiro, M. (1992). *Reading the postmodern polity: Political theory as textual practice.* Minneapolis, MN: University of Minnesota Press.

Spies, P. (2000). University traditions and the challenge of globalization. In S. Inayatullah & J. Gidley (Eds.), *The university in transformation: Global perspectives on the futures of the university* (pp. 19–30). Westport, CT: Bergin and Garvey.

Svetcov, D. (2000, September 11). The virtual classroom vs. the real one. *Forbes.* Retrieved from http://www.forbes.com/best/2000/0911/050.html

Tehranian, M. (1996). The end of the university. *The Information Society, 12,* 446.

The Economist. (2001, February 17). Online education: Lessons of a virtual timetable. Retrieved from http://www.economist.com/business/displayStory.cfm?Story_ID=505047

UNDP. (1999). *The human development report 1999.* New York & Oxford: Oxford University Press for the United Nations Development Programme. Retrieved from http://hdr.undp.org/reports/global/ 1999/en/pdf/hdr_1999_full.pdf

Van Eck, R. (2006). Digital game-based learning: Its not just the digital natives who are restless. *EDUCAUSE Review, 41*(2), 16–30.

Wiseman, L. (1991). The university president: Academic leadership in an era of fund raising and legislative affairs. In R. Sims & S. Sims (Eds.), *Managing institutions of higher education into the twenty-first century.* Westport, CT: Greenwood Press.

ERICA MCWILLIAM AND SHANE DAWSON

8. PEDAGOGICAL PRACTICE AFTER THE INFORMATION AGE

INTRODUCTION

Anticipating the future is as much the business of educators as it is of futurists. When we look at the concerns that teachers in the past have had about the future, it is clear that 'nay-saying' wins out over optimism or openness to change. America's National Association of Teachers (cited in Hill, 2007) record that, in 1703, teachers worried that students who used slate rather than preparing bark would run out of slate. By 1815, teachers worried that students were too dependent on paper instead of slate, and that the paper would run out. In 1917, teachers worried that students depended far too much on ink and had forgotten how to sharpen a pencil with a knife. By 1928, teachers complained that students depended too much on store bought ink and had forgotten how to make their own. Ball point pens were not acceptable to teachers in 1955—fountain pens only were to be used when submitting papers. Concerns that slide rules would eliminate problem solving skills emerged in the 1960s, and by 1980 panic set in around the numerical skills being lost because of the advent of the pocket calculator.

What we learn from this about teachers is that they are more likely to fear rather than embrace a future in which technological innovation is a key player. In an age increasingly dependent on, and ignorant of, science and technology (Martin, 2007), it is useful to imagine what we will make of our present educational fears in the next few decades—fears that text-messaging will be detrimental to young people's capacity to spell, fears that kids won't get a job because they don't understand what 'next–of–kin' means, fears that kids will lose the capacity to remember facts because they are so fast at finding them, fears that kids engage too much with games and not enough with 'work'.

Our interest in this chapter is not to give three cheers for technology; all its affordances come wrapped in barbed wire. However, we do seek to make a case for non-stupid 'yea-saying' in relation to the possibilities that new technologies afford twenty-first century educators. To do so we explore how 'content' and 'learning' are being transformed in the new millennium, and consider some quite precise ways in which schools and universities might be able to make practical, pedagogical moves to 'catch' the wave of technological change and ride it, rather than cling to the wreckage of traditional content and processes—even 'progressive' ones.

M. Bussey, S. Inayatullah and I. Milojević (eds.), Alternative Educational Futures: Pedagogies for Emergent Worlds, 133–147.

Much has been made, in recent times, of the extent to which we have seen one 'Age' of knowledge production end and another begin. Whether the advent of a new millennium provided the impetus, or whether it came from so much evidence of new patterns of social engagement emerging in a new generation, there is no doubt about the flurry of literature in recent years declaring the end of one sort of 'knowledge society' and the beginning of a new era. This new era—called variously the Conceptual Age (Pink, 2005), the Dream Society (Jensen, 1999), or the Economy of Icons (Sternberg, 1999)—is one in which knowledge, learners and learning are profoundly different, and it is a difference for which our educational institutions have been, and still are, thoroughly unprepared.

In what follows we indicate how 'content' and 'learning' are being transformed by the current surge of readily accessible information and communication technologies, and move on from these deliberations to explore practical, pedagogical moves schools and universities can make to catch the wave of change and ride it, rather than cling to the wreckage of traditional instructive content and process. We begin by considering the changing shape of 'content' i.e., of what counts as 'worth' learning. We then go on to explore new forms of social engagement and the new affordances they bring to a fresh understanding of how learners might engage optimally with 'content'. Finally we provide an indication of the sort of educational research that might inform pedagogical change in the short to medium term. We do all this in the context of the urgency that now attaches to pedagogical change and the entrenchment of our mainstream educational practices i.e., their capacity to stand as anachronistic sentinels defying external logic and yet anxious about the educational experience they offer to the 'Net' generation.

DISRUPTING 'CONTENT'

As a number of commentators have pointed out (e.g., Dator, 2005; Lessig, 2005), formal education remains deeply wedded to the written word. Indeed, Jim Dator goes further to argue that "seldom has a technology been the subject of more worship than the word is in literate cultures" (p. 202). The written word connotes more than the skills of knowledge access. As the capital 'w' ('Word'), it is imbued with moral purpose and as such achieves a status above and beyond a useful medium, skill or capacity.

If sacred texts are the purest examples of the call to the literal Word, secular texts like encyclopaedias have also achieved for the Word a revered status through which it has maintained a long and strong grasp on mainstream educational 'content'. While we certainly have seen tinkering at the edges of disciplinary 'content', what counts as worth knowing in schools and universities has remained very much wedded to the 'bookish' word: the word of the scientist, of the writer, the historian and so on. Thus, any parity of esteem of the sort that Lawrence Lessig (2005) argues should be afforded 'word', 'sound' and 'image' in digital times is still far from the value system that attaches to 'content'. 'Sound' and 'image' are very much garnish to the 'word' roast, unless located in the visual or performing arts. In most disciplines they remain fringe-dwellers on the edge of formal learning rather than part of its core business.

The resilience of the word–as–content is aptly illustrated by the longevity of the *Encyclopædia Britannica*. Despite all we know about the short shelf-life of knowledge and the speed with which scientific 'facts' become 'errors', The *Encyclopædia* still proudly claims itself as "an encyclopaedia created by experts, [and still] sought after by many [as] ... the gateway to knowledge and understanding" (http://www.britannica.com.au/, accessed 15 August 2007, emphasis added). As "the oldest continuously published reference source in the English language", and "the most authoritative encyclopaedia" in the world today, its presence is purported to signal value beyond a mere information repository. "Walk into a home or an office with the 2007 *Encyclopædia Britannica* on the shelf", its promotional material declares, "and you immediately know you're in a place where learning and discovery are respected ... [and where] ... [k]nowledge and information are cherished and enjoyed" (http://www.britannica.com.au/, accessed 15 August 2007). In other words, not just an encyclopaedia but a way of life!

For 'baby boomer' school children of the post-war years, *Encyclopædia Britannica* certainly had special significance, echoes of which linger in the marketing material quoted above. As a technology through which the legitimate form of content is, and is seen to be the 'authorised' word, the encyclopaedia may be considered a metaphor for the Information Age itself—information–as–knowledge that is crystalline and crystal clear, contained and containable, trustworthy and indisputable, readily available to all those who can read and write.

A key point here, in terms of formal education, is the word 'authorised'. This is what turns content into school curriculum and curriculum into a systemic syllabus. It is what frames the disciplines and the faculties of universities. The 'authorised' word locates the knower and the learner in very different spaces, vertically differentiated and clearly defined. It de-limits whose reading and writing is to be respected and revered. It is focused on a past in which reputations have been made rather than a future where reputations are yet to be forged. Thus the 'authorised' word is very much the medium for framing what Marc Prensky (2001) calls "Legacy content"—that is, content that "includes reading, writing, arithmetic, logical thinking, [and] ... understanding the writings and ideas of the past" (p. 4). It has little to do with "Future content" (Prensky, 2001) i.e., digital and technological knowledge like "software, hardware, robotics, nanotechnology, genomics ... [and also] ... the ethics, politics, sociology, languages and other things that go with them" (p. 4, emphasis in original).

Our interest is in imagining new forms of knowledge production and dissemination when the 'authorised' word ("Legacy content") that dominates in schools and universities is by-passed, as it increasingly is, by a Net generation that actively engages in co-creating 'Future' content—in editing, assembling and dis-assembling it. What pedagogical possibilities might arise when the command and control economy of knowledge creation and distribution finds its stranglehold on author/ity being weakened by the productive power of horizontal networks of individuals with a penchant for cutting and pasting ideas, patterns of words, sounds and images in millions of households and garages? In other words, how might formal learning environments become responsive to learners who are not at the end of a vertical supply and demand chain—not passive couch potato consumers but an active 'prod-users' (Lessig, 2005) of ideas and products, some of which may have wider commercial and/or scientific value?

To date there has been no radical re-working of the systems and the pedagogical practices that characterise mainstream education. This is so despite urgings about the need not simply for more education but better education for a changed world economy. This plea comes not only from social commentators such as Ken Robinson but also bodies like The National Center on Education and the Economy in the US (www.skillscommission.org) and the European University Association (www.eua.be). At the same time, moral panics continue to proliferate about the perceived loss of foundational skills in the young, as we have shown they have done for centuries. One way of understanding the panic is to appreciate the role that the 'authorised' word has in the moral training of young people. It is as if there is something fundamentally worthy about 'command and control' processes of instruction and allied testing, that young people will be 'better people' if they can recite the names of prime ministers and presidents in alphabetical order, or if they can write a 600-word essay in copy-book prose, as though some combination of Sir Francis Bacon and a quiz show champion would constitute the ideal global citizen/ knowledge worker for our times. Meanwhile, those who 'prod-use' Wikipedia (www.wikiepdia.org) as their preferred information source—and this number is increasing exponentially—do so with little regard for the trappings of academic authority or the moral panics that continue to emerge about anything sourced through the Internet. While the pre-publication scrutiny of content on the Internet as a whole cannot compete with the reputation and resources that continue to attach to the 'authorised' word, when it comes to expertise and editing, more interactive and shared knowledge resources allow for greater proportions of the public to contribute to the information sources. For instance, in answer to those who disparage the quality of information to be accessed online at sites such as Wikipedia, its advocates point to the speed and accuracy with which hundreds of regular pro-dusers can provide and update useful information, and can edit out 'bogus' or misleading information. This stands in sharp contrast to the lugubrious editing processes that need to be cranked up when *Encyclopædia Britannica* needs an error corrected. Moreover, Wikipedia's openness in terms of process also stands in contrast to the defensiveness of traditional editors when challenged on a particular point of 'fact'.

"LIQUID MODERN" LEARNING

However we might want to hold onto the myth of scientific certainty, "liquid modernity" (Bauman, 2000) does not allow author/ity to be monopolised by a handful of academic or scientific 'experts'—in other words, information wants to be free. Everyone can be publisher and editor, a producer and user of content knowledge. We are seeing not only the multiplying of sources of knowledge from 'outside' traditional knowledge domains, but also more openness to that knowledge from within social and scientific organisations, more combinations of in-house knowledge with external ideas, more co-production of knowledge and greater preparedness to jettison knowledge that does not tell in its applications. In this context, having 'the last word' is rendered at best suspect and at worst just plain silly.

New knowledge is being created at speed. According to Kevin Byron (2007), the full product cycle, from innovation to diffusion to stasis, was, in the 1970s, about 30 to 50 years in duration. By 2006, that cycle has now reduced in duration to about 5–10 years. The time taken to communicate with 50 million people has shifted from 30 years (Radio), to 13 years (Television) to 4 years (World Wide Web). Richard Florida, author of *The Rise of the Creative Class* (2002), argues that almost one third of the workforce are 'creatives', because they turn symbolic knowledge into economic and social assets. In so doing, their competitive edge depends on the speed with which they can make cultural products that are both novel and appropriate. The creative industries in which these workers will be predominant (many of which do not yet exist) are predicted by Daniel Pink, author of *A Whole New Mind* (2005), to be worth 6.1 trillion dollars in 15 years time. So speed matters, and those who can access and edit at speed have a greater potential to create and maintain valuable networks than those who cannot. For twenty-first century young people, the future is correctible (Inayatullah, 2007), available to be constantly re-invented, and all this can happen fast.

Along with the imperative for faster operational systems we are seeing a move away from content knowledge created by large scale commercial and research and development organisations. The move is to what is predominantly household driven innovation. The 'digital' shift from *authority* to *voice* is a shift that is evident in the communities of interest that provide the stories, identities and resources for building new communities—communities for co-creative communi-cation, communities of interest (e.g., eduspaces, BC campus), communities around user-generated content (e.g., flickr, My Space), user-defined collections (e.g., amazon, del.icio.us), and community interpretation (e.g., YouTube).

Meanwhile, formal education keeps promising to help young people reach their full potential while continuing with standardised curriculum, pedagogy and assessment models that have little to do with their futures, or indeed the future of learning. This is not to argue that theories of teaching and learning have not changed at all in recent decades. It is, however, to claim that schools are still organised through standard operational procedures that were produced in the Industrial and Information Ages of the nineteenth and twentieth centuries. They were not designed for content co-creation, new learners, or the new forms of engagements that digitally savvy young people call living. Unlike the Information Age, in which the core business was the routine accessing of information to solve routine problems, the new Age invests in, and springs from, unique cultural forms and modes of consumption that digital tools and communications are making possible.

Whether or not we agree that all this amounts to the first real generation gap since rock and roll (Robinson, 2007), it certainly makes unique demands of educators, just as it makes unique demands of the systems, strategies and sustainability of organisations. Put simply, educators are ill-equipped to respond, and the urgency of a more relevant response from schools and universities is increasing at an ever increasing rate.

NEW TIMES, OLD PEDAGOGIES

The vast majority of schools today continue to use structures and artefacts pertinent to the Industrial and Information Ages (Phillip, 2007). In organisational terms, schooling is a top-down hierarchy of command and control, with designated timetables, fragmented and specialised disciplines and classrooms designed to house 30 or so students, frequently at desks in rows facing black/whiteboards. Moreover, despite the tinkering with curriculum that we have seen in more recent times, teachers continue to work as singular 'content authorities'. Ask children to provide a picture of their experience of school, and the picture they are most likely to paint is 'blah blah blah' from the teacher at the front. Whether or not the blackboard has been replaced by a whiteboard, a 'transmission' culture of traditional curriculum remains dominant. While technologically-mediated tools have recently been conspicuously employed, the logic of their usage is predicated on pre-existing transmission-based models of pedagogy, i.e., Tools designed for new modes of social engagement serve fewer broader purposes than the transmission of "Legacy" content or the location of sites of information (Thompson, 2007; Williams, Coles, Wilson, Richardson, & Tuson, 2000). Thus, laptops, wireless access, data projectors and interactive whiteboards now merely 'stand in for' pens and paper, blackboard diagrams and print-based worksheets, despite the efforts of academic staff developers and a few maverick educators (Burnett & Dawson, 2005).

The command and control model of schooling clearly limits the sort of curriculum, pedagogy and assessment that can be enacted in a school. It is not a matter of 'blaming' school-based educators for this state of affairs but it is important to understand the 'double vision' that educational policy requires of its teachers. At a time when child protection legislation is central to any government policy related to children, teachers now have an expanded duty of care in which risk of any kind is to be minimised (McWilliam, 2003; McWilliam & Jones, 2005), while at the same time they are expected to provide an open, creative environment which encourages risk-taking. Schools must be on guard against the unfamiliar at the same time that they are supposed to welcome it. So the sort of risk-taking that is made possible through opening up schools remains in tension at all times with claims about 'safety first'. The fact that the push and pull of risk is a pendulum that swings back and forth in social life is a condition that we all now live with in a 'risk society' (Beck, 1992; Giddens, 2002), rather than a problem to be solved.

However, there is no assistance for schools to make a case that they are relevant to the cultural and social norms of the twenty-first century. Florida expressed his negative view of schools in his visit to Australia a few years ago.[1] A student of economic growth and social renewal in the US, Florida was responding to questions from an audience of Queensland academics, politicians, bureaucrats and students.

He had just finished a presentation about the importance of place in organising the sort of work that is done by 'the creative class'. According to Florida's empirical study of American economic trends, growth requires open systems that value social and cultural difference (tolerance), technology and talent (Florida, 2002, p. 249). Schools, by contrast, continue to operate as closed systems with traditional notions of accountability and performance expertise. While admitting that his research has been in economics, not education, Florida contended that schools are disconnected from the fizz and edge of the creative workplace and are likely to remain so.

Perhaps, then, it could be argued that the call to 'open up' to "Futures content" (Prensky, 2001) and its associated risk-taking and experimentation should just be ignored by those who really understand the nature of schooling and its limitations. To adopt such a position is very risky indeed, if Florida is correct in his assertion that 'openness' to an external and uncertain world is a fundamental disposition of those who would be part of "the creative class" (Florida, 2002). Closed systems which operate out of traditional notions of accountability and performance expertise are unlikely to lead to success in wealth creation or to social betterment.

There is no doubting the frustrations of many would-be school reformers who have bemoaned what they perceive to be strong resistance from teachers and administrators when trying to 'open up' schools to enable new experiences. In an article in *Campus Review*, "A new vision of learning environments" (Johnston, 2004), the frustration of one would-be reformer, Melbourne University doctoral student Andrew Bunting, is palpable: "At the moment we have stand-alone school buildings and whilst they're nestled out there in the community they're all behind cyclone fences. People aren't welcome because of things like stranger danger" (p. 12).

Bunting is convinced, however, that "contact and control can all be handled with today's communication technology and the increasing sophistication of on-line course delivery makes distance learning even more possible" (p. 12). While the panopticon possibilities of new technologies need hardly be reiterated, it is less clear what precisely this would mean in terms of taking full responsibility for enacting the expanded duty of care that is now *de rigeur* for all teachers of young people. The idea that more or different technology in/for schools can of itself solve this dilemma is naïve at best, given the moral panics that have been generated around children's access to the Internet, and the expense (and potential abuse) of mobile phones. Put simply, despite the fact that technology comes "with the friendliest of epithets" (Strathern, 1997, p. 317), each wave of techno-innovation brings with it a new set of risks that must be managed on behalf of the school community, and this in turn requires teachers and administrators to engage in yet another set of risk mitigation tasks. In short, the push to learning innovation and the pull to child protection through risk minimisation are contradictory imperatives that together shape the way that schools are organised and changed in the twenty-first century, for better *and* worse.

Beyond the problematic issue of 'risky' learning, we also have a pedagogical gap between how technological tools and resources are currently utilised and what research is telling us about optimal learning environments. Put simply, research tells us that optimal learning environments are not based on efficient 'couch potato' consumption of transmitted information but on social interactions within communities of interest. There is indeed a plethora of literature about the implementation and development of pedagogical practices across the education sector that focuses squarely on the importance of social interactions for optimising student learning. For instance, Vygotsky (1978), Bandura (1977) and more recently, Lave and Wenger (1991) and Seimens (2005) have developed learning theories emphasising the importance of socialisation in learning. Northedge (2003) likewise has argued that the embracing of social constructivist principles among educators has forced a shift in teaching practices from didactic teacher ('sage on the stage') to facilitator ('guide on the side'). What is critical here is the notion that learning is fundamentally a social activity and that pedagogy therefore, is about optimising the value of social engagement.

The shift from a transmission model of education to a social or community-centred approach is reflected in the move from absolute and verified knowledge as represented by *Encyclopædia Britannica* (EB), to community understandings as exemplified by Wikipedia. In essence the transition from 'sage on the stage' to 'guide on the side' has mirrored the transfer of information source from the authoritarian EB to the informal and communal online environment such as Wikipedia. While Northedge (2003) argues the importance of 'balancing' these pedagogical approaches, we would go further, arguing for pedagogical work that is appropriate to the role of "*meddler in the middle*" (McWilliam, 2005, p. 5). In this role teachers are not commanders, nor are they fully 'in control', just as the student is not a passive participant in the learning process but an active creator and sharer of 'curriculum' and the evaluation of learning outcomes. 'Meddling' teachers actively co-create learning resources with students, leading and following just as the students have opportunities to lead and follow.

BACK TO NATURE?

The concept of 'lead–and–follow' as a shared responsibility has been elaborated upon by us elsewhere (McWilliam & Dawson, In review). Students as leaders *and* followers in dynamic learning environments can be seen enacting the 'flocking' behaviour of birds, with individuals contributing collectively yet independently of fellow peers, in order to maximise efficiencies for achieving shared learning goals. As in 'swarming' behaviour (see Miller, 2007), command and control leadership is not the dynamic through which complex problems are solved and tasks allocated.

'Swarming' or 'flocking' or 'teeming' behaviour involves much more than this. Computer simulations of 'boids' (bird objects) (Thompson, 2006) demonstrate the behavioural principles that allow flocks or swarms to perform with more capacity (e.g., flying higher and faster) than the capacity of any one flock member. The deceptively simple rules involved—*separation* (the capacity to steer to avoid crowding others), *alignment* (the capacity to steer towards the average heading of the local flockmates) and *cohesion* (the capacity to steer to move towards the average position of local flockmates), ensure that each boid is aligned with and responsive to those flockmates in their immediate vicinity, as well as appropriately separate from other flockmates. The pedagogical implications of this are that team-based student 'self-management' needs to function in a way that does not interfere with others. At the same time, this is not a space of individual 'freedom'—there are 'good inhibitors' to behaviour that ensure any 'randomness' is always systematic, scanning for and reporting anything 'interesting'. All this purposive activity has the effect of reducing vulnerability to individual member failure, while at the same time generating "swarm intelligence" i.e., "amazing scheduling and routing capabilities" (Thompson, 2006) that are well beyond any individual capacity.

The Internet has made it possible to harness such 'swarm intelligence' more powerfully than any other technology. Yet while there has been much interest and investment in ICTs for learning, we have made scant headway in understanding what sorts of collaborations are now possible, and whether and how they might be systematically fostered in formal education. So what might pedagogy look like that is informed by 'bio-behaviour'?

While we acknowledge that human behaviour is much more complex than that of 'boids', we nevertheless see value in applying the principles of bio-behaviour to twenty-first century pedagogy. Some work has already commenced to apply these ideas to human teams at work within organisations (Thompson, 2006), but they are yet to be applied to educational environments. It may be that the very large numbers of users on the Internet militate against a self-managing 'local neighbourhood' forming and being sustained through its capacity to share, connect and co-invent. However, the numbers of students we teach in a particular discipline or 'class' should not be an inhibitor.

Recent research has begun to probe the social formations that university students co-create in their on-line learning (Dawson, 2007; Haythornthwaite, 2001, 2002). The sociogram of a sample class's interactions on-line in Figure 1 is a useful illustration of the emergence of what appear to be 'local neighbourhoods'— relatively stable groups of four, five or six individuals with strong peer–to–peer relationships. By contrast, it also shows that many individuals are disconnected or only tenuously connected to their peers.

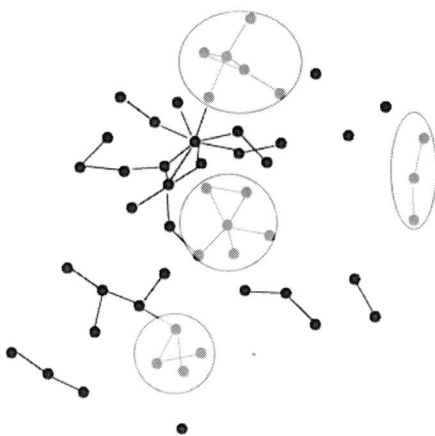

Figure 1. Sociogram of student discussion forum communication interactions[ii]

The sociogram illustrates not only localised neighbourhoods but also the key individuals *linking* potentially disparate student neighbourhoods into a networked community. These individuals act as 'border crossers' relaying, editing and assisting in the information flow throughout the entire network. Clearly the border crossers are taking on some of the typical roles of teachers, and their assistance is pivotal to the overall 'swarm intelligence' of the group as a whole. The sociogram also highlights those individuals with greater or fewer direct contacts in the network. From an educators' perspective this provides an opportunity to rapidly identify potential 'flockmates' that are disconnected and disengaged from the network.

There is much that we need to know about the presence or absence of 'local (student) neighbourhoods' in terms of the conditions of their formation, their temporal and spatial dimensions and how these factors impact on individual learning performance. In exploring these matters in future research, we may be able to provide the pedagogical support and direction through which more of our students can be active self-managers of their learning in active, purposive 'local neighbourhoods'. That is, we may be able to imagine and then create an environment in which 'group work'—currently the bane of many students' lives—is supplanted by rich dynamic processes of peer–to–peer learning as flockmates for whom the local neighbourhood works as a practical and sustainable source of—and support for—learning.

For the Net generation, the sharing of resources, content and information is already a central component of life (Oblinger & Oblinger, 2005). Novice online gamers seldom refer to instructional manuals for acquiring the rules, norms and vocabulary required to be an active and legitimate community member (Willett, 2007). They learn through discussions and online experiences with more skilled members, all of whom share, as flockmates, their passion for 'flying higher' in the game. This peer–to–peer dynamic carries through to all aspects of the Net generation's daily lives including their educational experiences.

In place of the skepticism brought by baby boomer educators to the usefulness of online technologies for learning (including worries about student plagiarism and lack of attention to print-based 'basics'), the Net generation is much more sanguine about fellow members re-creating and re-purposing prior learning resources. The sharing and co-production of learning resources within the virtual world has been possible because of the development of broad and effective social networks (Thompson, 2007). By developing friendly relationships in online blogging software such as MySpace and Facebook, users have the opportunity to identify the specific skills and characteristics that are required for participation within a dynamic team or 'local neighbourhood'.

Friends or flockmates are recruited through processes of self-promotion and exposure where individuals unabashedly display their daily lives, skills, interests and attributes in ways that may seem both narcissistic and dangerous to baby boomers. Yet this display does a particular kind of work in that it makes it possible to locate shared passions and thus who potential flockmates might be, as well as how they can be accessed. It seems that educators who capitalise on these generational characteristics of sharing, searching, rapidly evaluating, self-promoting, and synergising with peers, will be more likely to enact teaching and learning practices that imitate the forms of sharing and community that flourish in the virtual world.

Pockets of innovations may now be found dotting the formal learning landscape, yet most schools and universities continue to defy the trend away from singular top-down authority to the democratising imperative of 'giving voice'. Moreover, they remain domains in which the value of information accessed via the online environment is considered problematic in terms of its legitimacy as 'pure' disciplinary knowledge.

W(H)ITHER TEACHING?

Much has been written in recent times about the importance of 'communities' to learning (see for example: Bielaczyc & Collins, 1999; Lave, 1993; Lave & Wenger, 1991; Levine Laufgraben & Shapiro, 2004; Palloff & Pratt, 1999; Rovai, 2002). We would argue that the bulk of this literature remains vague about the precise work of setting up a robust 'peer–to–peer' environment. It has become a conceptual cul-de-sac rather than a pathway to better practice. So rather than continue to pile up the case for more or better 'communities of practice', we are seeking to explore further the value of bio-behaviour—and the language that attends it—in order to capture more precisely the social dynamics of optimal learning. All this helps us to think about the dangers and opportunities that exist in the author/ity of the teacher.

There is much that is exciting and still relatively unknown about the social world in which young people are increasingly spending their time and energies. As reported by Stephen Lunn (2007), the engagement of young people with new media has reached unprecedented levels and continues to show exponential growth. Australia MySpace, for example, has reached the level of 3.8 million profiles, while Facebook has grown 270 per cent in the past three months to about 150,000 profiles at the time of writing. It is not just that these sites are "worth billions" (Lunn, 2007), but that they are spaces where young people are practising the forms of navigation, networking and communication skills necessary to the 'creative worker' identity. Schools and universities whose curriculum, pedagogy and assessment remain 'outside' will be increasingly irrelevant to the modes of learning and social engagement that young people choose and to the future of their work. It is not that teachers should never instruct, or that facts should never be memorised. The point is that memorisation of facts by couch-potato consumers of information passed from a top-down 'authority' is a much less valuable exercise than it was a few decades ago.

We need to imagine a time in the not too distant future when students will have the Library of Congress implanted in their heads, a time when an Internet implant will allow our brains to be fully on-line, allowing every one of our students to download new knowledge and skills, a time when outdated knowledge can be deleted as updates arrive 24/7. It may be that the very word 'teacher' itself has a limited shelf-life, to be supplanted by knowledge facilitator, information technologist, creativity coach, all of whom work with learners whose predominant experiences are in virtual environments (Hill, 2007).

In preparing young people for these probable futures, adjustment, adaptation and habituation—the capacity to learn and reproduce appropriate social behaviours—will be increasingly unhelpful. Instead of opening up possibilities, what we learn and how we learn it—our current learning habits—continue to assume a fixed or predictable social world: one is which forms still ask for 'next of kin', in which handwriting is still important to employability, in which the basics are agreed and inculcated in schools.

When supply is linear and stable, when labour is shaped by relatively simple patterns of time and space, when consumption is a passive activity, then such behavioural and attitudinal habits make sense. In fact, they are the most likely means of achieving success. Get the routines right—the routines of thinking, of engaging, of problem-solving—and they will equip you well both now and in the future.

But these routines are deadly when the bottom falls out of the stable social world in and for which we learn. We have to imagine that learning itself—learning as we have come to enact it habitually—may no longer be particularly useful. The very habits that have served us so well in stable times are becoming impediments to social success, even to social survival. According to Zygmunt Bauman (2004), this is the contemporary social reality:

> Just as long-term commitments threaten to mortgage the future, habits too tightly embraced burden the present; learning may in the long run disempower as it empowers in the short ... 'Your skills and know-how are as good as their last application'. (p. 22)

For Bauman, educating in a "liquid-modern" social world means that the work of assembling and structuring new social relations is no more important than the work of "keeping them eminently dismantlable" (p. 22). Foundations cannot be relied upon as long term platforms for learning. We need to pay more attention to social relations among learners, teachers included, and to understand what it means to assemble, structure and dis-assemble these relationships in the interests of new learners. It is an exciting challenge for us all.

NOTES

[i] Florida, R. (2004). The Rise of the Creative Class, sponsored by the Hornery Institute, The Roundhouse Theatre, Kelvin Grove Urban Village, Brisbane, 22 March.
[ii] The data informing the sociogram (Figure 1) emerged from a study investigating the relationship between student sense of community and online communication interactions (Dawson, 2007).

REFERENCES

Bandura, A. (1977). *Social learning theory*. New York: General Learning Press.
Bauman, Z. (2004). Zigmunt Bauman: Liquid sociality. In N. Gane (Ed.), *The future of social theory* (pp. 17–46). London: Continuum.
Bauman, Z. (2000). *Liquid modernity*. Cambridge: Polity Press.
Beck, U. (1992). *Risk society: Towards a new modernity*. London: Sage.

Bielaczyc, K., & Collins, A. (1999). Learning communities in classrooms: A reconceptualization of educational practice. In C. Reigeluth (Ed.), *Instructional-design theories and models, Volume II: A new paradigm of instructional theory* (pp. 269–292). Mahwah, NJ: Lawrence Erlbaum Associates.

Burnett, B., & Dawson, S. (2005, September 29). *Aligned and resistant communities: Exploring new conduits for online engagement.* Paper presented at "OLT 2005: Beyond delivery", Brisbane, Australia.

Byron, K. (2007, January 8–10). *Defining boundaries for creativity.* Paper presented at "Creativity or conformity? Building cultures of creativity in higher education", Cardiff University.

Dator, J. (2005). Universities without "quality" and quality without "universities". *On the Horizon, 13*(4), 199–215.

Dawson, S. (2007). *Juxtaposing community with learning: The relationship between learner contributions and sense of community in online environments.* Unpublished PhD, Queensland University of Technology, Brisbane.

Florida, R. (2002). *The rise of the creative class.* New York: Basic Books.

Giddens, A. (2002). *Runaway world: How globalisation is reshaping our lives.* London: Profile Books.

Haythornthwaite, C. (2001). Exploring multiplexity: Social network structures in a computer-supported distance learning class. *The Information Society, 17*(3), 211–226.

Haythornthwaite, C. (2002). Building social networks via computer networks: Creating and sustaining distributed learning communities. In K. A. Renninger & W. Shumar (Eds.), *Building virtual communities: Learning and change in cyberspace* (pp. 159–190). New York: Cambridge University Press.

Hill, R. (2007, January 8–10). *Creativity is the currency of the new millennium in higher education.* Paper presented at "Creativity or Conformity? Building cultures of creativity in higher education Conference", Cardiff University.

Inayatullah, S. (2007). A post Howard–Costello scenario. *Journal of Futures Studies, 11*(3). Retrieved August 5, 2007, from http://www.jfs.tku.edu.tw/2011-2003/ES2002.pdf

Jensen, R. (1999). *The dream society: How the coming shift from information to imagination will transform your business.* New York: McGraw-Hill.

Johnston, S. (2004). A new vision of learning environments. *Campus Review, 7*(4).

Lave, J. (1993). Situating learning in communities of practice. In L. B. Resnick, J. M. Levine, & S. D. Teasley (Eds.), *Perspectives on socially shared cognition* (pp. 17–36). Washington, DC: American Psychological Association.

Lave, J., & Wenger, E. (1991). *Situated learning: Legitimate peripheral participation.* Cambridge: Cambridge University Press.

Lessig, L. (2005, January 18–19). *The vision for creative commons: What are we and where are we headed?* Paper presented as the keynote address at "Open Content Licensing (OCL): Cultivating the Creative Commons", QUT, Brisbane.

Levine Laufgraben, J., & Shapiro, N. (2004). *Sustaining and improving learning communities.* San Francisco: Jossey-Bass.

Lunn, S. (2007, July 27). Face to face in cyberspace. *The Australian.* Retrieved July 27, 2007, from http://www.theaustralian.news.com.au/story/2000,,22140064-22128737,22140000.html?from=public_rss

Martin, J. (2007). *The meaning of the 21st century: A vital blueprint for ensuring our future.* London: Transworld Publishers.

McWilliam, E. (2003). The vulnerable child as a pedagogical subject. *Journal of Curriculum Theorizing, 19*(2), 35–44.

McWilliam, E. (2005). Unlearning pedagogy. *Journal of Learning Design, 1*(1), 1–11.

McWilliam, E., & Dawson, S. (In review). Teaching for creativity: Towards sustainable and replicable pedagogical practice. *Higher Education.*

McWilliam, E., & Jones, A. (2005). An unprotected species? On teachers as risky subjects. *British Journal of Educational Research, 31*(1), 109–120.

Miller, P. (2007, July 1). Swarm theory. *National Geographic.* Retrieved August 22, 2007, from http://www7.nationalgeographic.com/ngm/0707/feature5/

Northedge, A. (2003). Enabling participation in academic discourse. *Teaching in Higher Education*, *8*(2), 169–180.

Oblinger, D., & Oblinger, J. (2005). Is it age or IT: First steps toward understanding the net generation. In D. Oblinger & J. Oblinger (Eds.), *Educating the net generation*. Boulder, CO: EDUCAUSE.

Palloff, R., & Pratt, K. (1999). *Building learning communities in cyberspace*. San Francisco: Jossey-Bass.

Phillip, D. (2007). The knowledge building paradigm: A model of learning for net generation students. *Innovate*, *3*(5). Retrieved July 28, 2007, from http://www.innovateonline.info/index.php?view=article&id=368

Pink, D. H. (2005). *A whole new mind*. New York: Penguin.

Prensky, M. (2001). Digital natives, digital immigrants. *On the Horizon*, *9*(5), 1–6.

Robinson, K. (2007, March 29–30). *The other climate crisis: Digital culture, demography and education*. Paper presented as the keynote address at the Digital Literacy and Creative Innovation in a Knowledge Economy Research Symposium, Queensland State Library, Brisbane, Australia.

Rovai, A. P. (2002). *Building sense of community at a distance*. Retrieved January 25, 2005, from http://www.irrodl.org/content/v3.1/rovai.html

Siemens, G. (2005). A learning theory for the digital age. *Instructional Technology and Distance Education*, *2*(1), 3–10.

Sternberg, E. (1999). *The economy of icons: How business manufactures meaning*. Westport: Greenwood Publishing Group.

Strathern, M. (1997). 'Improving ratings': Audit in the British University system. *European Review*, *5*(3), 305–321.

Thompson, J. (2007). Is education ready for web 2.0 students? *Innovate*, *3*(4). Retrieved July 28, 2007, from http://www.innovateonline.info/index.php?view=article&id=2393

Thompson, K. (2006). Enhance team performance by consistent individual behaviour. Retrieved April 27, 2007, from http://www.bioteams.com/2006/03/22/enhance_team_performance.html

Vygotsky, L. S. (1978). *Mind in society: The development of higher psychological processes* (M. Cole, V. John-Steiner, S. Scribner, & E. Souberman, Trans.). Cambridge, MA: Harvard University Press.

Willett, R. (2007). Technology, pedagogy and digital production: A case study of children learning new media skills. *Learning, Media and Technology*, *32*(2), 167–181.

Williams, D., Coles, L., Wilson, K., Richardson, A., & Tuson, J. (2000). Teachers and ICT: current use and future needs. *British Journal of Educational Technology*, *31*(4), 307–320.

Erica McWilliam is Professor of Education and Assistant Dean of Research in the Faculty of Education at the Queensland University of Technology. Her educational publications cover a wide spectrum, as is evidenced in her numerous publications on innovative teaching and learning, research methodology and training and leadership and management. She is currently series editor of 'Eruptions: New Thinking Across the Disciplines', an academic series for Peter Lang Publishing, New York. Erica is also an author and social commentator on some of the charming absurdities of corporate practice.

Shane Dawson is a Senior Research Fellow with the Centre for Learning Innovation at Queensland University of Technology, Australia. His research interests have focused on the application of data derived from institutional information and communication technologies (ICTs) to inform teaching practice. Shane's work has lead to the development of specific ICT-collected lead indicators of student sense of community and course satisfaction. Shane now leads an international project furthering the potential for data derived from Learning Management Systems to assist educators and administrators in the evaluation and monitoring of student engagement. Shane is also involved in developing pedagogical models for enhancing creative capacity in undergraduate students. He is currently investigating social network visualisation tools as a potential resource for teaching staff to better understand and evaluate student creative capacity.

MARCUS BUSSEY

9. ACCESS AND EQUITY

Futures of an educational ideal

Since its election in 1996, the Howard government has pursued an extreme version of neo-liberalism in its approach to education. The government has subjected education to market forces, and has made competition, choice, and accountability central priorities. These policy directions have affected all sectors of education in detrimental ways. This agenda has been taken up in narrow ideological ways and has threatened the social-democratic traditions in Australian education … In general, we have seen a shift from a view of education as a public good—central to the operation of a civil society—to a view of public education as a safety net operating in a system characterised by competition, stratification and individualism. The policies have reshaped public education—built on notions of universal access, diversity and democracy—and have marginalised programs addressing educational inequality. (Taylor, 2005, p. 8)

The neoliberal policy attack on access and equity and other pillars of the Australian social-democratic tradition that Sandra Taylor describes, has a long and noble history. The former Australian prime minister, John Howard, can chart his moral and intellectual roots back beyond his family's colonial roots to such Western luminaries as Socrates and Plato. The struggle to defend and develop concepts such as access and equity shares the same lineage, being rooted in the stand off between the Athenian citizenry and Socrates. In this contest Protagoras, the great sophist teacher parodied by Plato, can be seen to represent the opinion that education was of universal value and the right and responsibility of all citizens.

Neither Socrates nor Plato, nor for that matter the former Australian prime minister, share such an opinion. The Socratic position is that education is differential: it is an unspoken but firmly held belief that most people are unable to ascend to the heights of great minds and that culture, far from being universal, is the particular province of cultivated and cultured sectors of any community. In our age of political correctness this can no longer be stated so boldly, but in the Athens of Plato he could quite happily compare the average citizen to a donkey (Jaeger, 1939/1965, p. 307; James, 2005).

When exploring the futures of concepts like access and equity, it helps to place them in their historical and cultural context. It is here that we find the fears and hopes of cultures as well as the contested value systems that form the intellectual

M. Bussey, S. Inayatullah and I. Milojević (eds.), Alternative Educational Futures: Pedagogies for Emergent Worlds, 149–167.

and moral fabric of societies. From fear and hope, and the myths and metaphors that give them form, we come to understand why social expressions take the form they do when challenged in particular ways. Similarly, it is the dominant values of a culture that underwrite the definitions for what is possible and what is not and also set the limits of official knowledge and shape the nature of ignorance.

Throughout this article the historical standoff between Socrates and Protagoras will be used as a metaphor for the tension that lies at the heart of current definitions of access and equity and provide the context for thinking about the futures of such educational ideals.

AN ANCIENT WOUND

Werner Jaeger describes how education for the Sophists was a revolution that challenged patrician power. Their purpose in educating was to create good citizens. They posited that their vision was an advance on the earlier conception of education as a process of enculturation for the ruling patrician families. This tradition is represented by Protagoras, Hippias and Prodicus (Jaeger, 1939/1965, p. 308). Patrician education, which aimed at creating good leaders through the amassing of cultural capital, was aligned with power and fostered a high culture that was felt to be beyond the reach of the ordinary populace. Amongst the critics of popular education were Socrates, Plato and later Aristotle (the teacher of that archetypal great-man, Alexander the Great). The 'culture' in question, for both groups, was essentially political (Jaeger, 1939/1965, p. 300). Who had access to it was determined by the aims and political ideology of the leading educational thinkers of the day.

For Jaeger, this tension lay at the heart of Greek educational and cultural creativity. Protagoras, whom Jaeger describes as a proto-humanist, spoke of an egalitarian universal culture and developed the concept that "Man is the measure of all things". The patrician thinker Plato turned this idea on its head and posited instead that "The measure of all things is God" (Jaeger, 1939/1965, p. 301). By placing knowledge in a transcendent context, Plato strategically reinforced a dualism that fostered the splitting of humanity into two groups, the elite leaders who were gifted with culture, and the followers who were incapable of it. Plato offered a transcendent, yet authoritarian, culture and taught mostly nobles while Protagoras offered an immanent, egalitarian and universal culture and sought to bring his teaching to all.[i]

Both approaches saw education as essential for effective governance. To both threads of Athenian-Greek consciousness, culture was essentially political. The individual did not exist in a vacuum but was contextualised within the *polis* (James, 2005). All meaning came from their being a part of the functioning of the city. Political culture was 'universal', as social organisation, the sharing of values and ideals, was the culture that bound human beings of all walks of life together in an effective polity. In this way access was determined by the need to be equipped with the skills to participate in the life of the *polis*. Obviously, the elitist perspective had no need for the concept of equity because people were essentially unequal. In democratic Athens however, Protagoras and the other Sophists taught that equality was earned through education and demonstrated through civic engagement. Culture was the cement of the *polis*, and had universal application to both camps. Thus Jaeger concludes that:

> This conception of the nature of universal culture summarises the whole history of Greek education: ethics and politics taken together are one of the essential qualities of true *paideia* ... the close connection between higher education and the idea of society and the state is an essential feature of classical Greece. (Jaeger, 1939/1965, p. 300)

These two strands, the egalitarian and the elitist, have been in a constant dialogue ever since. Yet the balance has always been in favour of elites. This is not simply because Plato was its most eloquent advocate. Christianity too, with its equally pessimistic assessment of humanity, the 'fallen', as in need of constant rectification has perpetuated the distrust of authority for the crowd. Furthermore, Ziauddin Sardar has pointed out that the authoritarianism of Socrates has been a defining feature in both the Western and Islamic traditions. The question of educability lies at the heart of this tension and it goes back to the argument between Socrates and Athens. Socrates had argued we were not equal and all were certainly not educable to the same degree. The Athenian polity took and implemented the reverse position, namely that any cook could rule. Greek thought is stamped with this standoff and modern intellectual history in general, and educational theory in particular, perpetuates it. "Greek thought envelopes the ways of knowing as well as the very being of Western and Muslim civilisations. We live and breath it, it is our perpetual shadow, our eternal guide from the dark Cave into the world of reason and light, our road to reality" (Sardar, 1989, p. 3).

Roberto Calasso explores this tension further, pointing out that although the *demos* was a Greek discovery, it went hand in hand with their gift for subverting both freedom and justice via public opinion (Calasso, 1993, pp. 255–256), which acted as a form of popular authoritarianism. The contempt that Socrates had for the crowd was mutual. Thus, I. F. Stone observes that Socrates would not claim as his defence his entitlement to freedom of speech, that defining feature of the Athenian *polis*. Socrates treated that freedom with contempt and taught others to view the average citizen as little better than a donkey. Stone concludes:

> Socrates would have found it repugnant to plead a principle in which he did not believe; free speech for him was the privilege of the enlightened few, not of the benighted many. He would not have wanted the democracy he rejected to win a moral victory by setting him free.

> His martyrdom, and the genius of Plato, made him a secular saint, the superior man confronting the ignorant mob with serenity and humour. This was Socrates' triumph and Plato's masterpiece. Socrates needed the hemlock, as Jesus needed the crucifixion, to fulfil a mission. The mission left a stain forever on democracy. That remains Athens' tragic crime. (Stone, 1989, p. 230)

Education has been living with this 'stain' for two and a half millennia. It is deep and the tension is as alive and vigorous today as it was in the time of Socrates.

THE REASONS FOR EDUCATING

This historical overview reveals that the reasons for educating are linked with the way we educate, the range and scope of how we educate and the way we define the group we educate. Access in this sense becomes a question not just of delivery but of definition. Equity no longer refers to the single issue of a facilitated and selective access but to the systemic response to the human right to a rich, diverse and empowering education. At the risk of perpetuating a dualism, these two positions, encapsulated in the standoff between Socrates and the people of Athens, help us to establish the boundaries of the question: what does and can access and equity mean?

In exploring this question a spectrum of possible positions emerge. These positions are the result of attempts to resolve the wound of Socrates'' death. Socrates won a profound moral victory when he goaded the people into sentencing him to death. Were they right to do so? Did they prove their ignorance and pettiness by passing sentence? Is human nature essentially mean, sinful and vindictive?

If the answer is Yes, then education will focus on control and discipline, on what Gordon Tait calls 'individuation, differentiation, normalisation' (Tait, 2004). If however, the answer is No, then the focus will be on the child and their family, on holistic learning and on building strong critical and personal relevance into learning. If the answer is Yes, then access becomes a means of selection and assimilation, of the division of labour and of maintaining a belief in merit and of the rights of the individual over the collective. Equity, too becomes a differential concept, which when linked to the concept of merit rationalises the individual's, and whole sections of the populace's, inclusion or exclusion from power and wealth. If the answer is No, then access becomes a means of engaging with social division, the impoverishment of culture and the selective discrimination against various vulnerable groups within the community. Similarly equity, becomes a social justice issue as opposed to a neo-Darwinian tool and education becomes a vehicle for social renewal and a resource for community and regional enterprise.

Furthermore, if we were to step beyond the dualism implicit in much of Western thought and embrace the 'synthetic' position of many non-Western traditions, we find a space of possible interpretations and actions based on an entirely different set of principles. Such a space Edward Soja describes as a 'third space' in which hybridity of values and voices sets the scene for inclusive but not homogenised possible solutions to the tensions inherent in Western dualism (Soja, 1996).

Yoshiharu Nakagawa makes a similar point when he states that "Eastern philosophy does not see language as the all-embracing matrix or as the highest organ to grasp the universal laws (*logos*)" (Nakagawa, 2000, p. 148). The tension that is the hallmark of the Western educational tradition becomes a non-tension in this context. Access can mean openness and equity can mean fulfilment. In this context learning and unlearning become linked in a dance between ignorance and knowledge, both in this 'other' educational space holding a meaningful place within a seemingly paradoxical holistic educational setting.

The neohumanism at the heart of this position is a reformulation, one might say a transvaluation, of the Greek ideal as expressed by Protagoras and taken up two millennia later by Desiderius Erasmus and Thomas More. It offers a new critical dimension to educational thinking in which relationship and community are as important as analysis and individuation. When both positions are allowed to step out of the straight-jacket of binary logic, access must reconcile with the conceptual and social tension that there is no even playing field and equity must allow for both personal ability and structure to form fluid solutions to the personal and the social paradox that no two human beings are the same and therefore at some ultimate level the notion of equity is flawed.

The point here is that civilisations are networks of values that define our expectations and generate the reasons for human individual and collective action. The dualism at the heart of Western educational discourse is but one way of defining what is knowable and therefore real. Beyond dialectic there is the possibility of a third or neohumanist space that is a creative synthesis that is forever fluid and responsive to shifts in human and social order. This is the living space of cultural ordering where concepts are mutable and genealogical analysis opens the present up to its past.

Whose Definitions?

Institutions tend to be blind to history. Educational systems are no exception. This however does not exempt them from the play of history. As it stands, modernity has taken Socrates' side in the debate over human nature. This is why the issues of access and equity exist. Western society is not as free and liberal as our leaders would have us believe. Our educational institutions are dominated by systems that perpetuate exclusivity and inequity. Education is, we are told, about merit, excellence, performance and accountability and these concepts generate hierarchical, discriminatory and selective values. Furthermore neoliberalism, the ideological and economic structure of late modernity, perpetuates myths of ascendance and differential reward (Apple, 2003; Illich, 1971; Postman, 1969; Pusey, 1991).

This situation is maintained by the ahistorical nature of the educational gaze. From this neoliberal context the ideological struggles of the past are deemed to be over and modern education, for all its recognised problems, is heralded as one of the great victories of modernity. The subtext is simple: Why quibble about issues of access and equity when we are getting education to a vast and diverse population, meeting a vast array of needs and challenges and skilling our populations with new and exciting technologies, known in the trade as "essential learnings" and/or "multi-literacies"? The implication is that it is the future that education must respond to, not the past. The imperative, politicians and large tracts of the media would have us believe, is to prepare children for the threats, challenges and possibilities of a future that is essentially unknowable, yet darkly forbidding. Fear thus becomes the fuel for our educational conservatism.

Yet, from the expanded humanist position exemplified by Protagoras and the perspective of critical futures education, how education responds is moulded by its past, the choices made and the values that informed these choices. In this sense, the future becomes a magnet, the past the context and the emergent present provide a range of possibilities.

Still, to push our metaphor further, Socrates casts a long shadow. The modern state, threatened as it is by the dual forces of globalism and resurgent community action, stands in that shadow, and its perspective is shaped by unconscious assumptions about human nature being ignorant, lazy, short-sighted, chaotic, deceitful, etc. One logical response is to seek to extend control over this unruly nature via increased central control over education and other vehicles of civic and cultural cohesion. However, as James Scott dryly observes, "the administrator's forest cannot be the naturalist's forest" (Scott, 1998, p. 22). Similarly, the administrator's school cannot be the child's school.

For the administrative mind, control requires legibility, the quantification of natural space. So education, as an activity of the modern bureaucratic state, demands legibility (Scott, 1998, p. 183); it requires practices that enable schools, teachers and their students to be assessed, measured and quantified. Such practices become internalised and act as a form of social control. Foucault described this process by analogy to Bentham's panopticon, a revolutionary prison design that builds self-surveillance into the prisoner's psyche (Foucault, 1977). State surveillance via testing and reporting operates in this way, actively changing the way students and their teachers function (Meadmore, 2004, p. 27). Such self-regulation is only required when social institutions such as education are felt to be under-performing. The logic of neoliberalism, encapsulated on this occasion in the concept of 'performativity' is rooted in a lack of trust of the citizen/child/teacher and promotes the application of what Daphne Meadmore has called "disciplinary technologies" (Meadmore, 2004, p. 26). The need to measure the performance of schools is an administrator's response to the need to manage a populace, characterised by the flaws Socrates attributed to it, for a future that is described as unpredictable and complex.

The modern state's response is encapsulated in a recently released educational framework from the Australian state of Queensland. The focus here is to increase that state's competitive edge. The framework, from Education Queensland, opens with the following observation: "The world is changing rapidly. Queenslanders need to be highly skilled and educated to excel among their competitors overseas, and their skills need to be updated continually to keep pace" (Queensland Government, 2005, p. 1).

The future is used here not in the futures sense of an open domain to stimulate the emergence of what Richard Slaughter calls "social foresight" (Slaughter, 2004 p. 170ff), but as a tool for the further colonisation of social and personal space by the state. In the Australian context this escalation of bureaucratic surveillance in education has been described as a function of the nation's powerful, yet shadowy, elite to define the language and values of the populace (Connell, 2004). State intervention, through the promotion of reforms and the rewarding of performance, is an appropriate tool for this activity. This is important as concepts such as 'access' and 'equity' have been defined by policy in narrow quantifiable terms that fail to acknowledge the social aspiration inherent to them.

Damien Cahill (2004) stresses the central role that definition, the ability to define the real, has in the contestation of a hegemonic political/ideological landscape. Resistance today is often bound by the language and agenda of the state. Futures thinking helps to see beyond that agenda by proposing an analysis that acknowledges the roots of the present in the past, identifying the forces shaping the present and generating a sense of agency based on future images that acknowledge both that which is feared and that which is desired. Without such an approach we remain, as Cahill notes, bound by the rhetoric of those interests driving an aggressive, future-colonising agenda:

> Too often the language of the elite is being adopted by those resisting its agenda, and in doing so the words, ideas and the language of the powerful are accepted as the platform on which strategies are then mistakenly built. If it is accepted that the state is central to the program of neoliberalism then movements for change will be in a better position to strip away the propaganda behind such terms as 'free trade' and 'deregulation'. (Cahill, 2004, p. 84)

The same can be said of terms such as access and equity.

Mapping the Tension

Let's return for a moment to the Greeks. One way of interpreting the present and exploring the future is to look at the dualism expressed by the elitism of Socrates and the egalitarianism of Protagoras. The present set of educational ideals embodied in Western state education pay tribute to both and educational policy documents are stamped with both the authoritarian need to administer and control and the egalitarian wish to affirm the rights of the child and the innate drive to learn that lies at the heart of humanity (Bussey, 2001). Here we see that a consensus has been negotiated and a compromise arrived at. Reading such documents is like performing an archaeological dig in which we meet merit and access, excellence and equity, the vocational and the intrinsic, performance and process, information and knowledge. These terms define the central concerns and processes of education, but depending on whether the writer is placed in the Socratic or Protagorian traditions, the intent and practical result is different.

The thrust of the argument is that the mythic roots of civilisations, their ancient 'wounds', actually generate much of the instrumental logic that orders our cultural institutions. Cornelius Castoriadis reminds us of this when he describes the social imaginary[ii] the collective magma of humanity, as a set of forms: "A form—an *eidos* as Plato would have said—means a set of determinations, a set of possibilities and impossibilities that are defined starting from the moment the form is posited" (Castoriadis, 1997a, p. 103).

Of the social imaginary itself he notes:

> Social imaginary signification brings into being things as *these here* things, posits them as being *what* they are—the *what* being posited by signification, which is indissociably principle of existence, principle of thought, principle of value, and principle of action. (Castoriadis, 1997b, p. 313)

The dualism we are exploring as a process of the social imaginary is a social form in Castoriadis' sense—it demarcates the possible from the impossible while setting limits on the probable and the preferable (Bell, 1993). Form draws on deep narratives that, as Sohail Inayatullah points out, are often unconscious to the actors (Inayatullah, 2004, pp. 66–67). These forms order our reality by limiting the possible and establishing the criteria for measuring present activity. Despite periods of hegemonic constraint these forms are never unitary (Hetherington, 1997, p. 10), but contain within themselves the contradictions and tensions that, as Jaeger noted of the period of Greek democracy (Jaeger, 1939/1965, p. 300), are the source of a societies' creative energy.

Ernesto Laclau and Chantal Mouffe point to the fact that such forms of hegemony are rooted in deeply held images, at once plural and indeterminate, that institute the social (Laclau, 1992, p. 151). The definition of these forms is a field of contestation that constitutes the political. The twin poles of access and equity as represented by Socrates and Protagoras are in reality broken down. The political becomes a subjective process that concerns the ability to define. Hence Laclau and Mouffe assert, there can be no politics without hegemony:

> … politics as a practice of creation, reproduction and transformation of social relations cannot be located at a determinate level of the social, as the problem of the political is the problem of the institution of the social, that is, of the definition and articulation of social relations in a field criss-crossed with antagonisms. (Laclau, 1992, p. 153)

For Laclau and Mouffe it is the inner construction of the outer world that needs to be addressed when we are seeking to engage with the power of definition. This inner process is both richly inhabited by sign and signifier, but it is also paradoxically open and empty. Laclau sees this emptiness as the source of the force of any ideal (Laclau, 2002, p. 125). Richard Slaughter captures this process of interpenetration in a modification of Ken Wilber's four quadrant model in which each quadrant (the inner, outer, collective and individual) is seen to fold into the other (Slaughter, 2004, Image on p. 142).

This leads to a theoretical sensitivity to the creative process of the social imaginary and also to the appreciation of the "radical impossibility" of an end point to this process, be it a perfected democracy or a stable empire (Laclau, 2002, p. 128). It is too temping to place constructions such as authority and egalitarianism in mutually exclusive camps (Laclau, 1992). In fact they mutually interpenetrate one another. The naturalist's garden may not be the administrator's garden but they usually cohabit. Similarly, Socrates' life was spent in the vibrant intellectual world that was democratic Athens, he may have rejected it, but he also benefited from its vitality (James, 2005).

CLA OF THE ANCIENT STAIN

Laclau and Mouffe point to the problem of the institution of the social that takes place outside of the arena of the determinate. This is the arena of the symbolic in which collective 'mind' shapes and validates, and thus institutes, the real. This institution they see arising from the break down between the internal and external social world, a division which was in reality only a theoretical construct of nineteenth century Marxism as it focused on class relations (Laclau, 1992, p. 151ff). One way to explore this arena of the political imaginary is to apply causal layered analysis (CLA) to the standoff between Socrates and Protagoras (Inayatullah, 2004).

CLA is designed to unpack the social as it is constituted through the interplay of elements of the social imaginary. It begins with the area of the social Laclau and Mouffe call the determinate—that which is expressed through discourse and social process in the objective external world. The surface of this expression is the day–to–day *litany* that we hear in the mouths of politicians, read in headlines and see on the evening news. This is the unreflective disconnected social space that can be so easily manipulated by the powerful, the media and politicians. Below this level is the social-institutional that describes how society, or any organisation, functions as a *system*. There are two other areas that CLA interrogates and these are the layers of social reality that are not directly accessible on the external level. They constitute the deeper processes of social ordering around which society orients itself, instituting new forms of social relations as the narrative strands gain ascendency or loose ground to emergent alternatives. These are firstly the layer of *worldview* and discourse. This is constituted by the civilisational and hinges on ideology and discourse as a process for constituting the real and defining both the possible and that which is of value. Beneath this sits the *mythic–metaphoric* which represents the deep images, archetypes, memories and unconscious urges that drive and energise social expression.

The following table (Table 1) offers an analysis of the standoff between Socrates and Protagoras. Both figures take the form of an ideal type. The point is to reveal strands in the present that are recognisable as referents in the ongoing process of social ordering. In this sense CLA acts as an epistemic map that exposes what we might call the psycho-social DNA of a component of the current social and political order.

Such a schema provides an overview of some of the characteristics of both positions, although it is incomplete and partial and cannot be closed. As we are looking at the Greeks I sought out Greek-specific imagery for the mythic. The purpose of CLA is to expose the cultural, historical and epistemological roots at work in a specific context and offer an ontology of the social.

Table 1. The standoff between Socrates and Protagoras

	Socrates	Protagoras
Litany	Individual against the collective	Individual as part of the collective
	Noble Soul/Secular Saint	Nobility gained from Context
	Martyr to human pettiness and ignorance	Freedom always threatened by elitist aspirations of a minority
	Vision always at risk of succumbing to the dark	**Access** for all
	Access a mark of socio-economic status	Freedom = Responsibility
	Equity inimical to Freedom	**Equity** guarantees freedom
	Only the Great are Free	
	Everyone has their place	
System	Totalitarian/benevolent Dictatorship	Participatory democracy
	Plato's Guardians	Policy determined by consensus
	Hierarchy & Order	Flat structure
	Central control	Strong Community
	Individualism and merit	**Access** is a right
	Access is earned, it is a privilege	Wisdom is a collective attribute
	Wise Rule the Mob	**Equity** underpins social justice
	Equity threatens social stability and creativity	
Worldview	Culture is the badge of the Rulers	Culture is universal—it is our birthright
	Knowledge is 'power–over'	Knowledge is 'power–with'
	Security comes from strength of Ruler	Security comes from the Collective
	The Mob is Irrational/Nature is Irrational	The desire to control is irrational
	Wisdom is transcendent—**accessed** by the Sage	All Knowledge is within—**access** by education
	Hard work should be rewarded	Collective endeavour bears collective results
	Knowledge is unitary—absolute	Knowledge is partial-evolving
	Priesthood of Privilege	Community of Learners
	God measure of all things	'Man' the Measure of all things
	Equity is irrational, it is not supported by reality	**Equity** is rational, it creates a just reality
Myth–Metaphor	Delphic Oracle voice of transcendent knowledge	Prometheus gives the tools for our self development

Four Educational Futures

Through the use of CLA we begin to understand how various definitions of access and equity inform specific systemic and individual responses to the future. Here four differing forms of schooling are presented (Bussey, 2004) as ideal types in order to lay the foundations for our exploration of the concepts of access and equity as they function in each setting. The focus here is the emergent context. The typology offered draws upon current and emerging educational practice and spans a range of possible educational settings.

Fortress school is explored as the dominant short term possibility with recognisable features and clear roots in the Socratic-elitist tradition. It is already present in many ways today and, as was noted at the opening of this chapter, can be heard in the rhetoric of neoliberal policy. This model simply draws the present into the future as social division increases in response to the negative social, cultural and economic trends of a triumphal globalisation. The stresses inherent in such an historical process will increase all forms of social inequality and build a sense of isolation and antagonism into elite educational systems.

The multicultural school is considered as a future possibility in decline, many features have been trialled in educational systems in an ad hoc manner and are now the object of a sustained critique from conservative pedagogues, social commentators and politicians. Such schools can be seen to have roots in the Protagorian humanist tradition as they privilege culture as a birthright, access as a necessary ingredient for social solidarity and renewal and community over vested interest. Future decline of this type can be attributed in a large measure to the fact that multicultural principles are being forced into systemic contexts which are a direct product of elitist managerial practice and theory.

Virtual schools are a source of much excitement and speculation. They are much less immanent than either the fortress or multicultural school, both of which adopt as unproblematic many of the assumptions at the root of this type. There is an implicit elitism in the virtual revolution in general and in much thinking about virtual schooling in particular. This schooling therefore is linked to the Socratic tradition with its confidence in knowledge systems, its inherent virtual *versus* real world dualism and its insensitivity to the socio-economics of access and thus tacit acquiescence to a gated community of learners.

The eco-school is another emergent possibility. The ideology and idealism for such a possible future is certainly present today but such schools exist in many ways beyond the current construction of the real. They will have a deep commitment to sustainable social action which privileges community over isolated individual, responsibility over freedom, and participation over control. Many themes are present today in educational discourse yet the social structures needed to support them are rudimentary. They are strongly linked to the Protagorian tradition in that they value the collective as an extension of the individual, participatory engagement with questions of social and environmental concern, and learning as an ongoing collective engagement with personal and social reality. Yet they have the potential to move beyond humanism by affirming spirituality as a form of social action that has strongly integrative properties and the capacity to engage deeply with the forces that maintain the current imaginary institution of the real.

A CLA of Educational Futures

In applying the four educational futures sketched above to concepts of access and equity we find that a range of possible meanings emerge (see Table 2). The fortress school model with its emphasis on fear and intensification is a form of educational authoritarianism that currently dominates neoliberal thinking. It owes a strong debt to the authoritarianism of Socrates as indicated by the "Socrates+" at the bottom of its column. Rooted in our present it colonises the future through the propagation of a strongly hegemonic image of immanent loss of social, cultural and economic coherence in the face of a host of threatening 'unknowns'. Access here becomes a right and equity is the result of personal merit.

Table 2. CLA of educational futures

	Fortress School	Multicultural School	Virtual School	Eco-School
Litany	Schooling is out of Control, Survival of the Fittest	New 3 R's, Child as Global Citizen, Life is Complex	World full of Winners and Losers, Losers aren't on line	Learning and Living go hand in hand, we make our Reality
Systems Perspective	More Testing, Pressurise Teachers and Students for Excellence Schools of Merit	Centralised management, Smart Schools are flexible, Schools sell	Business/Government Mediate virtual world, Speed and Flexibility, Teachers as technicians	Decentralise, local communities define learning, "Capital" redefined
Worldview	Effective Management, Discipline	Plurality, Tolerance, Complexity	Individual Chooses Destiny	Unity amidst Diversity
Myth/ Metaphor	Schools are Knowledge Factories Socrates +	Global Village Protagoras –	Global Brain Socrates –	Eco-Commons of Gaia Protagoras +

Multicultural schools offer a less authoritarian response to the current social and educational climate. Such schools will contest the dominant fortress school for some time and may emerge again to shape a positive learning culture. This future is currently in retreat as aspiring multicultural schools are being forced into line by new legislation. Essentially they owe their roots to the idealism of the welfare state and also to liberal-humanist education. They are softly authoritarian, in that the welfare state was highly interventionist and centralised, yet they owe their intellectual roots to a humanist faith in the human beings' inherent curiosity and goodness, hence they are categorised as Protagoras–. Access in such a context is deemed relatively unproblematic, the door is always seen to be open and all are welcome. A raft of policy actions are offered to facilitate entry (i.e., there is an appreciation of structural barriers to access) and equity is defined as a right with considerable attention given to social forces of exclusion and the role of structure in the definition and maintenance of the real.

The virtual school, for all its claims to inclusivity, is highly selective. It has a systems view of knowledge and little real interest in the student as a learner, focusing instead on the student as a part of an information-generating web. It is softly authoritarian in that it is less interested in power and control than in the generation of knowledge as the new form of capital. Hence it receives a Socrates– classification. Access in this context is also deemed unproblematic, however there is little appreciation of the structural impediments to access and therefore the solution is simply one of money and skill. Equity is also a non-issue as the assumption is that all are equal online; gender, ethnicity and the like become invisible and therefore no longer inhibit the educational process.

The eco-school on the other hand values the student as an individual. Such schools will have a self-imposed charter to act as social change agents and will seek to strengthen community and sustainable praxis. Proto-typical eco-schools exist today although they account for a small fraction of the total educational system. They are usually holistic and even spiritual in orientation (Milojević, 2005), seeking to heal the psychic and cultural wounds inflicted on the Western psyche by the hyper-rationalism of modernity (Palmer, 1983/1993). They often tend to perpetuate the contemporary obsession with individualism and ego-identity, yet though their educational philosophies are diverse, they are all premised on the belief in the essential goodness of humans, and as such are classified as Protagoras+. Access in this context is a right that must be actioned through a shift in consciousness arrived at via a break with the modernist emphasis on utilitarian, neoliberal and individualist values. Equity too must be fought for, as it cannot simply be legislated but must be seen as a process not an end in itself.

Defining the Real

If we look at the level of myth and metaphor we come to understand the power of the deep image to frame the working realities of schools. Access and equity are seen to mean quite different things when placed in the context of their root myths. In the fortress school access is seen as a non-issue, the door in such schools is always open: all one need do is enter. Similarly, equity is defined as the result of hard work. In this context all are equal in the competition of life and thus we can all be winners. The fortress school is blind to the social processes that enable some while disabling others. Schools, defined as knowledge factories, are places of hard work and require constant scrutiny to run effectively.

In the multicultural school all are welcome. Access here is also unproblematic as there are many pathways in the global village leading to the school door. Equity hinges on ones' command of the knowledge economy and the embracing of and tolerance for difference which is a hallmark of the emerging global reality. Students are consumers and effectively earn knowledge shares through their own merit. Furthermore, such schools are sensitive to social processes that offer differential opportunity to students and seek to mitigate against such imbalances through an open door policy.

Virtual schools also find the concept of access unproblematic as they construct it in terms of access to information technology. In this setting money solves all problems and the only losers are those unable to log on. Social activism thus becomes a question of getting a computer into every home and computer banks into every classroom. For the global brain the construction of knowledge is unproblematic and equity is constructed as the freeing of the individual from their social and corporeal identity in cyberspace, where we are all equal.

In the eco-school we find access is defined as the extent to which we are able to free ourselves from external authority and construct pathways to learning via community. Equity in this context hinges on both the acknowledgement of the inherent worth of the individual and also on an appreciation of their social and ecological embeddedness. Education in the context of the global commons is a community resource that builds on empowerment.

The power to define the language that governs educational ideals such as access and equity is key to the control and maintenance of social processes. The neoliberal ascendancy of the past decade has successfully corralled education into the discourse of the fortress school, thus making it the most likely future. In colonising the future this discourse draws on the rhetoric, aspirations and processes of the multicultural, virtual and eco schools in order to forge a consensus of sorts, yet there is less and less interest in consensus as neoliberal politicians, academics and media successfully manipulate the litany of fear and anxiety.

It is the potential of the future to strike fear into the populace that is exploited by conservative governments with an eye on the State's bank balance and the next election. Capital is narrowly defined as GNP and community is regarded as a resource to be exploited. Here we find the power of litany used to draw on the ancient fears of populations all too willing to trade security in the present for preferable futures for their children. Thus, as Lewis Mumford observed many years ago, the irrational becomes the rational, and all social processes are subjected to the "ideology of the machine" (Mumford, 1934/1986, p. 132).

Towards a Wild History

Futures analysis, however, uncovers the rich range of myths that hold a place in the social imagination, and it is from this arena that alternatives to the present can emerge. When we redefine, we begin to transform the forms that maintain and order reality. Tobin Hart maps this movement when he links it to both the emergence of new categories and new self-definitions:

> To transform is to go beyond current form. This means growth, creation, and evolution, an expansion of consciousness. When education serves transform-ation, it helps to take us beyond the mould of categories, the current limits of social structure, the pull of cultural conditioning, and the box of self-definition ... (Hart, 2001, p. 12)

Philip Wexler also links it to the emergence of a living history. The educational gaze, shaken from its ahistorical blindness, becomes alive. This coming back to life of learning and being is rooted in our sense of self and community. Wexler observes that:

> If we need a 'wild' hunger to quench our ontological thirst, a dialogue with place that creates wholeness that we feel as ecstasy, then we also need a 'wild' history to satisfy our being in time. This is an active, living, remembered history and not a facticized accumulation of dead, inert otherness. (Wexler, 2000, p. 143)

Critical futures offers such a wild history in which the human engagement with the continuum of past, present and future brings us alive to the context of our being and the potential of our life to actively co-create the future we wish for our children. It is in this discovery of agency that the dissolution of the present neoliberal hegemony is to be found.

THE POLITICS OF FEAR AND HOPE

The potential for any reconstruction of the social lies in our ability to rediscover agency. It is important to realise that this fragile concept is caught (one might say bound) perpetually by a range of fears and drawn forward by a range, often less clearly defined, of hopes. Popular politics and the media are adept at manipulating the fears and hopes that are deeply rooted in all social constructions of the real.

To map our hopes and fears requires us to define the context that gives rise to these because, once again, each context is situated within its own social construction. If you were to ask: What does Socrates fear? you might answer, ignorance or freedom or perhaps, equality. For Protagoras the answer would be different, perhaps elitism or instrumentalism or radical individualism. At one level the answer is academic yet at another, deeply profound, as these iconic figures represent something of our reality today. They have a mythic power and authority that defines a set of human aspirations and concerns.

To better understand how definitions of access and equity are informed by social constructions of fear and hope we need to return to our four typologies, all of which are anchored in present value systems and cultural processes that stretch out into the future for 'radical' fulfilment.

In this future the fortress school is an embattled school. It focuses on the individual whose future is paradoxically the hope of the social. It fears the loss of freedom in the name of equality and sees learning as the building of armour so that the 'educated' adult can battle through life. The future for the fortress school is dark and menacing. Multicultural schools of tomorrow will fear fragmentation and the loss of coherence. They distrust competition and seek to balance the individual with the collective by acknowledging diversity. Those fighting for such schools will hope for a global world in which all have access to the benefits of education and can therefore contribute to the global village. The virtual school on the other hand will hope to get the entire world on line and fears luddites and the rediscovery of the body and relationship as the core of meaning. Finally the eco-school will fear technology and its ability to define reality. Those developing such schools will hope that individuals rediscover the cosmos and community and thus reinstate meaningful relating into the learning and living equation. Such schools offer a vision of the sacred in nature (as opposed to the end of nature) and of the unique place humans have within this. Technology in such a context will be both human and artificial and will weave seamlessly into learning and culture.

The power of fear as a tool for maintaining social order cannot be over-estimated, yet it can also act as a goad to positive social engagement. We have all experienced the politics of fear, as terror—both in its fundamentalist and state sanctioned forms—defines a whole set of current social relations. Yet it is in hope, the source of inspiration, that we find the power to transform the social. The politics of hope and fear need to be actively explored in order to redefine the current context. Hope here is of particular relevance.

Mary Zournazi sees hope as both a personal and social force that can effectively deal with the alienation and apathy that characterises the present neoliberal hegemony. She emphasises, however, that in the dominant political climate hope has been redefined, or constrained. There is, she says, a new context in which hope acts as a negative social force. Here, social order is reduced to minimal or impoverished settings in which, "for the benefit of our security and belonging, we evoke a hope that ignores the suffering of others, …[and]… create a hope based on fear" (Zournazi, 2002, p. 15).

Hope however can be much more, and Zournazi underscores this: "Hope can be what sustains life in the face of despair, and yet it is not simply the desire for things to come, or the betterment of life. It is the drive or energy that embeds us in the world—in the ecology of life, ethics and politics" (Zournazi, 2002, pp. 14-15).

In this context access and equity can link up with both personal and social aspirations that affirm human relationship and underscore a social commitment to justice and an ethical engagement with the powerful interest groups that benefit from maintaining a social imaginary that is divisive and exploitative. By exploring hope and fear and filtering concepts such as access and equity through this lens we develop more subtle and more robust understandings and strategies.

IMPLICATIONS FOR ACCESS AND EQUITY

To engage the causal strands that underpin current thinking on access and equity will require a shift in awareness and practice. These concepts are embedded in constructions of social reality and therefore cannot be simply dealt with in the abstract. This is the problem alluded to by thinkers such as Castoriadis, Laclau and Mouffe. To deal with access and equity outside of the question of context is to base the analysis on a "radical insufficiency" (Laclau, 1992, p. 151) that dooms attempts to legislate social justice in all its forms to failure.

We need to challenge the rules confining the definition of access and equity to narrow and instrumental policy processes. To do this we must realise that new rules need new roots (Myth/Metaphor) and that these roots may lie outside conventional wisdom and cultural conditioning. This is the possibility alluded to above as the 'third space' that generates new stories and draws on new cultural and civilisational imaginings. Humanism itself expresses the ideals at the heart of current thinking on access and equity, yet provides no capacity building structures to frame a redefinition of the discourse. Neohumanism provides a 'third space', human technology for reframing discourse on access and equity and also affirms the contemplative and spiritual ground for an engagement with human consciousness and the ethical and subjective roots of meaning. What emerges then is a new map and the processes outlined in the various layers of the causal analyses provided above act as sets of bearings in this process.

The central problem with any analysis of hegemony is that it usually remains in the realm of the theoretical and often is forced to use the terms and tools of the dominant knowledge system (Cahill, 2004). At present the neoliberal attack, described in the opening of this chapter, on the social-democratic traditions that have been the hallmark of Australian society for several generations is dominating the intellectual, moral and economic landscape that in turn defines the possible in education. To go beyond Sandra Taylor's critique of such an attack (Taylor, 2005) and to define new possibilities for the social will require us to clarify the causal roots of the neoliberal position. Only then can we actually begin thinking and acting in open-ended ways to create alternatives to the dominant system. Furthermore, when dealing with access and equity we must recognise that they are the products of specific civilisational, historical, social, economic and political processes.

How education engages with access and equity this century will be determined by how the interplay between the various contested educational futures is resolved. There are important and irreconcilable positions too that must be embraced in the movement towards greater access and equity in its most socially just context. For instance, there will always be a tension between the concept of freedom and that of equality. Similarly, there is a necessary tension between an individual's identity and their communal context, between biography and history, agency and structure. Such tensions are the source of the creative energy that defines social processes. They are politically charged by virtue of the fact that ideology seeks to define, maintain and control the construction of the real and what constitutes the valid.

The redefinition of access and equity hinge on our ability as individuals and groups to re-engage with alternative images of the social in order to activate memories, traditions and dreams founded on a trust in human agency. Only when we turn our backs on the long shadow of Socrates, and his disdain of the common-place and ordinariness of the human, will we be able to realise how much he (we) lost when he chose death over life.

NOTES

[i] We need to remember that 'all' meant all citizens—Athenian Greece, even at its most enlightened still had slaves (*helots*) and a large disenfranchised 'alien' population. Even so, both slaves and 'aliens' were given an education according to need and demonstrated ability.

[ii] "The symbolic orders of all societies have their actual centre of meaning in a world which is not merely perceived or rationally constructed, but rather in an imagined referential world, an imaginary. From it, society creates the interpretations and explanations which give it a unified meaning" (Honneth, 1986, p. 70).

REFERENCES

Apple, M. (2003). *The state and the politics of knowledge*. London/New York: Falmer.

Bell, W. (1993). Bringing the good back in: Values, objectivity and the future. *International Social Science Journal, 137*(August), 333–347.

Bussey, M. (2001). Sustainable education: Policy in search of a new language. *Journal of Futures Studies, 6*(12), 71–88.

Bussey, M. (2004). Educational scenario building: CLA as a tool for unpacking educational futures. In S. Inayatullah (Ed.), *The Causal Layered Analysis (CLA) reader: Theory and case studies of an integrative and transformative methodology*. Tamsui, Taiwan: Tamkang University Press.

Cahill, D. (2004). 'Getting the government off our backs'?: The ruling class and new trends in the state's management of dissent. In N. Hollier (Ed.), *Ruling Australia: The power, privilege & politics of the new ruling class* (pp. 70–86). Melbourne: Australian Scholarly Publishing.

Calasso, R. (1993). *The marriage of cadmus and harmony* (T. Parks, Trans.). New York: Alfred A. Knopf.

Castoriadis, C. (1997a). Anthropology, philosophy, politics. *Thesis Eleven, 49*(May), 99–116.

Castoriadis, C. (1997b). *World in fragments: Writings on politics, society, psychoanalysis, and the imagination*. Stanford, CA: Stanford University Press.

Connell, R. W. (2004). Moloch mutates: Global capitalism and the evolution of the Australian ruling class 1977–2002. In N. Hollier (Ed.), *Ruling Australia: The power, privilege and politics of the new ruling class* (pp. 1–23). Melbourne: Australian Scholarly Publishing.

Foucault, M. (1977). *Discipline and punish: The birth of the prison*. London: Penguin.

Hart, T. (2001). *From information to transformation: Education for the evolution of consciousness*. New York: Peter Lang.

Hetherington, K. (1997). *The badlands of modernity: Heterotopia and social ordering*. London and New York: Routledge.

Honneth, A. (1986). Rescuing the revolution with an ontology: On Cornelius Castoriadis' theory of society. *Thesis Eleven, 14*, 62–78.

Illich, I. (1971). *Deschooling society*. London: Pelican.

Inayatullah, S. (Ed.). (2004). *The Causal Layered Analysis (CLA) reader: Theory and case studies of an integrative and transformative methodology*. Tamsui, Taiwan: Tamkang University Press.

Jaeger, W. (1939/1965). *Paideia: The ideals of Greek culture* (Vol. 1, G. Highet, Trans.). New York & Oxford: Oxford University Press.

James, C. L. R. (2005). Every cook can govern: A study of democracy in ancient Greece. In D. Roussopoulos & C. G. Benello (Eds.), *Participatory democracy: Prospects for democratizing democracy* (pp. 332–347). Montreal: Black Rose Books.

Laclau, E., & Mouffe, C. (1992). *Hegemony and socialist strategy: Towards a radical democratic politics*. London: Verso.

Laclau, E., & Mouffe, C. (2002). Hope, passion, politics. In M. Zournazi (Ed.), *Hope: New philosophies for change* (pp. 122–148). Sydney: Pluto Press.

Meadmore, D. (2004). The rise and rise of testing: How does this shape identity? In B. Burnett, D. Meadmore, & G. Tait (Eds.), *New questions for contemporary teachers: Taking a socio-cultural approach to education* (pp. 25–39). Sydney: Pearson Education Australia.

Milojević, I. (2005). Critical spirituality as a resource for fostering critical pedagogy. *Journal of Futures Studies, 9*(3), 1–16.

Mumford, L. (1934/1986). *The future of technics and civilisation.* London: Freedom Press.

Nakagawa, Y. (2000). *Education for awakening: An eastern approach to holistic education.* Brandon, VT: Foundation for Educational Renewal.

Palmer, P. (1983/1993). *To know as we are known: Education as a spiritual journey.* San Francisco: Harper Collins.

Postman, N., & Weingartner, C. (1969). *Teaching as a subversive activity.* New York: Delta Books.

Pusey, M. (1991). *Economic rationalism: A nation building state changes its mind.* Cambridge: Cambridge University Press.

Queensland Government. (2005). *Queensland curriculum, assessment and reporting framework.* Brisbane: Department of Education and the Arts.

Sardar, Z. (1989). Against the common man: Authoritarianism and the greek intellectual heritage. *Muslim World Book Review, 9*(2), 3–15.

Scott, J. (1998). *Seeing like a state: How certain schemes to improve the human condition have failed.* New Haven, CT: Yale University Press.

Slaughter, R. A. (2004). *Futures beyond dystopia: Creating social foresight.* London and New York: Routledge/Falmer.

Soja, E. W. (1996). *Thirdspace: Journeys to Los Angeles and other real–and–imagined places.* Cambridge, MA: Blackwell.

Stone, I. F. (1989). *The trial of socrates.* New York: Anchor.

Tait, G. (2004). What is the relationship between social governance and schooling? In B. Burnett, D. Meadmore, & G. Tait (Eds.), *New questions for contemporary teachers: Taking a socio-cultural approach to education* (pp. 13–25). Sydney: Pearson Education Australia.

Taylor, S. (2005). Education—Private consumption or public good. *Green: The Magazine of the Australian Greens, 17*(Spring), 8.

Wexler, P. (2000). *Mystical society: An emerging social vision.* Boulder, CO: Westview Press.

Zournazi, M. (2002). *Hope: New philosophies for change.* Sydney: Pluto Press.

KATHLEEN KESSON

10. CULTIVATING DEMOCRATIC CHARACTER

Reconceptualising 'citizenship' for a partnership era

Each morning I turn on my public radio station and brace myself for the latest news of violence and aggression in the world. I am a citizen of a nation state, a powerful empire, perhaps the most powerful, militarily and technologically, of any nation in history. The current leader of my country asserts emphatically that we will be at war for the foreseeable future, and that we will not hesitate to use deadly nuclear weapons to protect 'our way of life'. I believe that he means here not just a way of life grounded in such principles as individual liberty, rational decision-making, and democratic process, but also a way of life characterised by materialism, increasing consumption, a voracious appetite for fossil fuels, and thus, the necessary economic domination of much of the rest of the world. I assume this because corporations based in my country, the United States, are recolonising the globe in their efforts to maximise profits, no matter what the cost in human and environmental well being. And in this they are supported by government policies in both Democratic and Republican administrations that favour 'free trade' agreements and other corporate interests over democratic decision-making. I am painfully aware that my 'way of life', brought to me by these corporations, which my leaders will defend with any force necessary, is made possible by tremendous actual and potential cost in human suffering and environmental degradation.

Perhaps our current leaders really do want a peaceful world. If so, their strategies indicate that they believe in "peace through strength" (Harris, 1988, p. 9). In a peace through strength model, the values of *militarism* dominate, values that support the use of force as a legitimate way to manage human affairs. There is a tremendous cost that comes with peace through strength: resources that might otherwise be used to mitigate the human suffering that is at the root of much of the violence in the world are channelled into the manufacture and stockpiling of weapons of mass destruction. These weapons find their way into the hands of dictators as well as terrorists and revolutionaries, enemies as well as friends, stable and unstable governments. The cycles of violence not only continue, they escalate towards an unthinkable future. It is clear to me that militarism is not a sustainable approach to peace. I want to change this, I want to do my part to bring the world more into balance, but as a citizen of this powerful nation, I feel increasingly helpless, except on a very local level, to influence the direction of my country toward a more just and peaceful world.

M. Bussey, S. Inayatullah and I. Milojević (eds.), Alternative Educational Futures: Pedagogies for Emergent Worlds, 169–185.

There are signs of hope. Recent elections in the US suggest that the electorate here has turned against the most blatant expression of global military domination (the war in Iraq) and people seem to be waking up to the problem of climate change and its connection to our patterns of consumption and energy use. The 'public' is notoriously fickle, and these cultural trends could easily be reversed by some dramatic event such as an economic downturn or another terrorist attack close to home, but it appears as if the moment is ripe for expanding the discourse on alternative visions of the future, and by extension, the discourse on alterative educational futures.

A 'PARTNERSHIP' FUTURE

Riane Eisler (1987, 2000, 2002) has defined two major paradigms of value and behaviour in today's world: the "dominator" model, which is characterised by relations of control, domination, manipulation, rapaciousness, and competition, and the "partnership" model, characterised by equity, caring, sustainability, non-violence, and justice. These models operate, according to Eisler, on both micro (family, relationship) and macro (nation states, global) levels. While perhaps oversimplified, these paradigms serve as useful models for thinking about where we have been as a society and where we want to go. Currently, dominator values seem ascendant and the hegemony of militarism complete as the world tries to find its way through the fear and confusion of these new times. But below the surface, in the town meetings and peace forums, in the many alternative publications, blogs, and web sites devoted to critical and courageous commentary, in local and community projects for sustainability and justice, and in the widespread individual and collective efforts to define a non-dogmatic, universal spirituality for a new era, the seeds of what she terms the "partnership society" sprout.

I am moved by the vision of a partnership society, a vision that would require a massive shift from the prevailing dominator values of cutthroat competition, greed, power and control to the values of care and compassion, of equity and global justice. And just as I often feel helpless, but still am stirred by this alternative vision, I know that young people, sometimes characterised as apathetic and self-centred, are also hungry for a meaningful vision of the future, one that is worthy of the investment of their time and their energy and their hope. As educators, we have a sacred trust to nurture this vision, and to provide our students with the knowledge and capacities that will enable them to take charge of their own destinies, to shape public policy, and to transform their society. If we are going to create a world in which citizens are not passive victims of dominator values, but active proponents of partnership values, then we must tend these seeds of hope carefully, and actively cultivate the skills and dispositions that will enable our children to live in accordance with these values. This paper is devoted to exploring the kind of citizenship education that I believe holds the most promise of promoting partnership values and behaviours.

COMPETING CONCEPTIONS OF DEMOCRACY, CHARACTER DEVELOPMENT,
AND CITIZENSHIP

At the core of every society is the collective character of its individuals. The collective is of course made up of individuals. So it is no surprise that educators and policy makers who want to shape the future of society concern themselves with character development. Periodically, concerns about citizenship and character education emanate from government, think tanks, and policy makers. The Bush Administration's *No Child Left Behind* policy (http://www.ed.gov/nclb/landing.jhtml) mandates a renewed emphasis on civic education and a return to the 'traditional' history curriculum in the context of their prescriptions for character education. According to this massive federal document, the Department of Education planned to launch a national campaign to promote character development and citizenship within schools, with an emphasis on reminding schools of their patriotic mission. Part of this initiative included high profile activities such as the Pledge Across America[i] to encourage patriotism. These efforts seem geared towards instilling unquestioning patriotism in US students, just as the narrow and prescriptive approaches to citizenship education during times of massive immigration in the early part of the century were designed to 'Americanise' the mostly southern European, Catholic immigrants.

At the other end of the political spectrum, more progressive educators have joined the debate about how to cultivate citizenship. The Forum for Education and Democracy:

> supports research, publications, and action projects which promote the democratic purpose of public education. The Forum works on behalf of a system of public education that is vibrant, equitable, and consistent (sic) with our belief in a government of, for, and by the people. We believe in and work for schools that nurture in all children the habits of heart and mind that make democracy possible. (http://www.forumforeducation.org/)

The Pledge Across America and the Forum for Education and Democracy represent genuine differences over what it means to be a citizen, about the nature of a pluralistic society, over the relative emphases on diversity and unity, and over the content and process of the social curriculum. Recent bitter debates over the history standards illustrate the kinds of meanings that are at stake.[ii] Framed in conservative/liberal educational terms, the opposing viewpoints pit people who prefer a traditional, 'facts-based', chronological history curriculum against those who advocate the teaching of 'inquiry' skills and a multicultural approach to the social studies. The traditional curriculum emphasises awareness of the textual artefacts of the US democracy, including the Constitution and the Bill of Rights, the "bonds in our political heritage that have brought Americans together" (Marciano, 1997, p. 33), loyalty to the existing political and economic system, patriotism, and acknowledgment that America is the standard bearer for liberty, democracy and freedom in the world. Proponents of the traditional approach to citizenship education worry about the current emphasis on cultural diversity that has, they say, fractured our national identity. They worry about the turn to a 'social history' that illuminates the daily life and struggles of historically marginalised groups (African–Americans, women, gays and lesbians), and about cultural 'relativism'. In very general terms, conservatives support the transmission model of education, a model that upholds the authoritative knowledge and values of the past. Liberals tend toward a curriculum that values critical thinking about authority so that students can "fulfill the democratic ideal of shared political sovereignty among citizens" (Salomone, in Ravitch & Viteritti, 2001, p. 222).

In these times of national crisis, of continuous war, and the erosion of civil liberties, we will likely see increasing educational efforts to forge consensus around 'traditional' values and national policies. Let us be reminded here of the etymological similarities between *patriarchy* and *patriotism*. At the root of both is loyalty to the father, or the fatherland. Traditional family values that place the woman as secondary, with primary responsibilities in the reproductive sphere, and national policies that emphasise loyalty over critical thinking are not unrelated. I believe that the call to return to the traditional curriculum represents little more than the effort to "manufacture consent" (a phrase coined by Walter Lippman and later used by Herman & Chomsky, 1988) to dominator values, so as to enable the continuing trajectory toward global economic and military domination. If we hold a different social vision, a vision of global peace and justice, we will need to offer up an alternative set of curricular aims and purposes. The ascension of partnership values will require us to think against the prevailing policy winds and direct our creative imaginations towards what it might mean to be a citizen of a partnership society. This will require rethinking many taken–for–granted aspects of modern education, including the necessary intellectual foundations for citizenship, the habits of mind necessary for critical analysis of issues, and the skills and dispositions that need to be cultivated in order to participate effectively in democratic life. If we are to bring a partnership society into being, then the democratic character we cultivate must necessarily be inclined towards strong democracy and active engagement in public issues. Here, I want to elaborate on this concept of *strong democracy*, and contrast that with our present *weak democracy*.

Scholars from different disciplines are now talking about a multi-faceted *crisis of democracy* (Trend, 1996). Factors they point to include the decline of voter participation, the growing gap between rich and poor, the globalisation of the economy, and the concentration of the media (McChesney, 1999), to mention just a few. This crisis of democracy is connected to a well-documented sense that our communities are losing their coherence and meaning. Bellah, Madsen, Sullivan, Swidler and Tipton (1985) point to individualism, isolation and fragmentation as root causes of the turn away from participation in public life. Robert Putnam, noted researcher on civil society and social capital, claims, "(t)here is striking evidence that the vibrancy of American civil society has notably declined over the past several decades" (1995, p. 65).

These problems are all connected to what might be called our 'weak democracy', a term applied to a citizenry that is content to limit their participation in governance to right to vote for people who will represent us in law making and governance. In one study, upper division college students were asked to list the most important citizenship skills they learned throughout their educational experiences. They invariably listed the five same 'skills': vote, obey the law, pay taxes, salute the flag, and say the Pledge of Allegiance (Andrzejewski, 1999, p. 3). I believe that this is a fairly accurate summary of what most students learn in their school experience about what it means to be a citizen, and that this is a fair characterisation of a system of democracy in which citizens are only minimally involved in governing themselves.

Given the multi-faceted crises in democracy, I want to suggest that a people who are only peripherally involved in their own governance are vulnerable to domination. A logical extension of this notion is that a weak democracy is consistent with the values of a dominator society. Hence, if we care about the future of democratic life and the development of partnership values, we need to shift from a *weak* notion of democracy to a *participatory* model, what Benjamin Barber (1998) calls *strong democracy*. These differing conceptions of democracy are contrasted in the following chart (Table 1).

Table 1. Conceptions of democracy

Weak democracy	Strong democracy
Citizens as consumers of government services, voters, and passive watchdogs to whom representatives are minimally accountable	Citizens as active, responsible, engaged members of groups and communities who participate in public affairs (Barber, 1998)
Private democracy	*Public democracy*
A tradition stemming from the philosophy of John Locke and later James Madison. Emphasises property rights and 'possessive individualism' (Sehr, 1997)	A minority strand in American democratic thought associated with Thomas Jefferson. Emphasises an engaged public involved in the affairs of government (Sehr, 1997)
Procedural democracy	*Deliberative democracy*
Emphasises the basic principles usually taught in civics classes: majority rule, due process, etc.	Emphasises free inquiry and debate over issues, aims at consensus
Formal democracy	*Deep democracy*
Emphasises voting, and participation in government through elected representatives	Emphasises democracy as a way of life characterised by empathy, equity, commitment, and connection (Green, 1999)

The conceptions of democracy on the left hand side of the chart represent a 'minimalist' approach to democracy, which characterises a population that is apathetic, cynical, ignorant, isolated and/or self-satisfied. A purely formal, or minimalist democracy, according to Judith Green, "is existentially unsustaining and culturally unsustainable, as well as ideologically subvertible" (1999, p. vi). The conceptions on the right side emphasise a more active, engaged population.

Moving from the currently dominant forms of private, procedural, formal, and weak democracy to the more robust participation suggested by public, deliberative, deep, and strong democracy implies important extensions of the concept and practice of democracy, broadening it from democracy within the constraints of the domination model to what democracy will, and can mean in the context of the partnership model. First, is an extension of rights and responsibilities to more and more citizens, many of whom have been marginalised or excluded in the past. One current example of this is the successful legislative campaign for domestic partnership rights by gay and lesbian citizens in Vermont and the extension of marriage rights to Massachusetts citizens. Second, it also suggests the extension of democratic practices to other cultural sites—from the voting booth into the workplace, the community, the school, the home. None of these extensions of democracy will occur without conflict, as we have seen from the various civil rights movements of the past. But while conflict in the dominator paradigm is enacted thorough such means as asserting authoritarian control, or through fear or violence, conflict in a partnership paradigm is resolved through the arts of deliberation, negotiation, and consensus building. Strong democracy in a partnership society will require a much higher level of participation and a deeper, more informed level of engagement with public issues.

SCHOOLING FOR DEMOCRATIC CHARACTER

Early progressive educators—John Dewey, Jane Addams, Lucy Sprague Mitchell, Caroline Pratt, Harold Rugg, Theodore Brameld, William Kilpatrick, and George Counts—were all committed to the idea of democracy as a moral way of living. In fact, the commitment to educating citizens for life in a complex democracy was most completely worked out by progressive educators in the early part of the twentieth century. In our frenzy to educate students for vocational roles in the emerging global economy, we have often forgotten this democratic mission of the schools. Dewey, Counts and other 'reconstructionists' believed that education had the capacity to reconstruct society by "creating individuals with a capacity for reflective thinking who will build a more equitable social order" (Harris, 1988, p. 23). Dewey thought that the identification of, and work on solving problems of social importance should be at the centre of a curriculum.

In more recent times, critical education scholars and social scientists—Apple, Anyon, Bourdieu, Freire, Giroux—have provided us with more sophisticated conceptual tools to bring to bear on social problems. 'Critical pedagogy' helps students critically question the dominant myths and ideologies that support inequitable and unjust social realities. Critical theorists introduced the idea of *hegemony*, or the way that one group dominates another through the control of knowledge. They revealed the nature of the *hidden curriculum*, or the way that the structures and processes of schooling perpetuate the dominant culture. They have helped us to understand the ways that the content of the curriculum reinforces a particular point of view, usually that of a dominant elite. Multicultural education provides us with some templates for understanding difference and celebrating the human diversity that makes up the world. Feminist theory has revealed the unhealthy power dynamics in patriarchal society, and provided practical pedagogical strategies for creating more equitable conditions. By themselves, these theories and practices have barely infiltrated modern education, with its increasing emphasis on test scores and adherence to externally imposed standards. But taken together, and combined with the important work in peace education by such scholar/activists as Betty Reardon (1978) and Ian Harris (1988), they inform a powerful democratic vision, capable of bringing us closer to the peaceful partnership society Eisler envisions. It is not coincidental that progressive education, multiculturalism, feminism, and critical pedagogy are all under attack from conservative educators who seek the return to the traditional curriculum and narrow versions of citizenship (see Ravitch, 2000).

Teaching for a strong democracy requires that we focus on the development of skills necessary for active participation in public life. Some of these skills involve critical thinking: the ability to think logically about issues and weigh evidence; the ability to question the motivations and interests underlying points of view, and detect bias; the ability to apply concepts to real life situations; the ability to 'stand outside' one's own value system, and understand it as socially constructed. All of these skills contribute to one's ability to come to just and justifiable conclusions about public issues.

In addition to the ability to think critically, citizens in a strong democracy must be able to deliberate about issues of concern. Deliberation requires interpersonal skills: the ability to listen actively and respond empathetically to the varied perspectives and opinions of others; the ability to negotiate differences; the ability to work together collaboratively and appreciate the varied skills and talents that others bring to a situation. Participation often calls up leadership capacities. Students who feel strongly about an issue need to have at their disposal the abilities to develop logical arguments, to write and speak coherently and persuasively, and the ability to make decisions that foster the 'common good', not just private gain.

In addition to outward motivation and the skills needed to participate in public problem-solving, the democratic character necessary for a partnership society has a tacit, internal dimension. John Dewey, America's most well known philosopher of democracy and education, spoke of democracy as more than just a government structure: "democracy is a way ... of personal life and one which provides a moral standard for personal conduct" (1989/1939, p. 101). Dewey knew, and tried to communicate through his writings that it is in the everyday interactions between people that a truly democratic culture blossoms. A more contemporary theorist of democracy, Judith Green, speaks of a deeper conception of democracy that:

> expresses the experience-based possibility of more equal, respectful, and mutually beneficial ways of community life and 'habits of the heart'—those characteristic, feeling-based, culturally shaped and located frameworks of value within which we perceive the world and formulate our active responses to it. (1999, p. vi)

Green's words speak to the tacit dimensions of deep democracy—the 'habits of the heart' that nourish the relationships upon which democracy must be based. These habits, or dispositions, include such attributes as a sense of connectedness and sociability, a sense of fairness and justice, care and concern for both friends and strangers, the desire to collaborate and work together to solve problems, the willingness to take the perspective of another, and the recognition of the fundamental equality of all people. In addition to this, a citizen of a deep democracy should be open-minded, and willing to incorporate new information into their belief system. They need to be self-confident, creative, and believe that they can accomplish things. They need to be free of the fear of conflict, and above all, they need to have a sense of humour to sustain them in the difficult work of building democracy.

The values of deep democracy—care, commitment, compassion and concern—are the very values necessary for the emergence of a partnership society. Imagine if our current leaders had all been educated to these 'habits of the heart'. Imagine that they used their public platforms to educate others to these habits of the heart. I am inspired by what I read about the emergence of a new sense of democratic possibility in the writings of such thinkers as Judith Green, Benjamin Barber, and Cornel West. These ideas, coupled with the passionate commitment of ordinary people like my neighbours and my teacher education students, make me hopeful that we can, collectively, effect change before it is too late.

DIFFERENT APPROACHES TO CITIZENSHIP EDUCATION

People of good will differ on how best to educate for democratic citizenship. Each of the approaches articulated below have strengths, and while all purport to educate students for citizenship, I believe that some are more promising than others in terms of educating for a partnership society.

The Academic Content Approach

This is the view that students develop into productive citizens through engagement with a rigorous, traditional (discipline-based) academic curriculum. According to Diane Ravitch, one of the proponents of this point of view, "democratic society itself is dependent upon the judgments of a majority, which suggests that everyone benefits by disseminating reason, knowledge, and civic wisdom as broadly as possible" (2000, p. 462). Though I agree with the ideal that 'high-status' knowledge should be widely available and accessible to all, I want to point out the obvious problems with a curriculum that is unrelated to student interests or concerns. To teach the academic disciplines without attention to the issues of student motivation, learning styles, and the multiplicity of 'intelligences' is to ignore Dewey's assertion that "the child and the curriculum are simply two limits that define a single process" (1964, p. 344).

Though I agree with theorists such as Paul Gagnon (1989) that an in-depth exposure to history and the humanities, for example, is crucial to the development of democratic citizenship, I worry that advocates of the academic content approach often present a one-sided view of history and culture. One of the most prominent advocates of this "liberal traditionalism" (Ravitch, 2000, p. 464) is E. D. Hirsch, Jr. (1996) who has attempted to define the 'canon'—what all students should know about Western culture—grade by grade. Critics of E.D. Hirsch's work point out that his canon privileges a particular (white, male, European, Christian, elite) cultural experience over a more diverse and representative set of perspectives. In a partnership society, the contributions of all people to our world need to be valued in the school curriculum, not just the achievements of those with dominator values.

Even more problematic, according to peace educator Ian Harris, is the idea that "traditional education glorifies war and does not teach pupils alternatives to war and violence" (1988, p. 27). This happens through the content of the curriculum, such as the emphasis on wars and military leaders in history, as well as through the process of teaching and learning. Students taught to assimilate information from their history textbooks, who are not encouraged to question the authoritative view, are not gaining the skill to question the policies of their government.

These serious concerns with the academic content approach do not diminish my interest in ensuring that all students, regardless of their perceived capacities, abilities, social class, or limited language skills, should have access to a curriculum rich in content.

Instillation of Loyalty and Patriotism

One school of thought popular in the nineteenth century, and obviously still dominant in some circles has as its main premise that "despite recurring problems and inequalities, the United States is and has been a democratic and humane society, in many ways the last and best hope for freedom and justice in the world" (Marciano, 1997, p. 31). Intellectuals such as Mortimer Adler (1987), William Bennett (1988), and Allan Bloom (1987) believe that students need exposure to the ideas of the Founding Fathers and the lofty ideals, such as duty, discipline, loyalty, obedience, and patriotism that have shaped our country. They acknowledge that there have been conflicts and contradictions along the way, but underemphasise our tragic past: the genocidal destruction of the indigenous people who were here before European colonisers, a system of slavery that lasted over a century, the suppression of women's political rights until 1920, the racism that blocked the achievements of African Americans until passage of the *Voting Rights Act* of 1965, and the exploitation of working people (Marciano, 1997). In his important work, *Civic Illiteracy and Education*, John Marciano documents the ways in which this approach to education indoctrinates youth, contributes to "historical amnesia" (1997, p. 196), and inhibits the development of critical thinking.

As noted earlier, the new federal educational mandate, *No Child Left Behind*, with its emphasis on the traditional history curriculum and activities such as the Pledge Across America, represents a mandate to educate for loyalty and patriotism. While I agree that attention to the ideals on which our society was founded—the ideals of liberty, equality, justice and rights—is important, I also believe that democracy is very much a 'work–in–progress', and that it is students' active engagement with such ideals, not merely an academic or doctrinaire acquaintance with them, that will influence their growth as citizens. And I agree with John Marciano (1997), Howard Zinn (1980) and Ronald Takaki (1993) who argue for the inclusion of diverse perspectives and a more honest and critical appraisal of our history in our curricula.

Study of How Governments Work

This approach equates politics with what governments and politicians do and understands the role of citizens as limited to voting or advocating for a particular interest or cause (Mathews, 1996, p. 270). A review of this type of civics education can be found in the CIVITAS report (Quigley & Bahmueller, 1991), published by the Council for Advancement of Citizenship and the Center for Civic Education. Some of the materials in this report assume that public apathy about politics is a sign of widespread satisfaction with the government.

Organisations like the Center for Civic Education are likely to play important roles in the new federal initiatives on citizenship education. Although I agree that it is important to understand the workings of power and decision-making, I believe that this approach to educating for democratic citizenship by itself encourages 'weak democracy'. However, when coupled with an active engagement with significant issues, the study of the way that governments work, and how power operates in our society, is a crucial component in citizenship education.

Critical Thinking and Moral Reasoning

Both the Second World War, with its fight against fascism, and the Cold War, with its fight against communism, alerted educators and policy makers to the need to educate students about how to resist propaganda. We "put our faith in 'critical thinking', meaning the ability to see through the manipulative arguments of our oppressors" (Mathews, 1996, p. 267). It was recognised that all political decisions were grounded in a particular set of values, so great attention was given to understanding the values of a democratic society. One aspect of this curricular intervention was called "values clarification"—a movement that generated its own heated controversies. Kohlberg (1996) and others promoted the idea that good civic education was the "stimulation of development of more advanced patterns of (moral) reasoning about political and social decisions and their implementation in action" (p. 211).

Through the 1970s and 1980s, there was less interest in agreeing on a core set of American values than there was in coming to terms with diversity, teaching creative uses of conflict, and conflict resolution. One of the best current examples of this educational approach is media literacy, a curricular intervention that teaches students to understand the kinds of social conditioning and yes—propaganda that bombard them through the media. Understanding the effects of images, advertising, and other media texts enables students to think critically about their world, understand the interests that operate in the shaping of consciousness, and resist corporate conditioning. In a strong democracy, citizens are called upon to work together to solve common problems, and critical thinking, reflective judgment, moral/and ethical reasoning, and conflict resolution are crucial to such efforts.

Direct Experience in Civic and Political Activity

Perhaps the most controversial of all the approaches, this method assumes, and many studies suggest, that students who experience active engagement with community service and direct political action are more likely to engage in civic activity later on in life (Berman, 1997, pp. 144–145). Berman notes a number of assumptions held by educators who advocate for this more active approach to civics learning. One is that students are not merely preparing for later citizenship, they *are* citizens now. Although they possess limited formal powers and privileges, they are quite capable of making genuine contributions to the welfare of their communities and the world. The second assumption, echoing Dewey's theory of experiential learning, is that genuine learning requires action to test the efficacy of one's theories about the world. A third assumption is that "students who are given greater responsibility develop a greater sense of responsibility" (ibid, p. 145). Research on 30 experiential education programs that included service–learning or community-based activity showed marked increases in student self-esteem, social competence, moral reasoning and social efficacy (ibid, pp. 145–146).

The most effective programs include a reflective component, so that students share their learning in discussions with their teachers and with other students. This last point reflects my belief that experiential learning activities, while often valuable in themselves, are strengthened by both a strong academic as well as a reflective component. Students volunteering at a homeless shelter or at a food distribution program benefit much more in terms of cognitive development if their curriculum includes a focus on the root causes of hunger and homelessness, and if they have ample opportunities to 'process' what they are learning both in terms of their first hand experiences and their encounter with rich academic content.

It should be clear from this limited review of existing approaches to citizenship education that there are many possible ways to educate for democratic character. I believe that the most effective approach is a comprehensive one that includes strong academic content, critical thinking and moral reasoning, active and collaborative engagement in political or civic activity, and meaningful reflection. In the stories below, drawn from research on students who are engaged in democratic problem-solving, you will see two very different examples of how students and teachers are actualising partnership values through the exploration of social problems.

NARRATIVES OF PRACTICE

Problem-solving through Literature

In a middle/elementary school in central Vermont, students in the 5th, 6th, 7th and 8th grades can take a class called Problem-Solving Through Literature, an alternative to a traditional English class (see Kesson, Koliba & Paxton, 2002). Using literary works, students identify with characters in the literature to gain insight into the character's situation, to learn how the character took action and developed strategies to deal with problems in life and, in many cases, how the character contributed to society. The students then apply what they learn from the characters to their own lives. The two teachers who oversee this project introduce students to metacognitive concepts such as Maslow's "hierarchy of needs" and Kohlberg's "stages of moral development", utilising these concepts in their analyses of literature and in reflecting upon their own experiences. Every topic of study has an activity that is based on academic considerations as well as personal exploration and involvement.

Students carry out various individually designed service–learning projects, often based on inspirational biographies of service-oriented individuals such as Eleanor Roosevelt. One student wrote a story and then published and sold it to get money for the battered women's centre. Some of them engage in teaching, such as the student who won a national award for teaching children with physical disabilities to ride horseback. By combining discussions about moral reasoning with the reading of literature and service–learning projects, these students learn the skills and dispositions of active democratic citizenship. They gain the ability to apply concepts to real life situations. These concepts are derived from the stories they read and applied to actions that they undertake as a part of their service–learning projects. By developing relationships with adult community mentors, students are afforded the opportunity to expand their intergenerational connections. This provides them with the "social capital" (Putnam in Ravitch, 2000, p. 58) that some researchers are now saying is so important to the cultivation of democratic character.

Service–learning is one important way that students develop the capacities of care, commitment, compassion, and concern so necessary to the cultivation of 'deep democracy'. In the next story, students carry their commitment to democracy even further, engaging in direct political action around issues of significant importance.

The Tar Creek Story

In a rural middle/high school in north-eastern Oklahoma, home to a population comprising numerous Indian tribal groups as well as whites, students participate in a service–learning club called the Cherokee Volunteer Society. The community in which these young people live is the site of one of the nation's worst hazardous waste sites, a result of extensive lead and zinc mining in the early part of the century. Tar Creek, which used to be a popular local site for swimming and fishing, runs orange in many places and neon green where sewage flows into it. The countryside looks like a surreal moonscape, dotted with acres and acres of toxic mine tailings, some 200 feet high. Abandoned mines honeycomb a 40 square mile site, sometimes collapsing leaving huge sinkholes. Cancer, kidney disease, and immune deficiency diseases are common in this small community.

In 1995, students in the service–learning club began investigating the environmental problems in their community using the Internet, primary source documents, interviews with community members, and on-site analysis of water and soil. The students began, from their research, to identify some causal connections between the contamination in their community, chronic (and in some cases terminal) illnesses in their families, and some of their own learning disabilities. These students, many of whom had been disengaged from school and learning, became informed, passionate activists, reaching across generational, cultural, and school/community boundaries to communicate their learning and facilitate problem-solving.

The students we interviewed as part of this research project (see Kesson & Oyler, 1999) have developed many skills and capacities working on these various projects. Clearly, they have mastered the art of identifying significant problems in their community. They have learned to carry out research in the public interest, and to share their new knowledge in a useful and appropriate way. In addition to the science and math concepts necessary to their understanding of the problems, they have learned a great deal about the structures of civic life: practical things like how to write to legislators, contact government officials, organise cultural events, circulate petitions, engage in peaceful protest (they have on occasion picketed polluters in the community), and about public relations. For their many appearances on television, radio, at community meetings and at local, state, and national conferences, they have had to hone their public speaking talents. The students are the proud authors of two anthologies of creative and expository writing about the history and current problems of Tar Creek, both of which have been published and distributed by the Cherokee Nation. The success of this project is indicated by the fact that it is sustainable (the project has been on-going for seven years now, despite changes in the student and teacher population). The school was chosen as a Leader School in Oklahoma for its admirable work in environmental education.

CONCLUSION

Both of the above stories deal in significant ways with questions of value. I highlighted them because I believe that they demonstrate approaches to citizenship education that foster partnership values. People get very nervous when they hear the word 'values' and the word 'education' in the same sentence. Whose values? they want to know. And rightly so. Any set of values represents contested terrain in education. As we have seen in the past, battles over such value-laden issues as diversity in the curriculum, quasi-religious school holidays, prayer in school, and sex education, to mention just a few, are fierce. Some people think that the curriculum and the teachers should be value-neutral, as if that were possible.

There is no getting around the fact that education in a pluralistic democracy is a complex moral undertaking. Indeed, educating for democracy is almost synonymous with educating for moral development. "Without a moral framework" asserts Stephen Goodlad, "there can be no such thing as democratic character, or indeed, democracy" (2001, p. 76). Kohlberg (1996), a leading researcher of moral development, concluded that civic, or political development was essentially a progression of increasingly complex moral thinking about the awareness of rights and principles of justice fundamental to our Constitution. Feminist scholars such as Nel

Noddings (1984) and Carol Gilligan (1982) have tempered this assertion with reminders that the 'ethic of care' is as important as the 'ethic of justice' in moral development.

In this chapter, I have tried to persuade you that the values of the partnership way share a great deal with emergent visions of a more participatory democracy. I have suggested that if we want to actualise the vision of a peaceful and just global society, we must make partnership values an explicit part of the educational discourse on moral development, character education, and citizenship. I have great faith in the capacities of teachers and other citizens to revitalise our democracy, in spite of the fact that dominator values seem stronger than ever. Those of us who teach, or as in my case, teach teachers, must go forth each day with this optimism, the faith that given the appropriate educational environment, students will grow up to be caring, critical thinkers who have a sincere interest in the welfare of humanity and want to do their part to make a better world. American civilisation, according to Cookson and Berger:

> ... is torn between two grand narratives. One narrative is based on manifest destiny, accumulation, and greatness. This is the America of the American eagle—proud, imperious, and even merciless. This grand narrative contrasts with the narrative of goodness. This American story is based on community, simple but sound values, and a fierce loyalty to justice ... If we pursue the narrative of greatness, our children will become economic and military warriors, blinded by pride of history and the struggle for dominance. If we help them learn the goodness narrative, they will create a just, humane civilisation, as the founders of the republic intended ... our children deserve an education worthy of their talent, hope, and goodness. (2002, pp. 149–150)

Fortunately, we educators are not alone in this task. Although the corporate media gives scant attention to grassroots democratic movements, there is undeniably a revitalisation of interest in building civil society. Thousands of NGOs and domestic civil society groups are organising to promote peace, environmental sustainability and global justice. Teachers who are part of this growing network of progressive activists find sources of strength, inspiration, and purpose to carry on the difficult, challenging, but rewarding work of educating young people to take an active role in transforming their society. If we are to bring about a partnership society, a civilisation based on a narrative of goodness, then we will have to form partnerships, locally, nationally and internationally with people who care about our common future. Perhaps the early progressive educators such as George Counts (1932), who challenged teachers to "build a new social order", overestimated the power of education in the transformation of the world. Then again, if education were not such an important site of social change, it would not be fought over so bitterly. People with dominator values understand the importance of education. I hope that people with partnership values will also make their voices heard in the coming debates over citizenship, character education, democracy, and the curriculum of our schools.

NOTES

[i] The Pledge Across America was organized by Celebration USA, a nonprofit organisation created to strengthen instruction on the basic principles of American democracy in America's classrooms. On 12 October, 2001, students, teachers, parents were encouraged to participate in a synchronized Pledge of Allegiance to demonstrate their patriotism.

[ii] For one perspective on the battle over the history standards, see Diane Ravitch, with Arthur Schlesinger, Jr. (1996, 3 April), The New, Improved History Standards, *Wall Street Journal*.

REFERENCES

Adler, M. (1987). *We hold these truths: Understanding the ideas and ideals of the Constitution.* New York: Macmillan.

Andrzejewski, J., & Alessio, J. (1999). Education for global citizenship and social responsibility. In K. Kesson (Ed.), *Progressive perspectives* (Vol. 1, Issue 2). University of Vermont, The John Dewey Project on Progressive Education. Retrieved from www.uvm.edu/~dewey

Barber, B. (1998). *A place for us: How to make society civil and democracy strong.* New York: Hill and Wang.

Bellah, R., Madsen, R., Sullivan, W. M., Swidler, A., & Tipton, S. M. (1985). *Habits of the heart: Individualism and commitment in American life.* New York: Harper and Row Publishers.

Bennett, W. (1988). *Our children and our country: Improving America's schools and affirming the common culture.* New York: Simon and Schuster.

Berman, S. (1997). *Children's social consciousness and the development of social responsibility.* New York: State University of New York Press.

Bloom, A. (1987). *The closing of the American mind: How higher education has failed democracy and impoverished the souls of today's students.* New York: Simon and Schuster.

Cookson, P. W. Jr., & Berger, K. (2003). *Expect miracles: Charter schools and the politics of hope and despair.* Cambridge, MA: Westview Press.

Counts, G. S. (1932). *Dare the school build a new social order?* New York: The John Day Co.

Dewey, J. (1989/1939). *Freedom and culture.* Buffalo, NY: Prometheus.

Dewey, J. (1964). The child and the curriculum. In R. D. Archambault (Ed.), *John Dewey on education* (pp. 339–358). Chicago: University of Chicago Press.

Eisler, R. (1987). *The chalice and the blade: Our history, our future.* San Francisco: Harper & Row.

Eisler, R. (2000). *Tomorrow's children: A blueprint for partnership education in the 21st century.* Boulder, CO: Westview Press.

Eisler, R. (2002). *The power of partnership: Seven relationships that will change your life.* Novato, CA: New World Library.

Gagnon, P. (1989). History's role in civic education: The precondition for political intelligence. In W. C. Parker (Ed.), *Educating the democratic mind* (pp. 241–262). New York: State University of New York Press.

Gilligan, C. (1982). *In a different voice.* Cambridge, MA: Harvard University Press.

Goodlad, S. J. (2001). Making democracy real by educating for an ecocentric worldview. In R. Soder, J. I. Goodlad, & T. J. McMannon (Eds.), *Developing democratic character in the young* (pp. 69–92). San Francisco: Jossey-Bass.

Green, J. M. (1999). *Deep democracy: Community, diversity, and transformation.* New York: Rowman & Littlefield Publishers, Inc.

Harris, I. M. (1988). *Peace education.* Jefferson, NC: McFarland & Co.

Hart Research Associates. (1989). *Democracy's next generation: A study of youth and teachers.* Washington, DC: People for the American Way.

Herman, E. S., & Chomsky, N. (1988). *Manufacturing consent: The political economy of the mass media.* New York: Pantheon Books.

Hirsch, E. D. (1996). *First dictionary of cultural literacy: What our children need to know.* New York: Houghton Mifflin Co.

Hoffert, R. W. (2001). Education in a political democracy. In R. Soder, J. I. Goodlad, & T. J. McMannon (Eds.), *Developing democratic character in the young* (pp. 26–44). San Francisco: Jossey-Bass.

Kesson, K., & Oyler, C. (1999). Integrated curriculum and service–learning. *English Education, 31*(2), 135–149.

Kesson, K., Koliba, C., & Paxton, K. (2002). Democratic education and the creation of the just and loving community. In J. S. Thousand, R. A. Villa, & A. I. Nevin (Eds.), *Creativity and collaborative learning: A practical guide to empowering students and teachers.* Baltimore: Paul H. Brookes.

Kohlberg, L. (1996). Moral reasoning. In W. C. Parker (Ed.), *Educating the democratic mind* (pp. 201–221). New York: State University of New York Press.

Marciano, J. (1997). *Civic illiteracy and education: The battle for the hearts and minds of American youth.* New York: Peter Lang.

Mathews, D. (1996). Reviewing and previewing civics. In W. C. Parker (Ed.), *Educating the democratic mind* (pp. 265–286). New York: State University of New York Press.

McChesney, R. W. (1999). *Rich media, poor democracy: Communication politics in dubious times.* New York: The New Press.

Noddings, N. (1984). *Caring: A feminine approach to ethics and moral education.* Berkeley, CA: University of California Press.

Putnam, R. (2001). Community-based social capital and educational performance. In D. Ravitch & J. P. Viteritti (Eds.), *Making good citizens: Education and civil society* (pp. 213–232). New Haven, CT: Yale University Press.

Putnam, R. (1995). Bowling alone: America's declining social capital. *Journal of Democracy, 6*(1), 65.

Quigley, C. N., & Bahmueller, C. F. (1991). Civitas: A framework for civic education. *National Council for the Social Studies Bulletin, 86,* Center for Civic Education.

Ravitch, D. (2000). *Left back: A century of failed school reforms.* New York: Simon & Schuster.

Reardon, B. (1978). *Militarization, security, and peace education: A guide for concerned citizens.* Valley Forge, PA: United Ministries in Education.

Salomone, R. C. (2001). Common education and the democratic ideal. In D. Ravitch & J. P. Viteritti (Eds.), *Making good citizens: Education and civil society* (pp. 213–232). New Haven, CT: Yale University Press.

Sehr, D. T. (1997). *Education for public democracy.* New York: State University of New York Press.

Takaki, R. (1993). *A different mirror: A history of multicultural America.* Boston: Little, Brown and Company.

Trend, D. (1996). Democracy's crisis of meaning. In D. Trend (Ed.), *Radical democracy: Identity, citizenship, and the state* (pp. 1–18). New York: Routledge.

Zinn, H. (1980/1995). *A people's history of the United States: 1492–present.* New York: Harper Perennial.

Kathleen Kesson is Professor of Urban Childhood Education at the Brooklyn Campus of Long Island University, where she teaches courses in the foundations of education and teacher research. She is co-author, with Jim Henderson, of Curriculum Wisdom: Educational Decisions in Democratic Societies *(2004) and* Understanding Democratic Curriculum Leadership *(1999), and editor, with Wayne Ross, of* Defending Public Schools: Teaching for a Democratic Society.

She is also the author of numerous book chapters, book reviews, and academic articles in such journals as Teachers College Record, Encounter: Education for Meaning and Social Justice, *the* Journal of Critical Education Policy Studies, English Education, Journal of Curriculum Theorizing, Curriculum Inquiry, *and the* Holistic Education Review. *Her interests are in the areas of democracy in education, critical pedagogy, aesthetics and education, and teacher inquiry and reflection.*

PART THREE

ALTERNATIVE FUTURES

PATRICIA KELLY

11. *GLOBO SAPIENS*—'WASTE OF TIME' OR WORK IN PROGRESS?

Sustainability education rhetoric is inspiring and the work is essential, but most teachers don't work in ideal contexts, so it is important to share our successes and failures. I share learnings from using Reflective Journals as a core strategy to support first year engineering students on their journey to becoming critically reflective, responsible, wise global citizens—*Globo sapiens*.

My six years' research showed that 65 per cent of students were Accepters, willing to change, 26 per cent were Converts from regarding the subject as a 'waste of time' to seeing it as beneficial and useful, and 9 per cent were Resisters all the way. Learnings included my own journey from using the term Resisters, to understanding some reasons behind 'resistings' and responding more effectively.

Analysis of Sense–Making guided interviews explained how and why particular students resisted or reconstructed their worlds when challenged. Positive, values-based outcomes emerged through the interviews in such terms as 'got connected', 'got respect', 'got insight', 'got inspired', 'got courage', 'got healing' and 'got transformation'. The study has international relevance because it was based in large, socially and culturally diverse vocational student cohorts who were required to study a sustainability-based subject. This will be a likely norm if all higher education institutions take this UN Decade of Education for Sustainable Development (DESD) seriously.

INTRODUCTION: WHAT DO WE HAVE TO DO THIS FOR?

The UN Decade of Education for Sustainable Development 2005–2014 supports teachers at all educational levels who are working towards societies that choose to 'survive' rather than 'fail' (Diamond, 2005). This is a huge responsibility if one considers the challenges involved in 'holistic, participatory' education for "peace, non-violence, human rights, democracy, tolerance, international and intercultural understanding ... cultural and linguistic diversity" (Thaman, 2006, p. 1). What can educators do?

Thaman contextualised her response in terms of Pacific island cultures. Most teachers have to bridge gaps between these urgent calls for change at global levels and the realities of our work locally with real students in imperfect settings (Apple, 2001 in Singh, 2002). We may want to teach more effectively for change or we may be asked to teach a new subject in new ways. Perhaps the students are not responding positively. They may resent both the topic and its teacher, expressing in the ways appropriate in each context, what do we have to learn this for? Why can't we do it the old way? Like me, you may find this hard to answer, feel that it is your

M. Bussey, S. Inayatullah and I. Milojević (eds.), Alternative Educational Futures: Pedagogies for Emergent Worlds, 189–201.

fault and that *everyone* thinks it is a waste of time. It is important to share our research findings because even influential educators like Thaman report criticism that "cultural literacy and intercultural issues" are "wishy-washy and a drain on resources" (2006, p. 14). This paper offers a short summary of some empirically research-based answers to these powerful and destructive criticisms.

My response is based on six years' doctoral research with large (300+), multicultural cohorts of first year engineering students studying a compulsory Professional Studies unit for one semester in an Australian university of technology. Over a 12 week semester, I used Reflective Journals (11 entries of 300 words) and online support (among other strategies) to create a supportive space or 'oasis'. I wanted students to feel confident to share the multiple 'knowings' they brought with them, if they chose to, as valued and valuable (Kelly, 2006a, 2006b).[1] This was based on my own values, as well as evidence that "harmonizing old way, new way" learnings is a more effective form of learning in cross-cultural contexts (Baker & Taylor, 1995). Each Reflective Journal was based on a Professional Practice and Communication lecture, associated readings and tutorials on topics aimed to encourage the development of sustainability professionals. Professional practice and communication was only one of three modules in the unit, BNB007, the other two being Generic Computing and Engineering Graphics. All modules culminated in a group project responding to the current United Nations International Year of (Water, Rice, etc). Personal journals are a powerful learning and teaching strategy and they are an integral aspect of UNESCO's interactive teaching materials, but they need to be used with caution. My work contributes to understanding how Reflective Journals, used effectively, can form part of a transformative pedagogy.

Here, I summarise and compare three possible guiding visions of the generic skills graduates need, including my preferred vision, *Globo sapiens*. These are analysed in more detail elsewhere (Kelly, 2006, 2007). I then explore the three main types of student responses, *Accepters*, *Resisters* and *Converts*, outline how these can be helpful and explain how I moved from seeing Resisters to 'resistings'. Based on the Sense–Making guided interviews with students, I offer some brief examples of how transformative learning occurred and the broader significance of several 'uses' to which they put their new learning. I conclude with a critical comment on the direction taken by most higher education institutions.

GUIDING VISIONS: GLOBALLY PORTABLE, GLOBALLY COMPETENT, *GLOBO SAPIENS*?

What sort of graduates do we want? What vision guides us? I originally used 'globally portable' as a catch-phrase because it linked to employment and I could 'justify' the approach to students and the faculty, as 'useful'. Globally portable is usually expressed in lists that include "Leadership skills, Fluency in English, Ability to work with others, Depth of work experience and Communications skills" (Frankenstein, 1997, p. 34). I became concerned that portability denoted an end 'product' in a marketised version of globalisation in which borders are porous in relation to the movement of capital and those able to create it, but resistant to people or ideas considered irrelevant, such as refugees, social justice or equity. Globally portable graduates or *Homo economicus* 'apply' their 'skills' to 'ends laid down' by their employers (Sharp & White, 1968, p. 15, cited in Kenway & Langmead, 1998, p. 30). The missing dimension in both workers and the term is the *integration* of values, ethics and responsibility. Education may engage the head and the hands, but there is no heart. This has led to skilled professionals who can design gas chambers, 'bomblets' designed to lure children to their destruction and 'mini-nukes' (Sterngold, 2003).

Table 1: The attributes of three possible graduate visions

Globally Portable: Homo economicus	Globally Competent: Homo globalis	Wise' Global Citizen: Globo sapiens
Gendered—male	Gendered—male	Gender inclusive
Attributes	Attributes (subsumes those of Global Portability +)	Attributes (subsumes those of Global Portability and Global Competence)
Leadership skills Fluency in English Ability to work with others Depth of work experience Communication skills Creativity (Frankenstein, 1997, p. 34).	Substantive knowledge Perceptual understanding Capacity for personal growth Ability to develop international, interpersonal relationships Ability to act as a cultural mediator (Wilson, 1994, p. 41).	S/he will be "… sensitive to the different ways we learn from each other and know the world" and "able to exercise imagination in order to "feel for and with the other" (Inayatullah, 2002; Brennan, 2005). S/he will show evidence of global consciousness (Markly, 2002, p. 340). S/he will be able to contemplate changes to their current way of life, rather than taking its continuation for granted. S/he will be capable of trans-generational thinking. S/he will be a person of courage/ "Critical being" (Barnett, 1997, p. 173) / "Parrhestiastes" (Foucault in Sidhu, 2006). S/he will work towards healthier futures, from the personal to the spiritual (Inayatullah, 2002).

This problem led me to 'global competence' or *Homo globalis* (global man) (sic). This broader term includes some awareness of an interdependent and multicultural world. This has been adopted by managers of transnational companies because of its potential to help avoid some of the risks of doing business in global markets.

From this perspective, cultural knowledge is only useful when it serves personal and company ends (Guirdham, 1999; Waddock & Smith, 2000; Sullivan & Tu, 1995). More useful understandings of global competence include Wilson's five attributes (1994) and the concept of graduates as citizens of a civil society (Annette, 2005; Crick, 2005; Nunan, George, & McCausland, 2000; Paranjape, 2000; Heath, 2000).

These concepts were useful but I saw deficiencies which encouraged me to develop a broader and more explicitly values-based vision from Malaska's term *Globo sapiens* (1997).[ii] I developed this in an education context to mean reflective, reflexive professionals united by a common sense of global responsibility, 'wise' global citizens. The core word is 'wisdom', which is rich in potential cross-cultural understandings and deserves more attention.[iii] By *Globo sapiens*, I mean graduates with not only the skills and attributes of Global Portability and Global Competence, but also with qualities and understandings that will prepare them to engage in thinking, dialogue and action around preferred, sustainable, critical and multicultural futures. *Globo sapiens* is one evolving, guiding vision, not an end in itself. As Table 1 shows, *Globo sapiens'* qualities build on and offer a more global form of Bellah's "democratic habits of the heart", "respect for others, self-respect, willingness to accept responsibility for the common good, willingness to welcome diversity and to approach others with openness" (1985, in Mezirow, 2000, p. 14).

HOW DID STUDENTS RESPOND?

My research findings are based on the results of three pre- and post- intervention questionnaires, two of which were paired for better comparison; Reflective Journals from consenting students between 2000 and 2004; and Sense–Making guided interviews with students from a variety of social and cultural backgrounds, including females, international and domestic students, mature-age students and school leavers. Although I will not detail them here, the surveys revealed that moderate to significant changes were taking place in students' attitudes to a variety of important issues, including cultural and gender issues and the importance of sustainability to the engineering profession.

I had no preconceived ideas of what, if anything, students' reflective journals might reveal in an Engineering context. The categories 'Accepters', 'Resisters', and 'Converts' are terms I used after similar responses emerged in the 1999 and 2000 journals (letting the data 'speak', in Grounded Theory terms). As Table 2 below shows, an average of 65 per cent of all students were *Accepters*, willing to change, 26 per cent were *Converts* from regarding the subject as a 'waste of time' to seeing it as beneficial and useful, and 9 per cent were *Resisters* all the way.

Accepters were either "willing" or "grudging". Willing accepters were optimistic and enthusiastic from the beginning, using words such as "hope", "positive", "ready" and "willing". Grudging Accepters were dubious about reflective journals but willing to try. This initial willingness, despite doubts, marked the difference between an accepter and a convert. Resisters, "angry", "arrogant", "threatened" or "unthinking", also tended to say similar things in similar ways. Early evaluations included comments which were rude, contemptuous, sarcastic and/or sexist. This is not unusual (Burrowes, 2001, p. 36). Although consistently the smallest group (average 9%), they confidently claimed to speak for the "overwhelming majority", who they asserted, disliked the unit, hated the journals and only wrote what they had to in order to pass. They saw no need to learn communication skills by communicating but preferred an examination in place of assessed tutorial exercises, Reflective Journals or projects.[iv]

Table 2: Numbers of Resisters, Accepters and Converts compared across five years

	2001 [316 total]	2002 [344 total]	2003 [429 total]	2004 [369 total]	2005 [335 total]
Accepters	93 = 66%	99= 71%	77= 56%	24 =63%	50 = 68%
Converts	35 = 26%	29 = 21%	47 = 34%	10= 26%	19 = 25%
Resisters	12 =9%	12 = 9%	13= 9%	4 = 11%	5 = 7%
	n= 140	n = 140	n = 137	n= 38	n =74
	45% cohort	39% cohort	32% cohort	10% cohort	22% cohort

Converts were the significant group, average 26 per cent of students, who realised and were able to acknowledge that even if they didn't like Reflective Journals or the unit, they had benefited.

> I will admit that I was one of many students that absolutely hated the idea of having to write a reflective journal week in week out about a topic that I probably hadn't thought about until it was presented in the lecture. Truthfully, I still do not like to take the time and sit done[v] and write the reflective journals. However, I can honestly say that I have gained so much from these journals and have learnt to truly express how I feel about these particular topics week in week out. (Male, ESB, 2002, Convert)

They could be "gradual" converts, who fitted Mezirow's 'incremental' model, "a progressive series of transformations in related points of view that culminate in a transformation in habit of mind" (2000, p. 21) or "sudden" converts. Mezirow's second or "epochal" level of transformation is "a sudden, dramatic, reorienting insight" (2000, p. 21).

WHY IS THIS USEFUL?

Challenges to the status quo, whether through gender, culture, age, content, teaching and learning styles, are correctly perceived as threats and may be strongly resisted by those who benefit most from its continuance (Tonso, 2001, p. 162). The reflective journals raised the issue of power in the learning environment because they created an equalising situation. Resisters exercise a powerful negative influence on others in lectures and online, because in cultural terms, they see only *their* perspectives or norms of behaviour, representing the dominant view so loudly and with such certainty that other students (and teachers) tend to believe it as well. For example, fear of expressing feelings was not peculiar to Resisters, but they were a large influence on it not being 'cool' to say something positive or praise the unit.

> Before I finish this journal, I'm going to reveal something about myself that I would never tell my mates. I've started to write personal journals about myself on a weekly basis. These journals are not for uni, but rather, for myself. SEE, BNB007 HAS HAD AN EFFECT ON ME and I'm positive that it is a good one. (Male, Bi-cultural, 2001, Convert) [emphasis in original]

It is important to recognise that the majority of students were Accepters, many of whom used the learning opportunities to move gradually or dramatically towards new ways of thinking or transformation. "Through this learning journey I have developed a new perspective on life" (Female, ESB, 18, 2004, Accepter).

Supportive relationships and environments play a crucial role in transformation (Taylor, 2000, pp. 307–8, Barnett, 1997, p. 164). We have to want to change and this 'conative' or motivational aspect is influenced by our relationships with those around us at various levels and how power is exercised in those relationships. Recent community research highlighted the "peer group's supportive impact" on "individual learning and confidence-building" (Taylor, 2005, p. 8). This is one compelling reason why Resisters should be made aware, in respectful ways, that their opinions are not those of the majority. A supportive environment also makes "possible a more confident, assured sense of personal efficacy, of having a self or selves—more capable of becoming critically reflective of one's habitual and sometimes cherished assumptions, and of having the self-confidence to take action on reflective insights" (Mezirow, 2000, p. 25).

> I thought this tutorial activity was extremely beneficial as it made me sit down and actually think about my traits and my strengths and weaknesses. Now that they have been brought to my attention, I can do something about them. (Male, ESB, 18, 2002, Accepter)

Among other benefits, the teaching approach supported students to 'feel' and the journals gave them opportunities to practice expressing those feelings: "I love to see improvements in everything … in particular myself. This subject helps me to feel comfortable about that" (Male, ESB, 2001, Accepter).

SENSE–MAKING: FROM RESISTERS TO RESISTINGS

The typologies were useful to gain a perspective on what had seemed like massive resistance, but without further research they could have stagnated into unhelpful 'labelling'. Reading the students' journals began my transformation as their teacher, but the Sense–Making-guided interviews enabled me to gain deep understandings of what lay behind some of the resistance and apparent transformations. Sense–Making (capitalised) is a meta-theory that also guides a methodology and methods (Dervin,

2003). It moves attention from nouns to verbs, seeing every moment as a move through space and time. In any given 'situation', we may confront a question or 'gap' and are either 'helped' or 'hindered' in our efforts to bridge that gap, leading to new 'uses' or 'helps'. 'Uses' are "the ways in which the individual puts the newly created sense to work in guiding his or her behaviour" (ibid, p. 256). Responses may also involve retreating or doing nothing. Establishing 'gaps' is useful for teachers because it helps to identify what questions students have and where in they occur in the learning process.[vi] As I moved my focus to the students' 'resistings', it helped me change from seeing "Resisters" as aggressive 'blockers', to considering what was blocking *them*. I then had the confidence to spend more time addressing these blocks and less on being defensive or blaming.

Since we need to be flexible in order to respond to a new moment, Dervin highlighted the need for procedures to undo "rigidities" (2003, p. 190). Changing behavioural practices requires both awareness and access to the same opportunities for 'repetitive practice' that created the behaviour in the first place. This is more complicated where rigidities indicate the site of damage from prior "oppressive and hurtful learning conditions" as was true for some interviewees. Change for them entailed not simply awareness and practice, but "a self-controlled consciousness raising process" (Dervin, 2003, p. 191) that is, "an act of individual emergence from past circumstances" (ibid). This was made clear in the way interviewee *Geoffrey*[vii] described the gendered process by which he had become alienated from his feelings to the point where he said "I've never really had to acknowledge that they exist until now":

> When you're a male, you grow up, you've always got to be macho, you can't really cry in front of people or really express your feelings, which means that writing a reflective journal about your feelings is extremely difficult, because you haven't actually decided whether they exist or not.

Highlighting 'resistings' rather than the attributes of Resisters, also acknowledged students' 'creativities' in making sense of their experience rather than the 'rigidities' that marked their behaviour. This avoided a negative and possibly self-perpetuating label for them. As I addressed their questions and confusions better, the resistings became less aggressive. Better identifying students' concerns and fears may have given them fewer reasons to feel defensive. The immediacy of electronic feedback also meant that they could complain or query something and get an answer rather than feeling like an invisible drop in a distant student sea.

Analysing the Sense–Making guided interviews allowed me to identify what sort of questions the interviewees had about the reflective journal process and the lecture topics and when support was most crucial. Sense–Making techniques also uncovered *how* and *why* particular students resisted or reconstructed their worlds when challenged. Positive, values-based outcomes emerged as "got connected", "got respect", "got insight", "got inspired", "got courage", "got healing" and "got transformation". "Got connected" was a significant use identified in previous research (Dervin, 2003). All but one interviewee (25/26) reported "uses" which I classed as "Got Connected, in relation to the identified 'questions' or gaps. Of 92 identified 'connectings' half were connecting to self and feelings (15%), or to others (37%). Other 'connectings' were to engineering (13%), to the issues (16%), to the environment, the world or life (14%) and to the past and future (4%). *Alex* connected "my life experience, my imagination and my work". *Yamaha* said, "You are touching people through who you are". Once 'connected' or more correctly, along with their connectings, students were helped to develop other "uses". There is only space here for two brief examples, one showing how a student "got courage" and one example of "got healing.

Courage is a "little-discussed phenomenon" that is essential to transformative learning (Taylor, 2000, p. 318). My study confirmed research identifying "four types of courage: to be, to believe, to feel and to do" (Lucas, 1994, cited in Taylor, 2000, p. 318). Associated aspects of courage are "encourage" and "discourage". Many more interviewees were encouraged (17) than discouraged (3). The journals encouraged students 'to have opinions' and to extend themselves. "... the articles that involved self-examination ... encouraged my thinking to turn inwards, and self analyse a bit" (*Bo*). "The agreement also encourages those reluctant to seek help on certain unit content to seek help and pass successfully in this unit" (*Fiza*).

My data reinforced Taylor's conclusion that transformative learning is not "autonomous and formal" but "more dependent on the creation of support, trust, and friendship with others" (2000, p. 308). For interviewee *Gir Bob*, the 'cultural sensitivities' lecture gave him the support and confidence to develop the courage "to be", while his comments reinforced for me as an educator, the power of formal statements about respect and diversity and the importance of being a diversity role model. In Sense–Making terms, it was a complete answer to my own question, "Why do I bother?" *Gir Bob* understood that "there would have been a racist in the lectures" and that the lecture was:

> getting it to one person and letting them know that their way isn't the only way and that the world is becoming more multicultural, just letting all those people know that there are other groups, that they see as minority groups, that they are in fact quite large and ... they think that they're only offending a small bunch of people but in fact they're, they're offending a mass, so just letting them know that this is out there. (*Gir Bob*)

It also encouraged students who wanted to change their racist attitudes. *Clarke*, a local English speaking background interviewee, had been sympathetic towards people suffering from racism but became more mindful in realising his dominant group privilege, "other people suffer, not me". His sympathy became empathy after his opinions were "reinforced" by the lecture on culture which, he said, "makes you want to make it better". Empathy nurtured and was, in turn nurtured *by*, successful team work.

Healing ourselves is an essential corollary of a healthy planet. Inayatullah argues that "health and healing" together are the defining dimension of the "next five hundred years ... (replacing 'strategy')", (2002, p. 142). Twelve of the interviewees or almost half (46%) reported experiences I identified as healing some past hurt, changing qualities they identified as not healthy for them, or a clearly expressed moving towards an integrated, holistic view of themselves. As *Alexander* expressed it, "I am a more complete human being". As I identified new "uses", particularly those discussed above, I could see the qualities of *Globo sapiens* they had developed or were developing.

Fien's research showed that while young people were aware of environmental issues, few were concerned enough to take the next step into action "for environmental protection in the future" (2004). The most significant indicator of a change of meaning perspective indicating transformation is "not only developing a revised frame of reference but a willingness to act on the new perspective" (Taylor, 2000, p. 297). So how do we foster transformative learning in an educational setting? (Taylor, 2000, p. 285). Transformations do not only follow a "disorienting dilemma" but can also occur from "integrating circumstances" (Clark 1991, 1993, cited in Taylor, 2000, p. 299). He summarised other characteristics of perspective transformation as a "revelation" including "new concepts of knowledge, mystical experience, personal power, and a redefined perspective followed by a sustained change" (Van Norstrand, 1992, cited in Taylor, 2000); "increase in personal power"; "spirituality"; "compassion for others"; "creativity"; "a shift in discourse"; "courage"; "a sense of liberation" and "a new connectedness with others" (cited in Taylor, 2000, p. 297).

Table 3 below lists examples of (epochal) transformation from the interviews, together with the characterising behaviour changes interviewees reported. I indicate in brackets which of these transformative categories each seemed to fit.

Table 3: Examples of transformation

Interviewees	Changes in "being" and "doing"
"Changed my life" [Alex]	"I read more—gives me something to do—gives me a chance to have input—makes me more a participant than a watcher—I participate rather than watch" [Alex]
	(Increased personal power/new connections)
"Just like reading those sorts of amazing facts, it hit me as a person, it hit me as a Pakistani, it hit me as an engineer, as a student, you know like, hey, might be able to make a difference to the world" [Fiza]	"… as an engineer I have a responsibility to conserve water, to respect the resources … to have a lot more respect for the world … I have a responsibility to the environment to the world … I can't have a long shower" [Fiza]
	(Revelation/increased personal power)
"that wasn't my responsibility"… I hadn't thought then just all of a sudden saw, Oh wow, I do have to worry about the environment. It is my responsibility" [Peter Parker]	"Made me a better engineer, a better person, more aware … who can better things for the long run" [Peter Parker]
	(Revelation/increased personal power)

CONCLUSION

Despite clear warnings, many universities proudly continue to hitch their wagons to the dying star of unsustainable, marketised futures, not noticing that the world they think they are serving is already moving in sustainable directions. "Relatively few institutions have made significant commitments to alter their campuses and even fewer have incorporated sustainability into their teaching and research" (Monastersky, 2006, p. 33).

My teaching aims were to set up a welcoming and respectful context for students with their diversities:
– to help them to communicate more effectively in writing, orally, interpersonally, interculturally;
– about issues that were important in the twenty-first century;
– as developing professional engineers;
– in a globalised context;
– but in a learning environment (oasis) that would nurture them to develop qualities and awarenesses enabling them to contribute to alternative, sustainable futures;
– as developing *Globo sapiens*, or wise global citizens and responsible professionals. My research showed that these aims were also the basis of a transformative pedagogy.

Whether we face "break-down" or "break-through" futures (Sterling, 2001, p. 22) will be influenced by graduates with the skills and qualities of *Globo sapiens*. Large, diverse, student cohorts, suddenly forced to study sustainability-based subjects, will be the norm if higher education institutions decide to take seriously this UN Decade. How many teachers and systems could confidently state that they understand the challenges such rapid change involves and are prepared to meet them?

ACKNOWLEDGEMENT

I am grateful to my colleague Professor Yoni Ryan, University of Canberra, for constructive comments which have improved this paper.

NOTES

i   The strategies are discussed in detail in the thesis, which is available online via Australian Digital Theses.
ii Malaska was describing the end product of a process by which new humans and non-humans would eventually coalesce into a new hybrid Internet progenitor "Grandpa and Grandma Internet", a "global mind with superior intelligence and wisdom" (1997).
iii Thaman contributes *"poto"*, meaning "wisdom and experience" with "intellectual, emotional and spiritual connotations" (Thaman, 1998 in Thaman, 2006, pp. 2-3). I engage with wisdom in more depth elsewhere (Kelly, 2006). See Tao (2004) for a Confucianist-guided approach to sustainability.
iv A similar group of 15 per cent "least amenable" to change have been identified in the general population and labelled "laggards" (Rogers, 1962, 1995 in Taylor, 2005, p.8).
v   Students' expression is uncorrected in all examples.

[vi] I cannot do justice to Sense–Making methodology here. As well as Dervin's book (2003), my understandings and comparisons of Sense–Making and my other methodology, causal layered analysis (Inayatullah, 1998, 2004) is detailed in other work (Kelly, 2005, Kelly, 2006).

[vii] (ESB, Male, 18) Students chose their own pseudonyms, italicised here. This admitted inability to express feelings was reported by female interviewees as well.

REFERENCES

Annette, J. (2005). Character, civic renewal and service learning for democratic citizenship in higher education. *British Journal of Educational Studies, 53*(3), 326–340.

Baker, D., & Taylor, P. C. S. (1995). *International Journal of Science Education, 17*, 695–704.

Barnett, R. (1997). *Higher education: A critical business.* Buckingham: SRHE and Open University Press.

Brennan, A. (2005). Globalization and the environment: Endgame or a 'new Renaissance'? In J. Paavola & I. Lowe (Eds.), *Environmental values in a globalizing world* (pp. 17–38). Abingdon, Oxford, UK: Routledge.

Burrowes, G. E. (2001). Gender dynamics in an engineering classroom: Engineering students' perspectives, *Engineering.* Australian Digital Theses Program: University of Newcastle, NSW.

Crick, R. D., & Wilson, K. (2005). Being a learner: A virtue for the 21st century. *British Journal of Educational Studies, 53*(3), 359–374.

Dervin, B., Foreman-Wernet, L., & Lauterbach, E. (Eds.), *Sense–making methodology reader: Selected writings of Brenda Dervin.* Cresskill, NJ: Hampton Press.

Diamond, J. (2005). *Collapse: How societies choose to fail or survive.* Melbourne: Penguin Group.

Fien, J. (2000). Young people and the environment: Implications of a study of youth environmental attitudes and education in the Asia-Pacific region for curriculum reform during the UN decade of education for sustainable development. UNESCO. Retrieved August 12 , 2006, from http://www.unescobkk.org/fileadmin/user_upload/esd/documents/workshops/kanchanburi/fien_young.pdf

Fien, J. (n.d.). *Teaching and learning for a sustainable future.* UNESCO. Retrieved August 12, 2006, from http://www.unescobkk.org/fileadmin/user_upload/esd/documents/workshops/kanchanburi/fien _tlsf.pdf

Foucault, M. (1984). *The Foucault Reader.* New York: Pantheon Books.

de Leo, J. (2006, May 1–3). Social and cultural perspectives of ESD: Cultural diversity and intercultural understanding with ESD. Paper presented to the UNESCO Expert Meeting on Education for Sustainable Development Reorienting Education to address Sustainability, Thailand. Retrieved August 12, 2006, from http://www.unescobkk.org/fileadmin/user_upload/esd/documents/workshops/kanchanburi/deleo_social.pdf

Frankenstein, J. (1997). The business of managing: The human factor. *Far Eastern Economic Review, 160*(37), 33–40.

Guirdham, M. (1999). *Communicating across cultures.* London: Macmillan Press.

Heath, P. (2000). Education as citizenship: Appropriating a new social space. *Higher Education Research and Development, 19*(1), 43–57.

Inayatullah, S. (1998). Causal layered analysis. Poststructuralism as method. *Futures, 30*(8), pp. 815–829.

Inayatullah, S. (Ed.). (2004). *Causal Layered Analysis Reader.* Tamsui, Taiwan: Tamkang University.

Inayatullah, S. (2002). *Questioning the Future: Futures studies, action learning and organizational transformation.* Tamsui, Taiwan: Tamkang University Press.

Kelly, P. (2008). *Towards Globo sapiens: Transforming learners in higher education.* Rotterdam: SensePublishers (Forthcoming).

Kelly, P. (2006a). Opening eyes and minds: teaching for social foresight in higher education. *Journal of Futures Studies, 10*(3), 1–14.

Kelly, P. (2006b). Letter from the Oasis: Helping engineering students to become sustainability professionals (revised). *Futures, 38*(6), 696–707.

Lowe, I. (2006, 1 August). Books: Climate change. *The Bulletin.* Retrieved November 11, 2006, from http://bulletin.ninemsn.com.au/article.aspx?id=141499

Kenway, J., & Langmead, D. (1998). Governmentality, the "now" university and the future of knowledge work. *Australian Universities Review, 41*(2), 28–32.

Malaska, P. (1997, 28 September–3 October). *Inventing futures.* Paper presented at the World Futures Studies Federation XV World Conference 'Global Conversations—What You and I Can Do for Future Generations', Brisbane.

Markly, O. W. (2002). Visionary futures: Guided cognitive imagery in teaching and learning about the future. In J. Dator (Ed.), *Advancing futures: Future studies in Higher Education* (pp. 330–341). Westport, CT: Praeger.

Mezirow, J. (2000). *Learning as transformation: Critical perspectives on a theory in progress.* San Francisco: Jossey-Bass.

Monastersky, R. (2006, November 29). Newborn in search of a niche. *The Australian,* 32–33.

Monbiot. G, (2006). *Heat.* Camberwell, VIC: Allen Lane (Penguin Books).

Nunan, T., George, R., & McCausland, H. (2000). Inclusive education in universities: Why it is important and how it might be achieved. *International Journal of Inclusive Education, 4*(1), 63–88.

Osamu, A., Deo, S., Elias, D., Fadeeba, Z., Gankhuyag, O., et al. (2005). *A situational analysis of education for sustainable development in the Asia-Pacific region/UN decade of sustainable development (2005–2014).* Bangkok: UNESCO.

Paranjape, M. (2000, September 1). Spirituality and globalisation. *Global Futures Bulletin,* 115.

Sidhu, R. (2006). *Universities & globalization: To market, to market.* Mahwah, NJ: Lawrence Erlbaum Associates Inc.

Singh, M. (2002). Rewriting the ways of globalising education. *Race Ethnicity and Education, 5*(2), 217–230.

Sullivan, S. E., & Tu, H. S. (1995). Developing globally competent students: A review and recommendations. *Journal of Management Education, 19*(4), 473, 421.

Sterling, S. (2001). *Sustainable education: Revisioning learning and change.* Totnes, UK: Green Books.

Sterngold, J. (2003, 21 May). Senate debates ban on small warheads 'Is half a Hiroshima OK?' losing Democrats ask. Retrieved from http://www.commondreams.org/headlines03/0521-10.htm

Tao, J. (2004). Relational resonance with nature: The confucian vision. In J. Paavola & I. Lowe (Eds.), *Environmental values in a globalising world: Nature, justice and governance* (pp. 66–79). London: Routledge.

Taylor, R. (2005, March 30). *Changing behaviour? New Zealand households learn to tackle practical sustainability (A working paper).* Paper presented at the EIANZ conference, Christchurch.

Taylor, E. W. (2000). Analyzing research on transformative learning theory. In J. Mezirow (Ed.), *Learning as transformation: Critical perspectives on a theory in progress* (Chapter 11). San Francisco: Jossey-Bass.

Thaman, K. H. (2006, May 1–3). Nurturing relationships: A Pacific perspective of teacher education for peace and sustainable development. Paper presented to the UNESCO Expert Meeting on Education for Sustainable Development Reorienting Education to address Sustainability, Thailand. Retrieved August 28, 2006, from http://www.unescobkk.org/fileadmin/user_upload/esd/documents/workshops/kanchanburi/thaman_pacific.pdf

Toh, S.-H. (2006, May 1–3). *Education for sustainable development & the weaving of a culture of peace: Complementarities and synergies.* Paper presented to the UNESCO Expert meeting on Education for Sustainable Development Reorienting Education to address Sustainability, Thailand. Retrieved July 28, 2006, from http://www.unescobkk.org/fileadmin/user_upload/esd/documents/workshops/ kanchanburi/toh_culture_of_peace.pdf

Tonso, K. (2001). "Plotting something dastardly" Hiding a gender curriculum in engineering. In E. Margolis (Ed.), *The hidden curriculum in higher education.* New York and London: Routledge.

Waddock, S., & Smith, N. (2000). Relationships: The real challenge of corporate global citizen. *Business & Society Review,* Spring, *105*(1), 47.

Patricia Kelly, FSEDA, is a critical futurist working in Higher Education. She has worked in cross-cultural curriculum development and academic staff development for the last 15 years. From 2006 to 2008 she managed a sessional staff development project for the University of Canberra. She is currently employed on a transnational education project for the University of Tasmania.

Her PhD used CLA and sense–making methodologies in her research into transformative education for engineering students. This work was published as Towards Globo Sapiens: Transforming Learners in Higher Education *(Rotterdam: Sense Publishers, 2008). She has published numerous papers relating to educating for sustainability. She is also interested in media education and has written numerous study guides for documentary films and videos.*

BASIL G. SAVITSKY

12. A TRANSFORMATIONAL PEDAGOGY FOR FUTURES STUDIES WITH A CASE STUDY IN BIODIVERSITY FUTURES

This chapter draws from activities and experiences in a one semester course on futures studies taught at Florida State University. The course is taught within the Department of Geography and Environmental Studies and is open both to seniors and to graduate students. During the first half of the semester, the 'inter-discipline' of futures studies is introduced, and nine specific tools are covered. Each tool is covered in a one hour lecture, and various individual and group homework assignments are geared to the implementation of specific tools. During the second half of the semester, pedagogy shifts from lecture to seminar, and various thematic topics are covered, including potential futures of energy, the environment, education, patriarchy and gender, youth, dissidence, and war and peace. The nine tools are applied to each of the specific themes and are an integral part of the term papers that students write on a futures topic of their choice. This paper reviews the nine tools and then covers the application of the tools to a single topic—biodiversity futures.

THE TOOLS

The nine tools include a mix of techniques drawn directly from the futures studies literature, models drawn from sociology, psychology, and religion, and methods that were developed by the author. The progression through the tools begins with techniques that are easy to apply and that are useful in organising a variety of facts, concepts, beliefs, and aspirations into a common framework to facilitate class discussions. As students master these first tools, more abstract and philosophical approaches are introduced. The first two tools are designed to facilitate a broad understanding of potential futures and to help develop the individual student's perspective on the future and on his or her relationship to perceived futures. The next four tools focus on institutional and societal change, and the last three tools emphasise the philosophical and metaphysical responsibilities of the individual. These nine tools were chosen based upon my previous experiences in three different classes—an earlier offering in futures studies, an information policy class, and a conservation geography class. The tools represent techniques that were most useful for students in internalising a variety of concepts and techniques that were valuable for me in the conveyance of deep sentiments in an academic context. Assignments

M. Bussey, S. Inayatullah and I. Milojević (eds.), Alternative Educational Futures: Pedagogies for Emergent Worlds, 203–221.
© 2008 Sense Publishers. All rights reserved.

associated with each of the tools alternate between individual exercises that are fairly straightforward to complete and group exercises that involve a bit more complexity.

Tool 1—The 200-Year Present

This approach was introduced in Boulding (1978). It places our current experience of the present day within the nexus of (a) information about the world that has been passed down to us from the elders we know personally, and (b) imagination about the world that we may exist in when we are elders and have grandchildren of our own. Students receive an individual homework assignment during the first week of class in which they are asked to interview their grandparents or the oldest people they know regarding the quality of their lives when they were children, the changes they have witnessed during their lives, their assessment of the world today, and their prognosis for the future. Students then partake in the first of four group assignments in which they rotate the duty of editor. In this assignment they compare the results of their individual interviews and synthesise their major findings in a brief report shared and discussed with the rest of the class via web-based discussion boards. Common themes that emerge include technological innovations, the speed of modern life, and changes in values associated with community, simplicity, or self-sufficiency. During the second homework assignment, individual students generate their own fantasy interviews playing the role of elder rather than interviewer, and have an opportunity to identify whether their vision of the future is optimistic or pessimistic. Generally, students find the first exercise to be very stimulating, but the second one to be challenging to the point of frustration. They are thus well-positioned for the use of the second tool that facilitates a more coherent organisation of their perceptions of multiple futures.

Tool 2—The 3 Ps (Probable, Possible, and Preferable Futures)

Amara (1981) introduced the concept of probable, possible, and preferable futures. I use a more narrow definition of each of these '3 Ps' than is commonly found in the literature. I define the 3 Ps using two continua between the probable and the preferable—a quantitative/qualitative continuum and a temporal continuum. The first continuum has the probable futures being those futures that are based primarily upon quantitative data. These futures are 'model-able', typically with computer software. The input to these models could include population growth rates (varying nationally), consumption trends of renewable and non-renewable resources (ranging from trees to oil and precious metals), and the capacities of pollution sinks (oceans, groundwater, and atmosphere). The output from these models is similar to the results generated by the simulations associated with *The Limits to Growth* (Meadows et al., 1972), *Beyond the Limits* (Meadows et al., 1992), and a variety of other approaches reviewed by Cole (1997). These types of models also address deforestation and fragmentation trends with output oriented towards projections of biodiversity loss. Likewise, a variety of global circulation models yield variable results in extent and timing of global warming. Although the variables and algorithms used in various models are debated by the scientific community, in general, the modeling approach has great credibility. On the other end of this first continuum is the conception of preferable futures. This work is done in a purely qualitative fashion. It is idealistic rather than realistic. Thus, there is a credibility continuum that is identical to the quantitative–qualitative continuum—the more qualitative and idealistic end of the spectrum of the 3Ps is the component that draws the references to futures studies as a crystal ball-gazing discipline.

The second continuum is temporal. Probable futures are typically short term forecasts (5 to 20 years) and are heavily reliant on the assumption that the near future will be very similar to the present. Thus, data and trends associated with present and recent conditions are useful in modeling, and the results are rarely controversial. It is within this domain that futures studies has much overlap with the discipline of planning and that futures studies got its initial disciplinary start. Preferable futures tend to span much longer periods. This may be due to the utopic nature of preferable futures—few believe that they can be reached any time soon, so 100 years or more would not be atypical for such futuristic 'visions'. Possible futures stand in the middle on both of these continua. They tend to mix quantitative and qualitative methods in an effort to go beyond the near future. There is a recognition that the element of surprise is more likely to be a factor in modeling the future, if the time span is in the order of 50 years. Thus, there is less confidence in the performance of possible futures, but they can be used to map out the range of conditions that can be anticipated. Such projects will often use the term plausible futures, not necessarily expecting any one of them to be privileged to occur, but knowing that any of them could occur. This approach is much less associated with predictions (as are probable futures) and more oriented to the deployment of scenarios. Typically, a variety of scenarios are generated using the worst-case and best-case outputs from the probable models to 'bookend' possible outcomes. The normative component of preferable futures is often more palatable within this context, because it is but one in a number of possible outcomes, and it is not perceived as excessively idealistic. Likewise, the need to pursue a utopic solution may become more apparent, because it is contrasted to a dystopic outcome. There is benefit to generating multiple scenarios between extreme conditions for several reasons. First, by identifying the best and worst case scenarios, there is a very good probability that reality will match something 'in-between'. Second, there is educational value to portraying a range of possible conditions, in order to display the range of outputs associated with modeled futures and to identify possible policy actions needed to avoid the worst-case results. Finally, 'muddling' towards the future is the most likely approach to be taken, unless surprise or crisis forces more serious changes. A centrist scenario is most likely to mirror the conditions of muddling. However, placing the centrist scenario in the context of extreme futures may provide policy guidance on signals of progress or deterioration if conditions associated with either extreme are encountered early.

Prior to the assignment for this tool, students are asked to broadly identify their topics for their term papers. Students are then assigned to groups with other students working on closely related topics. Each student is then asked to apply the 3 Ps to their paper topic. At this stage, students are not expected to collect or even know about all of the data sources that could be used to model their probable futures, but they are expected to ponder the data that would be needed. Likewise, students are not expected to generate multiple scenarios for possible futures, but they are expected to define the parameters that might be addressed in a single best-case and a single worst-case scenario. In terms of preferable futures, students relieve some of the frustration associated with the previous assignment both by developing a utopic future and by focusing on a single area rather than on multiple themes concurrently. Students are then asked to work as a group to synthesise their individual assignments, placing emphasis on the processes associated with each of the 3 Ps, rather than on attempting to summarise content associated with individual domain areas. These group documents are posted to the class website, and similarities and differences between group experiences are discussed. Typically, students find there to be a disconnect between probable and preferable futures that possible futures may or may not serve to bridge. Thus, students are well prepared to investigate the elements of individual and societal choices that have suddenly become more apparent in the degree of their impact upon future outcomes and that are an integral component of many of the following tools.

Tool 3—Reform, Transform, or By-pass

Changing the choices that we as a society make means changing the behaviour of our major institutions, whether those behaviours are market practices or governmental policies. This tool was influenced by a typology developed by Dahle (1998), and asks students to identify their degree of confidence in and loyalty to 'the system'. Transformers focus on changing the society, by-passers focus on building a new society, and reformers focus on changing the behaviour of the government and the market. Reformers tend to allow that the system is flawed, but they believe that it is reparable. Their motto is "you must work within the system to change the system". Transformers hold that the system is hopelessly broken and needs to be totally re-engineered, however they find that some of the parts in the existing system may be recycled. By-passers abandon the existing system to the extent that they possibly can and work towards the creation of alternative communities. By-passers tend to be apocalyptic, expecting imminent, or at least eventual, collapse of the system. If the operating myth is the phoenix to arise from the ashes, then by-passers expect to be a shaping force in the identity of the phoenix.

An individual assignment is provided in which students are asked to identify the category with which they most strongly identify, and to list examples of organisations or actions associated with each of the three categories. It should be noted that crossover categories (reformer/transformer or transformer/by-passer) are common and that students often indicate changes in their self-designation as the semester unfolds. Likewise, individuals may find that they are more predisposed to switch categories according to different lifetime phases, i.e., youth or retired may be more inclined to be by-passers, and householders may feel more obligated to the system during the peak of their careers. This tool is intentionally employed prior to Tool 4, because of the bias of the instructor for a transformative approach that becomes quite obvious in the presentation of the following tool.

Tool 4—Paradigmatic Trichotomies

This tool utilises the context of paradigm shifting to address the societal leverage that needs to be applied in order to successfully move away from possible dystopic futures and towards preferable utopic futures. The dominant paradigm associated with the worldview of corporate globalisation is disclosed as unsustainable and at the root cause of so many systemic failures; it is presented as an unwise culture that we must transcend (Slaughter, 1995). In order to reveal the nature of the dominant paradigm, we tend first to portray the historical antecedent to the current paradigm (whether it is perceived to be agricultural, tribal, or matriarchal) and then to select and champion an emerging body of thought that we hope will either displace the current model or be in position to carry humanity forward in the event of total systemic collapse. Thus, presentations of paradigm shifts are often trichotomised into the anachronistic, the current system, and the desirable. Three different trichotomies are examined, each characterising historical phases and cultural constituencies in a way that calls for societal transformation (Table 1). Each trichotomy can also be viewed as having past, present, and future components.

Table 1. Paradigmatic trichotomies

After Quinn (1999)	Abdullah (1999)	Ray and Anderson (2000)
Leavers	Keepers	Traditionals
Takers	Breakers	Moderns
Seekers	Menders	Cultural Creatives

The first trichotomy examined was put forth in the fictional Ishmael series (Quinn, 1992; 1996; 1997). In this typology, "leavers", or hunting and gathering members of pre-agricultural society are contrasted with "takers", who implemented a set of power relations that forced one class of people to till the land while another class kept the harvest under lock and key. In Quinn's model, the industrial revolution and information revolution characterised by Toffler (1981) as ushering in distinctive paradigms are simply different levels of impact of the consumption patterns and environmentally destructive behaviours of the taker mentality. Quinn (1999) does not call for a reversion to hunting and gathering, but he does call for an abandonment of the dominant culture through the creation of new tribal organisations; I define those who engage in the pursuit of this new culture as 'seekers'. The pedagogy of beginning with the leaver–taker–seeker trichotomy serves to place the concept of paradigm shifting in the broadest possible historical context. Additionally, it serves to exemplify the category of people who wish to change the impact of our current society by way of by-passing it.

The second model reviewed was developed in Abdullah (1999). This model has a temporal component to it, but seems more sociological than historical in its treatment of paradigms, in that it describes different constituencies that co-exist in modern society. The past is represented by the "keepers" who protect the 'old ways'. This includes indigenous peoples and the body of wisdom from which we should learn before it disappears altogether. The dominant society is comprised of "breakers" who are destroying the environment and the fabric of all other cultures and creating a homogenised culture full of violence and despair. The emerging category is that of the "menders". Menders do not envision a return to keeper ways, nor do they generally advocate abandoning the system, but rather believe in working within the system to heal the damage. The major principles that they work for are inclusivity and simplicity to create a world that 'works for all'.

The third model investigated is the "cultural creatives", defined by Ray and Anderson (2000). This team, comprised of a sociologist and psychologist, examined longitudinal survey data for over 100,000 Americans. They used these data to characterise an emerging set of values held by a group they labeled cultural creatives, an estimated 50 million Americans. These values include a global or synoptic perspective on issues such as the environment and women's rights, a propensity for the arts, self-actualisation and activism, and a reluctance to be pigeon-holed into either a liberal or conservative political party. The cultural creatives are contrasted to the mainstream "moderns" and to the conservative "traditionals". The moderns believe that the system is working well and that the status quo should be maintained. The traditionals hearken to simpler times and lament the fading sense of community, but also believe in strict lines of authority and fundamentalism.

Although they are by no means synonymous, the traditionals, keepers, and leavers share the minority perspective of the past. Modernists, breakers, and takers represent the present—they are in the majority, in power, clearly making a mess of things, and are often oblivious to the existence of the problem. Cultural creatives, menders, and seekers claim to represent the future, are also in a minority, will often cite the concept of critical mass, and can be expected to quote Margaret Mead on not underestimating what a handful of people can do to change the world.

In an individual assignment, students are first asked to identify examples (within the domain area of their paper topic) of activities, social processes, or organisations that are reflective of each of the components of the trichotomy of past, present, and future. Then they are asked to provide an essay response to the following questions: "Is a paradigm shift necessary to implement your definition of a preferable future in your domain area?", "Are we currently undergoing a paradigm shift or is this just rhetoric on the part of creative-mender-seekers?", "If a shift is underway, what evidence do you see to support that position?" and finally, "If a shift is not underway, what would be an example of an event that would indicate that we have actually begun to shift?"

Tool 5—Transformative Back-casting

This tool requires suspension of all dystopic futures. That we could fail as a species, and either foul our ecological planetary nest or destroy ourselves via our nuclear or bio-chemical arsenals, is conceded as a very real possibility. However, students are asked to set aside, just for the purposes of this exercise, all doubt, skepticism, and cynicism about humanity's ability to perform a full paradigm shift. Students are requested to recall their preferable futures and to imagine that we actually achieve a sustainable and harmonious existence on a planetary scale. What kinds of changes must have occurred in order for us to have reached such a transformation? Students are asked to work backwards from this utopic point, designing a flowchart or sequence of events that resulted in this desired future. Emphasis is placed upon the identification of potential 'early signals' of such a tide change including current organisations, websites, or individuals that could be harbingers of positive futures. Each individual is expected to bring their work within their thematic domain to their group, so that the group editor can summarise the similarities and differences in the approaches taken by the individual members. This document is then posted to the discussion board, in order to compare the results of different groups.

Tool 6—The Rail Ties

The metaphor of a railroad is used to characterise the parallel tracks of personal and societal transformation. The rail ties which both support and hold in place the rails of personal and societal 'work' are to be found in our communities, networks, and organisations to which we contribute. These ties provide a link between the individual and the entire world that: (1) helps to express and shape our individual identities, (2) enables us to do our part in crafting a world of our choosing, and (3) enables them to be experienced at a scale that is relationally meaningful and conceptually manageable.

This tool links societal change to the development of consciousness at the level of the individual. The tool builds upon a Buddhist concept, *paticca samuppada*, which refers to the dependent co-arising of all phenomena (Macy, 1991). Neither humanity nor the world is seen as dominant, but rather each is reflective of the other. The consciousness of humanity is mirrored in the world, but not from a causative or supernatural role. The evolution of the consciousness of humanity is tied to our relationship with the world. This includes our social context as well as the biophysical environment. Thus, one can only benefit the world by working on one's self, and one cannot work effectively on one's self in isolation. Therefore, the conscious soul daily travels between the spiritual vista of the mountaintop and the valley of human activity.

The doctrine of *paticca samuppada* provides a mechanism to begin to internalise the scientific paradigm shift that began in the early twentieth century. Comprehension by disciplines other than physics regarding the theory of relativity and the interchangeability of matter and energy has led directly to various exciting advances including chaos theory and systems theory in the natural and physical sciences. Likewise, within the social sciences, the theory of relativity has led indirectly to advances in postmodernism and to the unraveling of positivism. This makes for a condition that allows science to reevaluate the balance between the objective and the subjective, the inner and the outer, the personal and the planetary—all at the heart of the implementation of *paticca samuppada*.

The assignment associated with Tool 6 is the fourth and final group assignment. In this exercise, students begin by listing individuals that have had direct impact upon large numbers of people in the world. These tend to include people in a certain position, such as those currently in the papacy or the oval office, business leaders (such as Bill Gates) or those in film, television, or music industries (such as Steven Spielberg, Oprah Winfrey, or John Lennon). The second phase of the assignment is to identify people beyond family members that have been most influential in their lives. At this point, school teachers, mentors, religious leaders, and other sources of inspiration at the community scale are acknowledged. Finally, the students are asked to compile a list of the organisations in which they have been engaged during the course of their lives that have served, in any way, the advancement of society at large. Group summaries of the responses to these three questions are then posted to the class board for evaluation and on-line discussion.

Tool 7—The 4 Centres (4C)

This tool focuses on the individual, and works to identify methods for an individual to make conscious contributions to societal transformation. The tool is based upon a blend of three different systems in which developing consciousness is a central objective: the "fourth way" system, yoga, and Taoism (Table 2). The first system, the fourth way approach, is based upon the work done by Gurdjieff (Ouspensky, 1954; 1957). In this system, humans are understood to be such creatures of habit that we are like automatons only responding to stimuli, and we are far from crafting our world out of conscious choice. One of the tools for 'waking up' is to become aware of our three primary centres of experiencing life. These centres can be understood as epistemologies or ways of knowing and interacting with the world. The third epistemology, or way, is the one most dominant in our culture—the intellectual. The first way is physical. Individuals in whom the physical centre is strongest would rather learn by doing than listening and would much rather be engaged in an activity than talk about the plan. The second epistemology is emotional and is least honoured in Western culture. It should be noted that everyone uses all three centres constantly, but almost all individuals develop one centre to the exclusion of the other two centres. Although many of us develop a second centre to a reasonable degree, few of us are balanced in our instinctive, intuitional, and intellectual capacities. One metaphorical tale that helps students to retain the major characteristics of the four centres is from *The Wizard of Oz*. The scarecrow represents the intellect, the tin man depicts emotion, and the cowardly lion embodies physicality. Dorothy is unable to reach Oz and thus return home (consciousness) without the company and service of all three of her companions.

The fourth way approach fosters personal awareness of each of these centres in order to work from each one consciously, to bring the three of them into balance, and thus to open a fourth centre, one associated with consciousness.

The second system within the 4C tool is based upon yoga, specifically, four of the seven chakras that are located along the human spine (Dass, 1971). The first chakra is associated with human survival. The second chakra is associated with sexuality, relational skills, and emotions. The third chakra is associated with power and intellect. Although the numerous descriptions of chakras seem to differ on the details of the functions of the first three chakras, they seem to universally concur on the role of the fourth chakra—the heart chakra—as the seat of love. This is not to be confused with passion (*eros*), but is the unconditional love (*agape*) taught by the founders of the world's major religions. This spiritual love engenders devotion, bliss, and a sense of unity with others. Dass (1971) equates love with consciousness, but Gurdjieff and Ouspensky seem to focus more on consciousness than love. In other respects the four centres seem to run parallel with the first four chakras.

Table 2. Consciousness systems used in 4C tool

	4th Way (centres)	Yoga (chakras)	Taoism
C1/instinct/actions	Physical	Survival	Dualism prevails; Doing emphasised
C2/intuition/emotion	Emotional	Sexual/relational	
C3/intellect/thoughts	Intellect	Power/intellect	
C4/insight	Consciousness	Spiritual love	Unity prevails; Being emphasised

The third system used is Taoism. Here the dualism associated with active energies (yang) and receptive energies (yin) are understood to emerge from a non-dualistic or unitive state, the Tao. The Tao can be experienced through a type of knowing in which the person no longer feels separated from the object being known, the two are literally one. We have all had glimpses of this state of being when the ego disappears, when everything seems to be righted, and when it becomes fully apparent that the quality of life is more dependent upon perspective than circumstance. Maslow (1964) referred to these as "peak experiences" and built a psychology of self-actualisation around a life that stays at the peak. These flashes are what the perennial wisdom from many cultures tells us to be always available to us if we were but to be conscious. Actions that are motivated from an awareness of the Tao evoke harmony and restore balance—worthy goals for both the personal and planetary transformations addressed in the rail tool. Actions that emerge from within the constrained space of dualism are understood to reinforce rather than relieve problems. Emphasis is placed upon being rather than upon doing, with the most appropriate actions becoming evident from a perspective of unitive consciousness.

The 4C tool draws on each of these three systems. The primary assumption is that in working towards personal and societal change, our thoughts, feelings, and actions should be aligned and conscious, rather than imbalanced, automatic, or reactive. Additionally, actions that are guided from consciousness (flowing from the heart centre to the other centres) are more likely to be effective than thoughts, feelings, and actions that originate from the first three centres. The 4C tool makes a geometric shift to the chakric model, and thus makes it more synonymous with the fourth way approach. Rather than envisioning each of the first three chakras as they occur in the human body along the line of the spine, they are conceptualised as three points in a triangle, with each point being at the same level. This counters a very subtle notion that intellect (C3) is superior to instinct (C1) or intuition (C2) because it sits above the other two along the path to the 'higher' centres. The triangle is also used to exemplify the way we tend to go around and around endlessly from thought to feeling to action and back again. Further, one can conceptualise the fourth chakra as being centred between (balanced) and above (transcendent to) the other three chakras. The three-sided pyramid (illustrated in Figure 1) allows for the addition of the conscious perspective (C4) to bring life from a two-dimensional trap to a three-dimensional experience. Likewise, it characterises the quantum jump that needs be made to attain a unitive state, and the loss of perspective that occurs when one slips from the heart centre into a state in which attention gets 'stuck' in any one of the three lower centres.

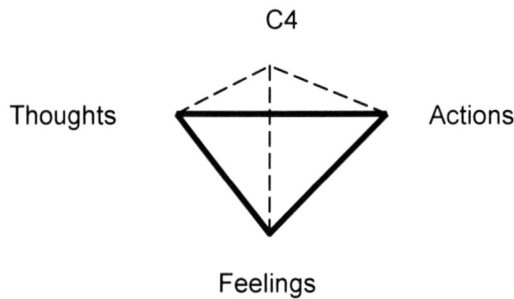

Figure 1. The three-sided pyramid

It should be noted that the C4 perspective is reliant upon each of the three base points. Thus, the mind is not to be denied, as is suggested in many spiritual paths, but balanced. Additionally, valorisation of the emotional centre over the intellectual centre is to be guarded against. Just as an excessively intellectual approach can be sterile or divorced from reality, an excessively emotional approach can succumb to the trap of dogma. In the 4C approach, nothing is to be taken upon faith, but rather positions should be grounded in experience and verified using the intellect.

The assignment associated with the 4C tool is three-fold. First, students are asked to identify their primary and secondary centres. Second, they are asked to describe (1) a single aha! moment, flash of transcendence, or a peak experience that they have had, and (2) the conditions that might have led to that experience or actions that may have been inspired as a result of that experience. Finally, students are asked to list actual or imagined examples of C1, C2, C3, and C4 interactions or perspectives associated with their specific thematic topics.

Tool 8—Metaphor, Myth, and Image

This tool is designed to evoke a variety of symbolic representations in order to see the past and present in the broadest terms possible and to identify patterns that might be useful in better envisioning the future. The metaphorical approach is introduced by looking at the historical development of human society within the context of human life stages. If we are in our adolescence (experimenting with our strength, enamoured with technology, prone to take risks, having a sense of invincibility, and often self-destructive), then there is hope that we may grow out of this awkward phase and into a more 'advanced' society. Another metaphor that is used throughout the semester is that of our species as a single critter—are we fouling our planetary nest?

Mythology is replete with useful lessons for envisioning futures dilemmas and potential solutions. The myth of the phoenix rising from the ashes has already been referred to in terms of societal collapse and resurrection. The myth of Icarus is viewed to ponder the role of technology as an unbridled force (Icarus was given wings crafted of wood, wax and feathers by his father Daedulus. Daedulus warned him not to fly too close to the sun, which of course he did and died after the wax melted.) What are the internal dangers of our current technologies (e.g., 250,000 years is a long time for plutonium waste to be contained)? Who are our elders, what are they saying about unbridled technological advances (e.g., genetically modified foods), and what do we risk if we fail to heed their warnings?

Imagery is very potent in its ability both to encapsulate a lengthy description and to evoke an emotional response. A few images from the twentieth century can be sequenced rapidly to reveal so much of the quality of the century—Model 'T' Ford, Kitty Hawk, swastika, mushroom shaped cloud, Einstein, Gandhi, Elvis, Mickey Mouse, Khrushchev banging his boot at the UN, the Beatles, peace sign, Woodstock, Martin Luther King, Jr., earth rise from Apollo 17, IBM and Apple Computer logos, the golden arches, Vietnamese monk performing self-immolation, teenage dissident facing down tank in Tiananmen Square, smart bomb hitting target during 1991 Gulf War, the Star Child from Kubrick's *2001*, etc. Processing visual imagery utilises a different part of the brain than verbal information and may increase our capacity for holistic thinking (Shlain, 1998). Combining a visual approach with metaphorical and mythical devices opens up a creative way for representing our current conditions and stimulates a long and broad view for examining potential futures. Likewise, the metaphor–myth–image tool can serve to link patterns that are perceived between domain areas. For example, when examining the energy and biodiversity domains concurrently, I am struck by the irony that the very carbon in the biomass of the life forms associated with the sixth major extinction wave 65 million years ago during the demise of the dinosaurs is now being unearthed to 'fuel' the industrial engine responsible for the population growth and consumption rates directly causing the biodiversity loss of the planet's seventh mass extinction.

In the assignment for this tool, students are first asked to list any metaphors and myths that exemplify their domain area and to draw or collect copies of any images that might be useful to supplement that list. Then they are asked to ponder their domain issue while reflecting upon the metaphors and myths and while looking at these images and to describe any new insights that they have had on their research topic as a result of this vantage point.

Tool 9—The Summit

This tool is designed for those in the class who have identified themselves as transformers (Tool 4). In many respects it is the internal side of the practice of *paticca samuppada* that was introduced in the context of the rail tie (Tool 6), which works on developing the external practice of *paticca samuppada*. By-passers and reformers could find it useful on a personal basis, but are less likely to find it relevant on the societal level. The summit tool is beneficial for transformers, because they are inclined to hold that anything less than the creation of an enlightened society is an insufficient level of change for the future of our species. Thus, enlightenment needs to be de-mystified and made much more accessible to the population at large or 'critical mass' will never be achieved. One approach to this end is the de-throning of the concept of enlightenment as a state to be achieved by a handful of masters. In contrast, enlightenment should be perceived as the journey itself, and there is a realisation that we are all on this journey together. In typical Zen fashion, one sees the summit when one realises there is no summit. This is also supported by process theology (Griffin, 2001), which perceives God as verb (the act of creating, seeking, or loving), rather than as noun (subject of creation or object of devotion).

The summit tool focuses on the integration of personal and societal levels and on the intersection of grand vision and tangible action. The metaphor of the summit is used for two reasons. First, it takes work to hike to the summit—the vista does not come without effort. Second, the summit is usually enjoyed in solitude or in the quiet company of a few fellow travellers. It is only by going deep within that we are able to develop the consciousness necessary to balance our thoughts, feelings, and actions. It is only by searching our souls that we know into which rail ties to channel our energies to link personal and societal transformation. However, there is also a lovely by-product of the journey to the summit—we are refreshed. The hubbub of the valley is distant and the din of the city is not heard. For a moment we are at peace and all is well. In fact, there is the notion that everything is perfect, just as it is. Nothing need be done. From this place, where being displaces doing, any action taken up is just as fine as any other. And the best action is the one that we simply are drawn to take, all the time recalling that nothing need be done. The operational adage is "chop wood, carry water, enlightenment, chop wood, carry water". Nothing changes in terms of behaviour after returning from the summit, but the perspective has shifted. We can carry the union internally attained while operating in the external world. The eagle embodies the type of vision needed in this tool—it can soar at great heights and take in a synoptic view and, at the same time, pick out a mouse on the landscape. Such a split level view enables us to concurrently look at both the probable future and the preferable future and to see reality but hold onto the ideal.

The assignment for the summit tool is optional. Students are instructed to identify what conditions might best serve their own internal journey, whether that be a solo wilderness camping trip, a day alone at the beach, or an afternoon or evening in which arrangements are made to have the house to one's self. While engaging in a long meditation, a day of reflection or a long stroll on the beach, students are asked to examine the story of their life, their talents, their distractions and 'detours', what they would do to serve if money were of no concern, and what they would like to have someone be able to say about them during a eulogy at their funeral service some 50 years in the future. Finally, students are asked to ponder whether they feel that they have found their calling, what obstacles need to be overcome to fulfill their lifework, and what bearing, if any, this perspective has on their research topic. Due to the optional and personal nature of this tool, assignments are not collected. However, an on-line discussion board is created on callings and lifework.

APPLICATION OF THE NINE TOOLS IN EVALUATING POTENTIAL FUTURES OF BIODIVERSITY

Although the application of the 200-year present through the interview and imagining processes is very general and works on multiple issues, there are a few observations that can be made upon domain-specific themes, such as biodiversity futures. The childhood of our elders still had frontiers, and knowledge of many wild places was brought to the attention of the public often only through the pages of *The National Geographic*. In 1900, only a handful of national parks had been formed. We operated in a frontier economy in which resources were perceived to be limitless and nature was more than capable of handling all of our wastes. Within the span of 100 years, we find the world to be rapidly filling, with all but a very few frontiers closed, resource limitations are apparent, and pollution of air, surface water, groundwater and oceans has surpassed levels of alarm. Terms such as sustainability, spaceship earth, greenhouse effect, and mass extinction have entered the common vernacular. Biodiversity loss seems to be acknowledged as a major global environmental issue, but international funding to prevent deforestation is but one piece of the international environmental budget, one that reflects the political reality that economic and military concerns far outweigh environmental concerns. Today, a growing proportion of forests is monocultural, existing purely for timber production. Scientists are scrambling to inventory what species are out there as thousands of species are slipping into oblivion before even being described. Numerous biodiversity hot spots have been identified around the globe and conservation efforts seem to be focusing on these areas, but remnant forests and wilderness areas are starting to look like an archipelago within a sea of urban and agricultural development. It is conceivable that our grandchildren will know a world where biological diversity exists in a natural state only in those select areas, and even these large 'zoos' may be more likely to be considered pharmaceutical mining reserves. Likewise, it is conceivable that science and technology will too regularly provide the last hope for some species via test-tube storage of DNA or some other form of genetic technology.

The 3P tool offers the possibility of offsetting probable futures with preferable futures, but let us examine first some of the quantitative methods that have been deployed in diagnosing probable biodiversity futures. One way to grasp the effect of the rate of change of human population growth on biodiversity is to look at a few global totals. In 1900, our species commanded 10 per cent of the world's terrestrial net primary productivity (NPP, or amount of biomass on the earth's surface), but in 1980 over 40 per cent of the NPP was used to support human consumption patterns (Vitousek et al., 1986). During the same timeframe that our demand for NPP increased fourfold, our population tripled from 1.6 billion to 5 billion. If this trend were to continue, human capture of 100 per cent NPP (nothing on land would live, but to serve us) would be reached by the time our population reached 12 billion, which some population growth models show occurring by the year 2100. As we move closer to this time, ecologists are likely to be asked how many and which species need to be preserved to ensure human survival, or to put it metaphorically, just how much of the web of life can we destroy before we die? We now move from the NPP model, which does not take into account such variables as population concentrations in urban areas or consumption patterns in specific countries, to more specific estimates, based upon trends associated with biodiversity hotspots. Conservative estimates of future biodiversity loss indicate that 10 per cent of current species will be extinct in 20 years. On the other extreme are projections that predict that 50 per cent of current species will be lost in 50 years.

Regarding preferable futures, we obviously have to halt population growth and the consumptive ways of our species. There are two ways that this could be accomplished—proactively through choice or reactively under duress. The first approach would entail an abandonment of the urbanisation our planet has gone through over the last 200 years with progress towards a low-impact settlement pattern. There would be extensive cooperative arrangements in housing, commerce, and recreation, and there would be ample green space. The problem here is that humanity would be uniformly spread over the planet and raw nature is likely to be replaced by gardens, parks, and zoos, none of which can approximate the species diversity found in undisturbed areas. In the second approach, humans could eliminate suburbs and concentrate more tightly in the cities and away from the remnant biodiversity. This gives natural areas a chance to continue to recover and spread. The problem here is that urbanisation is highly linked to consumption and it is unlikely that the net effect on nature can be curbed without severe rationing imposed from a centralised power.

In modeling possible biodiversity futures, the first assumption is that, in the near term, biodiversity will continue to hold a very low priority in policy circles with matters such as war on terrorism, attempts to buttress unsustainable economic growth, and protection of global markets holding much higher sway in the international arena. Thus, using a probable futures approach, current rates of population growth, suburban sprawl, and deforestation can all be expected to hold. The second assumption, also associated with a probable future, is that extinction rates are likely to continue for the foreseeable future at either a conservative or an exaggerated rate (it only makes a difference in timing not net effect) until the worst-case scenario is reached. Thus, the third assumption is that the preferable future associated with individual enlightenment cannot be reached unless there is massive societal transformation, which can only be expected through either total collapse of our planetary political and economic systems or through some form of surprise. An approach of 'muddling through' does not seem to be effective here, because it only delays the timing of ecological crisis, it does not prevent it.

So there are four choices for possible futures: (1) foul the nest, game over for humans, roaches win; (2) austere control, after the point of no return is recognised on an immediate and undeniable horizon, dystopia becomes reality; (3) phoenix from the ashes, human societal collapse occurs early enough for nature to survive in a form that is recognizable to us today; and (4) a surprise occurs and our society becomes more enlightened.

In terms of the reformer, transformer, and by-passer approaches to biodiversity, by far the majority of conservation activity is in the reformist context. Government agencies enforce conservation legislation and non-governmental organisations lobby for more strenuous law. Science oriented to study and protect biodiversity is funded through government agencies. No matter what radical influences an individual biodiversity advocate might have, their actions are typically directed to working through the system to minimise biodiversity loss, and there remains the hope that things can get better through such actions. The legacy of transformers in the conservation arena is scant, but could include such efforts as debt–for–nature swaps and ecotourism ventures. Likewise, there have been several integrated conservation and development projects (ICDPs) that have worked to empower local residents in park management. Yet, the most significant impact may be occurring through changing our consumption patterns, as in the voluntary simplicity movement (Elgin, 1981) or in the focus on greening industry, such as can be seen in industrial ecology. By-passers may contribute to the preservation of biodiversity within one corner of the world. However, they are more likely to be involved in simply adopting a lifestyle that is less ecologically destructive.

The past, present, and future emphases reflected in the paradigmatic trichotomies are useful in teasing out different constituencies within the conservation community. The influence of the preservation movement of the late 1800s can still be seen in purist attempts to maintain the sanctity of wilderness areas for their beauty and intrinsic value. The present modernist mode is reflected in conservation programs that are designed around utilitarian values—renewable resource extraction and recreation services are managed for their utility to the human system. The Green

Party, with its avowed alliance to systems theory, its ability to focus upon social and environmental issues, and its tendency to bring coalitio–ns to consensus (Graham, 1999) is indicative of a creative–mender–seeker mindset.

Applying a transformative backcast from a preferable future begins with envisioning a future in which the human system is in balance with the natural system—biodiversity loss would then occur at its natural rate. Such a society would have developed some form of world governance that is actually funded and empowered regarding environmental issues, at least those issues that need to be handled at global or international scales. One early signal, yet in our possible future, could be the creation of a global carbon tax, collected from countries that have the highest carbon emissions and distributed to those countries with the greatest carbon sinks. This would not only be a way to generate funds for environmental restoration, the distribution of the funds could provide an incentive for countries to receive carbon tax revenues by making their allocation contingent upon meeting deforestation standards. Another signpost of progress towards a transformative future would be the adoption of measures that would ensure corporate accountability. For example, if capital punishment were applied to a corporation guilty of intentionally taking life for profit, then its CEO would be fired, stockholders would lose their shares, and the assets of the corporation would go to a global justice fund (Morris, 1998). At that point one could imagine that ethical considerations regarding the environment would be more likely to influence corporate practices. One potential early signal is the institution of the round tables on environment and development that have been implemented in Canada—these are based upon multi-stakeholder, participatory, and consensual decision-making. Another contemporary early signal is the growing interest in the voluntary simplicity and the cultural creative movements.

The key with the rail tie tool is in seeing the connection between the individual and the societal at the community level. Each of the ventures listed above can be worked upon in any of a number of organisational contexts. The trick is to move beyond the paralysis of analysis and to take action. Commit to being an active part of the solution—sign a petition, get the panda bear sticker, buy a share in 1/32 of an acre of rain forest, visit the rain forest on an eco-tour. It does not matter what you do—just do something.

The 4 Center tool requires that any of those actions taken be performed consciously. It is difficult to describe the nature of thoughts, feelings, and actions that are imbued with consciousness, because it is such a subjective phenomenon, and only the individual can judge whether he or she is being conscious. However, regarding thoughts, feelings, and actions associated with biodiversity loss, it is possible to identify three examples of states in which instinct, intuition, and intellect are out of balance. For the first example, take the academic working on environmental issues. She may have had a strong passion that propelled her into the field, but in recent years she has spent most of her time 'up in her head' with little time or energy left to feel much of anything, let alone to take direct action on a specific issue. As another example, take the well-meaning activist who runs around from one cause to the next, definitely engaged, but not quite certain of the productive results associated with all of his activity. Or finally, examine the person who feels extreme despair about the condition of the environment, but really doesn't know what to do or where to begin, and thus remains literally overwhelmed and paralysed, knowing little and doing less, but definitely in command of a reservoir of energy waiting to be channelled.

Moving naturally to the tool of metaphor, myth, and image, it should be apparent that our culture is seeing the resurgence of a variety of earth-based symbols. I shall address only one. I hold that the most powerful icon of the twentieth century was the earth-rise over the lunar landscape and the associated familiar photograph of the home planet taken from Apollo 17. This image reached the consciousness of the planet at a very deep level. For the first time in our human history we saw our habitat from a fully synoptic view. We saw a water planet with swirling clouds and that onion-skin atmospheric layer—all afloat in a black sea of space. Concurrent with seeing the fragility of the planet, we also saw a globe without borders. Philosophically, the icon of the home planet has two possible motions of focus, externally radiating and internally oriented. External focus moves from the fragile atmosphere outward to the dark space surrounding the planet. This focus indicates how vulnerable we are should we destroy our life support systems, and the key word is unsustainability. This focus is inherently dominated by emphasis on biological and physical systems. It also tends towards doom saying which may be the psychological undoing of the environmental movement, in that excessive doom saying could erode credibility in scientific projections and catalyse environmental backlash. The internal orientation sees unity—one world, one people. Unity as a goal suffers from the magnitude of the mission, requiring a level of unprecedented human cooperation for which there is scant evidence for hope. However, one must wonder if sustainability can be reached without parallel political efforts. At a minimum, the two motions of focus of the planetary icon offer a balance between efforts in science and policy, as well as between nature and society.

The final tool, the summit view, inspires us to see the miracle of life, the perfection of the pattern of the diversity of life on this planet. We see the potentiality of humanity, both its barbaric and noble dimensions. We are compelled to return to the valley and take action to protect life on earth from ... ourselves. But first, we must bask, take in the view, and be healed, recalling that nothing need be done. It is imperative that we relax in the midst of apparent catastrophe. The Chinese word for crisis, *wei-ji*, is composed of two characters—danger and opportunity (Capra, 1982). We would do well to ponder both daily.

CONCLUSIONS

The nine tools have proven to be effective in providing a framework for introducing futures studies techniques, for evaluating societal change, and for giving students a methodology to expand and to develop their perspectives on the future. Likewise, the tools have furnished a common structure for students to compare, in depth, their sense of the future to that of their classmates. The flexibility of the implementation of the tools in both a generic fashion, introducing quantitative and normative approaches, and in specific application to a variety of thematic areas, indicated the strength of the approach. Revisiting numerous topics with the same set of lenses enabled students to articulate complex issues in a seminar format. Even the more philosophical tools seem to be approachable, and generally students report that they were both more positive about the future and felt more empowered in reaching preferable futures as a result of having taken the class. Synergy was generated by viewing issues through futurist, sociological, and philosophical tools. It should be noted that some tools took a while for students to comprehend. Thus, the incorporation of associated assignments and the coverage of one tool per week allowed students sufficient 'cook time' to internalise one tool before moving on to the next. The sequencing of the tools was of paramount importance, because of the inter-relationship between the tools and because of the ability to move into deeper territory as a result of having covering fundamental concepts earlier. At times, during the teaching process, I became very aware of the quality of the thin line between teaching and preaching. Two useful antidotes for transgressing in this domain were (1) a healthy dose of humility, not difficult to find, given the uncertainty of the times and of possible futures, and (2) a desire to balance my need for maintaining authenticity with the task of helping students craft their own visions of their futures.

ACKNOWLEDGEMENTS

I would like to thank the students in my Spring 2003 class of Geographies of the Future—not only for being willing to have these tools tested out with their participation, but for helping to create that space into which they emerged. I would also like to thank Kristin Stewart for her review of this manuscript and for her efforts in helping me evaluate the efficacy of these tools in their initial classroom implementation. I would like to thank Barney Warf for giving me the freedom to teach what I love and Sohail Inayatullah for encouraging me to write about the adventure. Finally, I would like to thank my anonymous reviewers for their constructive criticism.

REFERENCES

Abdullah, S. (1999). *Creating a world that works for all*. San Francisco: Berrett-Koehler.
Amara, R. (1981). The futures field: Searching for definitions and boundaries. *The Futurist, 15*(2), 25–29.
Boulding, E. (1978). The dynamics of imaging futures. *World Future Society Bulletin, 12*(5), 1–8.
Capra, F. (1982). *The turning point: Science, society, and the rising culture*. New York: Bantam.
Cole, S. (1997). Futures in global space//www.models.gis.media. *Futures, 29*(4/5), 393–417.
Dahle, K. (1998). Toward governance for future generations—How do we change course? *Futures, 30*(4), 277–292.
Dass, R. (1971). *Be here now*. New York: Crown.
Elgin, D. (1981). *Voluntary Simplicity: Towards a Life that is Outwardly Simple, Inwardly Rich*. New York: Morrow.

Graham, D. N. (1999). The theory of a transformational political movement: Green political theory. In S. Woolpert, C. D. Slaton, & E. W. Schwerin (Eds.), *Transformational Politics: Theory, Study, and Practice* (pp. 73–88). Albany, NY: State University of New York Press.

Griffin, D. R. (2001). *Reenchantment without supernaturalism: A process philosophy of religion.* Ithaca: Cornell University Press.

Macy, J. (1991). *World as lover, world as self.* Berkeley, CA: Parallax Press.

Maslow, A. H. (1964). *Religions, values, and peak experiences.* New York: Viking Press.

Meadows, D. H., Meadows, D. L., Randers, J., & Behrens III., W. W. (1972). *The limits to growth.* New York: Signet.

Meadows, D. H., Meadows, D. L., & Randers, J. (1992). *Beyond the Limits to Growth: Confronting Global Collapse, Envisioning a Sustainable Future.* Post Mills, VT: Chelsea Green.

Morris, D. (1998). Capital punishment for corporations? Institute for Local Self-Reliance. Retrieved from http://www.ilsr.org/columns/1998/092298.html

Ouspensky, P. D. (1954). *The fourth way.* New York: Knopf.

Ouspensky, P. D. (1957). *The psychology of Mans' possible evolution.* New York: Knopf.

Ray, P. H., & Anderson, S. R. (2000). *The cultural creatives: How 50 million people are changing the world.* New York: Three Rivers Press.

Quinn, D. (1992). *Ishmael.* New York: Bantam.

Quinn, D. (1996). *The story of B.* New York: Bantam.

Quinn, D. (1997). *My Ishmael.* New York: Bantam.

Quinn, D. (1999). *Beyond civilization: Humanity's next great adventure.* New York: Three Rivers Press.

Shlain, L. (1998). *The alphabet versus the Goddess: The conflict between word and image.* New York: Penguin

Slaughter, R. (1995). *The foresight principle: Cultural recovery in the 21st century.* Westport, CT: Praeger.

Toffler, A. (1981). *The third wave.* New York: Morrow.

Vitousek, P. M., Erlich, P. R., Erlich, A. H., & Matson, P. A. (1986). Human appropriation of the products of photosynthesis. *BioScience, 36,* 368–373.

Basil Savitsky holds a PhD in Parks, Recreation and Tourism Management. He spent nine years performing environmental research in a university setting and teaching computer mapping, conservation geography, and futures studies. He currently works as an educational consultant and is writing on the linkage between personal change and societal futures. His consulting work focuses on building emotional intelligence and on the provision of training to educators interested in asset development for youth at risk.

JULIE MATTHEWS AND ROBERT HATTAM

13. DID BUDDHA LAUGH?

A pedagogy for the future

This chronic dullness in school helps students become anti-intellectual. Their lives outside of school are humorous, and comedy is one way they experience their subjectivity. When learning is humorless and emotionless, it denies them two subjective values. (Shor & Freire, 1987, p. 163)

INTRODUCTION: ZEN, HUMOUR AND PEDAGOGY

Zen offers a form of praxis for living a life where humour is a significant resource. In Zen, humour provides a space for serious contemplation on existential concerns often repressed or silenced such as: embodiment as knowledge, impermanence, suffering and death. Humour and laughter have not always been welcomed in Buddhism and early Buddhist teachers regarded it as something to be avoided (Clasquin, 2001). The question of whether the Buddha laughed was an early scholastic debate. It was argued that Buddha frowned upon laughter because of its association with triviality, distractions and matters which evade deep and serious thinking (Heyers, 1973). In the great spiritual traditions of Christianity, Islam and Hinduism the sacred also has a longstanding association with serious minded devotional studiousness and humour and laughter is the antithesis to sacred scholarship.

The eccentric, outlandish and zany comic spirit of Zen Buddhism has become intrinsic to the tradition. This chapter takes the comedic dimensions of Zen teaching as a focal point to explore the humour as a pedagogy for the future. We are interested in how humour works as a creative practice of engaging with the art of being human; with intellect and subjective values, and with knowledge of life and death. Such a focus challenges the assumption that humour in education is either frivolous and trivial, or simply a means of promoting learner attention, motivation, comprehension, retention and facilitating positive teaching and learning relationships and environments (Powell & Anderson, 1985). This chapter is speculative, philosophical and makes no attempt to provide a thorough review of literature, or outline a theory of pedagogy that includes humour. Instead, we seek to offer a clarification and provocation which invites others to join a discussion about the role of humour in a pedagogy for the future.

In part, this chapter is a response to recent attempts in Australia to answer the question: what is good pedagogy? As examples, the New London Group (1996)

M. Bussey, S. Inayatullah and I. Milojević (eds.), Alternative Educational Futures: Pedagogies for Emergent Worlds, 223–233.

propose a 'pedagogy of multiliteracies' for designing social futures in late/fast capitalism and the Queensland Education Department have sponsored the development of the Productive Pedagogies (Lingard, Mills et al., 2000). We applaud these developments, given the paucity of vocabulary for pedagogy in an education context where teachers' work is increasingly instrumentalised and life in schools for students provides few opportunities for bringing academic knowledge into conversation with lifeworlds and the historical moment (Pinar, 2004). Unfortunately neither of these two models properly acknowledges the identity work that young people perform in schools (Wexler, 1992; Smyth & Hattam, 2004). That for too many young people, schooling is an alienating experience requiring the damping of emotion and self expression (Wexler, 1992). Schooling is organised around discourses where reason/cognition are privileged and split off from the affective/emotional and hence the 'art of being' (Fromm, 1992) or the "capacity to be fully human" (Wexler, 1996, p. 3) is presented as devoid of love, compassion and humour.

Our chapter could take many lines of flight in response to this critique, but we have chosen to focus specifically on humour, its absence in mainstream education debate and its potential towards developing a social consciousness beyond national loyalties and ideologies. We are aware that for many teachers, a pedagogy absent of humour is absurd, so why has humour received so little consideration in education? This chapter is interested in how we might understand the pedagogical role of humour; how might we think humour into our pedagogical vocabulary beyond instrumentalism and towards a practice that is open, creative and contemplative of therapeutic/pedagogical possibilities for moving education into engaging fully in the emotional and intellectual worlds of young people.

A starting point for a contemplation of humour and pedagogy is Critchley's (2002) *On Humour*. Critchley distinguishes between 'laughing at others' and 'laughing at oneself', arguing for the later as of value to self and society. 'Laughing at others' is based on malice and sustains the power relations of the status quo, whilst 'laughing at oneself' has therapeutic, and we would argue, pedagogical value also. We focus our attention on a resource not taken up by Critchley, namely Zen Buddhism, a tradition in which 'laughing at oneself' is a key pedagogical practice. The self, in Zen *is* the object of deconstructive work; that we take the *self* seriously is *the* habitual practice that requires unsettling and hence Zen as a pedagogy invokes humour as a way towards living what Critchley (1996) calls a post-deconstructive subjectivity:

> Post-deconstructive subjectivity would be a determination of the subject after deconstruction, a determination that succeeds the duty of deconstruction without lapsing back into the pre-deconstructive or classical conceptions of the subject ... (p. 39)

Unlike poststructuralism, Zen provides a pedagogy that takes us beyond simply theorising post-deconstructive subjectivity. It offers a means to experience non-self. This chapter also takes up Smith's (1999) challenge to go beyond the state of exhaustion, of intellectual and cultural impasse of Western views on identity and subjectivity, "stubbornly entrenched as the theoretical axis around which virtually all the defining concerns revolve" (p. 13). Certainly, for those of us interested in a critical futures orientated pedagogy, we at an impasse: having rejected the "clapped-out discreditable, historically superannuated ideology of Autonomous Man" (Eagleton, 1987, p. 47), the other alternative is the de-centred subject of the new identity politics. Whilst we have moved away from the essentialised irreducible *I* borrowed from Aristotle and further objectified by Descartes, to a more inclusive, pluralistic and decentred view of self, the point is that our projects—personal, social and educational—are still driven by a "profound desire for identity" (p. 15). The fiction of identity itself seems to be immune from the sorts of deconstructive practices that characterise critical/poststructuralist pedagogical work. Against the secularising impulse in Western education and scholarship, including critical theory and pedagogy, we argue that Zen Buddhism offers something beyond the *aporia* that appears to leave us no alternative than either suffer a neo-Nietzschean form of nihilism, or play along with late capitalism and consume our way out of disenchantment.

The chapter proceeds in this task with a discussion of the nature of Zen and its refusal of absolute and sacred scholarship. The second section of this chapter highlights Zen's moves to destabilise the self through the use of unexpectedly disarming pedagogies which use humour. We conclude by noting that our lives and work, what we teach and how we learn, are increasingly instrumentalised; certain forms of affective knowledge and values have been promoted and other forms of emotional engagement have been dismissed and disregarded. It seems to us that these directions are not only undesirable but disliked by most teachers and students. Education and pedagogy can be organised differently, not through more of the same sorts of emotional/affective distancing but through the redeployment of enduring pedagogical strategies.

WHAT IS ZEN?

Western philosophy has long been suspicious of 'pure reason'. In the Kantian tradition pure reason comprises metaphysical ideas and knowledge which appear beyond the limits of human experience. The dogmatism and capacity to self-justification of religion was one of Kant's prime suspects; in the twenty-first century it became a known guilty party. Kant's radical scepticism was not, however, uncalled for in the face of a Christian tradition where the Book and Word of God was deemed absolute and sacrosanct. But not all spiritual traditions are concerned with establishing their precepts above and beyond critique. Zen Buddhism is a case in point. Its iconoclasm is easily identified in constant re-edits and reinterpretations of *koans* and anecdotes and the practice of amending its own scriptures and commentaries, and stands in stark contrast to other traditions which regard the sacred as reproachless.

Of course there is more than one Zen Buddhism: Chinese, Japanese, Korean, Vietnamese, Soto, Rinzai, Pure Land, and we might even talk about an emerging Western Zen Tradition that draws on all of these.[1] For the sake of an introductory discussion, we can point to two types of Buddhism: one follows a graduated path to enlightenment that involves a gradual refining of conceptual understanding that is the basis for meditation, and the second (Zen) involves abandoning conceptualisation from the outset, seeking instead sudden enlightenment. There are variations on both of these themes, however Thich Nhat Hanh's definition derived from Bodhidharma's (the First Ancestral Teacher of Zen in China, circa fifth century) will suffice:

> [Zen is] a special transmission outside the scriptures, not based on words or letters, a direct pointing to the heart of reality so that we might see into our own nature and wake up. (Thich Nhat Hanh, 1995, p. 34)

Understood as a methodless method, Zen is not transmitted through scriptures but from 'mind to mind' in a manner that resolves the predicament of the "ego in ego-consciousness" (Martino, 1960, p. 145), reification and objectification. We repress the fact that we reify or objectify the world and ourselves, "forgetting" that reality is a construct of habitual "thought-props" (Loy, 1996, p. 65). For existentialism and psychoanalysis there is some-*thing*, an ego which engages in a process of self-reflection and repression of its own impending death. The self or ego *thing* is by nature anxious because of *its* fear of death. The ego is the *thing* that engages in the play of repression, feels guilt and engages in transference and projection. Anxiety then, is a characteristic of self, and is "not adventitious but essential to the self, not something we have but something we are" (p. 16). Not being able to see past the reification of self or ego, anxiety then is ontological and primordial. There can be no end to it.

A Buddhist critique understands hyperanxiety as not about repressing death but something more immediate. Our problem with death is "neither the threat of its actuality nor even its implications as impending possibility" (Loy, 1996, p. 52). Instead the problem arises because of a dualistic way of thinking, "a no-win game that the ego cannot stop playing because it is constituted by that game" (p. 52). A Buddhist view suggests that "life–versus–death is not the game the ego plays but that game whose play is the ego" (p. 21). That is, we impute self-existence, *thing*-ness, or some form of inherent existence onto the flux of our experience, which we grasp at and then cherish. But there is no-*thing* to grasp and cherish. "The sense–of–self that arises is a fiction" (p. 12). Thurman (1998) is instructive on this point:

> I questioned everything said by everyone ... except the one continuous report to myself that I was 'me'. I questioned who I was and why I held the opinions I held, feeling an urgent need to pin down my identity, but I never wondered if I was at all. (p. 2)

Out of a deluded form of forgetting, that Buddhism understands as a basic ignorance, we grasp at what is a mental construct, striving to become real by becoming some-*thing*. "The consequence is that the sense–of–self always has, as its inescapable shadow, a sense–of–lack, which it always tries to escape" (Loy, 1996, p. 12). We experience this sense–of–lack, that something is missing, that something isn't quite right, because the sense–of–self, which is a conditioned consciousness, struggles to become unconditioned, autonomous, or real. Anxiety "is generated by this fictional self-reflection for the simple reason that I do not know and cannot know what this thing I supposedly am *is*" (p. 21). But this project can never be completed because the ego-self is the effort or the struggle of awareness to objectify itself in order to then grasp itself: "what is grasped is confused with what grasps" (p. 12). Our hyperanxiety is "not something that the ego has, it is what the ego is" (p. 21).

For Buddhists, the solution to the problem of death–in–life is not a struggle against its terror but the practice of terror endured. Rather than sustain repression and its eternal return, projecting our lack onto others or introjecting it in guilt, the Buddhist path recommends abiding in the anguish with simple awareness. "One does not do anything with that anguish except develop the ability to dwell in it or rather *as* it; then the anguish, having nowhere else to direct itself, consumes the sense–of–self" (Loy, 1996, p. 57). Having deconstructed the sense–of–self in an existential sense we realise that there is no lack because there has never been any inherently existing and autonomous self that is separate from reality.

Zen practice then is a "straightforward, concrete assault upon the contradictory dualistic subject–object structure of the ego in ego-consciousness" (Martino, 1960, p. 154). And this contradiction can't be dealt using the logics we normally get by with.

HUMOUR AND PEDAGOGY

For the Zen master, humour gets under our guard to provide space for (serious) contemplation on issues commonly repressed and silenced. Humour is radically anti-essentialist and does not seek to ameliorate ego–angst, but completely undermine it.

Zen methods trigger 'the abrupt perception of absurdity' – early devotion of simple particulars, the "suchness and mystery of things beyond the schemas of intellect and value judgement". This runs against the grain of Western intellectual traditions whose quest it is to find reason and purpose (regardless of their pre-disposition to periodically collapse) in existence and to despair over absurdity and the "tragic absence of the good, the true, and the beautiful in everything" (Heyers, 1973, p. 102).

Heyers cites a contemporary Zen anecdote:

A roshi lay dying surrounded by his monks. The senior monk asked if he had any final words of advice or instruction. The old master opened his eyes and whispered "Tell them Truth is like a River". The wisdom circulated around the room till it reached the youngest monk who ask "What does it mean, 'Truth is like a river'?" Slowly the master opened his eyes and in a weak voice whispered, "OK, Truth is not like a river". (p. 103)

The anecdote provides a specific form of dualistic understanding that distorts the way we understand ourselves and others, and the Zen method often resorts to a whole range of unorthodox approaches to break through dualistic consciousness, to gain an intuitive form of understanding of self, and of direct realisation and hence beyond conceptualisation. Our acceptance, normalisation, naturalisation of this dualistic mind, once revealed, is often experienced with a laugh—that we finally get it—and also a release that humour/laughter creates. The ability of alternative philosophical positions to both be true and untrue demonstrates the futility of trying to comprehend reality by means of an intellectual system. It is not that existence is absurd (existentialism) or cogitatively meaningless (logical positivism) but that it is absurd to grasp after meaning and cling to reality by means of this or that philosophical system (Heyers, 1973, p. 104).

The method of revelation/realisation/enlightenment has been discussed by de Certeau (1986) in relation to Foucault's *Order of Things* where he writes in the preface: "This book first arose out of a passage in Borges, out of the laughter that shattered ... all the familiar landmarks of my thought". De Certeau draws attention to Foucault's efforts to extend "what it would be possible to think otherwise". For de Certeau, Foucault was on the look out for "some strangeness lurking there unnoticed" (in this case Borges) that when read, "take[s] the expected and codified by surprise"; that shatters "all the familiar landmarks of ... thought ... breaking up all the ordered surfaces and all the planes with which we are accustomed to tame the wild profusion of existing things" (Foucault, 1974, p. xv). Foucault often talks of "bouts of surprise, the sudden jubilatory, semi-ecstatic forms of 'astonishment' or 'wonder'" (de Certeau, 1986, p. 194). "Something that exceeds the thinkable and opens the possibility of 'thinking otherwise' bursts in through comical, incongruous, or paradoxical half-openings of discourse. The philosopher, overtaken by laughter, seized by an irony of things equivalent to an illumination..." (p. 194).

Humour "is produced by a disjunction between the way things are and the way things are represented... between the expectation and the actuality" (Critchley, 2002, p. 1) and upsets 'common sense' and is explained differently in the following three theories:

- Superiority theory is a perspective found in the work of Plato, Aristotle and Hobbes which sees humour as an effect of superiority achieved when others are disparaged or depreciated. Associated with ridicule, insult, sarcasm and in this form it offers little benefit for pedagogy.
- Relief theory in the work of Spencer, Darwin and Freud highlights the psychological basis of humour. Jokes and ambiguities are a cathartic way of releasing energy or suppressed and forbidden thoughts, and disguising or evading aggressive and sexual feelings and anxieties. Laugher opens up avenues of communication and enables students to see ordinary information in unusual patterns. Humour is thus a useful communication technique which develops positive rapport.
- Incongruity theory for Kant, Schopenhauer and Kierkegaard is the source of humour. The juxtaposition of odd inappropriate, inconsistent or unsuitable parts creates surprise and unexpectedness. For Kant humour "is the sudden transformations of a strained expectation into nothing" which derails the normal flow of thoughts (Morreall, 1987 cited in Critchley, 2002). This theory is of particular interest to a pedagogy for the future for it offers a means of demonstrating the indefensibility of present conditions.

In terms of humour as incongruity, examples include joke as 'anti-rites', that "mock, parody or deride the ritual practices of a given society" (Critchley, 2002, p. 5). Humour as incongruity must, however, be more than 'comic relief', it must show the "sheer contingency or arbitrariness of the social rites in which we engage" (p. 10). Certainly, we can find plenty of examples of this in the humour used by social movements. But it must involve more than simply laughing at power and its contingency. It must also move beyond ridicule and denigration which tends to be reactionary and can indeed reinforce the stereotypes by simply toying "with the existing social hierarchies in a charming but quite benign fashion" (p. 11). Likewise, comedy which scapegoats confirms the status quo through "denigrating a certain sector of society" or "laughing at the alleged stupidity of the social outsider" (p. 12). "Such humour is not laughter at power, but the powerful laughing at the powerless" (p. 12).

Critchley's distinction between laughing at oneself and laughing at others cited earlier provides a useful way to evaluate various forms of humour and it is this idea of laughing at oneself that we would now like to focus on. Critchley uses Freud as a way into his discussion on this point. Drawing on Freud's *Jokes and their Relation to the Unconscious*, Critchley argues that the act of laughing at oneself, of finding oneself ridiculous, is not a depressing act but, on the contrary, "gives us a sense of emancipation, consolation and childlike elevation" (2002, p. 95). Freud's argument is set up in his analysis of the difference between mourning and melancholia. Mourning is the response to the death of the beloved whilst in melancholia, the ego itself becomes an object. For Freud, melancholia is evidence of a splitting of the ego: that the superego emerges (as conscience) and denigrates the ego: the ego becomes "abject object" (p. 97). Critchley reminds us of Woody Allen's monologues. Problematically, the melancholic is understood to have "achieved a higher degree of self-knowledge than the rest of us" (p. 98) and we might consider the melancholic philosopher as example and think of Dostoevsky's underground man. "This is why humour is essential in philosophy" (p. 99). The way out for the ego is to find itself ridiculous; humour then is an antidepressant. "The subject looks at itself like an abject object and instead of weeping bitter tears, it laughs at itself and finds consolation therein" (p. 102).

In this sense then humour is a profound "cognitive relation to oneself and the world" (Critchley, 2002, p. 102). Humour not only makes the superego a less severe master, but saves the human being from the tragic hubris of the ego that imagines its own omnipotence and immortality. Critchley's analysis here, whilst not written through a Zen perspective, has strong resonance with the idea of struggling with ego-consciousness—laughing at self.

DID BUDDHA LAUGH, AND WHY WE NEED TO KNOW?

Humour is currently irrelevant in mainstream discourses on pedagogy. This absence is interesting given that current efforts to codify 'good pedagogy' seek to provide a vision for the future. As McWilliam observes, good teaching as professional work takes few risks, and takes itself and its texts very seriously (McWilliam,

1999, p. 175, also see her chapter with Shane Dawson "Pedagogical Practice after the Information Age" in this volume). Seriousness, in Christianity, Islam, Hinduism and Buddhism, has long been associated with the sacred, the devotional and with studiousness. The antithesis to sacred scholarship is humour, laughter comedy, triviality, and distraction.

The scholastic debate about whether Buddha laughed is thus of great interest to us in delineating a pedagogy for the future. Did Buddha frown on laughter because of its association with superficial pleasure, self-indulgence? Did he regard laughter as evading the deep and serious thinking necessary to understand sources of suffering such as ego, desire, attachment, ignorance and bondage (Heyers, 1973) or did he laugh? Did he laugh at himself and encourage others to do likewise? Did he cherish ego-displacing pedagogies which cultivated creative wonderment and illumination; did he welcome strategic use of paradox, irony, incongruity, unconventionality, the dissolution of dualisms, in the deployment of radical scepticism.

While many teachers would admit to using humour in various ways, serious consideration of its pedagogical possibilities and potentials are almost entirely disregarded in education (Teslow, 1995). Educational research into humour also underestimates its significance and where it has been investigated it is in terms of its use in promoting learner attention, motivation, comprehension and retention, or to facilitate positive teaching and learning relationships and environments (Powell & Anderson, 1985). Not only are teachers activating humour as a pedagogical ploy—and our claim is based on anecdotal evidence only—but students introduce humour into the classroom as their own tactic to make the experience less dull and boring. That students are acting out in classrooms is perhaps the single most significant aspect of classroom life: it motivates huge amounts of research—improving education for girls, 'what about the boys', concern about educational disadvantage of Indigenous students and less affluent students. And the interest has mostly centred on the ways that students resist classroom life through either rebellion or passivity. McLaren (1985) reminds us though that clowning is one form of resistance that doesn't fit neatly in these categories and one that provides educators with insights into 'good pedagogy'. In the first instance the class clown offers more than comic relief: they deconstruct the familiar and make us aware of "just how boring school really [is]" (McLaren, 1993, p. 161). They also reveal the "tenuousness and arbitrariness" (p. 161) of school codes and rules.

That is not to suggest that humour be included in codifications of pedagogy, because that would strip it of its pedagogical power turning it into a method, much like management consultants have done with notions of 'structured fun'. We want to suggest that the Zen Buddhist solution to the pain of being human establishes the groundwork of an alternative pedagogy for the future by providing a means of taking on the unknowable, insoluble. Like postmodernism and poststructuralism it recognises the significance of paradox, irony, incongruity, unconventionality and distancing; the dissolution of dualisms; and the deployment of radical scepticism—but then it takes a slightly different take on all of that!

The object of negation, the binary or dualism under deconstruction has yet to be identified by poststructuralism; the object is a trickster, an illusion, the ego itself, or that sense of sense that appear to us a stable, independent and permanent.

This would most certainly course preclude any attempt on the part of educationalists and bureaucrats to in-service, performance indicate or graduate attribute humor since: 'Nevertheless, you can not give courses to make teachers good humorists!' (Shor & Freire, 1987, p. 162)

NOTES

[i] There are Zen centres in most capital cities, "Western Roshis" (Aitken 1982), and it is now an impossible task keeping up with all the books being published about Zen. Of some note here of course, are the beat poets, many scholars are still referencing "Howl" (Gough, 2002), the Jazz minimalists such as John Cage, and Leonard Cohen often does Zen retreat. And how can we forget Pirsig's *Zen and the Art of Motorcycle Maintenance*? At least Pirsig was gracious enough to state that his book had nothing to do with Zen scholarship. There is also an emerging conversation between the psycho-sciences and Buddhism of various kinds and Zen is part of that (Loy, 1996a; Watson 1998).

REFERENCES

Abe, M. (1985). *Zen and Western thought*. Honolulu, HI: University of Hawaii.

Aitken, R. (1982). *Taking the path of Zen*. New York: North Point Press.

Barthes, R. (1982). *Empire of signs*. New York: Hill & Wang.

Carrette, J. (Ed.). (1999). *Religion and culture by Michel Foucault*. Manchester: Manchester University Press.

Clarke, J. (1997). *Oriental enlightenment: An encounter between Asian and Western thought*. London and New York: Routledge.

Clasquin, M. (2001). Real Buddhas don't laugh: Attitudes towards humour and laughter in ancient India and China. *Social Identities, 7*(1), 97–115.

Critchley, S. (1996). Prolegomena to any post-deconstructive subjectivity. In S. Critchley & P. Dews (Eds.), *Deconstructive Subjectivities* (pp. 13–46). Albany, NY: State University of New York Press.

Critchley, S. (2002). *On humour*. London and New York: Routledge.

de Certeau, M. (1986). *Heterologies: Discourse on the other*. Minneapolis, MN: University of Minnesota Press.

Eagleton, T. (1987). The politics of subjectivity. In *ICA Documents #6. Identity: The Real Me*. London: Free Association Books.

Florence, N. (1998). B*ell Hooks' Engaged pedagogy: A transgressive education for critical consciousness*. Westport, CT: Bergin & Garvey.

Foucault, M. (1974). *The order of things: An Archeology of the human sciences*. London: Routledge.

Fromm, E. (1992). *The art of being*. New York: Continuum.

Fromm, E., Suzuki, D. T., & De Martino, R. (1960). *Zen Buddhism and psychoanalysis*. London: Souvenir Press.

Gough, N. (2002). Voicing Curriculum Visions. In W. Doll & N. Gough (Eds.), *Curriculum Visions* (pp. 1–22). New York: Peter Lang.

Heyers, C. (1973). *The Laughing Buddha: Zen and the Comic Spirit*. Colorado: Longwood Academic.

Hooks, B. (1994). *Teaching to transgress: Education as the practice of freedom*. London: Routledge.

Hwu, W.-S. (1998). Curriculum, transcendence, and Zen/Taoism: Critical ontology of the self. In W. Pinar (Ed.), *Curriculum: Towards new identities* (pp. 21–39). New York , London: Garland Publishing.

Jacobson, N. (1981). *Understanding Buddhism.* Carbondale & Edwardsville, IL: South Illinois University Press.

Lingard, B., Mills, M. et al. (2000). Teachers, school reform and social justice: Challenging research and practice. *Australian Educational Researcher, 27*(3), 99–115.

Loy, D. (1996a). *Lack and transcendence: The problem of death in Psychotherapy, Existentialism, and Buddhism.* Atlantic Highlands, NJ: Humanities Press.

Loy, D. (Ed.) (1996b). *Healing deconstruction: Postmodern thought in Buddhism and Christianity.* Atlanta, Georgia: Scholars Press.

Martino, R. D. (1960). The human situation and Zen Buddhism. In D. T. Suzuki, E. Fromm, & R. D. Martino (Eds.), *Zen Buddhism and Psychoanalysis* (pp. 142–171). London: Souvenir Press.

May, R. (1996). Heidegger's *Hidden sources: East Asian influences on his work.* London: Routledge.

McLaren, P. (1985). The ritual dimensions of resistance: Clowning and symbolic inversion. *Journal of Education, 167*(2), 84–97.

McLaren, P. (1988). The liminal servant and the ritual roots of critical pedagogy. *Language Arts, 65*(2), 164–179.

McLaren, P. (1993). *Schooling as a Ritual performance: Towards a political economy of educational symbols and gestures.* London: Routledge.

McWilliam, E. (1999). *Pedagogical pleasures.* New York: Peter Lang.

Mistry, F. (1981). *Nietzsche and Buddhism: A prolegomena to a comparative study.* Berlin: de Gruyter.

Moreall, J. (1987). *The philosophy of laughter and humour.* Albany, NY: State University of New York Press.

New London Group (1996). A pedagogy of multiliteracies: Designing social futures. *Harvard Educational Review, 66*(1), 60–92.

Parkes, G. (Ed.) (1987). *Heidegger and Asian thought.* Honolulu: University of Hawaii.

Parkes, G. (Ed.) (1991). *Nietzsche and Asian thought.* Chicago: University of Chicago.

Pinar, W. (2004). *What is curriculum theory?* Mahwah, NJ: Lawrence Erlbaum Associates.

Shor, I., & Freire, P. (1987). *A pedagogy for liberation: Dialogues on transforming education.* South Hadley, MA: Bergin & Garvey.

Smith, D. G. (1999). *Pedagon: Interdisciplinary essays in the human sciences, pedagogy and culture.* New York: Peter Lang.

Smyth, J., & Hattam, R. (2004). *'Dropping Out', Drifting Off, being excluded: Becoming somebody without school.* New York: Peter Lang.

Teslow, J. L. (1995). Humour me: Call for research. *Education, Teaching, Research and Development, 43*(3), 6–28.

Thich Nhat Hanh. (1995). *Zen keys: A guide to Zen practice.* New York: Doubleday.

Thurman, R. (1998). *Inner revolution: Life, liberty, and the pursuit of real happiness.* New York: Riverhead Books.

Trinh T. Minh-Ha. (1992). *Framer framed.* New York: Routledge.

Turner, V. (1974). Liminal to liminoid, in play, flow and ritual: An essay in comparative symbology. *Rice University studies, 60*(3), 53–93.

Watson, G. (1998). *The Resonance of Emptiness: An inspiration for a contemporary psychotherapy.* Richmond, Surrey: Curzon.

Watts, A. (1960). *The spirit of Zen.* New York: Grove Press.

Welborn, G. (1968). *The Buddhist Nirvana and its western interpreters.* Chicago: University of Chicago Press.

Wexler, P. (1992). *Becoming somebody: Towards a social psychology of the school.* London: Falmer Press.

Wexler, P. (1996). *Holy sparks.* New York: St. Martins Press.

Zembylas, M., & Michaelides, P. (2004). The sound of silence in pedagogy. *Educational Theory, 54*(2), 193–210.

Julie Matthews is Associate Professor and Director of Research for the Faculty of Arts and Social Science, and a member of the Regional Sustainability Research Group, at the University of the Sunshine Coast, Queensland Australia. Her background is in sociology, anthropology and education. Her work is informed by postcolonial, feminist and Foucauldian theory and engages with groups and communities often marginalised or disregarded in mainstream research. She is currently working on projects looking at refugee education, reconciliation pedagogy and international education and she is exploring image-based methods and methodologies.

Robert Hattam is Associate Professor in the Hawke Research Institute at the University of South Australia. His research has focused on teachers' work, critical and reconciliation pedagogies, refugees, and socially just school reform. His theoretical work draws on critical sociology, critical anthropology, cultural studies, postcolonial theory and socially-engaged Buddhism. He has published in a range of journals including Pedagogy, Culture & Society, British Journal of Sociology of Education, British Educational Research Journal, *and* Discourse: studies in the cultural politics of education. *He has been involved in book projects with others that included* Schooling for a Fair Go, Teachers' Work in a Globalising Economy, *and* Dropping Out, Drifting Off, Being Excluded: Becoming Somebody Without School. *Recently he published a book entitled* Awakening-Struggle: Towards a Buddhist Critical Theory.

MARTIN HAIGH

14. THE SATTVIC CHOICE

An Indian contribution to education for a sustainable future

INTRODUCTION

The United Nations' "Decade of Education for Sustainable Development" (2005-2014) reflects an international desire to live together, harmoniously, within the means of our planet (Annan, 2001; Berry, 1999). The Decade proposes that education takes greater responsibility for tackling the causes of environmental degradation and helping learners realise that, collectively, the future is in their hands (UNESCO, 2004). It urges every educational institution to help learners achieve 'ecoliteracy', an understanding of the workings of our environmental life-support system and the realisation that their personal lifestyle decisions impact at every scale (Haigh, 2005).

Presently, the main environmental problem in the world is the Western way of life. The challenge for Education for Sustainable Development is to reconstruct some of the social beliefs that suffuse Western society such as: the right of every individual to maximise their immediate benefit from the world and that concern for the environment should be limited to its resource potential (Berry, 1999). Meanwhile, Western thought dominates the world, its economy, technology, science, and its media (Adams & Carfagna, 2006). Indeed, even in education, where multicultural perspectives are sometimes permitted, the discourse tends to be scripted by a neoliberal presumption that Western norms should prevail (Sidhu, 2004). The first target of Jonas Stier's (2004) critique of the ideologies of international education is 'Cultural idealism', interpreted as 'they should learn from us' and share the vision of a future shaped by technology, the market, and the exclusion of 'Others'—"women, non-Western cultures and Nature" (Milojević, 2005, p. 12). Stiers' other targets include 'academicentrism', which reifies an academic way of learning, and 'instrumentalism', which includes educational homogenisation—the creation of a common world educational structure that supports the current hegemony (Stiers, 2004). Gonzalez-Gaudiano (2005) has commented that even Environmental Education has, until recently, resisted the recognition of alternatives from outside its dominant milieu.

Today, many realise that Western culture, and the educational systems that support and reflect its beliefs, must transform. Ervin László, on behalf of the Club of Budapest, writes: "the world needs changing. It is not sustainable and sooner or later it will change. Predicting which way it will change is not the challenge... the challenge is for us to create a positive future" (László, 2002, p. 15). David Orr adds

M. Bussey, S. Inayatullah and I. Milojević (eds.), Alternative Educational Futures: Pedagogies for Emergent Worlds, 235–252.

that this is: "a crisis of values, ideas, perspectives and knowledge, which makes it a crisis of education, not in education" (Orr, 1994, p. 126).

Education for Sustainable Development (ESD) highlights the shortcomings of current Western education. A system oriented to creating and supporting an aggressive, competitive, 'me-first' society with a 'get-rich quick' mentality, which sets as its goal the maximisation of personal material wealth, is promoting attitudes that are strongly detrimental to the future (Berry, 1999). It is time to look outside for a better way, and this chapter seeks inspiration from an early challenge to Western globalised culture. This, the *sattvic* alternative, seems to suggest a path that leads through our current crises of environment, society and sustainability, toward a better, happier and more spiritually fulfilling future.

NEOVEDANTA EDUCATION

India's educational alternative grew up as a reaction to British Imperial education and its, not wholly unsuccessful, attempt to create British citizens in India after the fashion of the Roman Empire in Gaul. As Trevelyan advised the British Parliament: "Educated in the same way ... they become more English ... just as the Roman provincials became more Romans than Gauls" (Trevelyan, 1853). Of course, this system was motivated by commerce and the preservation of Imperial power. It was, as Swami Vivekananda later observed: "simply to get a lot of useful, practical slaves for little money ... a host of clerks, postmasters, telegraph operators, and so on" (Vivekananda, 1899, in Vivekananda, 1989, vol. 7, pp. 181–182). Its products: "westernized ... mercenaries ... mindless, soulless, directionless ... as if manufactured on an assembly line" (Sethi, 1979, p. 138).

Rooted in India's larger struggle for independence, resistance took the form of educational projects drawn from the ancient roots of Vedic culture (Sharma, 2002). From these, a new educational ideology evolved (Sharma, 2002). However, this Neovedanta education is a hybrid, emerging from an Indian episteme that has been heavily influenced by Western thought (Inayatullah, 2002; Sharma, 2002). Setting root in the wide array of modern social and religious movements, many international in scope, which have evolved from traditional Hinduism, it has matured into a viable educational alternative (Partridge, 2005). As Ivana Milojević argues, such discourses, which challenge the dystopian aspects of our present materialistic educational worldview, need to be considered by those engaged with educational development and policy (Milojević, 2005, p. 16).

The traditional themes that inform this Indian complex emerge from Vedanta, literally the 'end of knowledge', the teachings of the *Upanishads* that culminate the ancient Vedic scriptures, and also from Bhagavata Dharma, which is developed in later Vaisnava scriptures. The mix is leavened with ideas from science, socialism and Victorian notions of progress. Its leading modern luminaries include Swami Vivekananda, Nobel Laureate Rabindranath Tagore, Mahatma Gandhi, India's philosopher/President Sarvepalli Radhakrishnan, Sri Aurobindo and later international leaders such as Srila Bhaktivedanta Prabhupada, Maharishi Mahesh Yogi and Paramahamsa Yogananda. Its key text is the *Bhagavad-Gita*; it is no coincidence that most of those listed have written extensive commentaries on its verses (e.g., Gandhi, 1926).

THE THREE MODES OF EDUCATION

The *Bhagavad-Gita*[1] holds the keys to the educational alternative offered by Neovedanta's Bhagavata Dharma. This text, building upon Vedic precedent, proposes that the material world emerges from the imbalance of three qualities, whose relative proportions condition all aspects of matter and mind (*Bhagavad-Gita* 2.45). These are the three *Gunas*, three modes that govern all material existence. An analogy is a digital image, which is created from pixels of three primary colours. It matters not whether the image depicts Jaipur or Jordan, the colours are the same but, in different combinations, they create an image that observers take for reality.

Sattva guna, colour white, represents positive qualities: purity, serenity, harmony, tranquillity and harmony; *rajas guna*, colour fiery red, represents action, energy, engagement, attachment, desire, anger, acquisitiveness and greed; while *tamas guna*, black, represents negative qualities: ignorance, negativity, heedlessness, sloth, banality, heaviness and dullness (*Bhagavad-Gita* 14.5-18).

Everything in the material world is conditioned by the *gunas* combined in different proportions. However, when *sattva* and *rajas* are ignored or neglected, *tamas* overwhelms. When *tamas* and *sattva* are overpowered, *rajas* dominates. When, *rajas* and *tamas* are suppressed, *sattva* transcends (*Bhagavad-Gita* 14.10). The word *guna* means rope and all three bind to the world: *sattva* through goodness and happiness, *rajas* through lust, anger, greed and attachment to material possessions, *tamas* through ignorance and indolence (*Bhagavad-Gita* 14, 6-8).

Education may be interpreted in terms of the *gunas*. Learning is *tamasic* when learners are discouraged from thought, involvement or study and permitted only to memorise. By contrast, *rajasic* learning evokes energy and passion—it encourages classification, analysis, chauvinism and strategic creativity aimed at competitive personal advancement. Sattvic learning encourages learners to see things as a whole; it promotes synthesis, empathy, ethical understanding and deep learning (*Bhagavad-Gita* 18.20-22). To advance, it is necessary for learners to raise themselves above the thoughtlessness of *tamas*, beyond the emotive divisiveness and selfishness of rajas, and towards the harmony and serenity of a sattvic overview (12-13, 19-42).

In the *Bhagavad-Gita*, the *gunas* serve three functions. They provide a way of understanding the world—a means of interpretation; they provide a warning about the ways a person may become bound to self-destructive behaviour; and they provide a ladder—which spiritual aspirants may ascend through self-improvement and a better life-style. Climbing the ladder from *tamas* to *sattva*, of course, involves a far-reaching personal change, a new ethic, a new way of life, Bhagavata Dharma (cf. Tapasyananda, 1984, pp. 250–252).

The pedagogic key is that, while humans are the *gunas'* puppets, nevertheless, everything that the *gunas* colours, is, to some extent, coloured by the self. For example, giving a gift may be an act of goodness, promoting *sattva* (*Bhagavad-Gita* 18.5-6). However, if that gift is given without thought, inappropriately, to unworthy persons, then it is *tamasic*. If it is given in order to engineer future favours, then it is *rajasic*. Only if it is made, through a sense of duty, to a worthy cause and without regard for personal cost is it sattvic (*Bhagavad-Gita* 17. 21-23; 18.5-6). The point is that, in every small decision, there is a choice. There are always options that are more or less sattvic. As Tagore argued: "The highest education is that which ... makes our life in harmony with all existence" (Tagore, 1917, p. 116).

SELF-REALISATION AND *DHARMA*

The cultivation of *sattva guna* is a target for Neovedanta education. However, the ultimate aim of both Vedanta and Bhagavata Dharma is transcendence of the three *gunas* and all the trappings of the material world. The *Bhagavad-Gita*, a teaching of Lord Krishna, offers help to those embodied spirits who wish to return to their original, eternal, spiritual reality (*Bhagavad-Gita* 4.6-7; 18.64-66). This goal is called self-realisation, where that self is an eternal consciousness that is the foundation, source and cause of the universe. The purpose of life is to reconnect a personal self-conscious with consciousness of the universal self, the ultimate truth (Dandekar, 2005; Hiriyana, 1949). Gandhi's declared life-goals were "to realize God, to realize Self and to realize Truth ... three expressions for the same development" (Naess 1974, p. 34). Sri Aurobindo thought that such spiritual awakening, "Truth-consciousness' [was] the only way beyond Earthly ignorance and mis-Governance" (Nandakumar, 1988, p. 55).

Naturally, this worldview means that most schools of Vedanta, including the influential Vaisnava Acintya Bhedabheda School, recognise the material world as an aspect of Godhead (Tapasyananda, 1990). Vivekananda explains: "God is ... everywhere. He works through all hands, sees through all eyes ... lives in all life ... thinks through every brain. Man can become like God ... if he multiplies infinitely his centre of self-consciousness" (Vivekananda ca.1900 in Vivekananda, 1989, vol. 2, p. 35). Everything is the substance of God. Everything alive contains a spark of the Supreme. The material world is sacred, each human is embedded within it, and "All living beings are members one of another so a person's every act has a beneficial or harmful influence on the world" (Gandhi, 1884–1946, vol. 50, p. 218).

Of course, Gandhi's thinking was a direct ancestor of the ecocentric, 'Deep Ecology' philosophy that subtexts much ESD (Jacobsen, 1996). Deep Ecology builds upon the intuition that "I am One with Nature", which is achieved through a pedagogical process called "Ecological Self-realisation" (Devall, 1990). This three-step expansion tackles the way in which an individual defines their self. It strives to shift self-identity from ego to eco, from the personal self, through the self–as–part–of–a–social–group toward recognition of the ecological self, where that self is the community of all life (Naess, 1987, Haigh, 2006). Ecological self-realisation recognises that "The same stream of life that runs through my veins ... runs through the world ..." (Tagore, 1913, p. 69). Tagore found this world "a living thing, intimately close to my life, permeated by the subtle touch of kinship, which enhances the value of my own being" (Tagore, 1930, p. 99; Sinha, 1993).

Some Western commentators worry about Vedanta's subordination of the material world (e.g., Nelson, 1991). This is because the classical Advaita Vedanta of Sankara reduces the material world to an illusory superposition on true reality, the Universal Consciousness (Sharma, 2004). Of course, Western education reifies its own form of detachment. Teachers often pose as objective, world independent, observers—not invisible but separate from their objects of study. Such detachment obstructs ESD because it engages neither instructor nor student with the world but holds them at a distance (Haigh, 2005). For example, India's Western-style "National Curriculum Framework" worries that: "curriculum and success dynamics demand that [learners] shut out the real world ... and lock themselves up in the world of books" (NCERT, 2005, p. 117).

However, the *Bhagavad-Gita* considers inactivity *tamasic* and the sattvic lifestyle it commends is based on positive action in the world. Certainly, detachment of a kind is also required, but this detachment is not from action but only its personal material benefits. Sattvic action involves detachment, from selfish, *rajasic*, activity and from *tamasic* self-indulgent gratification and laziness. Sattvic action involves service undertaken as a matter of duty, because it is the right thing to do, regardless of its personal consequences. All India's Neovedanta educators accept this engaged ethos, all promote service to the world (Sharma, 2002). Tagore cast each learner as a "*visvakarma*", a world-worker, (Tagore, 1930, p. 42), who accepts responsibility to act for the welfare of all and who demonstrates the "union of education and life" (Tagore, 1961, p. 43). Vivekananda advised: "... teach the people first the means of procuring their food and clothing" (Vivekananda 1989, vol. 7, pp. 181–183).

BUILDING A SATTVIC EDUCATION

The *Bhagavad-Gita's* concept of sattvic education emphasises holism, synthesis, and rejects any reduction of the world to a collection of names and forms (*Bhagavad-Gita* 18.20-22). *Ekam evadvityam*, the 'catch-phrase' of Vedanta, is often translated as "all is One". However, achieving this sattvic condition, even from the platform of ecological self-realisation, is not easy. It demands a structured process of learning and personal development.

Commonly, this curriculum includes five key elements—all of which have direct value to ESD. First is the *acharya* concept, which proposes that teachers become role models. Second is experiential 'learning–by–doing' and reflective inquiry (Sharma, 1993; Gandhi, 1927-1929). Third is self-improvement, 'whole person, full character, education', which includes mental disciplines developed through yoga and meditation. Fourth is engagement with world-making though dutiful service, which may be effected through productive work, as practised by Gandhi, through service to the arts, as commended by Tagore, or service to the poor as demonstrated by Vinoba Bhave and Srila Prabhupada's "food for all" programmes. Fifth is the ethos of Bhagavata Dharma, which reifies truth, *ahimsa* (non-harming) with intolerance of iniquity and deprivation. Bhagavata Dharma's sattvic values rate spiritual above material wealth, humility above pride, while its doctrine of reincarnation contains the notion that one's present actions control one's future lives and so engenders respect for the future (*Bhagavad-Gita* 13.21, 14, 14-15). It also validates the need for self-sustainability and living within the means of the habitat, a practice that may be illustrated through Gandhi's overtly sattvic socio-economic system 'Sarvodaya'.

1. Acharya: *Leading by Example*

Traditionally, Vedic education involves service to a guru, who is both an *acharya*, a sattvic role model, and a teacher—required to issue instruction, but more importantly to respond fully to the questions posed by a learner, just as Lord Krishna responded to the questions of Arjuna in the *Bhagavad-Gita*. Everyone needs help, which in Vedic tradition, is provided by a guru, whose purpose is to provide a link between individual and immortal Self (Sivananda, 1998).

The duty and necessity for leadership by example is already widely debated in ESD workshops and it is a major challenge. David Orr writes "What is desperately needed are faculty and administrators who provide role models of integrity ... and institutions that are capable of embodying ideals wholly and completely in all of their operations" (Orr, 1991, p. 57).

Vivekananda agrees: "Without the personal life of the teacher, there would be no education" (Vivekananda, 1989, vol. 5, p. 224). Sunderlal Bahuguna, environmental campaigner and co-founder of the Chipko ("Hug the Trees") movement, echoes Gandhi's truth: 'My life is my message' (Bahuguna, 1987). Gandhi's disciple Acharya Vinoba Bhave's message was his 19 year walk through India's villages persuading village communities to donate land and labour to their poor, to resist oppression non-violently, and to live simply, self-sustainably and self-sufficiently (Bhave, 1986).

Srila Prabhupada (1896-1977), Founder-Acharya of ISKCON, the Hare Krishna movement, lived his version of Bhaktivedanta and his life remains a textbook for followers (Satsvarupa dasa, 1983). Indeed, ISKCON itself is the fulfilment of a request from Srila Prabhupdada's guru. Meanwhile, Srila Prabhupada, a guru for many, sets all gurus to work to alleviate the suffering of their followers, which he attributes to ignorance (*tamas*) and material attachments (*rajas*). Srila Prabhupada also stressed the importance of finding, not just a bona fide guru but The Guru, and described the many ways to distinguish a 'rascal', not least the *rajasic* trappings of personal pride and comfort (Prabhupada, 1989, p. 60).

In fact, the very activity of searching for this true guru is valuable because it brings the learner into contact with new ideas. For example, some Indian environmentalists have nominated Satguru Dattatreya, who, in the *Uddhava Gita*, has the signal honour of being quoted by Lord Krishna, as environmental guru for all Hindus (Dwivedi & Tiwari, 1987). Significantly, here, Satguru Dattatreya gains knowledge, not from any human or text but by observing the world around him, where he finds 24 gurus (Sivananda, 1998). In other Puranic texts, Sri Dattatreya teaches by creating experiential learning experiences for His supplicants and devotees; typically, placing them in scenarios where they are challenged to face down their own prejudices, and see beneath the surface appearances to the spiritual truth beneath (Haigh, 2007).

2. Experiential Learning: Experiments with Truth

ESD is about personal ethics and educator *acharyas* are urged to 'lead by being', which is no easy task. Fortunately, the lives of *acharyas* like Tagore, Bhave, Gandhi, Sarkar, Yogananda, Srila Prabhupada and others, provide both advice and consolation (e.g., Gandhi, 1927-1929; Bhave 1986, Satsvarupa dasa, 1983). All suffered setbacks. All made mistakes, *rajasic* and *tamasic*, but all progressed by a process of experimentation and experiential learning, which is typical of Vedanta's approach (Sharma, 1993). Former Gandhian sevak, Shrila Prabhupada argues: "Mahatma Gandhi ... dedicated his life to experimenting with Truth. Why only Mahatma Gandhi? Every one of us ..." should do the same (Prabhupada, 1958, in Prabhupada 1989, p. 38).

3. Whole Mind Education

For Swami Vivekananda, "The present system of education is all wrong. The mind is crammed with facts before it knows how to think ... I would learn to master my mind first and then gather facts if I wanted them ... control of the mind should be taught first" (Vivekananda, 1989, vol. 8, p. 280). Tagore considered that "the development of mind and body should go hand in hand with the development of the soul" (Roy, 2005). He founded his school, Santiniketan, "... under the shady trees [where a learner] is in a natural setting ... [and able to] fully express the hidden wealth of his individual endowment. True education can never be crammed ... from without; rather it must aid in bringing... to the surface the ... wisdom within" (Tagore in Yogananda, 1946).

Yoga and meditation, traditional Vedic techniques for controlling and developing the mind, are already part of daily life in the West. They aim to build mental focus, screen out distractions from the 'sea of life', and establish contact with "the God within" (Bernard, 2001). Paramahamsa Yogananda, who brought yoga to the US and to Gandhi, regarded yoga as a key educational discipline (Yogananda, 1946). Yoga involves constructive control of breathing, physical posture and mental control of the senses towards reconnecting of self and Self (Berry, 1992). However, in the West, it is popular because it helps practitioners relax, stay healthy, concentrate and function more effectively in everyday life (Berry, 1992). It has value for every system of physical education and as a more general antidote to the diseases of stress, currently at epidemic levels in the UK (NCERT, 2005).

Meditation, a related discipline, is also popularly employed as a way of reducing work–a–day stress. Decades of research have proven meditation's benefits that include enhancing readiness for learning, creative expression, spiritual development in primary education and short-term memory in university students (McLean,

2001; Tm.org, 2005). Medical benefits adduced include pain control, improved sleep patterns and reduced blood pressure, and in the psychological realm—enhanced self esteem, reduced stress, improved cognitive functions, greater empathy and happiness (Boniwell, 2006; Barrows & Jacobs, 2002). Its Vedic goal may be a higher consciousness but its initial exercises are valued in the classroom. A recent visualisation experiment at Brookes University found that many students had previously experienced its application in the context of religious studies at private schools. However, it is more widely deployed in professional management education. Internationally, the approach is most associated with the (hugely heterodox) Brahma Kumari movement and Maharishi Mahesh Yogi, guru of the Beatles and Natural Law (e.g., Fergusson et al., 1995). The Maharishi argues that knowledge is structured consciousness and education a change in consciousness, which mediation facilitates (Maharishi, 2005). The Brahma Kumaris emphasise sattvic values with the goal of peace (Jayanti, 2006). Their Living Values Educational Program launches with UNESCO's Delors Report (1996), whose foundations are: learning to do, learning to know, learning to live together and learning to be. The program focuses on the last, exploring and sharing an inner world of thoughts feelings and emotions, often using meditation as a tool (Tilman & Colomina, 2000).

4. Engagement with the World: The Visvakarma

Nevertheless, for Gandhi, Tagore, Bhave and Vivekananda, education requires active engagement. Tagore thought that involving his students in the creative arts and music, encouraging the dreamers of dreams, would help learners self-realise the integrity of humanity, Nature and the Divine (Sinha, 1993). Gandhi emphasised handicrafts, productive skills and economic self-sufficiency, while Vinoba Bhave and Vivekananda emphasised community service (Malik, 1961). Following the *Bhagavad-Gita*, Gandhi argued that "Education does not mean a knowledge of letters ... it means knowledge of duty ... True education lies in serving others ..." (Gandhi, in Rajput, 1998, p. 2). In recent years, service learning has become a major theme in the Community Colleges of the US. As in Neovedanta Education, the objective here is to combine community action and learning objectives, with the aim of transforming both the student and service recipient community. Again, this is accomplished by combining service work with activities that emphasise reflection, self-discovery, and mutual understanding (NSLC, 2004). The NSLC gives the example of students collecting litter from an urban stream bed, inherently a valuable community service, but when the trash is problematised and explained with recommendations for solutions, this is becomes service–learning, world-making in the sense of Tagore. Of course, constructive programmes uniting science, society, environment and the spiritual remain the rule for Bhagavata Dharma and Neovedanta education (Sharma, 2002). These programmes are overtly engaged in the task of trying to recreate heaven upon Earth, often citing Lord Krishna's Goloka Vrindavan as their ideal (Cremo & Goswami, 1995; Prime,

2000). However, the best documented are Gandhi's Sarvodaya and the Nai Talim, New Education, system that served it.

5. Values Education: Sarvodaya and Nai Talim

Today's Western educators measure the success of their graduates in terms of wealth and status. Bhagavata Dharma considers the accumulation of great wealth both antisocial and personally damaging because spiritual uplift is prevented by attachment to the material world. Environmentalist Vandana Shiva interprets the *Isa Upanishad*: "Take only what you need ... Do not take anything else for you know to whom it belongs" (Shiva, 2000, p. 133). This is why Gandhi sought to replace the concept of personal possession with a system of trusteeship.

Gandhi's version of ESD was *Sarvodaya*. This means the uplift of all, and its source is Gandhi's Gujarati paraphrase of John Ruskin's "Unto this Last". Here, Gandhi discovered three ethical pillars: that economy is good that benefits the good of all, a lawyer's work has the same value as a barber's in that all have the same right to earn their livelihood, and the life of labour, the life of the tiller of the soil, is the life worth living (Doctor, 1967).

Sarvodaya was built on five key values (Richards, 1982). First came Truth, a synonym for God, the goal of Self-realisation, and second, *ahimsa*, which means non-harming. The *Bhagavad-Gita* argues asserts the spiritual unity of all life, hence Gandhi campaigned against social prejudice and for the rights of all creatures. Third was *satyagraha*, the simultaneous realisation of Truth and *ahimsa* in the management of human affairs, which relied on 'Truth-force' to transform wrongdoers (Naess, 1974). Fourth was *swaraj*, self-rule—a term from India's struggle for independence, which Gandhi interpreted as self-control and proposed as a goal for each community and each individual. Fifth, *swadeshi* became "bread labour", a universal duty to engage in productive labour, which counters the prejudice that manual workers are inferior (Doctor, 1967). Bhave (1969) summarises Sarvodaya as: capable people directing their capacity to service of the people; people fully self-dependent and cooperative with non-violence as the social interaction. These ideals also emerge from Vaisnava scripture, especially the descriptions of Ramraj, the rule of Lord Rama in the *Ramayana* epic.

From today's standpoint, Sarvodaya thinking is startlingly progressive. Decades before ESD, it was a political economy that did not strive for growth but harmonious stability. It did not rely on trade (and the unsustainable transport of goods across huge distances) but emphasised sustainable local production. It did not reify material wealth but quality of life (cf. Berry, 1999). Gandhi's system also sought to avoid the environmental and social problems, which result from the endless quest for more possessions and sensual stimulation, by advocating a quiet and simple, sattvic, life-style; Gandhi's maxim, "live simply so that others may simply live", remains part of the Green catechism. Sarvodaya's system of trusteeship sought to eliminate the delusion of personal possession, which is the cause of *rajas* and so harmful to self-realisation.

Sarvodaya further promoted the concept of an egalitarian society by emphasising self-reliance, small scale enterprise and pluralism, so avoiding the social blight of class, caste, inter-community and employer-employee antagonism. Its commitment to non-harming, *ahimsa*, includes the search for non-destructive solutions to social problems, a deep respect for the rights of non-human living creatures and for the environment in general. Decentralisation, the idea of the democratic "village republics", sought to remove the possibility of oppression from distant administrations and bureaucracies and to link people more intimately with their own habitat. Gandhi argued "in serving the neighbour, one in effect serves the world" (Gandhi, 1932, in: Gandhi, 1884-1946, vol. 50, p. 218). Deep Ecology guru Naess comments: "Gandhi's utopia is one of the few that shows ecological balance, and today his rejection of the Western World's material abundance and waste is accepted by progressives of the ecological movement" (Naess, 1974, p. 10).

The point is emphasised in *The Economy of Permanence*, a pioneering book by Gandhian Sevak J. C. Kumarappa (1945), which links human civilisation to the three *gunas*, charting an evolution from *tamas*, through the *rajasic* present day, and towards a final advanced, spiritual, sattvic stage. This sattvic, Sarvodaya, "Economy of Service" would represent the:

> ... highest form of economy in Nature ... best seen in the relation between the young one and the parent. The mother bird will scour the jungle and risk its life in defending the young from its enemies. It functions neither for its present need nor for its personal future requirement, but projects its activities into the next generation, or generations to come, without looking for any reward. (Kumarappa, 1945, p. 9)

Attempts continue to be made to apply Sarvodaya to education both within India and outside (Tamatea, 2005). The best known is A. T Ariyaratne's, 15,000 village, Sarvodaya Shramadama programme in Sri Lanka (Kantowsky, 1980). Table 1 summarises this programme's development targets and indicates the way in which education, especially experiential service education, is embedded.

Gandhi regarded educational reform as a priority. His Nai Talim (New Education) sought a sattvic alternative to the British Imperial system, which he considered elitist, financially parasitic and producing graduates with unhelpful attitudes and irrelevant skills. Instead, Gandhi wanted a system that created free thinking people with relevant skills who would act locally and aspire transcendentally for liberation. Gandhi's Nai Talim sought the elimination of social problems and the creation of a local, self-sustainable productive base. It aspired to create sattvic reflective learners, skilled with useful knowledge, who were integrated into community life through engagement in productive work and who desired to undertake service for humanity. It tried to find self-realised acharya teachers, whose lives would be signposts that dissolved the need for words, often recruiting them from Tagore's Santiniketan (Sethi, 1979).

Table 1. Sattvic (Sarvodaya) development targets

Basic needs to satisfy	Social targets to address
1. Sattvic environment—clean, healthy, and sufficient—especially water	1. Sattvic society with motivation based on a respect for virtue, wisdom, moral strength, Truth, *ahimsa*, self-denial and a striving for self-realisation
2. Basic material wants: food—a balanced and adequate diet; shelter—housing; adequate energy supply, clothing; health care, communications	2. Material (and spiritual) self-reliance and self-sufficiency—including economic freedom through engagement with productive labour (*swaraj, swadeshi*) and service aimed at uplifting the physical, psychological and social environment, and removing social disparities
3. Cultural and spiritual needs: developed by 'whole person' education and through service and values learning	3. Engaging the Truth-force by harnessing sattvic qualities through community service and empowered, participatory self-governance

Source: after Kantowsky (1980, pp. 60-65); Herath (1998).

Gandhi's educational institutes were conceived as communities of learning, each deeply embedded within the context and concerns of their host community (Sethi, 1979, p. 138). Ever the practical politician, his first targets were the social problems of India's rural communities, especially poverty and caste. His system aspired to remove the disparities between town and village, which still draw people from the villages to swell urban slums, but it began with primary education in the villages.

Nai Talim was based on active learning. Rather than commencing with literacy, Gandhi's scheme began with learning by doing through agriculture and small scale production, typically handicrafts. Literacy came later, and so too other knowledge, developed as far as possible by strategies, now accepted as problem or project-based learning, which are widely used in medicine, engineering and (environmental) management.

Higher education would also be practically oriented and driven by active rather than passive learning strategies. It aspired to create 'world citizens', but also graduates who were grounded in India's own cultural roots (Narayan, 1969). Unlike Tagore, Gandhi did not seek to revive India's spirit through artistic and musical creativity. He had little time for the arts, especially in higher education, instead he emphasised self-sufficiency, arguing for example, that any agricultural college that could not provide for itself was not worth the name.

Of course, Gandhi was assassinated before his ideas were fully fledged. Serious attempts were made to implement his ideas during the 1940s and 1950s (Narayan, 1969). However, despite early support from India's Government, including its first President, Zakir Hussain, independent India's education gradually slipped back into well trodden paths.

CURRICULUM

The arguments concerning the means of delivering a sattvic curriculum are similar to those concerning ESD and 'ecoliteracy'. Options include the creation of separate specialist programmes, a core course—shared by all programmes, or learning exercises embedded within every programme. All of these options create problems; for example, one consigns ESD to an academic ghetto, another risks packaged tokenism and a third lip-service. Bonnett (2003), however, proposes that ESD should be adopted as a new ethos, a new frame of mind. The sattvic choice, which emerges from the ancient and neglected roots of ESD, provides a very similar ethos and framework, albeit without recourse to the traditional authorities of academic Western thought (Haigh, 2006). However, as in the difference between ecological and Vedic self-realisation, its scope is far greater.

Table 2. Ethos of the sattvic curriculum

	Sattvic	*Rajasic*	*Tamasic*
Worldview	Spiritual	Materialistic	Materialistic
Emphasis	Ethical	Competitive	Selfish
	Dutiful	Ambitious	Careless
	Means	Ends	Ease
Qualities	Peaceful	Energetic	Indolent
	Serene	Lively	Uninvolved
	Moral	Amoral	Immoral
Approach	Reflective	Engaged	Apathetic
	Active (*ahmisa*)	Active (*himsa*)	Passive
	Self-purification	Self-promotion	Self-indulgent
Objective	Assimilation	Acquisition	Avoidance

The sattvic choice provides an alternative ethos and a simple framework that could be applied to the benefit all education. This final section sketches out guidelines for curriculum design (cf. *Bhagavad-Gita* 16). Table 2 lists attributes of the three *gunas* that are relevant to curriculum design. The problem is to expunge *tamas* from the curriculum and develop *sattva*, while not becoming entrapped in *rajas*. Of course, *rajas guna* embraces qualities such as enthusiasm and creativity, which help develop *sattva*, albeit alongside aspects such competition, envy, greed and anger, which fuel *tamas*. The *Bhagavad-Gita* notes that *rajasic* activities tend to be enjoyable at the start but painful later, while sattvic activities are the reverse (*Bhagavad-Gita* 18. 24-26).

Equally, it is possible to sketch in a framework for the content of sattvic curriculum (Table 3). This stresses deep learning, reflective practice, ethical awareness and working for others rather than personal gain. It follows the Gandhian maxim that the means and the ends should be the same and the Delors' idea that people should work together toward mutual goals (Delors, 1996).

Table 3. Methodological framework for the sattvic curriculum

	Sattvic	Rajasic	Tamasic
Style	Holistic	Reductionist	Dogmatic
	Synthesis	Analysis	Fact-based
	Ethical debate	Problem-solving	Entertainment
Approach	Cooperative	Competitive	Collective
	Team	Individual	Book
Learning Style	Deep	Strategic	Surface
	Reflective	Operational	Minimal
Focus	Reflection	Exploitation	Avoidance
	Means	Ends	Immediate
	For All Today	For Me soon	For Me now
	Duty	Ambition	Gratification
	Welfare	Competition	Compliance

Translated as course content, in science, this might mean teaching more systems science and less about objects, such as rocks, plants and soils, in isolation. In religious studies, the sattvic curriculum would explore univeralism more than sectarianism; in social sciences—unities more than disagreements; in psychology—the positive; in arts—the uplifting more than the emotive or decorative; and in applied subjects—that which promotes human wellbeing more than immediate wealth. In the environmental disciplines, it would emphasise the unity of the human and environmental spheres, it would teach Gaia or Earth System Science, rather than merely cataloguing the environment's names and forms; in conservation, it would focus on the important rather than the merely pretty, and it would stress positive action for a sustainable future more than protesting about habitat degradation and decay. In engineering, it would aim to work within nature rather than seek to control or suppress it.

Discussion

The sattvic choice, developed through Bhagavata Dharma, offers a spiritual alternative and a way into the future that does not depend on material wealth, technology, or the suppression of 'others'. Instead, it offers learners both a personal ethic and a set of social values that is much more in tune with the needs of their environment and their descendents.

Today, most environmentalists believe the cause of our modern environmental problems is the human arrogance that puts human, often personal, welfare first and which is obsessed with the growth of material wealth (cf. Berry, 1999). The sattvic choice offers simple living, high thoughts and harmonious coexistence with all beings. Some Western educational philosophers look towards an environmental education for a Post-Humanist Age, albeit without reference to its non-European antecedents (Bonnett, 2003). In fact, decades ahead of its time, Gandhi's sattvic system for political economy, Sarvodaya, sought balance and stability not growth (Doctor, 1967). Like modern ESD, it emphasised sustainable local production rather than the unsustainable long distance transport of goods. It promoted social egalitarianism, small scale enterprise, decentralised governance, and pluralism. It also contained a deep philosophical underpinning, a window on the larger frameworks of Neovedanta education and Bhagavata Dharma (Gandhi, 1926).

Reviewers have asked if this sattvic alternative is a real option for secular education or just something appropriate to religious studies? The answer is that the approach is appropriate to any education that has deep concern for the person, their well being and the wellbeing of all in the future. Certainly, in the *Bhagavad-Gita*, the theory of the *gunas* is taught by God. However, subsequently, the same concept has been deployed in essentially atheistic philosophical systems such as Isvarakrsna's Samkhya and Sankara's Advaita Vedanta (Larson, 1979; Sharma, 2004). The message is that, while the *gunas* may lead towards the Supreme Self, this final revelation lies beyond the highest platform of *sattva guna*. The *gunas* themselves belong to the material world, where their recognition, as Gandhi and his Neovedanta associates demonstrate, provides an alternative approach both to environmental interpretation and world-making; an alternative that is overtly grounded in the personal, non-destructive and ethically validated lifestyle so urgently sought by ESD.

CONCLUSION

David Orr (1994, p. 53) writes that our world "... needs people who live well in their places ... it needs people of moral courage willing ... to make the world habitable and humane" (Orr, 1994, p. 53). Neovedanta education grew up to combat the *rajasic* ethos and *tamasic* effects of Westernised education that "most sophisticated danger ..." to a sustainable way of life (Saran, 1979, p. 367). In its place, they "propose a new education ... a new way of living" (Kumar, 1969, p. 6). Gandhi's message of simple living, self-sustainability, non-violence and 'making poverty history' anticipated much modern 'Green' thinking and was a direct ancestor of the ecocentric thought that underpins much ESD (Jacobsen, 1996). However, the larger aim of Bhagavata Dharma, to create thinking people who act locally and aspire transcendentally remains a sound foundation for ESD, much better than the 'me-first', 'get-rich quick' approach still promoted by much globalised education (Berry, 1999).

A sattvic curriculum recognises the ontological unity of everything, emphasises the learners' kinship with all living spirits and casts the learner's role, '*dharma*', as service in the world. *Sattva* is a condition of goodness, serenity, harmony and spiritual wellbeing. It contrasts with the *tamasic* indolence and self-indulgence and *rajasic* envy, ambition and greed that dominate modern human society. It is achieved through world-making service and experiential learning through service. Vivekananda asserted: "First, make the people of the country stand on their legs ... first let them learn to have good food and clothes and plenty of enjoyment—then tell them how to be free ..." (Vivekananda, 1899, in Vivekananda 1989, vol. 7, pp. 181–183).

Each sattvic learner is a would-be *visvakarma*, a world-maker. The nature of each learner's service in the world may be self-defined by their personal qualities and contexts but it always involves the active construction of a more sattvic habitat, a more sustainable future (Cremo & Goswami, 1995).

NOTES

[i] Scriptural sources—*Bhagavad-Gita* in translation: Bhaktivedanta Swami Prabhupada, A.C. (1972). *Bhagavadgita As It Is*. London: Collier Macmillan / New York: Collier; and Tapasyananda, Swami (1984). *Srimad Bhagavad Gita: The Scripture of Mankind*. Chennai: Sri Ramakrishna Math.

REFERENCES

Adams, J. M., & Carfagna, A. (2006). *Coming of age in a globalized world*. Bloomfield, CT: Kumarian.

Annan, K. (2001). *Secretary general calls for break in political stalemate over environmental issues*. United Nations Press Release: SC/SM/7739 15/03/01. Retrieved April, 2004, from http://www.un.org/News/Press/docs/2001/sgsm7739.doc.htm

Aurobindo Ghose. (1951). *The life divine*. New York: Sri Aurobindo Ashram.

Bahuguna, S. (1987). The crisis of civilisation and the message of culture in the context of environment. *Gandhi Marg—Journal of the Gandhi Peace Foundation, 9*, 451–468.

Barrows, K. A., & Jacobs, B. P. (2002). Mind-body medicine: An introduction and review of the literature. *The Medical Clinics of North America, 86*, 11–31.

Bernard, P. (2001). *La protection divine*. Oka, Quebec: Mystik Connexion.

Berry, T. M. (1999). *The great work: Our way into the future*. New York: Belltower.

Berry, T. M. (1992). *Religions of India: Hinduism, yoga and buddhism*. New York: Columbia University.

Bhave, V. (1986). *The intimate and the ultimate*. Totnes, UK: Green Books.

Bhave, V. (1969). The politics of non-violence. In S. Kumar (Ed.), *School of non-violence*. London: Martin Luther King Foundation.

Boniwell, I. (2006). *Positive psychology in a nutshell*. London: Personal Well-Being Centre.

Bonnett, M. (2003). Retrieving nature: Education for a post-humanist age. *Journal of Philosophy of Education, 37*, 551–730.

Cremo, M. A., & Goswami, M. (1995). *Divine nature: A spiritual perspective on the environmental crisis*. Los Angeles: Bhaktivedanta Book Trust.

Dandekar, R. (2005). Vedānta. In L. Jones (Ed.), *Encyclopedia of religion 14* (2nd ed., pp. 9543–9549). Detroit, MI: Macmillan.

Delors, J., et al. (1996). *Learning: The treasure within*. Paris: UNESCO. Retrieved December, 2006, from http://www.unesco.org/delors/delors_e.pdf

Devall, B. (1990). *Simple in means, rich in ends: Practising deep ecology*. London: Merlin Press–Green Print.

Doctor, A. H. (1967). *Sarvodaya: A political and economic study*. London: Asia.

Dwivedi, O. P., & Tiwari, B. N. (1987). *Environmental crisis and Hindu religion*. New Delhi: Gitanjali.

Fergusson, L. C., Bonshek, A. J., & Le Masson, A. (1995). Vedic science based education and non-verbal intelligence: A preliminary longitudinal study in Cambodia. *Higher Education Research & Development, 15*, 73–82.

Gandhi, M. K. (n.d.). *Sarvodaya, the uplift of all.* Ahmedabad: Navajivan Trust.

Gandhi, M. K. (1927–1929). *An autobiography or the story of my experiments with truth.* Ahmedabad: Navajivan Trust/Harmondsworth, UK: Penguin (1982).

Gandhi, M. K. (1926). *M K Gandhi interprets the Bhagavad Gita.* New Delhi: Orient-Vision Books.

Gandhi, M. K. (1884–1946). *In ministry of information and broadcasting (1958–1982), the collected works of Mahatma Gandhi* (85 vols.). New Delhi: Government of India.

Gonzalez-Gaudiano, E. (Ed.). (2005). Environmental education and education for sustainable development. *Policy Futures in Education, 3*, 239–308.

Haigh, M. (2007, September). *Sri Dattatreya's 24 gurus: Learning from the world in vedanta.* Paper presented at the 'Critical Perspectives on Religion and Environment conference, Birmingham.

Haigh, M. (2006). Deep ecology education: Learning from its vaisnava roots. *Canadian Journal of Environmental Education, 11*, 43–57.

Haigh, M. (2005). Greening the curriculum: Appraising an international movement. *Journal of Geography in Higher Education, 29*, 33–50.

Herath, H. M. D. R. (1998). Moral education for environmental protection: The sarvodaya model. In B. Saraswati (Ed.), *Cultural dimension of ecology.* New Delhi: Indira Gandhi National Centre for the Arts. Retrieved August, 2005, from http://ignca.nic.in/cd_07017.htm /http://ignca.nic.in/cd_07.htm

Hiriyana, M. (1949). *An outline of Indian philosophy.* London: Diamond.

Inyatullah, S. (2002). *Understanding sarkar: The Indian episteme, macrohistory and transformative knowledge.* Leiden: Brill.

Jacobsen, K. A. (1996). Bhagavad gita, ecosophy T and deep ecology. *Inquiry, 39*, 219–238.

Jayanti, B. K. (2006). *Practical meditation: Spiritual yoga for the mind.* London: Brahma Kumari World Spiritual University.

Kantowsky, D. (1980). *Sarvodaya: The other development.* Sahibabad, UP: Vikas.

Kumar, S. (1969). *School of non-violence.* London: Martin Luther King Foundation.

Kumarappa, J. C. (1945). *Economy of permanence.* Kashi: Akhil Bharat Sarva-Seva-Sangh Publications.

Larson, G. J. (1979). *Classical samkhya: An interpretation of its history and meaning.* Delhi: Motilal Banarsidass.

László, E. (2002). *You can change the world: Action handbook for the 21st century.* Clun, Shropshire, UK: Positive News.

Malik, G. (1961). *Gandhi and Tagore.* Ahmedabad: Navajivan Trust.

Maharishi. (1987). *Maharishi speaks to educators; Mastery over natural law by his holiness the Maharishi Mahesh Yogi* (4 vols.). Vlodorp, Netherlands: MTC.

Mashruwala, K. G. (1971). *Towards sarvodaya order.* Ahmedabad: Navajivan Trust.

McLean, P. (2001). Perceptions of the impact of meditation on learning. *Pastoral Care in Education, 19*, 31–35.

Milojević, I. (2004). *Educational futures: Dominant and contesting visions.* London: Routledge.

Naess, A. (1974). *Gandhi and group conflict: An exploration of Satyagraha's theoretical background.* Oslo: Universitetforlaget.

Naess, A. (1987). Self-realization: An ecological approach to being in the world. *Trumpeter, 4*, 128–31.

Nandakumar, P. (1988). *Sri Aurobindo: A critical introduction.* London: Oriental University Press.

Narayan, S. (1969). *Towards better education.* Ahmedabad: Navajivan Trust.

Nelson, L. E. (1991). Advaita vedanta and ecological concern. *Journal of Dharma, 16*, 282–301.

Orr, D. W. (1994). *Earth in mind: Our education, environment and the human prospect.* Washington, DC: Island.

NCERT. (2005). *National curriculum framework.* New Delhi: NCERT. Retrieved August, 2005, from http://www.ncert.nic.in/sites/publication/schoolcurriculum/NCFR%202005/contents1.htm

NSLC. (2004). *Service learning is* .... Scotts Valley, CA: National Service-Learning Clearinghouse. Retrieved November, 2006, from http://www.servicelearning.org/welcome_to_service-learning/service-learning_is/index.php

Partridge, K. (2005). *New religions: A guide*. Oxford: Oxford University Press.

Prabhupada, A. C., Bhaktivedanta Swami. (1989). *The science of self realisation*. Los Angeles: Bhaktivedanta Book Trust.

Prime, R. (2000). *Vedic ecology: Practical wisdom for surviving the 21st century*. Novato, CA: Mandala.

Rajput, J. S. (Ed.). (1998). *Gandhi on education*. New Delhi: National Council for Teacher Education. Retrieved August, 2005, from http://www.ncte-in.org/pub/gandhi/gandhi_0.htm

Richards, G. (1982). *The philosophy of Gandhi*. London: Curzon Press.

Roy, S. (2005). *The santiniketan environment*. Retrieved July, 2005, from http://www.visva-bharati.ac.in/Environment/santiniketan_environment.htm

Saran, A. K. (1979). On the promotion of Gandhian studies at university level. *Gandhi Marg—Journal of the Gandhi Peace Foundation, 1*, 363–381.

Satsvarupa Dasa, Goswami. (1983). *Prabhupada, your ever well-wisher*. Los Angeles: Bhaktivedanta Book Trust.

Sethi, J. D. (1979). *Gandhi today* (2nd ed.). Sahibabad, UP: Vikas.

Sharma, A. (2004). *Advaita vedanta: An introduction*. Delhi: Motilal Banarsidass.

Sharma, A. (1993). *The experiential dimension of advaita vedanta*. Delhi: Motilal Banarasidass.

Sharma, R. N. (2002). *Neo vedanta education*. New Delhi: Shubhi.

Shiva, V. (2002). Three principles to live by. In R. Prime (Ed.), *Vedic ecology: Practical wisdom for surviving the 21st century*. Novato, CA: Mandala.

Sidhu, R. (2004) Governing international education in Australia. *Globalisation, Education and Societies, 2*, 47–66.

Sinha, H. P. (1993). *Religious philosophy of Tagore and Radhakrishnan*. Delhi: Motilal Banarsidass.

Sivananda, Swami. (1998). *Guru tattva* (6th ed.). Shivanandanagar, Tehri-Garhwal, India: Divine Life Trust. Retrieved 1999, from http://www.SivanandaDlshq.org/

Stier, J. (2004). Taking a critical stance toward internationalization ideologies in higher education. *Globalisation, Societies and Education, 2*, 83–97.

Tapasyananda, Swami. (1990). *Sri Caitanya Mahaprabhu: His life religion and philosophy*. Madras (Chennai): Sri Ramakrishna Math.

Tagore, R. (1961). *Towards universal man*. Bombay (Mumbai): Asia Books.

Tagore, R. (1930). *The religion of man*. Rhinebeck, NY: Monkfish (2004).

Tagore, R. (1924). Foreword. In S. Radhakrishnan (Ed.), *Philosophy of the upanishads*. London: Allen & Unwin. Retrieved July, 2006, from http://www.cs.memphis.edu/~ramamurt/tagore_upanisad.html

Tagore, R (1917). *Personality*. London: Macmillan. Retrieved July, 2006, from http://www.learningnet-india.org/lni/data/publications/revive/vol4/part2.pdf

Tagore, R. (1913). *Gitanjali*. Retrieved August, 2006, from http://etext.virginia.edu/etcbin/toccer-new2?id=TagGita.sgm&images=images/modeng&data=/texts/english/modeng/parsed&tag=public&part=69&division=div1

Tamatea, L. (2005). The uses of Gandhi in education in Bali: Different responses to globalisation—implications for social justice. *Journal of Peace Education, 2*, 139-159.

Tillman, D., & Colomina, P. Q. (2000). *Living values: An educational program: LVEP educator training guide*. Deerfield, FL: Health Communications.

Tm.org. (2005). *The transcendental meditation program*. Maharishi Vedic Education Development Corporation. Retrieved June, 2006, from http://www.tm.org/discover/research/charts/index

Trevelyan, C. (1853). *The political tendency of the different systems of education in use in India*. London: Parliamentary Select Committee Paper.

UNESCO. (2004). *UN decade of education for sustainable development 2005–2014, international implementation scheme, draft*. Paris, UNESCO. Retrieved August, 2005, from http://portal.unesco.org/

MARTIN HAIGH

MARTIN HAIGH

education/admin/ev.php?URL_ID=36026&URL_DO=DO_TOPIC&URL_SECTION=201&reload=1099410445

Yogananda, Paramhansa. (1946). *Autobiography of a yogi*. Nevada City, CA: Crystalclarity. Retrieved August, 2005, from http://www.crystalclarity.com/yogananda/29.asp

Vivekananda, Swami (1989). *The Complete Works of Swami Vivekananda* (8 vols.). Calcutta: Advaita Ashrama.

Martin Haigh, a specialist in geographical education and co-editor of the Journal of Geography in Higher Education, *is Professor and University Teaching Fellow at Oxford Brookes University, Oxford, England. In 2004, he was elected President of the World Association of Soil and Water Conservation and, in 2002, helped draft the "Nairobi Declaration for the Year of Freshwaters 2003" which was endorsed by seven United Nations agencies.*

JENNIFER GIDLEY

15. BEYOND HOMOGENISATION OF GLOBAL EDUCATION

Do alternative pedagogies such as Steiner Education have anything to offer an emergent global/ising world? [i]

GLOBALISATION AS A HOMOGENISING INFLUENCE

One of the greatest obstacles to creating learning societies for the future is the model of Western culture—and by default, the model of education—being promoted by globalisation.

Sometimes called 'Americanisation' of the 'rest of the world', the processes of globalisation have amplified the modernity project. The primary tools of globalisation—other than economic 'development'—are mass education and communication technologies, particularly the Internet and the mass media ('virtual colonisation') (Gupta, 2000). Providing both opportunities and threats, globalisation's promoters argue that it is creating an improved economic climate within which educational, health and other socio-cultural 'improvements' will thrive. However, the 'development' model foisted upon the 'developing' world by the West, in the name of modernisation has been regarded for decades by many non-Western scholars, and anthropologists of development, as a second wave of cultural imperialism (Escobar, 1995; Lemish, Drotner, et al., 1998; Hunter, 2006). The realisation that globalisation has the power to exponentially increase cultural transgression has led me to coin the term "Modernity Project Mark II" to highlight its amplified effects (Gidley, 2001). On the other hand as feminist futures researcher Ivana Milojević points out, it also creates "opportunities for global transformation based on human unity" (Milojević, 2000). Such emancipatory opportunities will be addressed later in the chapter.

IS MASS 'EDUCATION FOR ALL' THE 'TROJAN HORSE' OF NEO-COLONIALISM?

Over a decade ago (1990), at the "Education for All" (EFA)[ii] meeting in Jomtein, Thailand, the World Bank put forward a model of education for the 'developing world'. This model has been heavily critiqued by a number of educationists and critical social theorists who cite it as being a further attempt to assert the values and culture of the Western materialist worldview (Jain, 2000).

It is well known that 'education' is a powerful method of enculturating—even 'brainwashing'—a people. A form of mass education that transplants an educational

M. Bussey, S. Inayatullah and I. Milojević (eds.), Alternative Educational Futures: Pedagogies for Emergent Worlds, 253–268.

model from one cultural system, such as Euro-American, into another very different culture while retaining the original standards and categories of knowledge, is tantamount to cultural genocide (Nandy, 2000).

While at first glance the goal of the meeting—"to universalize primary education"—might appear laudible, an unpacking of the details of how this is being implemented presents a dimmer picture. In regards to the World Bank's goal of increasing 'literacy levels' the concept of literacy itself has not been contested (Hoppers, 2000). And yet, in educational discourses in the 'Anglophone world' narrow conceptualisations of literacy have been undergoing serious critique from educationists and futures researchers for decades. The privileging of narrowly-defined 'textual literacy'—reading and writing text—over broader representations, such as 'social literacy', 'oral literacy', 'emotional literacy', 'futures literacy', 'spiritual literacy', reflects the pragmatic manifestation of narrowly defined conceptualisations of human intelligence. Diverse educational and psychological discourses that could underpin the possibility of broader literacies have arisen over decades. These discourses include notions of "postformal" thinking (Commons et al., 1982), "multiple intelligences" (Gardner, 1984), "cognitive holism" (Anderson, 1985), "holistic education" (Miller, 1988, 1990), and "imaginative and aesthetic education" (Read, 1943; Steiner, 1972; Schiller, 1977 (1795); Eisner, 1985; Arnheim, 1989; Egan, 1990). It is apparent that the World Bank has followed the trend in mainstream American education—which is still tied to the factory model—thereby overlooking the impact of these alternative discourses when designing the EFA programs. Furthermore, educational futures researchers, aware of the failure of the Western educational model to provide young people with confidence, hope, a sense of meaning and a love of life-long learning, have engaged in exploring alternative educational processes which transcend the narrow bounds of the three Rs (reading, 'riting and 'rithmetic) (Slaughter, 1989; Gidley, 1996; Hutchinson, 1996).

A reformulated twenty-first century 'Education for All' program that sought to honour cultural diversity and the complexities of a 'postindustrial' world, would investigate alternatives to the factory model of education. Critical, holistic, integral, postformal, and other 'postmodern' educational approaches may provide assistance in the transition from traditional forms of schooling—little changed since the inception of mass education—toward educational styles more suited to the complex current and emergent needs of a globalising world (Freire, 1972; Kotzsch & Colfax, 1990; Beare & Slaughter, 1993; Hutchinson, 1996; Wildman & Inayatullah, 1996; Egan, 1997; Kincheloe, 1999; Miller, 1999; Schwartz, 1999; Dighe, 2000; Inayatullah & Gidley, 2000; Horn, 2001; Sternberg, 2001; Thompson, 2001; Bussey, 2002; Fien, 2002; Gidley, 2002; Hicks, 2002; Milojević, 2002; Wilber, 2003; Esbjörn-Hargens, 2005). Additionally, perhaps it is also time for Western education to learn something from the 90 per cent of the world's oral cultures, referred to by Ong, who primarily use symbolic systems of meaning making transfer, such as story-telling, myth and dance while 'cultural memory' for this still survives (Ong, 1982). The later part of this chapter will discuss the potential contribution of alternatives to the traditional 'factory model' of education, by exploring one such alternative educational approach that arose in Europe yet maximises diverse learning processes (Steiner, 1965, 1967, 1972, 1976, 1981, 1982).

ENCULTURATION OR COMMODIFICATION: WHITHER OUR YOUTH?

Kincheloe (2002) points out that corporations are now the most prominent source of our cultural curriculum. No longer are schools, churches, and families dominant in the education of young people. Corporations are. (Steinberg & Kincheloe, 2004)

Although Joe Kincheloe's claim may at present apply mainly to America, before long it is likely to be the case globally. Since (at least) the European Enlightenment the West has claimed cultural superiority. With this self-imposed authority (at first European, now American), it has sought to 'develop' the 'underdeveloped world' according to its development discourses of 'deficit' and 'disadvantage' rather than 'diversity' (Dighe, 2000). This style of global monoculture underpinned as it is by Western scientific positivism, [iii] has in recent decades been amplified by the information technologies and the economic rationalist paradigm of commodification. Shirley Steinberg and Joe Kincheloe demonstrate how the corporatisation of our society and our culture of consumerism has led to the "corporate construction of childhood" and refer to the lack of understanding, pedagogy and contextualisation in this new "children's culture" (Steinberg & Kincheloe, 2004). Joseph Chilton Pearce takes this even further, pointing to several 'everyday' aspects of contemporary American (and increasingly global) life, that are contributing to deteriorating family and social structures (Pearce, 1992).

Like all great civilisations of the past that have reached their zenith before they begin to decay, the 'over-developed' Western culture, with its foundations rooted in scientific materialism[iv] has been for decades showing signs of decay. The litany of symptoms exhibited by many young people of the 'most developed' nations, exemplify this with great poignancy. Whilst discourses on 'global youth issues' have primarily focused on health and education in the 'developing' world, the emerging figures related to mental health issues for young people in the 'overdeveloped' world confirm that 'development' as part of the modernity project is seriously flawed. Research shows that many youth of the West are increasingly manifesting high rates of depression (15-24%), eating disorders and other forms of mental illness, (Bashir & Bennett 2000). Comparative studies (primarily OECD countries) indicate that when the figures for all mental health disorders are combined (including ADHD, Conduct Disorder, Depression, Anxiety, etc.) as many as 18–22 per cent of children and adolescents suffer from one or more of these disorders (Raphael, 2000). In Australia there have been increases in youth homelessness and school truancy which have created an underclass of 'street kids', disenfranchised by society, yet often by choice. Increasing numbers are committing suicide and other violent crimes at an alarming rate, and are expressing a general malaise, loss of meaning and hopelessness about the future (Eckersley, 1993; Gidley & Wildman, 1996). Youth suicides among young males (15-24) in Australia have doubled in the past 20 years (Mitchell, 2000). Sohail Inayatullah refers to these phenomena as symptoms of 'postindustrial fatigue' (Inayatullah, 2002). I call it 'the malaise of materialism'. Film director Peter Weir has described Western culture as a 'toxic culture', since violent school shootings incidents by and of fellow students in the US.

Before going further it might be worth considering what is missing from the Western materialist cultural model that may throw light on these issues. The epistemology of positivist scientific thinking that underpins Western culture follows both the empiricist and Cartesian traditions that developed during the European Enlightenment. More recently referred to as 'instrumental rationality'[v] it is a reductionist, materialistic mode of thinking which, in my interpretation, excludes such diverse ways of knowing as imagination, inspiration, intuition.

As the epistemology of the technologically advanced Western culture its global dominance of other cultures discounts the mythic, aesthetic, subjective, spiritual, traditional ways of knowing of most of the earth's cultures. Based as it is on a view of human nature that lacks a spiritual dimension (divorcing psychology from theology, science from ethics), all further fragmentations stem from this inherent tendency to segregate rather than integrate. Richard Tarnas refers to these developments as the "post-Copernican double bind" (Tarnas, 1991) where the dominant worldview led humans to experience the following three estrangements:

- cosmological estrangement from their home at the centre of the cosmos (with Copernicus declaring that the Earth was not the centre of the universe);
- ontological estrangement from their own being with the separation that came with Descartes' dictum "I think, therefore I am";
- finally, building on these new rational/materialist foundations came the epistemological estrangement from the philosopher Kant's proposition that all human knowledge is interpretive: that the "thing in itself" cannot be known other than through what is perceived by the mind that views it.

As a longer-term result of this cultural worldview, combined with the added pressures of increased mechanisation and globalisation, several major factors (inherent in the Western materialist cultural paradigm) have arisen in my view that have contributed to a failure of healthy enculturation of young people. These include the triumph of individualism/egoism over community; the colonisation of imagination; the secularisation of culture—and its counter response—fundamentalism of religion; and environmental degradation now a realistic fear for young people as 'global warming' has been firmly identified as a presence. These factors have been discussed in detail elsewhere (Gidley, 2002).

A major concern is that the implementation of mass education based on a monocultural Western model, with its homogenising and corporatising cultural influence, is likely to bring with it these factors as well.

EMANCIPATORY POTENTIAL OF GLOBALISATION

On the other hand, from a Taoist perspective, everything contains the seed of its opposite. Hence, even whilst the globalisation project ("Modernity Project Mark II") threatens to be potentially more damaging in its colonising and homogenising power than Modernity Project Mark I, it also holds the potential for the greatest emancipation (Gidley, 2001). It is suggested by Bhandari that what is needed is to be able to distinguish between the hegemonic and emancipatory potential of the diverse strands of modernity (Bhandari, 2000). There are several emerging opportunities that can be harnessed. Some of these, paradoxically, co-exist within the Western model itself:

- The inherent focus on individualism in the Western cultural worldview as discussed above can be transformational if used selflessly, for the greater good. Individual human agency then becomes a powerful force to counter the homogenising effects of a dominant monoculture.
- The counter-materialistic, alternative streams within the Western educational and cultural paradigm that have developed in parallel with mainstream culture, become ever more active the stronger materialist culture becomes (e.g., the educational alternative discussed below).
- The networking potential of free human beings to use global networks for the common good is beginning to be harnessed. For example, it has also enabled the authors discussed earlier to publish and circulate their book on the Internet thereby promoting their concerns about globalisation globally (Jain, 2000)!

Processes need to be put in place that will foster the potential of globalisation to increase these opportunities to encourage diversity. Policy, research and practical processes have been suggested by Jan Visser (2000).

RECLAIMING WISDOM AS A GOAL OF EDUCATION

The industrial worldview that underpins mainstream education in the West, and thereby the processes instituted by the World Bank in its EFA agenda, has not only been critiqued by educationists in the developing world. Much of the youth futures research over the past decade has demonstrated that many young people in the industrialised world have become fearful of the future, disempowered and disenchanted by the education system (Slaughter, 1989; Eckersley, 1995; Gidley & Wildman, 1996; Hutchinson, 1996). These futures researchers recommend more holistic, integrated teaching methods using imagination (to be elaborated later), pro-active social skills (such as conflict resolution, cooperative learning methods) and specific futures methodologies (such as creating scenarios, visualising preferred futures, action plans).

It has been argued by some educational futurists that the limitations of the instrumental rationality of Western scientific positivism has rendered it as being well past its 'use-by date'[vi] as a viable dominant epistemology for the future (Wildman & Inayatullah, 1996). The 'global problematique'[vii] has become so complex that a worldview based on instrumental rationality with its fragmented disciplines and specialisations is no longer able to cope with finding solutions.

I propose that what is needed are integrated education systems at both the school and tertiary levels which are underpinned by higher order knowledge systems and inclusive—or integral—cosmologies (Gidley, 2006). These may include the traditional, indigenous knowledge systems of many cultures, as well as such spiritually-based cosmologies, or 'perennial philosophies' as may be found to underpin several alternative education approaches found in the West, (for example, the underpinning philosophy of Steiner education, discussed below). Such systems reclaim wisdom as the goal of learning and transformation as the goal of a learning society. There is also an emerging movement from within the psychology discipline to identify and acknowledge *wisdom* as a construct, and even a goal of education (Arlin, 1999; Sternberg, 2001; Sternberg, 2005). In addition, the emergence of integral consciousness as a higher-order, 'post-formal' or 'post-rational' mode of thinking is being fostered by Ken Wilber's Integral Institute in the US (Wilber, 2004), which draws inspiration from the pioneering work of Sri Aurobindo Ghose in India (Aurobindo Ghose, 1990 (1914)), and Jean Gebser in Europe during the middle of the last century (Gebser, 1991). Some implications of this integral approach for futures in education are discussed elsewhere in this volume: "Integral Perspectives to School Educational Futures".

While it is becoming increasingly vital that school and university education are underpinned by such higher order knowledge systems and integral cosmologies, this is by no means to suggest that education (and learning) are confined to schools, colleges and universities. The industrial, factory model of education as schooling being confined to factory-like buildings for persons between the ages of four and twenty-something, must urgently be regenerated by spatial and temporal expansion into life-long learning in physical, architectural and social spaces that breathe with the community. The creative imagination required to foster such transformations has been for too long impeded by the limitations of the reductionist school education model. It will be shown later in this article that cultivation of imagination in education enables young people to have more positive, creative and empowered visions of the future. This would seem to be an important step in creating learning societies with wisdom as their vision.

TOWARDS VISIONS OF A TRANSFORMED SOCIETY

If I were to begin to envision a future transformed society it would be far removed from the monocultural variety that globalisation is attempting to impose. There would be no one 'ideal society' as the meta-narratives of communism, national socialism and late capitalism have tried to institute.

The critical value of cultural 'diversity' to the survival of human society as a whole would be paramount. This diversity would be found *between cultures* (for example, Chinese and Ayurvedic medicines would be equally valued with Western allopathic medicine, so that genuine dialogue between practitioners could actually discover which approach best suited which situation). Some beginnings are being made in Australia with the establishment of holistic medical practices that integrate paramedical (e.g., massage, physiotherapy) and non-Western practices (e.g., acupuncture) into traditional medical clinics. Dommers and Welch have explored the development of 'systems maps' for general practitioners to facilitate more integrated health service models (2001). In addition, the diversity would be found *within cultures* whereby the plurality of possible ways of knowing would be encouraged at all levels of education, including university learning. This would involve a revaluing of the arts, the practical skills, and contemplative processes as being of equal value with the rational in contributing to an integral knowledge paradigm for the future.

However, such a vision could not be implemented without great struggle. There is much powerful vested interest in maintaining the status quo whereby the few who play Monopoly with the vast majority of the world's power and wealth cling desperately to their monocultural myth of globalisation that commodifies and homogenises all values into the economic 'bottom line'. In the same way that it has taken decades for the world's scientists to admit that disregard for the environment had resulted in global warming, it may also take more decades before the grassroots visions suggested here will develop the critical mass that is needed for trans- formation into a learning (rather than consuming) society. In the vision presented here, the economic bottom line would be superseded by what has become known as the 'triple bottom line' where the impacts of any enterprise/policy on the environment and the social/human are equally valued with economic impact. Taking this even further, Sohail Inayatullah has introduced the concept of spirituality as the 'fourth bottom line' (Inayatullah, 2006).

To summarise, this vision of a transformed society would no longer represent a hegemonic, linear and hierarchical global monoculture based on the endless acquisition of fragmented 'bytes' of information, but rather, a pluralistic, multi- layered network of cultures within societies, committed to nurturing diverse, meaning-centred, integrated, wisdom-based cultures.

A key question is: How might we educate children and young people across the globe to facilitate this vision?

AN 'ALTERNATIVE' APPROACH THAT FOSTERS 'EDUCATION FOR WISDOM'

On a visit I made to Nepal a few years ago, while trekking in some reasonably remote Himalayan villages, some children took me by the hand when they discovered that I was, at that time, a teacher. They excitedly ran me away to show off with pride their new school. It was a dark little square room with straight rows of seats, a blackboard, and some white chalk with each child having a little piece of black slate so they could 'learn to write'. I tried to look happy for them while inwardly wondering how it is that only the driest crumbs of the Western educational model, that is already failing our own children in droves, could be being offered to these lively Nepalese children. I now wonder if this is what is meant by 'education for all'. And I'm certainly not suggesting that this could be improved by giving these little schools a couple of computers as well. Having been involved for 10 years in founding, pioneering and teaching in a Rudolf Steiner school in rural Australia, I have guided numerous children from their sixth/seventh year to puberty. As a responsible participant in their (and my) joyous learning of every imaginable subject through stories, drawing, painting, singing, movement, drama, music, poetry, mythology and play, I knew learning could be otherwise. And surprise, surprise! The children also became literate in the process—and not just literate in the narrow sense. Rather they developed what I would call broad literacies (to read for meaning, to write creatively, to share, to respect nature, to imagine worlds beyond their immediate one, to have social confidence and to love learning).

The educational processes described here are not necessarily new, but were indicated for their significance in a child's education by Rudolf Steiner (1861– 1924), in Europe in the 1920s. Steiner, already a century ago, was decrying the limitations of the Western materialist cultural model. He was a scientist, philosopher, artist and visionary who contributed significantly to the fields of education, agriculture (biodynamics), medicine and the arts, lecturing and writing extensively on all imaginable subjects in the first quarter of last century. Arguably a futurist and macrohistorian, he called for science to be reunited with art and metaphysics through 'spiritual science'. In addition to valuing the conceptual/ rational development of the child and the practical, real life context of education (also recommended by John Dewey), Steiner strongly emphasised the cultivation of the imagination through aesthetic, artistic processes and highly valued the use of oral language through poetry, drama and story telling (Steiner, 1964; Dewey, 1972).

The educational movement that has grown out of Steiner's initiative has resulted in the establishment of hundreds of schools worldwide. Considered by many of its proponents to be an educational model, this problematic belief has become one of its weaknesses, as some interpreters of Steiner's approach can be quite dogmatic about processes. In fact, Steiner repeatedly stated that he was not laying down dogma, but rather elucidating knowledge of the wisdom of humanity (anthroposophy) to be creatively worked on by the artistry of each individual teacher:

> All instruction must therefore be permeated by art, by human individuality, for of more value than any thought-out curriculum is the individuality of the teacher and educator. It is individuality that must work in the school. (Steiner, 1967, p. 142)

From my reading of Steiner, I believe that he intended individual educators to use his teachings as a basis from which to be creative themselves and to reinvent the processes for different contexts (temporal and geographic). There is still a great deal of untapped potential in this area, as the temptation of many communities is to transplant a nineteenth century German educational 'model' into every cultural context.

The conceptual approach of Steiner education is an integrated approach to the development of the child. In particular, the cultivation of the student's vivid and healthy imagination (compared with just the dry, abstract intellect) is considered to be extremely important. The foremost tool for this in Steiner schools is the use of story-telling as a pre-eminent medium of teaching. Stories and pictures are used with small children to introduce the letters and numbers, and with older ones to teach anything from sewing to complex mathematical and scientific concepts. The individual subjects, where possible, are integrated rather than segregated (e.g., geometry may be integrated with biology through studying flower and leaf patterns; maths may be woven into music lessons; and also important social and moral lessons can easily be integrated with stories of great characters from history), while the content where possible is presented thematically. In addition, the recognition of the fundamental interconnectedness of all things as a way of knowing and learning aligns this approach with many indigenous and other non-Western epistemologies. This integrated approach is supported today by recent literature on the importance of contextualising knowledge and proponents of situated learning, not to mention the movement for the development of integral consciousness, discussed further in this volume. The creative arts are also widely used to promote intrinsic motivation, encourage self-esteem and help to give meaning to the subject matter.

The contemporary research supporting the use of imagination, metaphor and visual artistic approaches to education as an adjunct to abstract intellectual methods has its historical context for Western thinking in the Platonic stream of philosophical thought that values aesthetic education. More broadly, the social, cultural and psychological context for the use of image, myth and metaphor is supported by the psychological and literary works of Carl Jung and Joseph Campbell. Essentially these writers critique the Euro-centric Cartesian[viii] position of the importance of solely rational modes of thinking at the expense of other forms of human expression, emphasising modes such as symbological, contemplative, depictive and mythogenetic (Campbell, 1968).

In terms of learning theory, Harry Broudy argues for the crucial role of imagery and imagination in forming part of what he calls the *allusionary base* of learning. Here he refers to the conglomerate of concepts, images, and memories available to us to provide meaning in what we hear or read. Relating more to the connotative (aesthetic/symbolic) rather than the denotative (scientific) functional use of words, Broudy explains that this context of meaning may be richly developed through poetry, literature, mythology and the arts, and is essentially the stock of meaning with which we think and feel (Broudy, 1987). Several contemporary educationists also emphasise the significance of cultivating imagination in education (Sloan, 1983; Eisner, 1985; Neville, 1989; Egan, 1997). Could it be that the lack of meaning experienced by many Western youth today is related to an education that lacks imagination, and other non-discursive ways of knowing?

To test my intuition that Steiner educated students may have a different relationship to the future from their mainstream educated cohorts, I undertook some research on views and visions of the future with the senior secondary students of the three largest Steiner schools in Australia (Gidley, 1997). The findings suggested that the young people who had been educated within this approach are more positive and hopeful towards the future and more empowered that they can effect change, than their mainstream educated counterparts (Hutchinson, 1992). In spite of having been exposed to similar, negative images of the future of the world expressed in their expectation of the 'probable future', they appear to have emerged from this 'hidden curriculum' with their idealism and social activism intact. Unlike many young people who have difficulty imagining a very different future (other than the standard 'techno-fix' solution to problems), the Steiner students' visions of their preferred futures were very richly developed and also strongly focused on improved social futures (Gidley, 2002). In this research it was also found that the Steiner educated students placed human agency at the centre of the change that needs to happen if we are to prevent global catastrophe. They listed qualities such as personal development, activism, changes in values (less greed, more spirituality), and future care as some of the ways that humans, including themselves, need to change (Gidley, 1998).

It is proposed here that in any given situation, at least two layers of education are occurring:

- the education provided by the school/schooling system;
- the meta-layer of education (the 'hidden curriculum') provided by the tacit messages of society/culture, in particular through the mass media, much of which provides negative, fearful images of 'the future'. These messages are of course rapidly colonising the image life of youth globally as a result of the processes of globalisation discussed in the beginning of this chapter. (Gidley, 2002)

It is suggested here that with 'mainstream educated' youth there is a consistency between the two layers of education in that the style and operation of most mainstream schooling reinforces and supports many of the tacit, negative messages of society. These messages of course are also embedded in the educational models implanted through the EFA agenda. It is further argued that this consistency between the messages of school and society may leave the students insufficient opportunity to create alternative images of the future either consciously or tacitly. This raises the question: How are mainstream schools today, in the West and their carbon copies in the 'non-West' balancing these destructive societal messages about the future for our young people?

By contrast, alternative approaches such as Steiner education provide artistic, imaginative, values-based, meaningful educational experiences and processes which provide a counter balance to the often fragmented, abstract, violent, meaningless and pessimistic messages of our culture provided through the mass media.

A Personal Comment on Strengths and Weaknesses of Steiner Education

It may appear that I have biased, overly positive views of Steiner education, however I am not without critique of how it is applied in some settings. There has been an increasing interest among some 'mainstream' educators to explore alternatives. In addition to my own research discussed above, numerous studies have been undertaken in the US and the UK in the last two decades to investigate the Steiner/Waldorf approach, from both 'inside' and 'outside' (Almon, 1992; Uhrmacher, 1993; McDermott et al., 1996; Armon, 1997; Easton, 1997; Glockler, 1997; Miller, 1997; Oberman, 1997; Ogletree, 1997; Uhrmacher, 1997; Woods et al., 1997; Smith, 1998; Astley & Jackson, 2000; Miller, 2000; Nicholson, 2000; Woods & Woods, 2002; Woods et al., 2005). It is beyond the scope of this paper to evaluate this research. Instead I will offer a personal comment as to its strengths and weaknesses from my experience working with this approach. It is my observation that overall the students develop a strong, intrinsic motivation for learning; a balanced repertoire of practical, artistic, and social as well as academic skills; a positive self-esteem, regardless of whether they are academically 'bright' or not; a broad cultural awareness; and a love of, and respect for, nature. As my research shows, Steiner educated students also have a sense of confidence and empowerment that they can create a more positive, equitable and just future and a sense of responsibility that humans (indeed they, themselves) are the key to the future health of society and the planet.

On the other hand, I have seen children who for whatever reason did not thrive in this approach, and I have seen teachers and even whole schools which became too narrow, dogmatic and even 'cultish' in their interpretation of Steiner's ideas. Many of the Steiner schools worldwide, even in Australia and South East Asia, continue to use primarily Euro-centric content rather than local, culture specific material, at best severely limiting the richness of educational experience, at worst contributing to cultural colonisation. In my observation many Steiner teachers, through a combination of 'over zealousness' and pedagogical arrogance, have become too out-of-touch with contemporary educational thought, thereby missing some of the pockets of positive change occurring globally which may help to keep them 'current'. Finally, some aspects of the overall 'hidden curriculum' of schooling generally, also occur in Steiner schools. In particular, these schools seem to fall prey to the institutional mentality of teachers (i.e., the school becomes their world), the hierarchical posturing and politics that can occur between individuals, and last but not least, the lack of meta-questioning about whether schools, *per se*, need to exist at all.

EDUCATION FOR TRANSFORMATION IN AN EMERGENT GLOBAL/ISING WORLD

The research described should not be interpreted in any way to suggest that all students ought to be attending Steiner schools, but rather to suggest that a real dialogue of pedagogies, such as that occurring in this collection, might open general education (and EFA) to additional processes that may empower students to create a wiser and more positive future world. If organisations such as the World Bank are serious about developing educational processes 'for all' that will underpin healthier outcomes for young people and for societies in general, the current emphasis on narrow literacies and 'head knowledge' would need to be balanced by 'heart and hand' processes.

If we seek to foster the conditions in which learning societies might flourish, educational processes for the future would need to be more integral, artistic, imaginative and proactive, enabling the students (of all ages) to feel more committed and empowered to create cooperative, diverse, wise futures for all.

Integrated educational processes, regardless of their cultural origins, can provide endless sources of material for life-long learning which is inclusive of all cultural and ethnic content and diverse processes of implementation. Examples include: Steiner education, neohumanist education, Montessori education and Integral education. Such an integrated 'head, heart and hands' approach is ideally suited for a much broader implementation, beyond schools, as a catalyst for a learning society. This is of course providing that tendencies, inherent in any such philosophy, towards spiritual arrogance and fundamentalism, can be overcome in human nature.

And that begins with each one of us.

NOTES

i   This article is based on an earlier paper called "Education for All", or "Education for Wisdom", which was an invited chapter for the book *Unfolding Learning Societies: Deepening the Dialogues*, Vimukt Shiksha Special Issue, April 2001. I had been asked by a group of educators from Shikshantar, Udaipur, in India, to present my interpretation of how Steiner education might assist in providing an alternative to the 'factory model' of education being promoted by the World Bank's "Education for All" agenda and whether it might support the development of a 'learning society'. Other than a few editorial changes to title and subtitles, and the addition of a few research detail updates, the content and voice are largely unchanged as they are still relevant and appropriate for this topic, from my current perspective.

ii   In 1990, delegates from 155 countries, as well as representatives from some 150 organisations, agreed at the World Conference on Education for All in Jomtien, Thailand (5–9 March 1990) to universalize primary education and massively reduce illiteracy before the end of the decade.

iii   'Positivism'—empirical scientific thinking, which arose and flourished in the West after the European Enlightenment and has since been the dominant mode of academic discourse.

iv   The term 'scientific materialism' was characterised by Alfred North Whitehead as the foundational 'tradition of thought' underlying 'modernity' the civilisation that now dominates the globe (see Gare, 2002).

v   The term 'instrumental rationality' was coined by Jürgen Habermas to distinguish it from what he called 'communicative rationality' as part of his theory of 'universal pragmatics' (see Habermas, 1979).

vi   'Use-by date'—this term is used to define the last date by which commodities such as food products are safe to be eaten. Its use here alludes to the commodification and packaging of knowledge and learning in the Western model as if they were products to be consumed rather than processes to be engaged in; that is, Western scientific positivism is 'no longer safe for human consumption'.

vii   'Global problematique'—is a complex, interdependent set of problems, where the existence of a particular problem is systematically bound into (and dependent on) the existence of other problems.

viii   'Cartesian'—derived from the philosophical position of Rene Descartes, "I think, therefore I am".

REFERENCES

Almon, J. (1992). Educating for Creative Thinking: The Waldorf Approach. *ReVision, 15*(2), 71-78.

Anderson, J. (1985). *Cognitive Psychology and its Implications*. New York: W. H. Freeman and Co.

Arlin, P. K. (1999). The Wise Teacher: A Developmental Model of Teaching. *Theory into Practice, 38*(1), 12-17.

Armon, J. (1997). *The Waldorf Curriculum as a Framework for Moral Education: One Dimension of a Fourfold System*. American Educational Research Association Annual Meeting, Chicago.

Arnheim, R. (1989). *Thoughts on Art Education*. Los Angeles: Getty Centre for Education in The Arts.

Astley, K., & Jackson, P. (2000). Doubts on Spirituality: interpreting Waldorf ritual. *International Journal of Children's Spirituality, 5*(2), 221-227.

Aurobindo Ghose, S. (1990 (1914)). *The Life Divine*. Pondicherry, India: Lotus Light.

Bashir, M., & Bennett, D. (Eds.) (2000). *Deeper Dimensions: Culture, Youth and Mental Health.* Culture and Mental Health: Current Issues in Transcultural Mental Health. Parramatta: Transcultural Mental Health Centre.

Beare, H., & Slaughter, R. (1993). *Education for the Twenty-first Century.* London: Routledge.

Bhandari, V. (2000). The Artifice of Modernization: Postcoloniality and Beyond. In M. Jain (Ed.) *Unfolding Learning Societies: Challenges and Opportunities* (p. 120). Udaipur: Shikshantar—The People's Institute for Rethinking Education and Development.

Broudy, H. S. (1987). *The Role of Imagery in Learning.* Los Angeles: The Getty Centre for Education in The Arts.

Bussey, M. (2002). From Youth Futures to Futures for All. In J. Gidley & S. Inayatullah (Eds.) *Youth Futures: Comparative Research and Transformative Visions* (pp. 65-78). Westport, CT: Praeger.

Campbell, J. (1968). *The Masks of God: Creative Mythology.* New York: Penguin Arkana.

Commons, M. L., Richards, F. A., et al. (1982). Systematic and Metasystematic Reasoning: A Case for Levels of Reasoning beyond Piaget's Stage of Formal Operations. *Child Development, 53*(4), 1058-1069.

Dewey, J. (1972). *The Early Works, 1882-1898* (Vol. 5). Carbondale and Edwardsville, IL: Southern Illinois University Press.

Dighe, A. (2000). Diversity in Education in an Era of Globalization. In M. Jain (Ed.) *Learning Societies: A Reflective and Generative Framework.* Udaipur: Shikshantar—The People's Institute for Rethinking Education and Development. Available online at: http://www.learndev.org/dl/VS3-00q-Diversity.PDF.

Dommers, E., & Welch, D. (2001). An Australian GP Futures Conference. *Journal of Futures Studies, 5*(3), 173-182.

Easton, F. (1997). Educating the Whole Child, "Head, Heart and Hands": Learning From the Waldorf Experience. *Theory into Practice, 36*(2), 87-94.

Eckersley, R. (1993). The West's deepening cultural crisis. *The Futurist*, 8-20.

Eckersley, R. (1995). Values and visions: Youth and the failure of modern Western culture. *Youth Studies Australia, 14*(1), 13-21.

Egan, K. (1990). *Romantic Understanding: The Development of Rationality and Imagination, Ages 8-15.* London: Routledge.

Egan, K. (1997). *The Educated Mind: How Cognitive Tools Shape our Understanding.* Chicago: The University of Chicago Press.

Eisner, E. W. (1985). *The Educational Imagination: On the Design and Evaluation of School Programs.* New York: Macmillan.

Esbjörn-Hargens, S. (2005). Integral education by design: how integral theory informs teaching, learning and curriculum in a graduate program. *ReVision, 28*(3).

Escobar, A. (1995). *Encountering Development: The Making and Unmaking of the Third World.* Princeton: Princeton University Press.

Fien, J. (2002). *Teaching and Learning for a Sustainable Future.* Paris: UNESCO.

Freire, P. (1972). *Pedagogy of the Oppressed.* Harmondsworth: Penguin.

Gardner, H. (1984). *Frames of Mind: the Theory of Multiple Intelligences.* New York: Basic Books.

Gare, A. (2002). The Roots of Postmodernism: Schelling, Process Philosophy, and Poststructuralism. In C. Keller & A. Daniell (Eds.) *Process and Difference: between Cosmological and Poststructuralist Postmodernisms* (pp. 31-54). New York: State University of New York Press.

Gebser, J. (1991). *The Ever-Present Origin.* Athens, OH: Ohio University Press.

Gidley, J. (1996). Wings to the future: Imagination and education. *New Renaissance, 6*(3), 9-11.

Gidley, J. (1997). Imagination and Will in Youth Visions of their Futures: Prospectivity and Empowerment in Steiner Educated Adolescents. *Education, Work and Training.* Lismore: Southern Cross University. Available online at: http://www.swaraj.org/shikshantar/ls2_gidley.pdf

Gidley, J. (1998). Prospective Youth Visions through Imaginative Education. *Futures, 30*(5), 395-408.

Gidley, J. (2001). Globalization and its Impact on Youth. *Journal of Futures Studies, 6*(1), 89-106.

Gidley, J. (2002). Global Youth Culture: A Transdisciplinary Perspective. In J. Gidley & S. Inayatullah (Eds.) *Youth Futures: Comparative Research and Transformative Visions* (pp. 3-18). Westport, CT: Praeger.

Gidley, J. (2002). Holistic Education and Visions of Rehumanized Futures. In J. Gidley & S. Inayatullah (Eds.) *Youth Futures: Comparative Research and Transformative Visions* (pp. 155-167). Westport, CT: Praeger.

Gidley, J. (2006). Spiritual Epistemologies and Integral Cosmologies: Transforming Thinking and Culture. In S. Awbrey, D. Dana, V. Miller, et al. (Eds.) *Integrative Learning and Action: A call to Wholeness* (pp. 29-53). New York: Peter Lang Publishing.

Gidley, J., & Wildman, P. (1996). What are we missing? A review of the educational and vocational interests of marginalised rural youth. *Education in Rural Australia Journal, 6*(2), 9-19.

Glockler, M. (1997). A New Educational Paradigm: Identity of Vital Functions and Thinking Activity. *Research Bulletin, 2*(2).

Gupta, P. (2000). Liberating Education from the Chains of Imperialism. In M. Jain (Ed.) *Learning Societies: A Reflective and Generative Framework*. Udaipur: Shikshantar—The People's Institute for Rethinking Education and Development.

Habermas, J. (1979). *Communication and the Evolution of Society*. Boston: Beacon Press.

Hicks, D. (2002). *Lessons for the Future*. London: Routledge.

Hoppers, C. O. (2000). Turning the Monster on its Head: Lifelong Learning Societies for All. In M. Jain (Ed.) *Unfolding Learning Societies: Challenges and Opportunities*. Udaipur: Shikshantar—The People's Institute for Rethinking Education and Development.

Horn, R. (2001). Post-formal design conversation: designing just and caring educational systems. *Systems Research and Behavioural Sciences, 18*(4), 361-371.

Hunter, J. (2006). Anthropology of Development Discussions. In J. Gidley (Ed.) *Anthropology Essays*. Maroochydore, QLD.

Hutchinson, F. (1992). *Futures consciousness and the school: Explorations of broad and narrow literacies for the twenty-first century with particular reference to Australian young people*. Armidale NSW: University of New England.

Hutchinson, F. (1996). *Educating Beyond Violent Futures*. London: Routledge.

Inayatullah, S. (2002). Youth Dissent: Multiple Perspectives on Youth Futures. In J. Gidley & S. Inayatullah (Eds.) *Youth Futures: Comparative Research and Transformative Visions*. Westport, CT: Praeger.

Inayatullah, S. (2006). Spirituality as the Fourth Bottom Line. *New Renaissance, 12*(2). Available online at: http://www.ru.org/122-Inayatullah-spirituality.htm.

Inayatullah, S., & Gidley, J. (Eds.) (2000). *The University in Transformation: Global Perspectives on the Futures of the University*. Westport, Connecticut, Bergin and Garvey.

Jain, M. (Ed.) (2000). *Unfolding Learning Societies: Challenges and Opportunities*. Udaipur: Shikshantar—The People's Institute for Rethinking Education and Development.

Kincheloe, J. (1999). *The Post-Formal Reader: Cognition and Education (Critical Education Practice)*. New York: Falmer Press.

Kotzsch, R., & Colfax, J. (1990). Waldorf Schools: Education for the Head, Hands and Heart. *UTNE Reader, 41*(2).

Lemish, D., Drotner, K., Maigret, E., Stald, G., & Liebes, T. (1998). Global Culture in Practice: A Look at Adolescents in Denmark, France and Israel. *European Journal of Communication, 13*(4), 539-556.

McDermott, R., Henry, M. et al. (1996). Waldorf Education in an Inner-City Public School. *The Urban Review, 28*(2), 119-140.

Miller, J. P. (1988). *The Holistic Curriculum*. Toronto: OISE Press.

Miller, R. (1990). *What Are Schools For? Holistic education in American culture*. Brandon, VT: Holistic Education Press.

Miller, R. (1997). "Partial Vision" in Alternative Education. *SKOLE: The Journal of Alternative Education, XIV*(3), 27-33.

Miller, R. (1999). Holistic Education for an Emerging Culture. In S. Glazer (Ed.) *The Heart of Learning: Spirituality in Education* (pp. 189-201). New York: Putnam.

Miller, R. (2000). Education and the Evolution of the Cosmos. In R. Miller, *Caring for New Life: Essays on Holistic Education*. Brandon, VT: The Foundation for Educational Renewal.

Milojević, I. (2000). Globalization, Gender and World Futures. Unpublished ms.

Milojević, I. (2002). Futures of Education: Feminist and Post-Western Critiques and Visions. PhD Thesis. School of Education. Brisbane: University of Queensland.

Mitchell, P. (2000). *Valuing Young Lives: Evaluation of the National Youth Suicide Prevention Strategy*. Melbourne: Australian Institute of Family Studies.

Nandy, A. (2000). Recovery of Indigenous Knowledge and Dissenting Futures of Universities. In S. Inayatullah & J. Gidley (Eds.) *The University in Transformation: Global Perspectives on the Futures of the University* (pp. 115-123). Westport, CT: Bergin and Garvey.

Neville, B. (1989). *Educating Psyche: Emotion, Imagination, and the Unconscious in Learning*. Melbourne: Collins Dove.

Nicholson, D. W. (2000). Layers of Experience: Forms of Representation in a Waldorf School Classroom. *Journal of Curriculum Studies, 32*(4), 575-587.

Oberman, I. (1997). *The Mystery of Waldorf: A turn–of–the–century German experiment on today's American soil*. Annual Meeting of the American Educational Research Association Chicago, Electronic Data Resources Service (EDRS).

Ogletree, E. J. (1997). Waldorf Education: Theory of Child Development and Teaching Methods. University of Chicago.

Ong, W. (1982). *Orality and Literacy; The Technologisation of the World*. London: Methuen.

Pearce, J. C. (1992). *Evolution's End: Claiming the Potential of Our Intelligence*. San Francisco: HarperSanFrancisco.

Raphael, B. (2000). *Promoting the Mental Health and Well-Being of Children and Young People*. Canberra: Commonwealth Department of Health and Aged Care.

Read, H. (1943). *Education through Art*. London: Faber and Faber.

Schiller, F. (1977 (1795)). *On The Aesthetic Education of Man—In a series of letters*. New York: Frederick Ungar Publishing.

Schwartz, E. (1999). *The Millennial Child: Transforming Education in the 21st Century*. New York: Anthroposophic Press.

Slaughter, R. (Ed.) (1989). *Studying the Future: An Introductory Reader*. Melbourne: Commission for the Future, Bicentennial futures education project.

Sloan, D. (1983). *Insight-Imagination: the Emancipation of Thought and the Modern World*. Westport, CT: Greenwood.

Smith, P. (1998). Essentials of Waldorf Education Study. *Research Bulletin, 3*(1), 1-2.

Steinberg, S., & Kincheloe, J. (2004). *Kinderculture: The Corporate Construction of Childhood*. Boulder, CO: Westview.

Steiner, R. (1964). *The Arts and Their Mission*. New York: The Anthroposophic Press.

Steiner, R. (1965). *The Education of the Child: Lectures, 1909*. London: Rudolf Steiner Press.

Steiner, R. (1967). *Discussions with Teachers, Lectures, 1919*. London: Rudolf Steiner Press.

Steiner, R. (1967). *The Younger Generation: Education and Spiritual Impulses in the 20th Century (Lectures, 1922)*. New York: Anthroposophic Press.

Steiner, R. (1972). *A Modern Art of Education, Lectures, 1923*. London: Rudolf Steiner Press.

Steiner, R. (1976). *Practical Advice to Teachers: Lectures, 1919*. London: Rudolf Steiner Press.

Steiner, R. (1981). *The Renewal of Education through the Science of the Spirit: Lectures, 1920*. Sussex: Kolisko Archive.

Steiner, R. (1982). *The Kingdom of Childhood: Lectures, 1924*. New York: Anthroposophic Press.

Sternberg, R. J. (2001). Why Schools Should Teach for Wisdom: The Balance Theory of Wisdom in Educational Settings. *Educational Psychologist, 36*(4), 227-245.

Sternberg, R. J. (2005). Older but not Wiser? The relationship between Age and Wisdom. *Ageing International, 30(*1), 5-26.

Tarnas, R. (1991). *The Passions of the Western Mind.* New York: Random House.

Thompson, W. I. (2001). *Transforming History: A Curriculum for Cultural Evolution.* Great Barrington, MA: Lindisfarne.

Uhrmacher, B. P. (1993). Making Contact: An Exploration of Focused Attention between Teacher and Students. *Curriculum Inquiry, 23*(4), 433-444.

Uhrmacher, B. P. (1997). Evaluating Change: Strategies for Borrowing from Alternative Education. *Theory into Practice, 36*(2), 71-78.

Visser, J. (2000). Rethinking Learning: Implications for Policy, Research and Practice. In M. Jain (Ed.) *Unfolding Learning Societies: Challenges and Opportunities.* Udaipur: Shikshantar—The People's Institute for Rethinking Education and Development.

Wilber, K. (2003). The Integral Approach. Available online at: ww.integralinstitute.org/approach.cfm.

Wilber, K. (2004). Introduction to Integral Theory and Practice: IOS Basic and the AQAL Map. Available online at: http://www.integralnaked.org.

Wildman, P., & Inayatullah, S. (1996). Ways of Knowing, Culture, Communication and the Pedagogies of the Future. *Futures, 28*(8), 723-740.

Woods, G., O'Neill, M. et al. (1997). Spiritual Values in Education: Lessons from Steiner. *The International Journal of Children's Spirituality, 2*(2), 25-40.

Woods, P. A., Ashley, M. et al. (2005). *Steiner Schools in England.* Bristol: Department for Education and Skills.

Woods, P. A., & Woods, G. (2002). Policy on School Diversity: Taking an Existential Turn in the Pursuit of Valued Learning? *British Journal of Educational Studies, 50*(2), 254-278.

Jennifer Gidley is an educational psychologist and futures researcher with the Centre for Children and Young People, at Southern Cross University, Lismore, Australia. She is also an advisor to the Integral Education Centre of Integral University, Boulder, Colorado, and a Research Fellow at the Global Dialogue Institute at Haverford College, Philadelphia. As well as founding and pioneering a Steiner School over ten years, she has researched and published widely on youth futures and educational transformation, including co-editing two books: The University in Transformation… *(Bergin & Garvey, 2000) and* Youth Futures: Comparative Research and Transformative Visions *(Praeger, 2002). Currently, she is researching the evolution of consciousness, focussing on the visionary wor/l/ds of Rudolf Steiner and Ken Wilber.*

BILLY MATHESON

16. CREATIVE PEDAGOGY

Narrative approaches and a neohumanist philosophy of education

The idea that we can teach people how to be creative speaks to a fundamental paradox underpinning the humanist philosophic tradition. While most of us accept that people have the capacity to learn, change and develop, the concept of an 'essential self' that remains constant throughout our lives still informs most people's folk psychology. The belief that each of us is born with certain innate gifts and talents— such as creativity—still informs most people's understandings of life and identity (White, 2001b).

Working as a lecturer in the creative industries has impressed on me the importance of making space around students' understandings of identity, in order to allow new creative competencies to be developed and new and alternative identities to be inhabited. This process requires students to research the narratives they live by and to design and develop stories that can carry them into the future.

This paper explores the relationship between futures studies and narrative approaches and how they can mutually inform a neohumanist philosophy of education.

The concept of 'cultural reproduction' through education is used to describe current educational and social paradigms. Alternative pedagogic frameworks are considered—based on the work of humanist educators Paulo Freire and bell hooks— and these are compared using four futures scenarios.

Humanist understandings of life and identity inform many of our ideas about both mainstream education and creative pedagogies such as futures studies. In the final section of this paper, the Narrative model is used to critique the traditional humanist concept of human nature and to present a neohumanist vision of personal development and collective learning.

INTRODUCTION

Contemporary Anthropology has made this shift from positivistic emulation of the hard sciences towards a more literary narrative approach, what [Clifford] Geertz calls thick description; a storytelling approach that stresses the narrative relationships among specific details rather than generic laws or universal details. (Ogilvy, 1996, p. 42)

M. Bussey, S. Inayatullah and I. Milojević (eds.), Alternative Educational Futures: Pedagogies for Emergent Worlds, 269–283.

In 1996 I bought a book called *New Thinking for a New Millennium*. Reading Richard Slaughter's introduction it became apparent to me that there was a field of investigation called futures studies (Slaughter, 1996). The direct and conscious nature of the contributors' relationship with the future was refreshing to say the least. I felt that here was a movement with a strong emphasis on positive change that was attempting to be both academically valid *and* open-ended and original in its structures and thinking.

During my undergraduate study of industrial design, I felt very strongly that I was engaged with the construction of the future, however, reading *New Thinking...* I felt that not only was my own knowledge of the future lacking, but that the approach of the design school I was attending was similarly inadequate. My friends and I were busy designing the tools, vehicles, and other consumables of the future without any real consideration of what that future might hold.

Issues like the state of the environment, population growth, climate change, new patterns of employment, and population demographics were never seriously engaged with in the way that *New Thinking...* advocated. Although I did not have the words at that time, I was aware at some level that we had been taking a lot for granted. In short, we were busy designing for a future, based on the assumption that our world would essentially stay the same.

My sense of being engaged with the future has not changed now that I am a lecturer; what has changed is that the focus of my creative work has indeed changed from things to relationships. It is my students who will construct the future, creating the next generation of material and visual culture for our society. As a lecturer in the creative industries my primary concern is helping students to develop their own unique visions for the future. In doing this work I am frequently reminded of Ogilvy's belief in the importance of "a storytelling approach that stresses narrative relationships" (1996) and his vision for an interdisciplinary futures studies in *New Thinking*.

NARRATIVE APPROACHES

> To exist humanly, is to name the world, to change it. Once named, the world reappears to the namers as a problem and requires of them a new naming. (Freire, 1972, p. 61)

Paulo Freire's words eloquently describe the importance of being able to understand and describe the world in our own terms. As the Ogilvy paper pointed out, the profound value of the narrative *interpretation* of reality over the scientific paradigm's *explanation* of reality is that it openly invites creativity and diversity; in fact, narrative interpretation relies on these qualities. The narrative construal of reality returns authority—literally 'authorship'—of people's lives back to the people whose life and identity are being described.

Recently there has been a proliferation of interest in narrative approaches, especially in the areas of adult education and psychotherapy, two disciplines particularly concerned with the issue of human development. Storytelling engages people, both teachers and students, at the deep level of their own experience rather than through abstract or disembodied ideas. Storytelling invites us to connect our seemingly isolated individual experiences with those of our fellow classmates, and with larger social and cultural histories and structures. In this way, narrative approaches allows people to experience themselves both as autonomous individuals and as members of a cultural group, and in the process often create powerful experiences of unity and belonging.

Marsha Rossiter describes the role of the adult educator in the Narrative process:

> First, the teacher is a character in the learner's story. Second, we are what Randall calls the "keepers" of the learner's story, by which he means that we provide a safe environment in which learners can tell their story; we 'receive' their story. Third, the educator or learning helper can function as an editor or critic, helping the learner to question what kind of story they are telling and to identify the assumptions that are driving it. And finally, the educator can assist as a co-author with learners as they fashion a revised self-narrative that is more inclusive of the realities of their lives. (Rossiter, 1999, p. 68)

Narrative and storytelling are powerful tools to create knowledge and identity. More specifically they create situated knowledge of 'the self–in–relation–to' other people, history and places. This approach to teaching represents a radical shift away from the commonly accepted view that part of the teacher's role is to determine what and how the student should learn (Illich, 1972).

In his book *Narrative Schooling: Experiential Learning and the Transformation of American Education*, Richard Hopkins expresses the potential of narrative to create new understandings of our own development: "Our narratives are the means through which we imagine ourselves into the persons we become" (Hopkins, 1994, p. xvii). For me this clearly articulates the relevance that narrative approaches have to the field of futures studies. Both are methodologies that enable groups of people to imagine themselves in the society they want, through the generation of probable, possible and preferable future scenarios.

CREATIVE PROCESSES

> What is the point of education? Is it to socialize young people so they can fit into the fabric of society? Is it to train a workforce? Is it to introduce young people to the greater possibilities that life has to offer? These are ... [all legitimate questions] ... But they leave out the most profound purpose that education might have: helping young people learn how to create the lives they truly want to create. (Fritz, 2000, p. 167)

Robert Fritz has been developing his vision for Creative Processes Education since the early 1970s. Developing pedagogies that will foster something as multi-layered as creativity obviously requires a similar multi-layered approach. As a starting point on this journey, two layers of meaning that are important to this paper are those of content and structure. While many aspects of Fritz's pedagogy clearly emphasise individual autonomy, he engages more than most with the role that culture plays in shaping the creative process:

> Many well-meaning people think that they have asked their children or students what they want to create, but they haven't really. They have asked a subtle variation: 'Of the things we've made available to you, what do you want?' Notice the difference. 'What do you want to create?' asks the young person to consider his or her overall life goals, values aspirations, and dreams. The second version begins by providing a menu of acceptable possibilities, and then says: 'From what is available to you, pick something.' What if the goals and dreams they truly want aren't on the menu? (Fritz, 2000, p. 169)

Working in the creative industries, my students are constantly asked to be creative, always within pre-existing structures and limits—for example a project brief or course outline—but also within broader boundaries of what various institutions (school, university or corporation) and their representatives (teachers, lecturers, employers or clients) want. This is often dependant on the cycles of fashion and ultimately on perceived financial viability in the context of a capitalist global economy. The content of Art and Design courses asks students to expand their thinking, to think 'laterally' or 'outside the square' (to use two fashionable phrases) and there are a number of straightforward techniques that facilitate this development. In doing this work, students often find powerful reconnections with ways of being creative that have not been experienced since pre-schooling.

What invariably happens, however, is that at some point in this process students find that their new creative vision—the content of their education—comes into direct conflict with a series of structural restrictions. The most visible and immediate authority students encounter is their tutor who may or may not value them or their ideas. Another common structure that students push against is the requirements of the project brief that may or may not be open to interpretation. These are followed by other parameters that are less visible, like the course outline and the way courses—both elective and core—are structured which are non-negotiable, the values and tenets of the institution which are sacrosanct, and finally an educational/societal paradigm of which most people are completely unaware.

I have found it useful to put these ideas in front of students early in their first year of tertiary study. Fritz's writing is clear and accessible, and frames these issues in terms of 'freedom of choice' in a way that most students find appealing. Asking these simple yet far-reaching questions seems to be enough to encourage in most students some consideration of how society tacitly and explicitly limits the range of alternatives from which we make our decisions.

The nature and origins of these educational and societal structures is seldom the focus of Primary or Secondary education. Consequently students and teachers lack an awareness of how to negotiate institutional structures and to set their own parameters for creative development. By the time students reach the Tertiary level the boundaries of what is acceptable have usually ceased to be visible to the average young person.

The path I have taken to try and imagine alternatives to the way we learn and teach has required me to firstly accept a view of education, society and culture as mechanisms for the 'reproduction' of the status quo—i.e., education, society and culture as they exist now. From this perspective radical social change is not a struggle, we just need to stop busily reproducing the present paradigm.

CULTURAL REPRODUCTION

Theories of cultural reproduction have been described by the Austrian-American educational philosopher Ivan Illich in *Deschooling Society* (1972), and by the French sociologists Pierre Bourdieu and Jean Claude Passeron in *Reproduction in Education, Society and Culture* (1977). Bourdieu and Passeron argue that the democratic ideals promoted by universities serve to obscure the hereditary nature of class privilege, and that this social stratification is perpetuated though the inculcation of an 'ideology of merit' and individual achievement. They describe the modern university as:

> ... a privileged instrument of bourgeois sociodicy that confers on the privileged the supreme privilege of not seeing themselves as privileged [and] convinces the disinherited that they owe their scholastic and social destiny to their lack of gifts or merits, because in matters of culture, absolute dispossession excludes awareness of being disposed. (Bourdieu & Passeron, 1990, p. 210)

The metaphor of a child's playpen seems appropriate to this discussion about suitable limits and the possibility of a pedagogy of transgression. This metaphor exposes the paternalistic belief that restrictive structures are imposed on us for our own good, to protect us from our selves and the world outside. In our present educational system both teachers and students are encouraged to 'play', to learn and experiment, but within safe and accepted limits. The existence or origin of these limits is usually not discussed or experienced until boundaries are transgressed, either accidentally or deliberately. As a consequence we don't even come close to transgressing boundaries later in life, for fear of what might happen.

Bourdieu and Passeron state, somewhat frustratingly, that it is impossible to expose the structure of power relations without perpetuating the same power relations we are tying to expose:

> The idea of a PA (pedagogic action) exercised without PAu (pedagogic authority) is a logical contradiction and sociological impossibility; a PA which aimed to unveil, in its very exercise, its objective reality of violence and thereby destroy the basis of the agents pedagogical authority, would be self destructive ... The paradox of Epimenides the liar would appear in a new form: either you believe that I'm not lying when I tell you that all education is violence and my teaching isn't legitimate, so you can't believe me; or you believe I'm lying and my teaching is legitimate, so you still can't believe me when I tell you its violence. (Bourdieu & Passeron, 1990, p. 12)

Other writers on education, such Paulo Freire, are less pessimistic. Freire similarly believed that "Education must begin with the resolution of the teacher–student contradiction, by reconciling the poles of the contradiction so that both are simultaneously teachers *and* students" (1972, p. 53).

For Freire, resolving this contradiction was not impossible. The process of resolution does, however, mean devolving pedagogic power to the students, by asking them to be creative with the nature of education itself, and being responsible for creating their own project briefs, course outlines, program structures, and eventually institutions. In other words we must cease trying to re-form the status quo and start authoring our own narratives of the future.

Seeing the content of education, society and culture as separate from the structures that are responsible for its reproduction, it becomes possible to imagine the 'production' of culture through a learning process oriented towards structural awareness and change, rather than the inculcation of normative values and the 'reproduction' of culture as it currently exists. This analysis allows us to then speculate as to the nature of a future based on cultural production and the nature of a pedagogy that would actively promote the creation of new cultural forms.

THE LAND OF THE LONG NOW

What follows are four snapshots of the future of my country. Each scenario considers the relationship between education, cultural reproduction and structural awareness in order to explore the role that education for creativity can play in the development of future societies, and what such pedagogies might involve. I describe these futures using four indicators: the mode of institutional delivery of education; the relationship between knowledge and power; the level of structural awareness encouraged by the curriculum; and the role that creativity plays in each future.

The first two scenarios presented are considered as status quo options, based on social democratic and free market ideologies. According to the 'eco-feminist' analysis of Maria Mies and Vandana Shiva, both capitalism and socialism are status quo because they both view the "... achievement of human happiness as basically conditional on the expansion of material goods' production" (Mies & Shiva, 1993, p. 16). The plurality of status quo scenarios seeks to show how these supposedly oppositional ideologies can both teach creative processes content within their existing structures, in ways that leave those structures largely unchanged. The third scenario is a partial change option, predicated on power sharing between indigenous and colonial cultures, and the fourth and final scenario is a 'paradigm shift' scenario, that while largely unknown/unknowable, is conceived on the premise of an emergent *culture of creativity*.

Kiwi Corp ™

The first of the status quo options is a 'corporate future' that presupposes the continued implementation of new right free market economic reform. The defining trend in my country during the last 20 years has been the restructuring of the economy according to the free-market ideology. Successive governments have sold state owned assets and infrastructure and implemented variations on the policies of the Thatcher and Reagan administrations in the UK and the US.

- Following the privatisation of all remaining publicly owned assets, education is offered through private training institutions at market rates, and through in-house corporate-run training programs.
- Knowledge in this society is privately owned and traded as a commodity in order to advance professional development and career. Power derived from the level of private intellectual property at the disposal of corporations or individuals, and is perceived to be a reflection of individual merit.
- Structural awareness would vary between private universities that offer specialised education to a wealthy elite and private technical institutions that are solely designed to deliver vocational training, where potential workers train at their own expense. The capitalist structure of this future society would continue to be accepted as a given. All research would be market driven and there would be an absence of social analysis that traditionally has been the function of the humanities.
- Creativity is encouraged for those who will be in management and leadership positions, in order to develop the potential of capitalist structures and facilitate the constant expansion and growth of markets for private financial gain.

In this paradigm, economic expansion is achieved through the further exploitation of non-renewable resources. Writing in 1972 Ivan Illich described how "... all of today's futuristic planners seek to make economically feasible what is technically impossible, while refusing to face the inevitable social consequence: the increased craving of all men for goods and services that will remain the privilege of a few" (Illich, 1972, p. 52).

The Third Way

In 1999 New Zealand voted in a 'centre left' coalition government. This reflected contemporary trends in North America and England towards the 'third way', or centrist policies of the Clinton/Blair Democratic and New Labour administrations. This second status quo scenario suggests a continuation of this movement and the eventual restoration of social democratic political ideals. In this future, core national infrastructure could eventually be nationalised and universal access to social services, like health and education, would be reinstated and paid for through various forms of taxation.
- State-run education is delivered through a centralised state school system. In this scenario a multicultural approach is taken within a singular and culturally specific educational model, reflecting the ideal of unity and the construction of a national identity.
- Knowledge in this society is state owned and made universally available because of what it can contribute to the national welfare. It is acquired though institutional processes and is directed back through institutions that have the power to act to improve the society as a whole. Power is something nations and institutions have, and individuals derive power from membership of these collective groupings.

- In this future, social structures are examined by agencies of government, such as universities, and strengthened to increase social security and to better cater for societies' needs. Structural awareness is enhanced through a renewed emphasis on social studies leading to a revival of the humanities and the increased structural awareness that the social sciences provide.
- Creativity is still encouraged at government and administrative levels to get the most out of socialist structures and to provide an increased standard of living and social development.

While a social democracy may embody the egalitarian, classless society that many people would like to see in this country, it still involves many fundamental inequalities and coercion due to the need to maintain a status quo. Noam Chomsky, who has written extensively on the coercive nature of institutions, describes this tendency to use education to control a population:

> From the early days of the school system there was a tendency to foster creativity and independence of thought [because] you want people who are going to be in decision-making positions to be able to think and to have ideas. On the other hand you want them to be deeply indoctrinated and not to challenge authority and institutional structures. For the rest, the end goal ... [of education] ... is to turn you into a docile, passive worker. (Chomsky, 1994, p. 139)

Aotearoa New Zealand

The antithesis to these mono-cultural status quo options is a 'bi-cultural' future that I describe as a partial change scenario. Since the annexation of this land by England in 1840, Maori have actively asserted the right to self-determination guaranteed in *Te Tiriti o Waitangi/The Treaty of Waitangi*.

This future is based on the successful implementation of meaningful power sharing and the creation of dual sovereignty between Settler and First Peoples, Pakeha/Tauiwi and Maori. Rather than eliminating difference from an existing structure, successful de-colonisation relies on the dominant culture 'allowing' another structure to operate parallel to it, establishing a bi-cultural society. The influence of cultural values and social structures of Maori on Pakeha, combined with the development of a truly multicultural framework *within* Pakeha society, combine to encourage cultural diversity and to reconfigure the social structures of this country.

- Education is re-invented to reflect the plural values of both treaty partners, resulting in education being delivered through a combination of traditional European style state schools, Kohanga reo, Wananga, alternative schools, and community initiatives.
- Knowledge is seen being largely synonymous with tradition, and as coming from ancestors and the past. Such wananga/knowledge is communally owned and held. Power is understood as the right to self-determination, directly derived from an ability to enact the knowledge held within individuals and communities.

While knowledge may be culturally *specific* and an issue of identity, the *sharing* of power is fundamental to bi-cultural relationship in this future.

- A curriculum based on the implementation of meaningful power sharing between Maori and Settler cultures—as outlined in *Te Tiriti O Waitangi*—requires a deep awareness of the cultural frameworks and social structures of both treaty partners. For this to be possible education would be built on bi-lingual and bi-cultural frameworks.
- Creativity is encouraged to foster a sense of identity, through art, crafts, sports, performance and other cultural activities, and this is done within the existing cultural frameworks and the traditions of the respective treaty partners.

This partial change scenario seeks to demonstrate the culturally specific nature of the current paradigm. Although this future represents a radically new social order, I describe it as a partial change scenario because it is based on the pluralist *reproduction* of two *existing* cultures within one new structure. In saying this it is not my intention to diminish the importance of the bi-cultural project. As Vandana Shiva points out, this may be necessary for the growth of both majority and minority cultures:

> Ghandi clearly formulated the individuality of freedom, not only in the sense that the oppressed of the world are one, but also in the wider sense that the oppressor too, is caught in the culture of oppression. Decolonisation is therefore as relevant in the context of the colonizer as it is in that of the colonized. (Shiva, 1993, p. 264)

A crucial question facing educators in Colonial/Settler societies is how members of dominant cultural groups can relate with the knowledge base of Tangata Whenua and other indigenous cultures in ways that don't constitute a further (neo) colonisation. Sohail Inayatullah reinforces this point when he says "… the West has prospered precisely because it has been able to be diverse enough to appropriate the symbols of others without changing its essential world-view". The challenge of this bi-cultural future is that the dominant culture will have to change its essential worldview. In New Zealand this could lead to the development of new cross-cultural competencies and related understandings that will be of enormous value to this country and the world.

Te Tai Ao/The Natural World of Change

Completing the thesis, antithesis and synthesis model is a speculative 'paradigm shift' scenario. A decade ago the United Nations Environment Program conference in Thessaloniki, Greece, expressed the urgency felt then by people concerned with climate change:

> The question is how long can we wait to make the changes to education we now need, regardless of how broad or how deep these required changes need to be. The challenge is tremendous—one of unprecedented scope, scale, and

complexity—and we have to do this in a climate of sweeping economic, social, technical and political change. (UNESCO-UNEP, 1997, p. 16)

As the twenty-first century unfolds most indicators suggest that there are many ongoing issues of survival that we need to respond to by changing how we conduct ourselves in the world. If we are to develop healthy social processes, create a sustainable and holistic future, we will need to re-weave binaries such as student and teacher, past and future, the personal and professional, formal education and informal learning, theory and practice. The holistic project is a vast undertaking, one that cannot be achieved in personal or intellectual isolation. For this reason the focus of this future pedagogy is learning how to 'think together'.

- In this future, learning could be facilitated through a diverse range of independent individuals, community-based student/teacher councils, as well as the full spectrum of already existing organisations.
- The relationship between knowledge and power is core to understanding the multi-layered nature of education in this future. Knowledge is explored as a whole system that both shapes and is shaped by the people that inhabit it. Power relationships are understood as both generative and problematic, and learning discernment between having power over others and having power with others in relationships is seen as central to collective thought processes.
- The concept of curriculum evolves to engage the whole person in a learning journey. Student and teacher become synonymous co-creating the courses they participate in. Social and cultural structures can be playfully reconfigured as and when required to meet ever-changing societal and cultural needs as perceived by the people who inhabit them.
- In a culture of creativity, education ceases to be fixed to certain institutions and to be seen as separate from other cultural activity. In this respect, terms like education, school, teacher, student, may no longer be appropriate. As a founding principle of these future societies, creativity is understood as being vital to human growth—both to our collective as well as our personal development— and to the well being of the whole community.

This fourth scenario presupposes a future society that has accepted the need for radical change at a structural, rather than a superficial level. To achieve a societal paradigm that is meaningfully different I believe we need to imagine a future society dedicated to growing a new *tradition of creative change*.

The best that can be said for any system is that it is (a) effective in doing what it claims to do, and that (b) that it leads to its own demolition via the liberation of those who employ it to reach new conclusions, fresh in sights, and real inner and outer growth. (Stewart, 1987, p. 19)

Innovation and tradition combine in praxis—creating wisdom—and that feeds back, permeating the process, avoiding rigidity and driving further cycles of creative change and development.

THE LIMITS OF CHANGE

Education is paradoxically both a sadly neglected and a vigorously contested space. The idea of a preferable future for the role that education plays in our society is obviously highly political because the education of the next generation of voters, consumers, parents, workers, and activists, will profoundly shape the effectiveness and consciousness of these groups. Whether we see education as a process of indoctrination or liberation will necessarily depend on our personal beliefs and experiences.

While changes to the content of the present curriculum—like the inclusion of creative processes or futures studies—offers many exciting and positive possibilities, their effectiveness as promoters of social change is often diminished and in many cases defeated by the fundamentally conservative nature of the institutions that we try to deliver them through.

While individual teachers and schools are able to create new kinds of learning environments, extending this quality of education throughout the present education system will not be easy, as David Orr, Professor of Environmental Studies Program at Oberlin College, in Ohio points out:

> What would it mean for educational institutions to meet this challenge? For one thing, it would mean fostering, in every way possible, a broad and ongoing dialogue about concentrated economic power and the changes that would be necessary to build a sustainable economy. I know no safe way to conduct that conversation that would not threaten the comfortable, or risk loosing some of the institutions financial support, a sensitive topic when the cost of a college education is becoming prohibitively expensive. (Orr, 2002, p. 96)

What the four scenarios presented above hopefully convey is the magnitude of the task ahead even to create the conditions for the "broad and ongoing dialogue" that Orr is asking for. Each of the first three futures has an internal logic and set of core beliefs about what is necessary for the survival of that culture. While this is possibly true of the fourth scenario also, the important thing to notice is the willingness to question the necessity of our present ways of doing education. In that future we are open to questioning culture itself and learning to consciously create new cultural forms.

In his book, *On Dialogue* British physicist and philosopher David Bohm describes the relationship between dialogue and questioning the status quo:

> Now if you can question it and say, "Is it absolutely necessary?" then at some point it may loosen up. People may say, "Well maybe it's not absolutely necessary." Then the whole thing becomes easier, and it becomes possible to let that conflict go and to explore new notions of what is necessary, creatively. The dialogue can then enter a creative new era. I think this is crucial. (Bohm, 1994, p. 23)

What would it look like to question what is "absolutely necessary" in contemporary Western culture? What would I need to make some room around in my own thinking in order to "enter a creative new era"'? To reflect on these questions more deeply we might need to take a look in the mirror.

SELF AS NARRATIVE

The modern self, the 'I' at the centre of the humanist worldview, assumes itself to be a free intellectual agent and that its thinking process is now largely free from coercion by historical and cultural circumstance: "In his work Descartes offers us a narrator who imagines that he speaks without simultaneously being spoken" (Sarup, 1993, p. 1). Renaissance humanism continues to inform many of our contemporary ideas about life and identity, and consequently the way we approach education. Philip Wexler, Professor of Education and Sociology at the University of Rochester, describes this tendency to collapse these complex issues of cultural identity into the concept of the autonomous individual:

> The creation of individualism has been going on a long time. So, in this culture of individualism, all the social and cultural processes are carried inside the self-question. So take the self-questions of: 'What am I thinking?' 'What's going to become of me?' 'What's my relation to this and that?'. All of these are in my view deeply social, cultural and historical questions. But because we are so individualistic, they are coded and translated into the language of the self, and worked out in the medium of the self. So the self is where the action is. But it's not just about the self, it's about history and civilisation and evolution and collective processes. (Wexler, 1995, p. 95)

The Australian psychotherapist Michael White is one a growing number of people working in the field of human development who traces many of the difficulties they experience in practice back to the humanist worldview that has underpinned Western thought for hundreds of years:

> In contemporary Western culture, humanist discourses have become pervasive in the shaping of our taken–for–granted understandings of most expressions of life. These understandings provide naturalistic accounts of life and identity. In them, identity is taken to be the product of nature, of human nature; a nature made up of "essences" or "elements" that are to be "found" at the centre of who one is. (White, 2001a, p. 28)

The humanist discourses that White refers to above assumes that certain ways of thinking and understanding are 'natural' or 'essential' parts of being a human, rather than being learned behaviours or manifestations of specific cultural values. This has led to the projection of Western developmental goals and cultural values (humanism) onto all people (humans) regardless of 'race, religion or creed'.

Of more concern to this project is the way that through this process Western cultural values have become largely invisible to Western people. We have become blind to our own part in the diversity of the whole. David Bohm calls the ability to be aware of ourselves 'propreoception'. He argues that in the West we have lost the capacity for propreoception of thought, and therefore of culture:

> I am suggesting, however, that thought is a system belonging to the whole culture and society, evolving over history, and it creates the image of an individual who is supposed to the source of thought. It gives the sense of an individual who is perceived and experienced. This would be conducive to the next step, which is for thought to claim that it only tells you the way things are and then the individual inside decides what to do with the information. (Bohm, 1996, p. 71)

Bohm manages to articulate the difficulty we face when we try to think about our own thinking:

> You may look at this and try to reason and see what is wrong ... The very "wrong" things, which we should be looking at are in the one who is looking, because that is the safest place to hide them. Hide them in the looker and the looker will never find them. (p. 72)

As a process tool he offers the technique of 'suspension' of judgement. In this way, thoughts and collective values aren't stopped, suppressed or ignored; rather he suggests that they can be suspended in front of us, visible to us but no longer dictating our responses. In doing this we can come to look at 'ourselves' and realise that, while we might be attached to these ideas, we are also more than these ideas. Or, in Bohm's words: "We are trying to get deeper, to the very essence of the whole process that is behind the self, or the observer" (Bohm, 1996, p. 73).

The idea of a 'process that is behind the self' seems like a potential doorway to a reinvention of humanism and the ideology of an essential self that defines who we are and what we can be.

CONCLUSION

Human history is rich with examples of the ways in which humanist and liberation philosophies—and the educational movements they have informed—have succeeded in giving people a voice, often in the face of direct opposition from conservative authority. Telling our story can be a powerful strategy for empowerment, whether in the context of individual psychotherapy, or a significant social movement seeking greater autonomy and self-governance.

> In contemporary societies there is a struggle for interpretative power, and the prevailing ideologies limit the means by which individuals understand their material experiences. The modern culture-industry robs individuals of 'languages' for interpreting self and world by denying the media for organising their own experiences. (Sarup, 1993, p. 186)

In creative pedagogy such narrative approaches make this process of telling our stories central to the design of people's learning journey. It is vital that we make this journey available to all people, not just those of us fortunate enough to be involved in the creative industries and who have access to multimedia communication tools and digital storytelling technologies.

While giving people an opportunity to 'interpret self' is an important first step, I am suggesting that we need to go further than this if we want to create the conceptual space necessary to constructively engage with shared visions for the future. In taking this opportunity to deconstruct the naturalistic account of identity that is coded into the modern self, narrative approaches challenge the humanist belief that peoples current identity conclusions constitute the truth of who they are (White, 2001a).

The emergent neohumanist philosophy of education challenges and extends traditional humanism's faith in the redemptive potential of education by asking us to engage with the intentional transformation of consciousness. Beckoning to us from the other side of the crisis of identity is the possibility that we can overcome centuries of intellectual isolation and learn to 'think together'.

The process craft of this new way of learning requires us to hold both individual and collective awareness at the same time. If we can learn the art of *presencing* both our own experience and the experiences of others then we can participate in the flow of meaning between part and whole (Senge et al., 2004).

> I think that when you get strong enough, as it were, that you can stand firm in a distracting environment, then you're strong enough to begin to look at the infinite … I think that then there is the possibility of a transformation of consciousness, both individually and collectively. It's important that it happens together—it's got to be both. (Bohm, 1996, pp. 94-95)

At this point in our collective journey it seems that we are being challenged with the need to reinvent the very culture that grew us. We are being asked to evolve.

REFERENCES

Bohm, D. (1996). *On dialogue*. London: Routledge.
Bourdieu, P., & Passeron, J. (1990). *Reproduction in education, society and culture*. London: Sage.
Bruner, J. (1996). *The culture of education*. Cambridge, MA: Harvard University Press.
Chomsky, N. (1995). A conversation with Noam Chomsky. *Dulwich Centre Newsletter, 2&3*, 138–144.
Freire, P. (1972). *Pedagogy of the oppressed*. London: Penguin Books.
Fritz, R. (2000). Teaching structural tension. In P. Senge (Ed.), *Schools that learn: A fifth discipline fieldbook for educators, parents, and everyone who cares about education*. New York: Doubleday.
Hooks, B. (1994). *Teaching to transgress*. New York: Routledge.
Hopkins, R. L. (1994). *Narrative schooling: Experiential learning and the transformation of American education*. New York: Teachers College Press.
Illich, I. (1972). *Deschooling society*. London: Coyar and Boyers Ltd.
Inayatullah, S. (1998). Listening to non-western perspectives. In D. Hicks & R. Slaughter (Eds.), *Futures education*. London: Kogan Page.
Mies, M., & Shiva, V. (1993). *Ecofeminism*. London: Zed Books.
Ogilvy, J. (1996). Futures studies and the new sciences: The case for normative scenarios. In R. Slaughter (Ed.), *New thinking for a new millennium* (pp. 26–83). London: Routledge.

Orr, D. W. (2002). *The nature of design: Ecology, culture, and human intention*. New York: Oxford University Press.

Rossiter, M. (1999). A narrative approach to development: Implications for adult education. *Adult Education Quarterly, 50*(1), 56–71.

Sarup, M. (1993). *An introduction to post-modernism and post structuralism*. Athens, GA: The University of Georgia Press.

Senge, P., Scharmer, O., Jaworski, J., & Flowers, B. (2004). *Presence: Human purpose and the field of the future*. Cambridge, MA: SOL.

Shiva, V. (1993). *Monocultures of the mind*. London: Zed Books.

Slaughter, R. A. (Ed.). (1996). *New thinking for a new millennium*. London: Routledge.

Stewart, R. J. (1987). *Music and the elemental psyche*. Wellingborough, Kent: Aquarian Press.

Wexler, P. (1995). A conversation with Philip Wexler. *Dulwich Centre Newsletter, 2&3*, 95–101.

White, M. (2001a). Narrative practice and the unpacking of identity conclusions. *Gecko: A Journal of Deconstruction and Narrative Practice, 1*, 28–55.

White, M. (2001b). Folk psychology and narrative practice. *Dulwich Centre Journal, 2*, 8–30.

Billy Matheson, MEd (Adult Education) Massey University, BDes (Industrial Design) Victoria University, is a lecturer at the Centre for Creative Technologies at the Wellington Institute of Technology in Wellington, New Zealand. His current research projects include cybernetics and systems thinking, community development approaches to creating sustainable futures, and prototyping a cross sector change tool for social entrepreneurs. He is involved in several learning communities that use open space and dialogue processes to explore and develop alternative learning environments.

JENNIFER GIDLEY AND GARY HAMPSON

17. INTEGRAL APPROACHES TO SCHOOL EDUCATIONAL FUTURES[i]

INTRODUCTION

Regarding school education, research to date arising from the transdisciplinary field of futures studies includes three major areas:

- research with young people (mostly in school settings) which explores their views and visions of the future;
- the teaching of futures concepts, tools and processes in school settings;
- speculative research into transformative educational models and approaches facilitated by futures/foresight thinking.

The first area provides a context for how young people see themselves in regard to 'the future' and why 'futures' processes are so valuable for them. The global scope of this area—more typically called 'youth futures'—has been well documented in the book, *Youth Futures: Comparative Research and Transformative Futures* (Gidley & Inayatullah, 2002). The second area includes an analysis of the current 'state of play' in futures education *in* schools. A comprehensive literature review has recently been undertaken on this area, including examples of 'good practice' at the primary and secondary levels (Gidley 2004). The third area points to a possible future of 'futures education' which goes beyond the teaching of 'futures' as isolated lessons or subjects to where foresight is an integral part of the conceptual schema rather than an 'add-on'.

This chapter will initially explore some issues relating to the latter—more transformative—area, futures *of* school education, in particular from the perspective of the term 'integral' as used by Ken Wilber. Secondly, there will be an exemplary case study of how the four quadrants component of Wilber's integral framework has been used to analyse the present state of play of futures education *in* schools.

THE INTEGRITY OF 'INTEGRAL'

'Integral' means 'inclusive, balanced, comprehensive' … The integral approach does not advocate one particular value system over another, but simply helps leaders assemble the most comprehensive overview available, so that they can more adequately and sanely address the pressing issues now facing all of us. (Wilber, 2003)

Let us take a brief look at 'integral'. From a historical perspective, 'the spirit of integral' or 'integral intent' can be seen to have formed part of the leading edge of human consciousness for over 2000 years. Whilst the 'deep structure' of 'integral

M. Bussey, S. Inayatullah and I. Milojević (eds.), Alternative Educational Futures: Pedagogies for Emergent Worlds, 285–303.

intent' can be seen to have maintained 'integrity' through time, its 'surfacing' at any given time can be seen to have required adaptability of form—in particular, in relation to socio-cultural conditions. Moreover, as collective human consciousness has generally evolved, new understandings can be seen to have been taken on board. In this way, we can identify, so to speak, the evolution of 'the integral avant garde' (Wilber 2003).

The use of the term 'integral' or 'integrative' has become increasingly common in leading edge approaches to many disciplines. Some significant twentieth century and contemporary writers—other than Wilber—who were working from a substantially integral perspective include Rudolf Steiner, Michael Polanyi, Jean Gebser, Sri Aurobindo Ghose, Ervin László, Ashok Gangadean, and William Irwin Thompson. An important basis of the idea in its varied forms is that the complexity of the present times requires higher-order forms of thinking that go beyond the narrow specialisations of instrumental rationality. Integral approaches include multiples ways of knowing, being and acting in the world.

Wilber's own use of the term, 'integral' can be traced back to usage by both Sri Aurobindo Ghose and Jean Gebser. The first—and largest—integral tertiary institution in the US is the California Institute of Integral Studies (CIIS), founded in 1968, based on the Integral approach developed by Sri Aurobindo Ghose. Several other centres of integral studies have emerged in the last decade in the US, including Ken Wilber's Integral Institute (www.integralinstitute.org).

Wilber's framework provides a broad conceptual territory in which an integral analysis might take place. At the same time, due consideration should be given to domains of 'integral' other than *analysis per se* in which other 'contenders' can be seen to be of value.

Several other educational approaches have used the term 'integral education', such as:
- Michael Bakunin, a Russian Marxist, who coined 'integral education' in 1869 as an attempt to overcome classism in society.
- Dr Karan Singh (Indian Integral Education).
- Rey Juan Carlos University in Madrid, Spain.
- The Catholic Church in Africa and Sri Lanka.
  or 'integrative learning', such as:
- Community of Integrative Learning and Action (CILA).
- American Association of Colleges and Universities' (AACU) 2005 conference on Integrative Learning: Creating Opportunities to Connect.

It is beyond the scope of this chapter to discuss all of the above interpretations of 'integral education'. However, with regard to school education, an 'integrally aware' perspective such as Steiner's (discussed below) can be seen to provide rich rewards regarding possible research from the domain of an *already-established approach with integral intent*. This should not be taken to imply, however, that such already-established approaches can not be critiqued in relation to a possible imbalance or neglect of certain integral dimensions (with additional understanding that there can be a dissonance between educational theory and its implementation in educational practice). Indeed, such a critique of educational approaches should form a significant part of the process of conceptual mapping needed to understand what a well-formed 'integral education' might look like.

This process can be seen to form part of 'preferred future' scenarios for school (and non-school) education. Through integral understanding, it can be seen that an important feature of these preferred scenarios is the move away from the overarching quality of fragmentation to that of integration.

FUTURES *OF* SCHOOL EDUCATION—FROM FRAGMENTATION TO INTEGRATION

Perhaps we ought to consider the notion that the purpose of education be reconceptualized as the facilitation of people's search for meaning, wholeness, transcendence and an understanding of our individual roles in the human evolutionary journey. (Rogers, 1998)

Critical Speculation about Education for the Future

Over the past decade a number of educational futurists have developed a critical approach to what they see as the pedagogical implications of the disturbing responses of Western youth to their futures. Critical speculation about alternative forms of education makes some clear recommendations about better preparing youth for a rapidly changing and uncertain future, while also considering the needs of future generations. These futures researchers recommend more holistic, integrated teaching methods using imagination, visualisation, pro-social skills and specific futures methodologies (Bjerstedt, 1982; Galtung, 1982; Slaughter, 1989; Beare & Slaughter, 1993; Tough, 1993; Slaughter, 1994; Hicks & Holden, 1995; Hutchinson, 1996).

In a comprehensive conceptual review of current global dimensions of change and consciousness shifts required to prepare young people for the twenty-first century, Australian educational futures researchers Hedley Beare and Richard Slaughter list a number of educational features (see Table 1) that they recommend schools incorporate to better prepare young people for the future (Beare & Slaughter 1993).

As yet, the suggestions and guidelines put forward by Beare and Slaughter have not been applied by educational futures researchers in an integrated fashion in an educational setting that could then be studied. However, these ten educational features listed in Table 1 are remarkably consistent with the Rudolf Steiner approach, with at least eight of the ten points being key features of Steiner education. So, in effect, the guidelines suggested by Beare and Slaughter, with the exception of the specific futures methods and tools, are already being implemented in Steiner schools around the world. Not surprisingly, this speculation of futures researchers was born out in research with Steiner-educated students, where it was found that this 'integrally aware', artistic, imaginative approach to education did facilitate a more confident, proactive and hopeful futures outlook in young people (Gidley, 1998, 1998, 2002). More detailed findings are discussed in the next section.

Table 1. Educational futures research—Guidelines for teaching and preparing young people for the twenty-first century

---

* 1. Appropriate Imagery—choosing metaphors with care and imagination

* 2. Teach for Wholeness and Balance—holistic paradigm

* 3. Teach Identification, Connectedness, Integration—epistemological interconnectedness

* 4. Develop Individual Values—value the individual

* 5. Teach Visualisation—development of the picturing imagination

6. Cultivate Visions of the Future—cultivate images and visions of futures

* 7. Empowerment through active hope—distinguish between faith and hope

* 8. Tell Stories—use story telling and mythology as powerful teaching tool

* 9. Teach and Learn how to Celebrate—celebrate festivals

10. Teach Futures Tools—encourage and use futures tools and methods

---

Source: Beare & Slaughter (1993)
* The asterisked points all refer to important features of Rudolf Steiner Education (Gidley, 1997)

Integral Approaches to Education

In parallel with the growing concerns of educational futurists about the need to transform school education in the ways discussed above, there is the emergence of the movement towards contemporised integral understanding mentioned earlier.

We believe the integral movement with its various currents and facets has the potential to facilitate transformative development in human consciousness. Its implications for educational futures should not be overlooked. With regard to the application of Wilber's integral theories to school education, conceptual development has begun at the Integral Education Centre—a branch of the emerging Integral University. In terms of existing school educational approaches, the importance of going beyond the factory model of schooling to more integral, artistic and spiritually-based approaches was already foreseen a century ago by

Rudolf Steiner (and others) in Europe (Steiner, 1965, 1982) and by Sri Aurobindo Ghose in India, who actually coined the term 'integral education' (1930, 1990 (1914)). Furthermore, the wisdom-based theories of these two leading edge educationist have been being implemented around the globe for between 50 (in the case of Aurobindo's system) and 80 years (in the case of Steiner education). While it is beyond the scope of this paper to further investigate the educational approach of Sri Aurobindo, the research with Steiner-educated students discussed below is the only known research demonstrating how an apparently more integral approach to education actually fosters foresight and personal empowerment towards creating one's own preferred future.

Research Findings from Steiner Education

Since Steiner education is arguably one of the few educational approaches in the Western educational arena that points towards an integral model, research findings can throw light on what a more integral approach to mainstream education can hope to achieve. Steiner education provides an integrated balance of intellectual/ cognitive, artistic/imaginative and practical/life skills education, grounded in a dialectical epistemology, ontology and cosmology. Although Steiner did not use the specific term 'integral', the educational approach he initiated can be seen to closely resemble the meaning of 'integral' in the sense that Wilber uses it. As well as consciously emphasising Plato's Goodness (ethics), Beauty (aesthetics) and Truth (science)—across all levels of schooling—these three aspects are constantly interwoven through the 'head, heart and hands' approach to all the teaching and learning. Also, reflecting a convergence between Steiner's and Wilber's approaches, Steiner pedagogy works from a deep understanding of the levels of development of the human being as they unfold both developmentally within an individual's life (ontogenetically) and also for humanity as a whole (phylogenetically) through the evolution of culture and consciousness. Although it is beyond the scope of this chapter to go into this in detail, the 'levels' that Steiner describes include several 'higher dimensions' similar to those described by Wilber, Aurobindo and others. Correspondences and divergences between these two approaches are being elucidated elsewhere by Gidley (2006).

Steiner was a polymath—scientist, philosopher and artist—who contributed significantly to a multiplicity of fields. He had a macrocosmic perspective on time in relation to the evolution of human culture and consciousness and with considerable foresight he initiated the educational approach discussed here in 1919 (in Germany).

In a study of senior secondary students in the three largest Steiner schools in Australia, it was found that Steiner students were able to develop richer and more detailed images of their 'preferred futures' than mainstream students (Gidley, 2002). About three-quarters of the Steiner students were able to envision positive changes with regard to the environment and human development and almost two-thirds were able to imagine positive changes in the socio-economic area. In much of the other research young people had general ideas about positive things they would like to see happen, but were unable to translate them into concrete detail

(Hutchinson, 1992) It was also found that the Steiner educated students were not disempowered, like many young people, by their realistically negative views of the 'probable' future, but rather had a strong sense of activism that they could change things for the better (Gidley, 1998).

In addition, when the Steiner students came to envisioning futures without war, the content of their visions primarily related to improvements in human relationships and communication, through dialogue and conflict resolution, rather than a 'passive peace' image. Furthermore, 75 per cent of the Steiner students came up with many ideas on what aspects of human development (including their own personal development) needed to be changed so that their aspirations for the future could be fulfilled. These included more activism, changes in values, spirituality, future care and better education (Gidley, 1998). Finally, this study appears to be the only one with young people where social futures has emerged so strongly as a way to solve problems, as compared with the more commonly occurring 'technofix' solutions.

Additional 'Integrally Aware' Educational Approaches

In addition to the educational approaches of Sri Aurobindo Ghose in India (more recently spreading to other countries) and Rudolf Steiner (with several hundred schools operating globally), numerous other 'integrally aware' educational approaches have arisen. Most have been in response to the increasing fragmentation and commoditisation of education found in the 'factory model' promoted in the West. Although beyond the scope of this paper, attributes of alternative approaches to education—as well as mainstream perspectives—could be conceptually mapped according to various dimensions of integral understanding. This clearer picture would facilitate an integrating dialogue between educational approaches. An attempt to elucidate the territory that might need to be covered in such an integral mapping exercise has been developed elsewhere (Hampson, 2004). The approaches briefly discussed below also need to be considered.

Neohumanist education stems from the understandings of P. R. Sarkar (b. 1921), and the science of Tantra Yoga. In 1935, Sarkar developed the multi-faceted organisation Ananda Marga—"the Path of Bliss"—dedicated to 'uplifting' humanity. In addition to education, the organisation includes such domains as: humanistic economy and collective welfare, women's emancipation, the arts, ecology, and intellectual renaissance. The Centre for Neohumanist Studies comments:

> Neohumanist education pedagogy applies the philosophy and principles of Neohumanism. Educators aspire to exemplify these values in their personal lives, in the classroom, and in their interactions with the students, colleagues, parents and the community. These principles include:
>
> – Holistic Personal Development
> – Cardinal Human Values and Universalism
> – Neohumanism and Universal Love
> – Astaunga Yoga

- Applied Learning—Knowledge of Self and the World
- Individual Evolution, Movement and Motivation.
  (http://www.cns.hr/e_philo.htm)

Another educational pioneer—Maria Montessori (b. 1870)—has left a very influential and growing legacy to the world: Montessori's is a comprehensive educational approach based on the observation of children's needs in a variety of cultures. It specifically includes an understanding of children's natural learning tendencies as they unfold in "prepared environments" (www.montessori-namta.org/NAMTA/geninfo/concepts1.html). Specially prepared materials are seen to help facilitate the cultivation of concentration, motivation, self-discipline, and a love of learning. There are now thousands of Montessori schools worldwide (http://www.montessori-namta.org/NAMTA/geninfo/whatismont.html).

Ron Miller has conceptually brought together the alternative approaches of Steiner, Montessori, Krishnamurti and others under the more general banner of 'Holistic Education', drawing out commonalities such as the importance of considering the moral, emotional, physical, psychological and spiritual dimensions of the developing child as well as the intellectual. Direct engagement with the environment and the development of a sense of wonder are also seen by Miller as important common attributes (Miller, 1999).

Another youth and futures-positive educational approach has been developed by Riane Eisler, called partnership education (Eisler, 2001). It is an integrated framework for primary and secondary education, which has three interconnected components:
- Partnership process (how we teach and learn).
- Partnership structure (the kind of learning environment).
- Partnership content (the actual educational curriculum).

In addition, an important movement that has gathered momentum over the past decade is the 'Education for Sustainability' or 'Sustainable Education' movement (Fien, 2002). Related to this and often incorporated under its banner is the 'citizenship education' focus. The 'sustainability in education' movement was primarily initiated as a response by educators to the Earth Summit—the UN Conference on Environment and Development held in Rio de Janeiro, Brazil in June 1992. Although it is a new evolving concept, it is also embedded in an understanding of indigenous approaches to education. Many of the key features of the sustainable education approach have been incorporated into the work of futurists David Hicks and Cathie Holden. They have extended the sustainable education territory and their futures work into the citizenship education focus in the national curriculum of the UK (Hicks, 2001; Holden, 2002).

FUTURES *IN* SCHOOL EDUCATION—PAST, PRESENT AND FUTURE

Part of the soul-work of learning is the development of images of desired futures; images that may be expressed in music, art, words or other aesthetic venues. (Rogers, 1998)

As a 'subset' of 'futures *of* school education', many educational futurists like to focus on the specific role of futures concepts and methods *in* school education. There are a number of ways in which we could analyse the progress of futures *in* education over the past four decades. Based on Slaughter's emerging integral futures model (Slaughter, 2003), this paper presents a case study of how an integral analysis can be undertaken. It attempts to analyse the state of play in futures in education today according to a four quadrants analysis that is part of the integral scheme developed by Ken Wilber (Wilber, 2000; Wilber, 2003; Wilber, 2004).

Since much of the early 'futures in education' work was concerned with survey studies of young people's probable views of the future, it sits within the empirical tradition which was strongly developed in the US. The next wave of futures in education work incorporates the bulk of the work to this day. Much of the teaching about futures (concepts, methodologies and tools) included in futures courses and syllabi is related to moving beyond the idea of the 'probable future' to include consideration of the 'possible' (imaginative, creative, alternative) and the 'preferred' (critical, ideological, values-based). The latter relates to the second phase of the futures field, originating in Europe and evolving into the critical futures tradition. Hicks' work is strongly grounded in this approach (Hicks, 2002).

However, one of the limitations of this aspect of futures in education is that most of the futures in education work has been undertaken in the US, the UK and Australia, and is thereby very biased by its 'Anglo-Saxon Western' orientation. Even though much of the discourse around 'possible futures' concerns open, creative, imaginative, flexible processes, much of the work as yet is limited by Western paradigm metaphors. However, Ivana Milojević's research makes a major contribution here, particularly in its consideration of indigenous educational futures (Milojević, 2002). This relates to what Slaughter calls the third wave of futures work, which he describes as still developing and as being "more diffuse, international, and multicultural" (Slaughter, 2003). An attempt has been made to address the gap in the literature on this multicultural area of futures in education, in the book *Youth Futures* (Gidley & Inayatullah, 2002). However, this was mainly focused on the youth views and visions aspect of futures with less focus on teaching futures. Some of Inayatullah's work begins to touch on this area of how to teach futures in education using concepts and tools and metaphors which are viable in a range of alternative cultural settings (Inayatullah, 1995, 2002). Much more research needs to be done in this area.

The empowerment-oriented educational futures work (prospective futures) is the fourth area in our typology. In mainstream futures literature it is rarely considered an area in its own right. While Slaughter's voice was one of the strongest in developing the futures field beyond the empirical—to include the critical— Inayatullah's voice is probably one of the strongest in developing the futures field into its third iteration which he calls the cultural (Inayatullah, 1990; Ramos, 2003). Although empowerment-oriented (prospective) futures studies was pioneered in Europe by Berger, Bjerstedt and Boulding, it seems that emphasis on this aspect may be the special contribution of Australia to the futures in education field. Wildman's coining of the term 'futuring' to represent this more engaged, activist approach, is a case in point. In our view this is the area where futures in education and youth futures research overlap, particularly if they are undertaken by em-powerment oriented teachers/researchers. It is interesting to note that Inayatullah's most recent work also includes a fourth 'action research' dimension to his futures framework (Inayatullah, 2004).

In the framework presented here, the empowerment/action research futures would be the fourth iteration and integral futures would be the fifth. It is vital that the futures studies field keeps abreast of rapid new developments in all fields of knowledge when constructing its own frameworks.

A Four Quadrants Analysis of Futures in Education

Despite the apparent complexity of Wilber's framework, useful understanding may arise from consideration of one aspect, such as the four quadrants (Figure 1). In its simplest form the four quadrants represent the inner and outer dimensions of individual and collective perspectives:
- Upper Left—Inner aspect of individual (intentional, psychological).
- Upper Right—Outer aspect of individual (behavioural, physical).
- Lower Left—Inner aspect of collective (meaning systems, culture).
- Lower Right—Outer aspect of collective (social systems, society).

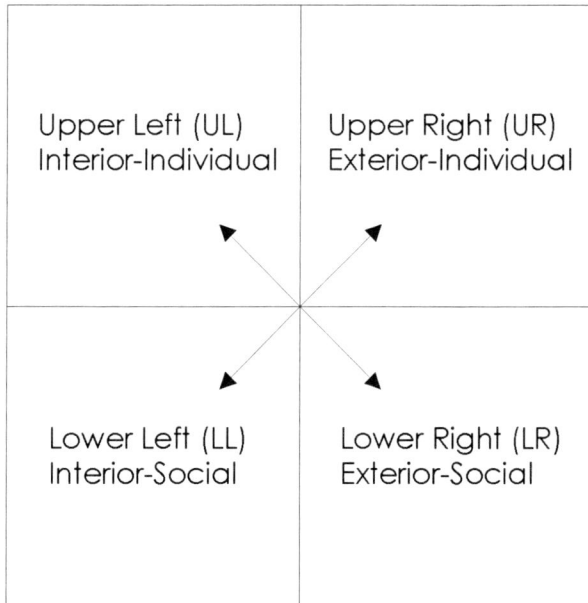

Upper Left (UL) Interior-Individual	Upper Right (UR) Exterior-Individual
Lower Left (LL) Interior-Social	Lower Right (LR) Exterior-Social

Figure 1. Wilber's four quadrant model

Other Integral Considerations

In addition to four quadrants, brief mention will be made here of other aspects of the integral approach. Firstly, the integral approach carries an injunction to 'practice' (as a complement to theory) (Wilber, 2000). An example here would be the empowerment-oriented methodologies already mentioned. Secondly, a 'four quadrants' analysis should be seen as one part of a 'full spectrum' analysis, which would require us to also look at "all types, all states, all streams, and all waves" (Wilber, 2000, 2004).

"Types" refers in this instance to different personality types. It may also be seen to refer to gender. "States" of consciousness include waking, dreaming, sleeping, altered, and meditative. "Streams" or "lines" refer to the different aspects of our being such as the cognitive, ethical, empathic, creative, socio-emotional, communicative, spiritual, kinaesthetic, mathematical, sexual and musical.

Taking the upper left (UL) quadrant, the emphasis in school education and in futures in school education has been with developing cognition. "Streams" support developments in psychology that indicate there are multiple ways of knowing (artistic, contemplative, practical etc.) and that all are important for a balanced education (Gardner, 1996). In the lower left (LL) quadrant, streams can represent different cultures and sub-cultures as discussed below.

"Waves" refers to the different 'levels' of development occurring within an individual or society. For example, an important "stream" to consider in an analysis of the education process would be the different value-systems and worldviews that may be held by pupils, teachers and administrators. This particular developmental aspect may be investigated through the Spiral Dynamics model based on Clare Graves' pioneering work and developed by Don Beck and Christopher Cohen (Wilber, 2000). Although consideration of the waves of development is essential for a full integral analysis, space does not permit a due elaboration in this present article.

It is, also important to recognise that these developmental levels exist within each of these quadrants (i.e., in the UL there is individual psychological development; in the LL there is cultural evolution; in the UR there is the more scientific view of physical evolution, and in the LR there is the development of society and civilisational history). Wilber argues that there is a need to harmonise all aspects if the whole system is to remain in balance: "An increase in exterior or social development can only be sustained with a corresponding increase in interior development of consciousness and culture" (Slaughter, 2003). Wilber also claims (along with many other integral theorists) that at the present time there is emerging a major transition in culture and consciousness (related to what has been referred to as the emergence of an integral age, as discussed earlier). Yet many key social institutions such as schools and many workplaces (and the key stakeholders in them) are not changing sufficiently or appropriately in relation to this potential cultural transformation, to keep a balance within the system as a whole.

The question remains for this paper—How can a four quadrant analysis assist the futures studies field in framing issues regarding 'futures *in* schools'?

The Upper Right (UR)—Individual Exterior ('Behaviour')

The most obvious thing that emerges when examining the futures in education work to date is that most of it has been working within the upper two quadrants. It is primarily about introducing concepts and tools that will increase an individual's knowledge base (UL) and ideally their behaviour as well (UR). Although much of the work is done in classes and small groups, it is still primarily focussed on the development of the individual. Indeed, the ongoing problems with getting sufficient support from school systems to keep initiatives going may stem primarily from the lack of work to date within the collective quadrants—cultural (LL) and social (LR) systems. How this could be done will be part of the research focus below. In particular, the upper left quadrant (inner and developmental aspect of individual) lends itself to much greater extension by the futures in education field.

The Upper Left (UL)—Individual Interior ('Psychology')

Psychological processes. Although much of the work in teaching futures is concerned with the upper left quadrant—the domain of the psychological—little research has been done into what psychological processes we are dealing with when we are teaching futures. Apart from Martha Rogers drawing our attention to the fact that futures work involves the heart and soul (Rogers, 1998), and a small pilot study which looked at the impact of futures visioning on clinical hopelessness and depression (Gidley, 2001), little has been done that has consciously linked futures processes and psychological processes. Yet the two are obviously intimately related. In this sense even the best futures work has been largely unconscious of its own processes and thereby ignores the development of its own UL quadrant. Peter Hayward's research is crucial in beginning to explore this terrain (Hayward, 2002, 2003).

And while the empowerment-oriented research is clearly involved in bringing what is learned from futures lessons (UL) into some unity with the individual's outer behaviour and actions (UR), we have not really studied how this comes about.

Ways of knowing. Still in the upper left quadrant, one of the streams is different ways of knowing. The emphasis in all school education (and also to a large degree in 'futures in education') has been with developing the cognitive faculties. This is only one way of knowing. Current developments in psychology indicate that there are multiple ways of knowing and that all are important to a balanced education (Gardner, 1996). So, more attention to different lines or ways of knowing (artistic, contemplative, practical, etc.) will be another area of potential development for futures in education.

Individual development. There is also a need to consider developmental aspects within the upper left quadrant. Over the last two decades several researchers from within developmental psychology have been exploring notions of developmental stages beyond Piaget's formal operations. Such stages are variously referred to as "postformal", "postconventional", "postrational", "fifth order", "unitive" (Commons, Richards et al., 1982; Commons, Armon et al., 1990; Kohlberg, 1990; Kegan, 1994; Yan & Arlin, 1995; Arlin, 1999; Baltes, Staudinger et al., 1999; Cook-Greuter, 2000). The implications of this are enormous for education as a whole and futures in education specifically.

The Lower Left (LL)—Collective Interior ('Culture')

Cultural development. One could also consider the possibility of an integral vision for the future of humanity.

Evolution of consciousness research points to the idea that human nature as a whole is currently mirroring what developmental psychology is uncovering in individual development. This research explores the emergence of a broader cultural movement beyond the intellectual, rational, mental mode of operating into postformal, post-conventional, 'second-tier', integral (and more spiritual) ways of thinking and being (Aurobindo Ghose, 1930; Steiner, 1966; Gebser, 1991; Wilber, 1996; Thompson, 1998; Wilber, 2000; Combs, 2002; Gidley, 2006a). Within this developmental aspect—as applied to the evolution of culture and consciousness—it is also interesting to distinguish between what Wilber calls the 'leading edge' of humanity and the 'centre of gravity' of humanity. "With less than two per cent of the population at second-tier thinking, second-tier consciousness is relatively rare because it is now the 'leading edge' of collective human evolution" (Wilber, 2000). Reflection on such a framework would be very valuable for futurists.

Expressing futures. Looking at the cultural quadrant (LL), we can see a lack of development of futures' cultural resources and artefacts. How many movies, songs, plays and art shows have arisen from the futures field? Although there are plenty of science fiction movies and books, most of these are dystopian. Rather than 'futures' as 'just another social science lesson', we need to enter youth culture through music and film—and to inspire young people to help with this. The computer game model may be an ideal way of introducing futures concepts.

Cultures. Also in respect of the cultural quadrant, streams can represent different cultures and sub-cultures. This is an under-represented area in educational futures. For example, what do educational futurists in Australia know about how our indigenous children and youth frame the future? What metaphors would they use? Are the materials we use suitable or do we need new ones? Apart from Milojević's and Inayatullah's work and a few other studies which look at young people's future visions in a range of countries, there is very limited futures in education work that has been recorded in non-Western settings (Inayatullah, 1995, 2000, 2002; Milojević, 2002, 2003).

Social futures. Still examining the lower left quadrant, another area that has been largely ignored in futures research is social futures. This is really the more inner, culturally-based aspect of social futures, concerned with how people relate to each other, how we connect with each other (LL). Galtung pointed out some years ago that when we hear the term future we seem only able to think of technological futures. There is much scope for development in this quadrant. This could go hand in hand also with more emphasis on developing an ethically-based, values-focused cultural component to education.

Lower Right (LR)—Collective Exterior ('Social Systems')

School systems. In addition, there is the lower right (LR) quadrant that again has been largely overlooked in much of the futures in education work. To what extent have educational futurists working in schools attempted to work with "the nature and dynamics of the relevant societal structure and systems?"(Slaughter, 2003), including the school and education system itself (e.g., analysis of classroom dynamics, school internal politics, etc.).
And if we keep the four quadrants in mind, this will also include as Slaughter points out:
– the specific ways that the various stakeholders construct meaning and significance (UL)
– culturally derived perspectives, rules and systems of meaning (LL)
– people's concrete skills, behaviours and actions (UR)
Perhaps it has not been for want of trying that this has not occurred. However, the beauty of an integral model such as this is that it makes the gaps more obvious. If this latter omission could be addressed, it may become possible to encourage schools and education departments to make use of existing futures resources (knowledge base, personnel) to enrich their current 'fashion-statement' futures interests.

Technology. In the LR we may also question the increasing use of technology—notably computers—in schools. Such is the prevalence of this issue, the term 'futuristic schools' is often limited to mean 'high-tech schools'. The increased usage of technology is not without its potential problems, however. A number of studies have begun to explore potential psychological and physical damage to children from long exposure to television screens and computer monitors (Healy, 1998; Grossman, Degaetano et al., 1999; Benoit, 2000; Grossman, 2000; Large, 2000). Initial findings suggest a link, for example, between screen viewing and myopia ('short-sightedness').

'Integration'

Finally, even in the most innovative of areas of educational change and trans-formation on the planet today, there is a tendency toward division and fragmentation rather than inclusion and integration. There are different schools of 'progressive' educational thought that are not necessarily even informed about each other let alone joining forces. This indicates that a very deep philosophical bridging needs to occur in our contemporary world. The importance of Wilber's valorisation of the process of "transcending *and* including" can help facilitate such a bridging.

What is it that holds us to the divisiveness of the fragmented view? Jean Gebser would see it as being the deficient part of the mental mode of thinking (Gebser, 1991). Good analysis does not necessarily produce good synthesis. Until we have fully conceptualised and then developed integral consciousness we will be forever limiting our own (individual and cultural—inner and outer) 'forward views'. The challenge for us all is how do we move beyond this conundrum? What is meant by 'integral consciousness', in all its possible domains and dimensions, is still at an early stage of human understanding but is certainly something with which futures educators need to concern themselves (Hampson, 2004). From the struggle of futurists to stretch our own foresighting capacities to understand where human consciousness is going in the future, will arise insights into how to transform education so it better prepares youth to create an authentic integral future.

WHERE TO FROM HERE? POSSIBLE RESEARCH AREAS

As demonstrated in the integral analysis above, a number of gaps have been identified in the research and practice of educational futures. Subsequently, a number of research focus areas and some specific questions have been formulated which, if undertaken, would greatly broaden and deepen the potential impact of this work.

A sample of these is given below.

1. Psychological dimensions.
- Further psychological research is needed into futures thinking/foresight.
- Psychological implications of futures processes on clinical depression and hopelessness in young people need to be more fully explored.
- Further research is needed on the implications of the correlation between age and increasing pessimism.
- Why are boys more passive and technologically oriented in their preferred futures images? And why are they more susceptible than girls to clinical levels of hopelessness? Can positive futures visioning help to reverse this?
- Why are Steiner students more empowered towards creating their preferred futures than mainstream youth and does this apply to students from non-Steiner alternative schools?

2. Diverse ways of knowing.
- How can futures in education help to keep 'non-cognitive streams' open?
- How could music be used as a futures tool?
- Is there a place for more poetry, dance and theatre in futures in school education?
- Is there a place for contemplative practices?
- How could Integral Transformative Practices be more fully integrated into school education?

3. Socio-cultural diversity.
- What kind of research could inform futures in education processes so that they could be more inclusive of non-Western cultural values?
- How can futures in education foster the co-existence of a tapestry of different cultures on a global scale?
- How can we best explore alternatives to hegemonic conceptions of education (Milojević, 2003)?
- How can the Western mono-cultural model be more enriched by indigenous, Indian, Chinese, etc., educational models?

4. Cultural resources.
- There is a need to develop a resource bank of what cultural material (movies, literature, music, computer games) already exists which presents *positive* futures.
- Who will write the futures fiction of the future? Need it be 'science fiction'?
- How can young people be encouraged to write their own 'alternative futures fiction'?
- Is it possible to explore a popular form of expression of futures that appeals to student populations?

5. Human/social futures.
- What images of future humans are the media presenting?
- Why do technology futures figure so strongly in youth futures research?
- What are the emerging issues relating to over-use of technology in education?
- How can the various stage theories of moral development throw light on our framing of social futures?
- Why do Steiner students have such a strong emphasis on social futures?
- What might widen and deepen young people's capacity to imagine better social futures?

6. Tackling the social systems.
- How are futures approaches currently being used in school systems and how could they be improved?
- Given that the 'future' is a current fashion in education, how can education systems be informed of the knowledge base of futures studies as a resource?
- Can the futures field provide strategies to better support teachers who wish to use innovative approaches?
- Who are the key power brokers in national curriculum initiatives? How can they be informed of futures studies resources?
- How might futures best evaluate alternatives regarding educational administrative structures in education?
- How can futures in education contribute to better communication and a re-evaluation of roles and expectations in teacher–teacher/teacher–pupil/ pupil–pupil relationships? How might we regard the prevailing internal politics in schools?

7.   Developing integral consciousness.

− What is the significance of Ken Wilber's integral framework for educational transformation globally?
− How might a Spiral Dynamics analysis inform futures in school education?
− How can alternative approaches to education such as Steiner schooling (Steiner, 1981) or Aurobindo's integral education (Aurobindo Ghose, 1930) best inform futures in education?
− Is imagination one of the qualities necessary to develop an integral consciousness? If so, how can imagination be fostered by futures in education? What existing research is available on the cultivation of imagination in education?
− What other existing organisations or networks are working towards an integral education approach with or without a futures perspective?
− Are there any existing cross-cultural visionary worldviews based in an integral paradigm?

CONCLUSION

Our preferred futures *of* school education include the ongoing development and strengthening of futures *in* school education. It also includes an imperative to develop more integral approaches.

Futures research indicates that Steiner-educated students display significant differences to mainstream students both in having more positive visions of the future and also in feeling more empowered. Pertinently, it is suggested that this difference is because Steiner education is more *integral* than mainstream education. It is also suggested that substantive research into other non-mainstream educational approaches may well prove similarly insightful.

A use of Wilber's four quadrant analysis is also demonstrated with regard to futures in school education. New—potentially fruitful—avenues of research have now become apparent, many of which carry within them seeds of educational transformation.

NOTES

 A number of voices could be adopted in writing about this area. For the purposes of this paper, we have chosen to 'locally embody' an interpretation of Thomas Berry's (1988) *post-critical naïvité*.

REFERENCES

Arlin, P. K. (1999). The wise teacher: A developmental model of teaching. *Theory into Practice, 38*(1), 12–17.
Aurobindo Ghose, S. (1930). The graded worlds. In S. Aurobindo Ghose (Ed.), *The riddle of this world*. Pondicherry, India: Sri Aurobindo Ashram.
Aurobindo Ghose, S. (1990 (1914)). *The life divine*. Pondicherry, India: Lotus Light.

Baltes, P. B., Staudinger, U. M., & Lindenburger, U. (1999). Lifespan psychology: Theory and application of intellectual functioning. *Annual Review of Psychology, 50*, 471–507.

Beare, H., & Slaughter, R. (1993). *Education for the twenty-first century*. London: Routledge.

Benoit, M. (2000). The Dot.Com kids and the demise of frustration tolerance. In C. Clouder, S. Jenkinson, & M. Large (Eds.), *The future of childhood*. Gloucestershire: Hawthorn Press.

Berry, T. (1988). *The dream of the earth*. San Francisco: Sierra Club Books.

Bjerstedt, A. (1982). *Future consciousness and the school*. Malmo, Sweden: School of Education, University of Lund.

Combs, A. (2002). *The radiance of being: Understanding the grand integral vision: Living the integral life*. St Paul, MN: Paragon House.

Commons, M. L., Armon, C., Kohlberg, L., Richards, F. A., Grotzer, T. A., & Sinnott, J. D. (Eds.). (1990). *Adult development: Vol. 2, Models and methods in the study of adolescent and adult thought*. New York: Praeger.

Commons, M. L., Richards, F. A., & Kuhn, D. (1982). Systematic and metasystematic reasoning: A case for levels of reasoning beyond piaget's stage of formal operations. *Child Development, 53*(4), 1058–1069.

Cook-Greuter, S. (2000). Mature ego development: A gateway to ego transcendence. *Journal of Adult Development, 7*(4), 227–240.

Eisler, R. (2001). Partnership education in the 21st century. *Journal of Futures Studies, 5*(3), 143–156.

Fien, J. (2002). *Teaching and learning for a sustainable future*. Paris: UNESCO.

Galtung, J. (1982). *Schooling, education and the future*. Malmo, Sweden: Department of Education and Psychology Research, Lund University.

Gardner, H. (1996). Probing more deeply into the theory of multiple intelligences. *NASSP Bulletin, 80*(583), 1–7.

Gebser, J. (1991). *The ever-present origin*. Athens, OH: Ohio University Press.

Gidley, J. (1997). Imagination and will in youth visions of their futures: Prospectivity and empowerment in steiner educated adolescents. In *Education, work and training*. Lismore: Southern Cross University.

Gidley, J. (1998). Prospective youth visions through imaginative education. *Futures, 30*(5), 395–408.

Gidley, J. (1998). Youth futures: Transcending violence through the artistic imagination. In S. Inayatullah & P. Wildman (Eds.), *Futures studies: Methods, emerging issues and civilizational visions. A multi-media CD ROM*. Brisbane: Prosperity Press.

Gidley, J. (2001). An intervention targeting hopelessness in adolescents by promoting positive future images. *Australian Journal of Guidance and Counselling, 11*(1), 51–64.

Gidley, J. (2002). Holistic education and visions of rehumanized futures. In J. Gidley & S. Inayatullah (Eds.), *Youth futures: Comparative research and transformative visions*. Westport, CT: Praeger.

Gidley, J. (2004). *Futures in education: Principles, practice and potential*. Melbourne: Foresight Institute.

Gidley, J. (2006a). Spiritual epistemologies and integral cosmologies: Transforming thinking and culture. In S. Awbrey, D. Dana, V. Miller, P. Robinson, M. M. Ryan, & D. K. Scott (Eds.), *Integrative learning and action: A call to wholeness* (pp. 29–53). New York: Peter Lang Publishing.

Gidley, J. (2006b). *The evolution of consciousness and its implications for education: An integral gaze at the visionary wor/l/ds of Rudolf Steiner and Ken Wilber*. PhD Research being undertaken at Southern Cross University, Lismore, Australia (ongoing).

Gidley, J., & Inayatullah, S. (2002). *Youth futures: Comparative research and transformative visions*. Westport, CT: Praeger.

Grossman, D. (2000). Teaching kids to kill. In C. Clouder, S. Jenkinson, & M. Large (Eds.), *The future of childhood*. Gloucestershire: Hawthorn Press.

Grossman, D., Degaetano, G., et al. (1999). *Stop teaching our kids to kill: A call to action against TV, movie and video violence*. New York: Random House.

Hampson, G. (2004). *The emerging spirit of integral*. Unpublished manuscript. Brisbane.

Hampson, G. (2004). *Toward the facilitation of appropriate transformation in education*. Unpublished manuscript. Brisbane.

Hayward, P. (2002). Resolving the moral impediments to foresight action. *Foresight*, *5*(1), 4–10.

Hayward, P. (2003). Foresight in everyday life. In *AFI monograph series*. Melbourne: 42.

Healy, J. M. (1998). *Failure to connect: How computers affect our children's minds—and what we can do about it*. New York: Touchstone.

Hicks, D. (2001). *Citizenship for the future: A practical classroom guide*. Surrey: World Wildlife Fund-UK.

Hicks, D. (2002). *Lessons for the future*. London: Routledge.

Hicks, D., & Holden, C. (1995). *Visions of the future: Why we need to teach for tomorrow*. London: Trentham Books.

Holden, C. (2002). Citizens of the new century: Perspectives from the United Kingdom. In J. Gidley & S. Inayatullah (Eds.), *Youth futures: Comparative research and transformative visions* (pp. 131–142). Westport, CT: Praeger.

Hutchinson, F. (1992). *Futures consciousness and the school: Explorations of broad and narrow literacies for the twenty-first century with particular reference to Australian young people*. Armidale NSW, University of New England: 410.

Hutchinson, F. (1996). *Educating beyond violent futures*. London: Routledge.

Inayatullah, S. (1990). Deconstructing and reconstructing the future: Predictive, cultural and critical epistemologies. *Futures*, *22*(2), 115–141.

Inayatullah, S. (1995). Futures visions for South-east Asia: some early warning signals. *Futures*, *27*(6), 681–688.

Inayatullah, S. (2000). Alternative futures: Methodology, society, macrohistory and the long-term future. In *Tamkang chair lecture series*. Tamsui, Taiwan: Tamkang University.

Inayatullah, S. (2002). Youth dissent: Multiple perspectives on youth futures. In J. Gidley & S. Inayatullah (Eds.), *Youth futures: Comparative research and transformative visions*. Westport, CT: Praeger.

Inayatullah, S. (Ed.). (2004). *The Causal Layered Analysis (CLA) reader: Theory and case studies of an integrative and transformative methodology*. Tamsui, Taiwan: Tamkang University Press.

Kegan, R. (1994). *In over our heads: The mental demands of modern life*. London: Hravard University Press.

Kohlberg, L. (1990). Which postformal stages are stages? In M. Commons, C. Armon, L. Kohlberg, F. A. Richards, T. A. Grotzer, & J. D. Sinnott (Eds.), *Adult development, Volume 2: Models and methods in the study of adolescent and adult thought* (pp. 263–268). Westport, CT: Praeger.

Large, M. (2000). Out of the box. In C. Clouder, S. Jenkinson, & M. Large (Eds.), *The future of childhood*. Gloucestershire: Hawthorn Press.

Miller, R. (1999). Holistic education for an emerging culture. In S. Glazer (Ed.), *The heart of learning: Spirituality in education* (pp. 189–201). New York: Putnam.

Milojević, I. (2002). *Futures of education: Feminist and post-western critiques and visions*. PhD Thesis. Brisbane: University of Queensland.

Milojević, I. (2003). Hegemonic and marginalised educational utopias in the contemporary western world. *Policy Futures in Education*, *1*(3), 440–446.

Ramos, J. M. (2003). *From critique to cultural recovery: Critical futures studies and causal layered analysis*. Melbourne: Foresight Institute.

Rogers, M. (1998). Student responses to learning about the future. In D. Hicks & R. Slaughter (Eds.), *World yearbook of education 1998: Futures education* (Chapter 15). London: Kogan Page.

Slaughter, R. (1989). What is futures education? In R. Slaughter (Ed.), *Studying the future: An introductory reader* (pp. 10–20). Melbourne: Commission for the future, Bicentennial futures education project.

Slaughter, R. (1994). Why should we care for future generations now. *Futures*, *26*(10), 1077–1085.

Slaughter, R. (2003). *Integral futures—a new model for futures enquiry and practice*. Melbourne: Foresight Institute.

Steiner, R. (1965). *The education of the child: Lectures, 1909*. London: Rudolf Steiner Press.

Steiner, R. (1966). *The evolution of consciousness as revealed through initiation knowledge: Lectures (1923)*. London: Garden City Press.

Steiner, R. (1981). *The renewal of education through the science of the spirit: Lectures, 1920*. Sussex: Kolisko Archive.

Steiner, R. (1982). *The kingdom of childhood: Lectures, 1924*. New York: Anthroposophic Press.

Thompson, W. I. (1998). *Coming into being: Artifacts and texts in the evolution of consciousness*. London: Macmillan.

Tough, A. (1993). What future generations need from us. *Futures*, December, 1041–1050.

Wilber, K. (1996). *Up from Eden*. Wheaton, IL: Quest Books.

Wilber, K. (2000). *A theory of everything: An integral vision for business, politics, science and spirituality*. Boulder, CO: Shambhala.

Wilber, K. (2000). *Sex, ecology, spirituality*. Boston: Shambhala.

Wilber, K. (2000). Waves, streams, states and self. *Journal of Consciousness Studies, 7*(11–12), 145–176.

Wilber, K. (2003). *The integral approach*. Retrieved from www.integralinstitute.org/approach.cfm

Wilber, K. (2004). *Introduction to integral theory and practice: IOS basic and the AQAL map*. Retrieved from http://www.integralnaked.org

Yan, B., & Arlin, P. K. (1995). Nonabsolute/relativistic thinking: A common factor underlying models of postformal reasoning? *Journal of Adult Development, 2*(4), 223–240.

Gary Hampson is a PhD candidate at the Centre for Children and Young People, Southern Cross University, Australia. His research topic is postformal epistemologico–educational trans/formation. He is an advisor to the Integral Education Centre of Integral University, Boulder, Colorado, and a Research Fellow at the Global Dialogue Institute at Haverford College, Philadelphia. He describes himself as a life artist.

303

IVANA MILOJEVIĆ

18. CONCLUSION

Developing futures literacy

ISSUES

Like most books on educational futures, the writers in this selection make the following foundational points: the world is changing at a rapid rate and has been changing for some time; educational institutions, on the other hand, are not, or at least not as much as they should/could be. Alternatively, educational institutions and practices have been changing in a direction that has very little to do with pro-active engagement, social change and future oriented thinking. Rather, in most places, educational change has occurred as a reactive response to protect and solidify a model whose use–by date has long expired.

Another point that several authors in this collection make is that the majority of educators and the institutions within which they work contribute to some of the current 'global problematique'. This they may do directly or, as it is most commonly the case, indirectly, by being passive, conservative and status quo maintenance oriented. For example, Dator argues that not only has education, as it is commonly practiced in our word/print-based era, been complicit in destroying traditional pre-print forms of literacy, wisdom and ways of learning, it was indeed researchers, educators and professors that have been instrumental in inventing various weapons of mass destruction, selling their research to the highest bidder. As another theorist and educator argues:

> We all know by now that many things on which our future health and prosperity depend are in dire jeopardy: that modern life has succeeded in threatening climate stability, the resilience and productivity of natural systems, the beauty of the natural world and both biological and cultural diversity. It is worth noting that this is not the work of ignorant people. Rather, it is largely the results of work by people with BAs, BScs, LLNs, MBAs and PhDs.

> The modern Western education system—which has successfully replaced indigenous forms of education throughout the world—prepares students almost exclusively for an urban existence, and dependence on fossil fuel and global trade. Children are taught from an early age how best to compete. But they are not taught how best to live in a truly sustainable society. (Orr, 1999, p. 166)

The change from oral-based traditions and from learning through watching, listening and doing towards the current model of learning through reading and

M. Bussey, S. Inayatullah and I. Milojević (eds.), Alternative Educational Futures: Pedagogies for Emergent Worlds, 305–314.

writing of decontextualised information (Dator, 2002) has been massive. And even though some benefits of print-based literacy are obvious, this shift has also come with a cost. The very act of reading an alphabet reinforces linear, abstract and predominantly 'masculine' type thinking, argues Leonard Shlain (1998). As well, this process has happened at the expense of holistic, concrete, visual and 'feminine'-based thinking, learning and teaching. Over the long term, this massive shift also meant the end of image and Goddess-based cultures and the beginning of the long reign of patriarchy and misogyny (ibid). The shift has also perhaps encouraged fragmentation/specialisation *versus* integral approaches in education (see Gidley and Hampson, this volume). Further massive social trends that were not possible without print-based literacy and education include industrialism, scientific rationalism and specialisation, even colonialism and globalisation.

Aren't we thus correct to expect that the latest digital, communication innovation is to have an equally shattering effect on the very structure of our societies, as well as education in general and pedagogy in particular? Most authors in this volume would say "Yes", however, none would agree that this is by any means the only challenge/opportunity both education and global society are facing. Rather, of equal if not more significant importance are possible shifts from nation-based frameworks to globalism (see chapters by Inayatullah, Bussey, Hicks and Gidley); from Western imperialism to wider cultural influences (see chapters by Haigh, Bussey, Matthews and Hattam); from industrialism to sustainability-based paradigm and from monoculture to bio-diversity (see chapters by Kelly, Savitsky, Slaughter); from patriarchy to gender partnership (see the chapter by Kesson); from materialism to spirituality (see chapters by Bussey, Inayatullah and Haigh); from violence-prone to peace cultures (Kesson); totalitarianism and elitism to more authentic democracy and equity (see chapters by Kesson and Bussey); from 'truth'- and transmission-based to 'facilitation'-based approaches to knowledge; from information society to a dream society of icons and images (see chapters by Dator, Savitsky, McWilliam and Dawson); from boring/tedium to fun-based approaches to teaching and learning (see chapters by Dator, Matthews and Hattam); from elitist and/or mass-based to niche and communal-based educational institutions (see chapter by Bussey); from certainty to radical scepticism/questioning and narrative approaches (see chapters by Matthews and Hattam, Matheson); from *tamasic* (materialist/crude) and *rajasic* (hyper extroversal, fragmented) towards *sattvic* (subtle and spiritual) education (see Haigh); and from fragmentation to integration and holism (see Gidley and Hampson).

All these are not, by any means, givens but rather current possibilities and options for the future as well as choices we could collectively make. Having said that, some of these possible shifts are clearly preferred by the majority of authors—usually those that move from the analytical and fragmented to the synthetic and empowering whilst avoiding reductionist binaries. Whatever the particular issue and preferred vision of each individual author, there is a general consensus that a transformation of current educational systems and practices needs to take place. As well, there is a commonly shared desire that this transformation—or these changes—are to be socially beneficial, positive and constructive.

PROCESSES

But teaching futures is not easy. The transformative potential is there (Kelly, Savitsky, Hicks), but so is the danger of reinforcing the very thing the teacher is trying to challenge. During a class in which I examined issues of global violence and focused on the alternatives to structural and environmental violence in particular, I was asked by a student: "Isn't it already too late? Aren't we naïve to think improvement of our societies is really possible? Haven't we just become more 'sophisticated' in how we kill and destroy?"

Directing our attention to current trends and global events it is hard not to at least partially agree with Dator when he writes: "Nature is dead and dying everywhere". Or with the realisation that during our era of a "peace through strength" (Kesson), security and "safety-first" (McWilliam and Dawson) obsessed world any innovation is bound to be coopted and stripped of its true meaning to reinforce the very system it wants changed. Or that new technologies and globalisation are creating as many problems as, if not more than, they are trying to solve. Or that rather than weakening, the patriarchal project for the future is continuing unabated—and so are continual colonisation and imperialism by Western culture and by several selected societies, whether through military interventions, global policies or encouragement of rampant consumerism.

There is a very thin line indeed between educators' responsibility to raise awareness of contemporary social issues so as to inspire positive individual and social development/change, and the danger of enhancing the dominant narratives of 'nothing can be done' hopelessness. Our societies, cultures and mainstream educational practices currently occur within a context of collective and perpetual denial. 'No worries mate, she'll be right' may be a uniquely Australian colloquialism but this phrase is reflective of a more global propensity to continue with 'business as usual', status quo attitudes and behaviours. And the majority of educators seem to be complicit in this process, if not outright conservative, "more likely to fear rather than embrace a future in which technological [as well as other type] innovation is a key player" (McWilliam and Dawson). As explained by Cuban (2001, p. 153), change takes far longer to implement in formal education than in, for example, business or private households because: "… schools are citizen controlled and non-profit. As systems, they are multipurpose, many-layered, labour-intensive, relationship-dependent, and profoundly conservative". The external pressures do not help either, as explained by Moorcroft (2008):

> Risk taking and innovation are difficult at the best of times: in public sectors where evidence based policy and public accountability are the rule, innovation is even more difficult … Most national education systems are dominated by public sector services strapped for cash: they also face the same challenges as service industries the world over as new technologies, new ways of working and new sources of competition take hold.

But even if all educators were 'progressives' and enthusiastic about educational change and reform they would still need to deal with other education stakeholders, including P & C committees and various ministerial boards. While education, especially in the West, has often been looked upon as the *utopian measure par excellence* (Hertzler, 1965) and even a means of salvation, many utopian desires to solve social problems through education invariably fail as education cannot do what society does not want it to do. If, for example, the overall society predominantly desires discipline and order, education focuses on firmly locating bodies and minds in place via teaching of particular knowledge and skills to achieve this overarching desire/aim. As Foucault's work clearly demonstrates, an educated subject that is 'governed' becomes a self-regulated subject, therefore successfully fulfilling "the practical needs of schools, businesses, and society as a whole for discipline and order" (Cromer, 1997, p. 118). Too many students all over the world still worry about how not to 'get in trouble', 'keep quiet', be obedient, able to be 'on task' and 'stay in line'. In that sense, Foucault's critique further concludes that the current mainstream educational structure is not dissimilar to that of other disciplinary institutions such as production lines, prisons, psychiatric hospitals and the army (Foucault, 1977). No wonder then that even the most progressive of educators would at least occasionally feel hopeless and like wanting to give up or give in.

PEDAGOGIES FOR EMERGENT FUTURES

The development of futures literacy may be helpful in addressing these difficulties and challenges. Some elements of futures literacy—tools, methods and transformative pedagogies—are offered by all authors throughout this book. Particularly useful may be the overviews by Inayatullah and Savitsky. But each individual chapter offers some insight into how to deal with the previously discussed propensity to remain 'part of the problem' or 'give up'. Knowledge based on futures studies— theories and methods—can help both our students and teachers/educators, including ourselves, to move beyond "cycles of cynicism" (Jones, Haenfler & Johnson, 2001) towards those of hope.

For example, the futures triangle can help locate and understand the issue but also our own place within a broader scheme of things. We can use this tool to locate ourselves on a 'pull of the future'/'weight of history' trajectory. We can also then accept others for their own contribution; if we are more inspired by desired futures and less by weight of history and social structure, making us either utopians or reformists, we could start by acknowledging those that fall more into 'the box' of traditionalism and conservatism (see Figure 1). We can then add the concept of 'disowned' futures (see Inayatullah) to investigate what each one of those visions is missing. As well, Galtung's 'transcend' method (www.trascend.org) can be added when the need for negotiation between visions arises. At the very least, the futures triangle enables us to understand the overall system, other people and our place in it. It can help us not get completely disillusioned when the reforms we worked hard on are co-opted and appropriated by the system. It can also help us understand that even though some changes are too slow, or sometimes go 'one step forward two steps back', it is the overall movement towards preferred futures that we can choose to focus on. This tool also enables us to acknowledge that the gratification of our desire for social and educational change may not occur immediately but instead take generations; yet we are an important link in that chain. By seeing an overall picture we can choose to segment the 'status quo' and 'back to basics' approaches as well as the "resisters" (Kelly) and see them not as defining the 'way of the world' but as only one force influencing our presents and futures.

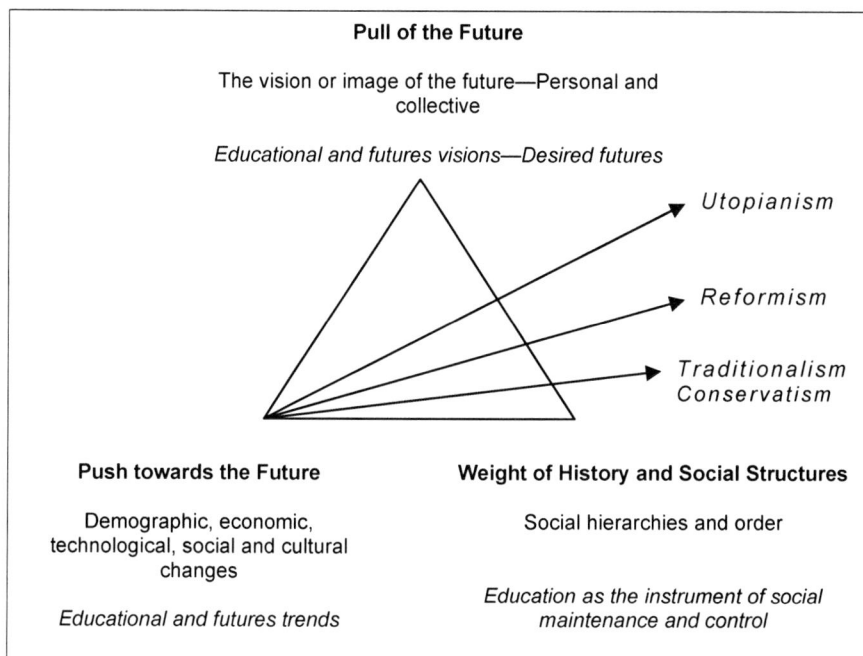

Adapted from Inayatullah (2002, p. 186)

Figure 1. The futures triangle

Thus, when faced by students' questions of "Isn't it too late?" and "Can anything really be done?", as well as by my own dilemmas, I re-focus attention on the possibilities rather than on detrimental trends, negative histories and harmful actualities. I also draw attention to preferred futures and the role of this concept as an active principle in the present. Lastly, I invite the 'lightness of being' that comes with the realisation of us not being 'the general managers of the universe' but rather an important part of a broader processes of envisioning and creating positive, constructive and beneficial alternatives.

I also have the option to quickly outline archetypal scenarios and show that 'the collapse'-based scenario of regression—things getting worse and there is imminent anthropocide or even omnicide—is just one option. I can then locate this option within a long historical tradition of dystopianism or apocalyptic doomsday mythic/ archetypical stories such as millennialism, eschatology, and various other religious teachings on the 'end of time' and point out that, despite numerous claims to the contrary, we are still here and that many of us are, historically speaking, enjoying rather privileged existences. I can then run an exercise in envisioning preferred futures in which this privileged existence is extended across humanity and other living beings. The next step is to go back to 'remember' how this happened via the backcasting method. Lastly, I ask participants to take responsibility for pro-actively choosing to create/participate in events that got us there, to our collectively imagined desired futures.

Other options available to me include deepening the 'worse case scenario' future through CLA to show in which ways 'litany' and the deep worldview and myth/metaphor are interlinked, how system and structure contribute and how, most importantly, alternative worldviews and stories can create different insights and solutions (see chapters by Inayatullah and Bussey). I can give examples of 'emerging issues' that have previously dramatically changed particular trajectories (i.e., the collapse of the Berlin Wall, the events of 9/11). This then opens up the option of investigating various alternatives: from alternative energy sources to the establishment of global sustainability and peace oriented governance. As well, I can utilise the futures wheel to show how small, incremental events could possibly have major direct and indirect consequence, for better or worse. Or I can use the 'four quadrant model' to show the link between inner and outer, individual and collective spaces (see Gidley & Hampson). Or the four centres tool (Savitsky) that links our physical, emotional, intellectual and spiritual selves. In a nutshell, I can utilise methods that address students' questions and dilemmas in a systematic way and in line with the 'zone of proximal development'; the methods that enable them to make a "conscious contributions to societal transformation" (Savitsky). This is extremely important because I am also aware that if I choose to 'preach' about the present and future problems and some possible solutions, as is often the case when our thinking is inspired by particular social activism (i.e., environmentalism, feminism, post-colonialism, peace movement), I would 'lose' most of my classroom. Instead, I can choose to share my own 'discoveries' and much more importantly, I can utilise futures methodology to facilitate the process of students making their own.

In this task I am well supported by previous work done by my colleagues who wrote extensively on how to generate informed and strategic optimism as well as the active hope as an antidote to pessimism, cynicism and passive hope through external salvation (i.e., Hutchinson, 1996; Hicks, 1994, 1998, 2001; Boulding, 1995). In this book, most essays offer some insight into this process. More specific are discussions by David Hicks, Marcus Bussey, Patricia Kelly, Basil Savitsky and Jennifer Gidley. But the sources of hope can be found in each and every contribution. The following section outlines some of those sources of hope, specifically those that may be both indicators and drivers of the coming of a very different global society.

HOPE

As asserted by Inayatullah and Bussey in the introductory chapter, the aim of this book is not to provide a blueprint but rather "visions that create new categories that change the direction of reality". This, as well as the insistence on diversity of visions and futures, is in line with the postmodern insight that: "providing a solution, ideal or utopian hope ... would set limits on possibilities for the future ... [this also means assuming] a position of political authority (intellectual as center)" which is declined on ethical grounds (Fendler, 1999, p. 185). But even postmodernism is, to a degree, a utopian philosophy (Doll, 1995, Siebers, 1994). Not only can the postmodern vision be characterised by its focus on heterogeneity, multiplicity, difference and equality (not of sameness, but of differences), but it is also utopian in a sense that "postmodernism wants what has been lacking ... it is about desiring ... not about being 'nowhere'... but [rather] 'elsewhere'" (Siebers, 1994, p. 23):

> Utopianism demonstrates both a relentless dissatisfaction with the here and now as well as bewilderment about the possibility of thinking beyond the here and now... Postmodernists, then, are utopian not because they do not know what they want. They are utopian because they know that they want something else. They want to desire differently.

So even though the authors in this collection may not necessarily agree about what they collectively want, they would most likely agree about what they do not want. In addition to the previously mentioned postmodern "not-wanting" of sameness, uniformity, hierarchy, authoritarianism and totalitarianism of any kind, the list of non-wanting at the level of a society would also most likely include nationalism, imperialism, industrialism, patriarchy, elitism and violence-based cultures. Furthermore, it is highly likely that the authors would also not want for educational system imperatives to remain about "power, control, economy and efficiency" (Slaughter, 2004, p. 195) or about 'expert' teachers transferring knowledge to "relatively ignorant" 'learners' (Beare, 2001, p. 1). In sum, such an educational not-wanting has in this book been nicely summarised by Marcus Bussey in his description of a non-desired classroom which is: limited, violent and punitive; teacher driven and authoritarian; not about learning but about dull transmission and idle memorisation; selfishly individualistic or segregated; exclusive, fundamentalist or closed; competitive, time driven, output obsessed and assessment oriented.

To move beyond the not-wanting of contemporary global society and education requires imagination, creativity, insight and daring. Above all what is required is re-focusing from thinking about and practicing what *is* or *has been* to what *could be*. In this *could be* lies potential for transforming selves and societies, for generating informed optimism, strategic utopianism and active hope.

WHAT COULD BE

To start with, education *could be* about *fun*. Learning could be through humour and play; whether one utilises digital (Dator, McWilliam and Dawson) or social (Matthews and Hattam) technologies is less critical than whether one has the courage to engage with this process. Even within current structures we could have *Laughing Classrooms* (Loomans and Kohlberg, 1993). Learning through humour, fun and play may not be neat, organised and easily 'assessed'. Rather, such teaching and learning recognises "the significance of paradox, irony, incongruity, unconventionality and distancing; the dissolution of dualism; and the deployment of radical scepticism" (Matthews and Hattam). Such an educational process is interactive and engaging. It connects learning with both entertainment as well as life (watching/doing/ participating) in general. It utilises story-telling (Matheson, Gidley), aesthetics, icons, images, myths and metaphors. It values the personal experiences of participants and self-reflection (as in laughing at self not at others). It deals with issues commonly repressed and/or silenced. It can help alleviate both educational as well as existentialist angst which is critically important in times of rising depression, suicide and other mental health disorders amongst (primarily OECD-based) youth (Gidley). "Show me the fun" (Dator) could be a motto of the not–so–distant future student and educator.

Education could also be about the *holistically educated subject*. Throughout history, the educated subject has variously been conceptualised as obedient, competent worker and/or capable, effective manager; nation–state citizen; wise elitist; and more recently as *Homo economicus*, *Homo globalis* or techno wiz. But the educational 'outcome' could also be a subject that is critically reflective, responsible and a wise global citizen (Kelly); *Sattvic* long–life learner (Haigh); a more complete, balanced individual that is also more informed, politically active and in charge of one's own life; Sarkar's neohumanist (Bussey) or '*Sadvipra*'; 'unconditioned', 'self-aware, centred', 'total, whole integrated, free, happy, joyful, blissful and peaceful human being' (Milojević, 2005, p. 215). In this process education can also utilise the "self as narrative" (Matheson) or look at self and identity as works in progress or, perhaps, even question the very existence of one's self (Matthews and Hattam). Alternatively, the educated subject can also be conceptualised as an emerging eco-self; as not only postmodern hybrid but also as Lynn Margulis's (1998) "symbiont" self or Lifton's (1993) "protean" self. The former debunks any notion of 'individuality' and 'independence', given our symbiotic relationship with other living beings, free-living species that entered into symbiotic relationships with us and became microbiotic components of our very own cells and bodies. The latter representation helps us assert "our organic relationship to each other and to nature" (Lifton, 1993, p. 13):

> That assertion, for symbolizers like ourselves, is a matter of the psyche, of the imagination. We can come to feel what we (according to our best scientific categories) are: members of a common species. We can experience, amidst our cultural diversity, that common humanity. The diversity is integral to the process, as: "We are multiple from the start".

The emerging eco-self challenges anthropocentric, individualist versions of what humanity is about. Instead of competition between species—survival of the fittest—which is reflected in most nationalistic histories taught in most educational institutions, this different paradigm is fundamentally about the move from hierarchical and competitive design into futures/presents that promote cooperation and respect for difference. Educating driven by the vision of holistic, symbiotic, spiritual, eco selves that are also a works in progress is about transformative education at its best.

This educational process is also about creating situated knowledge of "the self–in–relation–to" other people, history and places (Matheson). The self that is asked to evolve (ibid) becomes an active participant in a broader society. Thus education could also be about *authentic participatory democracy*. Education that helps create a truly democratic knowledge economy and that is of "universal value and the right and responsibility of all citizens" (Bussey). The aim here is to reclaim wisdom as the goal of learning and transformation and as the goal of a learning society (Gidley). Which leads us back to invoking the educational process best described as "integral, artistic, imaginative and proactive", so as to create cooperative, diverse, wise futures for all (ibid). It also leads us to assert that education could also be about *connection*. Through stories that connect (Slaughter), through narrative approaches (Matheson), through acknowledging spatial and temporal dimensions of the curriculum (Hicks), unity and spiritual love (Savitsky), "partnership" content, structure and process (Kesson and Eisler, 2000) and fostering a community of learners (Bussey), such education will help create radically different societies. Education that connects may utilise the *Sarvodaya* system that seeks balance and stability, self-reliance and self-sufficiency and focuses on community service and empowered, participatory self-governance (Haigh). It may utilise a higher order knowledge system, integral and spiritually-based cosmologies and perennial philosophies (Gidley). In a nutshell, education that connects is inspired by and aims to create "a pluralistic, multi-layered network of cultures within societies, committed to nurturing diverse, meaning-centred, integrated, wisdom based cultures" (ibid). It is based on the development of "'broad literacies': reading for meaning, writing creatively, sharing, respecting nature, imagining worlds beyond own immediate one, having social confidence and loving learning" (ibid). And wherever and whenever one is engaged in education about connection, the key is to remember that one is not alone, but connected with other people, nature and/or 'Spirit'. All this means creating and connecting with a different cosmology, different stories about humanity and what societies are to be about. Education remains a key to both understanding why alternative futures are necessary as well as to what may be our own role in creating such alternative, desired futures.

While my summary of selected educational possibilities presented in this book ends here, educating through hope and for hopeful futures does not and should not. So whoever and wherever you are, we hope you go beyond the mere dissatisfaction with today's education and choose to proactively engage with future possibilities of improved educational practices that inspire you.

REFERENCES

Beare, H. (2001). *Creating the future school*. London: RoutledgeFalmer.

Boulding, E. (1995). Image and action in peace building. In E. Boulding & K. Boulding (Eds.), *The future: Images and processes* (pp. 93–117). Thousand Oaks, CA: Sage.

Cromer, A. H. (1997). *Connected knowledge: Science, philosophy, and education*. New York: Oxford University Press.

Cuban, L. (2001). *Oversold and underused: Computers in the classroom*. Cambridge, MA: Harvard University Press.

Dator, J. (2002). *Advancing futures: Futures studies in higher education.* New York: Praeger.

Doll, B. (1995). Post-modernism's utopian vision. In P. McLaren (Ed.), *Postmodernism, post-colonialism and pedagogy* (pp. 89–101). Albert Park, Australia: James Nicholas Publishers.

Eisler, R. (2000). *Tomorrow's children: A blueprint for partnership education in the 21st century.* Boulder, CO: Westview Press.

Fendler, L. (1999). Making trouble: Prediction, agency, and critical intellectuals. In T. S. Popkewitz & L. Fendler (Eds.), *Critical theories in education: Changing terrains of knowledge and politics* (pp. 169–189). New York: Routledge.

Foucault, M. (1977). *Discipline and punish: The birth of the prison.* New York: Pantheon.

Hertzler, J. O. (1965). *The history of utopian thought.* New York: Cooper Square Publishers.

Hicks, D. (1994). *Preparing for the future: Notes and queries for concerned educators.* London: Adamantine Press Limited.

Hicks, D. (1998). Identifying sources of hope in postmodern times. In D. Hicks & R. Slaughter (Eds.), *Futures education: World yearbook of education 1998* (pp. 217–230). London: Kogan Page.

Hicks, D. (2001). Learning about global issues: Why most educators only make things worse. *Environmental Education Research, 7*(4), 413–425.

Hutchinson, F. P. (1996). *Educating beyond violent futures.* London: Routledge.

Inayatullah, S. (2002). *Questioning the future: Future studies, action learning and organizational transformation,* Tamsui, Taiwan: Tamkang University Press.

Jones, E., Haenfler, R., & Johnson, B. (2001). *The better world handbook: From good intentions to everyday actions.* Gabriola Island, British Columbia: New Society Publishers.

Lifton, J. (1993). *The protean self: Human resilience in an age of fragmentation.* New York: Basic Books.

Loomans, D., & Kolberg, K. (1993). *The laughing classroom: Everyone's guide to teaching with humor and play.* Tiburon, CA: Kramer.

Margulis, L. (1998). *Symbiotic planet: A new look at evolution.* Amherst, MA: Sciencewriters.

Milojević, I. (2005). *Educational futures: Dominant and contesting visions.* London: Routledge.

Moorcroft, S. (2008). Trend alert: Education facing a revolution? *Insight* on-line Newsletter. Retrieved February 6, 2008, from www.shapingtomorrow.com

Orr, D. (1999). Education for globalisation. *The Ecologist, 29*(3), 166–169.

Shlain, L. (1998). *The alphabet versus the goddess.* New York: Viking.

Siebers, T. (Ed.). (1994). *Heterotopia: Postmodern utopia and the body politics.* Michigan, MI: The University of Michigan Press.

Slaughter, R. (2004). *Futures beyond dystopia: Creating social foresight.* London: RoutledgeFalmer.

Ivana Milojević is a researcher and educator with a background in sociology, gender, peace and futures studies. Ivana is currently teaching the Introduction to Peace and Conflict Studies course at the University of the Sunshine Coast, Australia, where she is also an adjunct researcher. In 2007 and 2008 she received a fellowship to teach the introductory course "Futures Studies from Feminist/Gender Perspectives" to MA and doctoral students at the Center for Gender Studies, Novi Sad University, Serbia. She has previously taught peace and futures education, as well as globalisation and education at the University of Queensland. Her other affiliations include being Research Director of metafuture.org (www.metafuture.org) and she is a faculty member/Associate of Prout College www.proutcollege.org.

Ivana's recent publications include: Alternative Futures of Education: Dominant and contesting visions *(London: Routledge, 2005);* Neohumanist Educational Futures *(co-editor, with Inayatullah, S. and Bussey, M.) (Tamsui, Taiwan: Tamkang University Press, 2006) and a special issue of* Futures *on feminism/gender (ed. with Hurley, K. and Jenkins, A.) (2008).*

Printed in the United Kingdom by
Lightning Source UK Ltd., Milton Keynes
139667UK00001B/57/P

9 789087 905118